This is a study of the foreign policy views of Arthur James Balfour (1848–1930), British Prime Minister and Foreign Secretary, which examines his understanding of foreign relations, his perception of contemporary foreign and Imperial affairs, and his prescriptions for British policy. The book spans international thought, diplomatic history, and biography. Theory is, however, not divorced from practice, still less practice from people.

In elucidating Balfour's mind, the author touches on most of the major issues of four decades of international history and some fundamental questions of international relations. Little attention has been paid hitherto to Balfour's political thought, but here he is shown as an intellectual with a deep and coherent philosophy, which led him to emphasise the importance of Anglo-American partnership in world affairs.

D1715001

BALFOUR AND FOREIGN POLICY

BALFOUR AND FOREIGN POLICY

The international thought of a Conservative statesman

JASON TOMES

CAMBRIDGE
UNIVERSITY PRESS

PUBLISHED BY THE PRESS SYNDICATE OF THE UNIVERSITY OF CAMBRIDGE
The Pitt Building, Trumpington Street, Cambridge, United Kingdom

CAMBRIDGE UNIVERSITY PRESS
The Edinburgh Building, Cambridge CB2 2RU, UK
40 West 20th Street, New York NY 10011–4211, USA
477 Williamstown Road, Port Melbourne, VIC 3207, Australia
Ruiz de Alarcón 13, 28014 Madrid, Spain
Dock House, The Waterfront, Cape Town 8001, South Africa

http://www.cambridge.org

First published 1997
First paperback edition 2002

A catalogue record for this book is available from the British Library

Library of Congress Cataloguing in Publication data
Tomes, Jason.
Balfour and foreign policy: the international thought of
a Conservative statesman / Jason Tomes.
p.   cm.
Includes bibliographical references and index.
ISBN 0 521 58118 4 hardback
1. Balfour, Arthur James Balfour, Earl of, 1848–1930 – Views on
foreign relations.   2. Conservatism – Great Britain – History –
20th century.   3. Great Britain – Foreign relations – 1901–1936.
4. Great Britain – Foreign relations – 1837–1901.   5. Great Britain
– Intellectual life.   I. Title.
DA566.9.B2T66   1997
327.41–dc20   96-19709   CIP

ISBN 0 521 58118 4 hardback
ISBN 0 521 89370 4 paperback

Contents

Acknowledgments

The author gratefully acknowledges financial support from the ESRC and Martin Tomes. His thanks go to Don Markwell and Philip Waller of Merton College, Oxford, for their valuable encouragement and advice; to Nuffield College, Oxford, for facilitating his research; and to all others who have assisted him. Quotations from the papers of A.J. Balfour are by permission of the Fourth Earl of Balfour. Acknowledgment is also due to the Bodleian Library, the British Library, the Controller of HM Stationery Office, the Earl of Crawford, the Clerk of the Records of the House of Lords, the Public Record Office, the Marquess of Salisbury, the Warden and Fellows of New College, Oxford, and the Scottish Record Office.

Abbreviations

BDFA	*British Documents on Foreign Affairs: Reports and Papers from the Foreign Office Confidential Print* 1st Series Part II (University Publications of America 1989)
BP	A.J. Balfour Papers, British Library
CID	Committee of Imperial Defence
Conference	*Conference on the Limitation of Armament, Washington, 12 Nov. 1921 – 6 Feb. 1922* (Washington: Government Printing Office 1922)
DBFP	*Documents on British Foreign Policy 1919–1939* 1st Series (London: Her Majesty's Stationery Office 1947–85)
FRUS	*Papers relating to the Foreign Relations of the United States* (Washington: Department of State)
Grosse Politik	*Die Grosse Politik der Europäischen Kabinette 1871– 1914* (Berlin: Deutsche Verlagsgesellschaft für Politik und Geschichte 1922–7)
Hatfield	3rd Marquess of Salisbury Papers, Hatfield House
HCD	*House of Commons Debates* 5th Series
HLD	*House of Lords Debates* 5th Series
LPCW	M.W. Weisgal (ed.) *The Letters and Papers of Chaim Weizmann* Series A (London: Oxford University Press 1968–)
PDeb	*Parliamentary Debates* 3rd and 4th Series
PRO	Public Record Office
SRO	Balfour of Whittingehame Muniments, Scottish Record Office

Introduction

This is a study of the foreign policy views of Arthur James Balfour (1848–1930), sometime British Prime Minister, Foreign Secretary, and Leader of the Conservative Party. It examines his understanding of international relations, his perception of contemporary foreign and Imperial affairs, and his prescriptions for British policy. It thus spans international thought, diplomatic history, and biography. Theory is not divorced from practice, still less practice from people.

There exist five posthumous biographies of Balfour.[1] The best overall coverage of foreign policy is to be found in the first, notwithstanding that it was published in 1936 and written by his devoted niece. Blanche Dugdale was conscientious and well informed. She was also a woman of strong convictions, a fervid Zionist, and a stalwart of the League of Nations Union. (Balfour kept his real opinion of the LNU from her for fear that she would burst into tears.)[2] Her interpretation set the tone for her successors. Two further works, on Balfour and the British Empire, are of limited scope and depth.[3]

Balfour was once described as the Cyrano de Bergerac of British foreign policy – 'celui qui souffle et qu'on oublie.'[4] He does feature in all the diplomatic histories of the period, but rarely as a focus

---

[1] Blanche Dugdale *Arthur James Balfour* (London 1936); K. Young *Arthur James Balfour* (London 1963); S.H. Zebel *Balfour* (Cambridge 1973); M. Egremont *Balfour* (London 1980); R. Mackay *Balfour* (Oxford 1985).

[2] N.A. Rose (ed.) *'Baffy'* (London 1973) pp. xvi and xix; Balfour to Cecil, 4 June 1923, Cecil Papers 51071A f. 89.

[3] H.E. Bärtschi *Die Entwicklung vom Imperialistischen Reichsgedanken zur modernen Idee des Commonwealths im Lebenswerk Lord Balfours* (Aarau 1957); D. Judd *Balfour and the British Empire* (London 1968). There is also C.B. Shannon *Arthur J. Balfour and Ireland 1874–1922* (Washington 1988).

[4] A.L. Kennedy *Old Diplomacy and New 1876–1922* (London 1922) p. 365.

of attention. A wide and generous scattering of passing references is the norm. This reflects his status. He was long a British policy-maker of undoubted prominence. He was never *the* British policy-maker of acknowledged dominance. If Salisbury, Grey, and Lloyd George might be said to have topped the bill, Balfour has a strong claim to head the supporting cast. The comparative brevity of his premiership and tenure of the Foreign Office belies the magnitude of his involvement. For forty-odd years he belonged to the inner circle of politicians who mattered, and his views were respected to the extent that he came to be regarded as an authority on international affairs. He is in consequence a significant statesman from momentous times.

The years 1890–1930 witnessed the zenith of the British Empire. Never was there more red on the map. The British people had grown fully conscious of their global leadership. Yet this very awareness was due in part to the intensification of international rivalry. The culmination of four centuries of Western imperialism was a situation in which no Great Power could extend its interests without interfering with those of another. The modernisation of Russia appeared to endanger British India. Germany had attained pre-eminence in Europe and aspired to more. There was still the possibility of France becoming overambitious. Japan was embarking on expansion in the Far East. Great wealth and growing foreign trade made the United States of America a potential force throughout the world. The weakness of the Habsburg, Ottoman, and Manchu Empires created persistent instability. Then a war of unprecedented scale convulsed the whole international system, accelerating technological and political change, and spawning a new ideological challenge in the form of Bolshevism.

The proliferation of threats and the advancement of modern weaponry caused the costs of defending the British Empire to spiral, while the relative strength of the British economy declined. Defence expenditure was further restricted by rising popular demand for social provision. Thus developments at home and abroad combined to straiten external policy. Government ministers faced increasingly difficult choices, while theorists pursued long-term solutions down the divergent paths of internationalism and autarky. British ascendancy in world affairs, consolidated after the Napoleonic Wars, was less and less to be taken for granted. With hindsight, we know it was already on the wane.

The factors which determine the changing role of one nation in relation to others are exceedingly multifarious: geographical, diplomatic, military, industrial, agricultural, financial, commercial, technological, educational, intellectual, moral, religious, ideological, institutional, party political, biographical, etc. Of the writing of books there is no end, and this one may seem at first sight a negligible addition to the monstrous pile. Let it however be said, without contradiction, that this is a book at once narrow and broad. It is narrow in that it elucidates the mind of a single man, who, though influential for a time, was no 'world historical figure'. It is broad in that, in so doing, it touches on most of the major issues of four decades of international history and some of the fundamental questions of international relations.

The human world is too complex for its politics to be understood fully by anybody, but practical statesmen need at some level to try and make sense of the muddle. This book is an examination of how one did. People respond to situations as they see them. Their images of reality are coloured by their preconceptions and customary patterns of thinking. Even though the connection between political thought and political action cannot be established with certainty, a key to the explanation of British policy is surely provided by the way its makers perceived the world.

The thinking of this particular policy-maker was unusually profound and coherent, moreover, for it rested on a deliberate philosophical basis. It was also distinctively conservative. Should some of his ideas be found to possess inherent interest, so much the better.

The high appraisal of Balfour's political thought given here may possibly surprise some readers acquainted with previous books about him. It is worth considering why.

By general admission, Balfour was an intellectual. A great many learned societies welcomed him on account of his political standing, but his participation in several was real and his presence seldom incongruous. He was a Fellow of the Royal Society, of course, and President of the British Academy. In private life, too, he enjoyed the company of eminent scholars and scientists. Philosophy was his discipline, and he wrote it in earnest throughout his life. *A Defence of Philosophic Doubt* (1879), *The Foundations of Belief* (1895), *Theism and Humanism* (1915), and *Theism and Thought* (1923) are proof of his capacity for sustained abstract thought and of the importance which he attached to it.

Is he then an acclaimed political thinker in the history of British Conservatism? He is not. The subject-matter of his philosophical treatises was never explicitly political. The speculative mind which very publicly pondered the bases of theology, science, aesthetics, ethics, and even economics was rarely observed to venture near the theory of politics. Thus little was revealed of the political thought of an otherwise notably thoughtful person. It remained unclear how his intellectual life related to his politics at all.

Biographers have dodged the question – because Balfour dodged it himself. He generally chose to give formal expression to his opinions either at an abstruse philosophical level or else at a practical political one. What kind of thinking he used to link the two levels (if any) was never set out in a treatise-cum-memo or explained in a lecture-cum-speech. On this point, indeed, the enquiries of Mrs Dugdale elicited only banter. When she asked for the essence of Toryism, he answered, 'to do what seems to be the right thing in a given case'. He declined her request for guiding principles in politics, saying, 'the more effort has been made to produce those abstract rules, – the greater has been the confusion and controversy'.[5]

Are we then to assume that Balfour was devoid of serious political ideas? Elsewhere he suggested that the highest success in politics required a power of dealing both with principles and with practical problems.[6]

'The last of the Athenians', Baldwin called him. 'The philosopher of statecraft and the statesman of philosophy' was another graceful epitaph.[7] His most eulogistic biographer – Kenneth Young – likewise itches to hail a philosopher-statesman, but a philosopher *and* a statesman is all he manages to show.[8]

There has consequently been a tendency to dismiss the philosophical side of Balfour as a dilettante irrelevance. Worldly-wise political historians, unimpressed by his donnish airs and graces, have stripped the statesman down to an adaptable executive

[5] Dugdale *Balfour* vol. II pp. 404–5.
[6] A.J. Balfour *Essays and Addresses* 3rd edn. (Edinburgh 1905) p. 220.
[7] Ian Malcolm *Lord Balfour* (London 1930) p. 123.
[8] Young *Balfour* pp. 59–60 and 155–6. Young deserves credit for at least paying due attention to the philosophical work of Balfour and wondering how it fitted in with his politics, even if he lacks substantial answers. The biography by Mackay, sub-titled *Intellectual Statesman*, is not especially concerned with Balfour's thinking.

politician of rather colourless aspect. The power of his intellect is acknowledged with reference only to points of style and technique: lucidity, logic, critical subtlety, cold calculation, and an incurable habit of seeing both sides of a question.

This interpretation fails to solve the puzzle. If Balfour were simply a smooth political operator, what can explain his stubbornness in respect of Ireland and Zionism? These are precisely the issues most often associated with him. Was he a pragmatic placeholder with streaks of unaccountable obstinacy? Such an estimate is likely to satisfy only those who routinely take the view that Conservatives, no matter how cerebral, have nothing to offer but expedients and prejudices.

Alan Taylor described the 'detestable' Balfour as *both* 'cynical, unprincipled, and frivolous' *and* 'that rare thing in politics, an intellectual extremist'.[9] It appears that neither admirers nor detractors have presented an integrated view.

This study insists on seeing Balfour whole – as a deep-thinking politician with effective principles. He did not offer them up on a plate, but, when they are sought out and pieced together, his approach to international relations demonstrates a continuity of belief and application from his formal philosophical writings to his actual political practice.

The scheme of this book will naturally not commend itself to everyone. Some analysts discount the role played by politicians in history, which they prefer to explain purely in terms of impersonal forces. British foreign policy is to them a function of the economic and strategic position of the nation. This doctrine, in its extreme form, is surely to be set aside with the metaphysics of determinism. To commonsense observers it is evident that the personal element cannot be altogether excluded. The broad lines of national development set the parameters of feasible policy. Within them, political leaders make choices which are not intrinsically less 'free' than those of everybody else.

This conceded, policy-makers may yet be studied primarily as products of their environment. Some historians fasten on social and cultural influences. They trace the reactions and reasoning of British statesmen of this period to class consciousness, the public school ethos, *fin de siècle* pessimism, and so on. This kind of general-

---

[9] A.J.P. Taylor *From the Boer War to the Cold War* (London 1995) pp. 55 and 57.

isation may be useful and informative within its proper limits. Balfour did himself display many attributes of the stereotype: 'a cool, detached view of politics, a global perspective, a distaste for mere trade, for the *nouveaux riches*, and for foreign governments which did not follow the gentlemanly code'.[10] He has been called 'the best example in modern British history of the aristocrat in public life' and even 'a typical product of the Eton incubator'.[11] His manners were indeed aristocratic – the more so, perhaps, because he was not quite a fully-fledged aristocrat. ('Odd how the middle class blood will out', observed a disparaging titled relative.[12]) Scrutinise the alleged embodiment of a human type and idiosyncrasy is certain to be discovered. This country land-owner was happier on a bicycle than on a horse. Public school left him with a *dislike* of team games and classics. He grew up in the second third of the nineteenth century, but felt no partiality for it in retrospect. In literature, his favourite was Jane Austen. In music, his idol was Handel. He said that the intellectual celebrities of his youth – Mill, Carlyle, Comte, and Newman – failed to arouse his enthusiasm.[13] If individual tastes cannot be inferred with confidence from the facts of class and generation, still less can a detailed correlation with individual views on national priorities and the world order be constructed. This book does not purport to characterise the outlook of a representative specimen.

Other historians concentrate on connecting the words and deeds of statesmen to the political situations in which they worked. Tactical manoeuvres within and between parties and departments are the centre of interest. Successful politicians are assumed to profess whatever opinions they need to profess in order to remain successful – and personal conviction is a redundant concept. This postulate raises difficult questions about belief and communication with implications beyond the practice of professional politicians. How are 'real' independent opinions to be distinguished from 'artificial' instrumental ones? Is there any meaningful distinction? Are ulterior motives universal? What is denoted by integrity? This is not the place to attempt answers. Adherents

[10] P.M. Kennedy *The Realities behind Diplomacy* (London 1981) p. 60.
[11] Sir Arthur Salter *Personality in Politics* (London 1948) p. 25; L. Mosley *Curzon* (London 1961) p. 204.
[12] Lady Robert Cecil, cited in K. Rose *The Later Cecils* (New York 1975) p. 136.
[13] A.J. Balfour *The Nineteenth Century* (Cambridge 1900) p. 12.

of the tactical mode of analysis may be able to interpret the contents of this book in accordance with their assumptions, but they will observe that it is not written with these in mind. The author takes the view that (i) some expressed beliefs are clearly more instrumental than others, and (ii) that the preponderance of Balfour's expressed beliefs about foreign policy is rather less so (in relation to the norms of high-level politics in general). This is not at all to deny that the pursuit of power plays a large part in political life or to doubt that the expectations of supporters constrain leaders. It is simply to suggest that such considerations do not apply with equal force to all politicians and all kinds of political activity.

Balfour never cultivated a close personal following. Founding his career on family patronage, he sustained it by holding himself a little above the fray and impressing people with his superiority. Every strategy imposes its own restrictions, but this most self-conscious of power-brokers did not sacrifice his individuality. His partisan and factional operations were marked by exceptional ingenuity – and a detachment so obvious as to be a serious political weakness. Colleagues and constituents admired his skill and appreciated his condescension. They did not understand him. His successor, Bonar Law, heard that Balfour thought it 'an advantage to have a leader who was not intellectually much superior to the rest of the party he led'.[14] A politician so aloof was quite capable of manufacturing expressions of belief to advance his cause while all the time retaining and developing his own views. Behind this facade there was a building. Balfour did think for himself – and judged when it was appropriate to impart his thoughts.

Foreign affairs are remote by definition. Balfour believed that they were best considered on their own terms at a remove from domestic political contests. This was an ideal, unrealisable even by himself, but the belief was widely held in governing circles. Thus, while party considerations inevitably continued to play a part in the framing of public speeches on foreign policy, many major issues were simply not seriously addressed in public speeches. Parliamentary involvement was often superficial as a result. Given that foreign affairs were not usually a continuous factor in internal Cabinet politics either, the policy-making pro-

---

[14] Thomas Jones *Whitehall Diary 1916–1925* ed. K. Middlemas (London 1969) vol. I p. 222.

cess did preserve a considerable degree of autonomy from outside pressures.[15] Within the policy-making coterie, there was
consequently significant scope for the expression of personal
conviction.

Thus it is possible to derive from what Balfour wrote, and what
others with direct knowledge wrote about him, a collection of opinions on external policy which is not a mere rag bag of instrumental remarks but amounts to a body of practical thought. The con-
sistency of his approach points to a system, indeed, though it
would be inappropriate to attempt a schematic exposition of it.
That he ever formulated such a thing in his own mind is doubtful,
and no one can now construct one in his name.

Even far less ambitious inferences are open to fundamental
objection. How *dare* anyone presume to draw conclusions about the
outlook of another person on the basis of incomplete material
which cannot always be taken at face value? And yet everyone
does. It is by such imperfect means that social relations between
human beings are doomed to operate. All we can know of what
other people think is gleaned from what they say and do. Insofar
as we impute beliefs and desires to the living, we can with equal
justification impute them to those who once lived. Only two essential points distinguish the latter procedure: there is no chance
of our obtaining additional information at will by creating test
situations, and we can publish our interpretation without fear of
contradiction at first-hand.

There was a time when dead British statesmen were routinely
granted a generous measure of indulgence by historians of their
own nationality. This excessive respect for persons bred an understandable reaction. It can seem as if only political leaders of super-
human perception could satisfy some latter-day critics. It is all too
easy to forget that historical figures were real people to whom
justice should be done. A marginal amount of unconscious misrep-
resentation yet remains unavoidable. Balfour once said: 'I am sure
I am always more or less happy when I am being praised, and not
very uncomfortable when I am being abused; but I have moments
of uneasiness when I am being explained.'[16] He was addressing
the Parliamentary Press Gallery at the time, so it is uncertain

[15] Kennedy *Realities behind Diplomacy* pp. 50 and 59.
[16] A.J. Balfour *Opinions and Argument* (London 1927) p. 44.

what caused him the sharper unease: explanation that was wide of the mark or explanation that was spot on.

The modern historian is better placed than the average Edwardian journalist to produce an accurate interpretation. He has access to virtually all official papers and a significant amount of correspondence. Balfour could normally draw up a Cabinet memorandum on foreign policy without radical pretence, and the frankness of his letters naturally varied according to his relation to the recipient.

This study relies on these private sources, but does not ignore public statements. To assess the full range of Balfour's international ideas requires a full range of material. Many of his books, essays, and addresses on topics more or less remote from current affairs yet have a bearing on the larger questions of politics. They help counteract the inevitable bias of ministerial documents towards emphasis on short-term executive thinking. No autobiography exists to clarify or cloud the picture – a posthumous fragment, written for financial reasons at the age of eighty, is impersonal almost to the point of uselessness.[17] Extensive transcripts from a life-time of speech-making are available in *Hansard* and the press. Balfour's speeches, almost invariably all his own work, were usually extemporised from notes scrawled on the back of an envelope, which meant both a halting delivery and a refreshing absence of polished rhetoric. The constraints on him were many and often obvious. He is not to be found gratuitously threatening the unity of his party, his country, or the Empire, or giving needless offence to foreign governments, or outraging popular sensibilities. International affairs received especially bland and careful treatment. Parliamentary and platform speeches nevertheless contain suggestive and characteristic touches, be they general ideas or telling phrases, which illustrate the mind of their creator. The same may be said to a lesser extent of diplomatic notes drafted by Balfour.

All documents need to be considered critically in their context and in conjunction with other material. Where there is evidence that Balfour was saying something which he did not believe, his statement is discounted. Where there are specific grounds for suspecting that he was doing so, those grounds are indicated. Elsewhere, his sincerity is left unchallenged. Any attempt to delineate

---

[17] A.J. Balfour *Chapters of Autobiography* (London 1930).

with greater precision than this the balance between political pressure and personal inclination in the formation of an expressed opinion would be a questionable undertaking at best. Let him speculate who will. In so much the historian has to use his judgment, but ultimately his readers must exercise their own.

CHAPTER 1

Biographical survey

Born in 1848, the eldest son of a wealthy Scottish landowner, Arthur Balfour was orphaned when seven years old. In the absence of his father, his maternal uncle assumed greater prominence. The uncle was Robert Gascoyne-Cecil (1830–1903), later Third Marquess of Salisbury, Conservative Prime Minister, and Foreign Secretary. In maturity, Balfour acknowledged that this association had probably affected his whole life and character.[1] Certainly it was commonly reckoned a factor in his political advancement – 'Bob's your Uncle!'

After Eton and a second in Moral Sciences at Trinity College, Cambridge, he dallied in cultivated society and envisaged an exclusively philosophical career. Salisbury intervened with the offer of a safe seat, however, and Balfour entered Parliament in 1874.

His maiden speech was two-and-a-half years coming and followed an eight-month world tour. (He did not leave Europe again for four decades.) When Salisbury became Foreign Secretary in 1878, he made Balfour his Parliamentary Private Secretary, in which capacity he attended the Congress of Berlin. He spoke a little in defence of Government foreign policy, but it was in the 1880 Parliament that he began to make his name.

Although considered for Under-Secretary for Foreign Affairs, he found himself at the Local Government Board in 1885.[2] Next year he became Secretary for Scotland and joined the Cabinet. The year after that he won eminence as a resolute Chief Secretary for Ireland. Even the epithet 'Bloody Balfour' enhanced his standing

[1] 'The Prime Minister at the Mansion House' *Times* 16 Oct. 1902 p. 5.
[2] R. Harcourt Williams (ed.) *Salisbury–Balfour Correspondence 1869–1892* (Hertford 1988) p. 121.

with all but the Irish Nationalists who bestowed it. His uncle's faith was vindicated and further promotion assured. He was Leader of the Commons and First Lord of the Treasury 1891–2, and to these posts he returned in 1895.

There was a deep sympathy between Balfour and Salisbury. Both intellectual conservatives, they thought alike on many matters (from the indispensability of religion to the scope of arbitration treaties) and a precise delineation of their differences would require detailed comparison. The nephew was much fonder of metaphysics, and his conservatism was the more Romantic. Salisbury belittled national sentiment and 'corporate entities'. Foreign policy seemed to him largely dictated by material interests.[3] Balfour never said such things.

Salisbury seconded Balfour to direct the Foreign Office for days or weeks at a time, while the Under-Secretaryship was held by a frustrated George Curzon. (Over the next thirty years, 'Dear Arthur' and 'Dear George' were often to be at odds over foreign policy – they were such 'friends' that neither could resist criticising the other behind his back.) When Salisbury was ill in 1898, Balfour was Acting Foreign Secretary for two extended periods in March–April and August. This dual leadership was not without its tensions. Balfour did not think Salisbury was managing the Chinese crisis well. Salisbury was angry that Balfour made the Anglo-German Agreement on Portuguese Colonies.[4] They did not feel quite the same way about the Spanish-American War. The younger man tactfully deferred, but he increasingly sympathised with those in the Cabinet who desired a change in British policy. In 1900, he helped ease Salisbury from the Foreign Office in favour of Lord Lansdowne, who inaugurated a new era with the Anglo-Japanese Alliance of January 1902.[5] Balfour's own

---

[3] Lady Gwendolen Cecil *Life of Robert, Marquis of Salisbury* (London 1922–32) vol. I p. 108 and vol. IV p. 267; P. Smith (ed.) *Lord Salisbury on Politics* (London 1972) pp. 26 and 53–5; M. Pinto-Duschinsky *The Political Thought of Lord Salisbury* (London 1967) pp. 12, 25, 54–74, and 134. Pinto-Duschinsky argues that Salisbury upheld 'Empirical Conservatism', i.e. a political philosophy based on liberal empiricist and utilitarian assumptions, but tempered by caution and pessimism.

[4] W.S. Blunt *My Diaries* (London 1919–20) vol. I p. 357; Z.S. Steiner *The Foreign Office and Foreign Policy 1898–1914* (Cambridge 1969) p. 26; Alice Balfour's diary, 11 Aug. 1898, SRO GD 433/2/224; A.L. Kennedy *Salisbury 1830–1903* (London 1952) p. 318.

[5] G.E. Buckle (ed.) *The Letters of Queen Victoria* 3rd Series vol. III (London 1932) pp. 606–7.

succession awaited the end of the Boer War. He became Prime Minister on 12 July 1902.

Lansdowne remained Foreign Secretary. A characteristic practitioner of old diplomacy, he was punctilious, cautious, and pragmatic. 'I shouldn't call him clever', said Balfour (who had been his fag at Eton), ' – he was better than competent.' Diffident by nature, the Foreign Secretary sought frequent reassurance from his Leader, who commented and criticised in a friendly fashion.[6] 'You can't expect the P.M. *not* to interfere in Foreign Office business', Balfour always maintained. He claimed to have worked in perfect harmony with Lansdowne, who praised his unremitting attention to foreign affairs.[7] Together they dealt with Anglo-Russian rivalry in Asia, concern over German ambitions, the Alaskan frontier dispute, the Russo-Japanese War, and, most famously, the *Entente Cordiale*. Balfour also created the Committee of Imperial Defence to co-ordinate military, naval, and foreign policy. In 1905 it seemed that his greatest claim to fame was to have broken the tradition of indifference to defence.[8]

Unionist politics were meanwhile convulsed by Joseph Chamberlain's divisive advocacy of Tariff Reform. While his party fought among itself, Balfour clung to office – partly because he considered his likely Liberal successor, Campbell-Bannerman, unfit to handle foreign complications[9] – but desperate ducking and weaving on trade policy earnt him an enduring reputation for slippery insubstantiality. When he declined 'to profess a settled conviction where no settled conviction exists' during a fiscal debate in 1903, he coined a phrase which has stuck. Some people accept Birkenhead's appraisal of Balfour as one of the greatest intellects ever to engage in British politics. Others prefer Curzon's gibe that he possessed 'the mind of a marshmallow'.[10] Balfour did once joke:

[6] Steiner *Foreign Office* p. 46; Egremont *Balfour* pp. 162–63; Notes by Sandars, [*c*. 1929], Sandars Papers c. 771 ff. 70–2 and 330.
[7] E.W. Edwards 'The Prime Minister and Foreign Policy – The Balfour Government', in H. Hearder and H. Loyn (eds.) *British Government and Administration* (Cardiff 1974) pp. 202–14; Sir Austen Chamberlain *Down the Years* (London 1935) p. 209; 'Lord Lansdowne on Foreign Affairs' *Times* 7 Nov. 1905 p. 6.
[8] 'Mr. Balfour and Imperial Defence' *Times* 13 Sept. 1905 p. 6.
[9] M.V. and O. Brett (eds.) *Journals and Letters of Reginald, Viscount Esher* (London 1934–8) vol. II p. 56.
[10] 10 June 1903, *PDeb* 4th Series vol. 123 col. 575; J. Campbell *F.E. Smith, First Earl of Birkenhead* (London 1983) p. 251; Mosley *Curzon* p. 157.

'I am a thick-and-thin supporter of nothing, not even of myself',[11] but Lord D'Abernon perceived the truth: 'the reality of belief was much stronger than the superficial appearance. There were profound convictions on a limited number of subjects, and these were proof against the assaults of time or argument. Admittedly, fundamental convictions were few in number, but even outside these Balfour was tenacious rather than changeable.'[12]

He was safe enough when he told reporters: 'it is my good fortune to be a consistent thinker, and, therefore, I am never dismayed or embarrassed when previous utterances of mine are referred to'.[13] The 'No Settled Convictions' tag was born of his agility at walking the tight-rope of party unity. It survived because he made a habit of qualified expression. This was his fastidious (sometimes Jesuitical) method for allowing political adaptability while retaining personal integrity. It was also in part the deliberate practice of a philosophic sceptic. In an age when the unprecedented growth of knowledge was threatening to blind Western civilisation to the vastness of its residual ignorance, Balfour refused to add to the common stock of false certainties. He was also psychologically disinclined to strong emotional commitment.

Committed he certainly was to the practice of politics. The resignation of his Government on 4 December 1905 was followed by heavy electoral defeat, but Balfour soldiered on as Leader of the Opposition through six turbulent years, fighting Liberal reforms and campaigning for faster 'Dreadnought' building. Two more lost elections and recriminations over the Parliament Act finally precipitated his resignation as Conservative leader on 8 November 1911.

Any impression that he intended to withdraw from public life was soon dispelled. His particular interests – Ireland, defence, and international affairs – dominated the political agenda 1911–14, and he could see himself as Foreign Secretary in the next Conservative Government.[14]

The War recalled him to the front rank of working politicians. He was invited in October 1914 to rejoin the Committee of Imperial Defence, which, renamed the War Council, soon became

---

[11] 'Mr. Balfour in Manchester' *Times* 11 Jan. 1900 p. 10.
[12] Viscount D'Abernon *Portraits and Appreciations* (London 1931) p. 43.
[13] Balfour *Opinions and Argument* p. 45.
[14] 15 Nov. 1912, Lord Riddell *More Pages from my Diary* (London 1934) pp. 101–2.

an inner Cabinet. Coalition in May 1915 ended his anomalous constitutional position and made him First Lord of the Admiralty. Optimistic about ultimate Allied victory, he recommended preserving the Fleet and tightening the blockade, while maintaining a defensive position on land. It would then be a matter of waiting for the Germans to wear themselves out in futile offensives.[15] To impatient colleagues (and the popular press) this fabian strategy appeared fainthearted. Lloyd George included in his December 1916 ultimatum to Asquith a demand that Balfour be dismissed. When the ensuing crisis was over, Lloyd George was Prime Minister and Balfour was Foreign Secretary. 'There are many things to consider in the formation of a Government', Lloyd George explained, 'and the placing of Balfour at the Foreign Office was of incalculable assistance to me' – for with him came solid Conservative support. The appointment still provoked criticism.[16]

Balfour has been called 'England's unknown Foreign Secretary',[17] but the 'Balfour Declaration' on Palestine is well remembered, and the 'Balfour Mission' to the USA was celebrated at the time. He helped determine policy towards the Russian Revolution and, from January to September 1919, attended the Paris Peace Conference – as second plenipotentiary on the Council of Ten until June, and then as Head of the British Delegation. He was thus a signatory of the Treaties of Versailles and St Germain, but to the press 'the delegates of Liberia and Siam were by comparison world figures'.[18]

If Balfour was a shadowy figure 1916–19, it was largely because Lloyd George always stood in the limelight, having proposed from the first to take a direct interest in Foreign Office business. One voice among many in the policy process, Balfour was not a member of the five-man War Cabinet, although free to attend whenever he wished (which was more often than not).[19] Lloyd George liked to hear his analyses, adding: 'His mind is opposed to action, but

---

[15] Lord Bertie *The Diary of Lord Bertie of Thame 1914–1918* (London 1924) vol. I p. 336; Memo. by Balfour, 1 Feb. 1915, BP 49712 ff. 144–8; Memo. by Balfour, 27 Dec. 1915, PRO CAB 42/7 No.5 (Annexe).
[16] Lloyd George to Gwynne, 8 Dec. 1916, Lloyd George Papers F/22/4/2; 'How to Lose the War' *Daily Mail* 9 Dec. 1916 p. 4.
[17] H. Nelson *Land and Power* (London 1963) p. 4.
[18] 'E.T. Raymond' [E.R. Thompson] *Mr. Balfour* (London 1920) p. 200.
[19] Lloyd George to Gwynne, 8 Dec. 1916, Lloyd George Papers F/22/4/2; Dugdale *Balfour* vol. II pp. 241–2.

I can decide, and such a discussion is of the utmost value.' This encapsulates their relationship, which was cordial enough on the mutually patronising basis which reconciles very different personalities: each sincerely admired the other for qualities which he himself lacked, while never doubting that his own attributes were somehow superior.[20] Lloyd George did not scruple to bypass or over-rule his Foreign Secretary. Balfour recognised 'the Little Man's' failings: he was impulsive, he did not adequately gauge the depths of his own ignorance, he was frankly a very bad diplomatist – but he was far the best Prime Minister available, so the patriotic course was to provide him with all help and guidance.[21]

The eclipse of a Foreign Secretary in war-time seemed understandable. His failure to re-emerge come the peace did not. What sort of Minister 'day by day pulled the extinguisher more firmly down on the head of his own Department'?[22] A geriatric one, it is often assumed. Balfour was sixty-eight in December 1916 and a little hard of hearing. A rest-cure at Eastbourne was not a dashing start to a Foreign Secretaryship. Yet this man had another decade of political life ahead of him and still played tennis in his eightieth year. Despite life-long martyrdom to severe colds and mild hypochondria, he seemed to take to his bed *less* frequently after middle age. His deserved reputation for absent-mindedness was nothing new either, and he rather played up to it.[23] The peculiarities of his incumbency owed more to personality than to age.

Balfour was on his own admission a lazy man. Though energetic on occasion, he had no patience for drudgery and disliked heavy reading.[24] State papers were often skimmed, and his comments on them were notoriously brief and uninformative. In 1915 he had asked for a job which entailed no onerous office work.[25] Placed

---

[20] J. McEwen (ed.) *The Riddell Diaries 1908–1923* (London 1986) pp. 234, 21, and 238; Jones *Whitehall Diary* vol. 1 p. 201.

[21] Balfour to Cecil, 12 Sept. 1917, Cecil Papers 51071A ff. 45–6; Alice Balfour's diary, 20 Nov. 1917 and 4–5 Dec. 1918, SRO GD 433/2/136 pp. 8 and 15.

[22] Mosley *Curzon* p. 207.

[23] R. Jenkins *Asquith* (London 1964) p. 518; Lord Rayleigh *Lord Balfour and his Relation to Science* (Cambridge 1930) p. 36; J. Vincent (ed.) *The Crawford Papers* (Manchester 1984) pp. 212 and 392; Ian Malcolm *Vacant Thrones* (London 1931) pp. 29–30.

[24] 'Lord Balfour's Memoirs' *Times* 9 Oct. 1930 p. 15; Balfour *Opinions and Argument* p. 174; Rayleigh *Balfour* pp. 11 and 15.

[25] Ronald Storrs *Orientations* (London 1945) p. 260; J.T. Shotwell *At the Paris Peace Conference* (New York 1937) p. 122; Harold Nicolson *People and Things* (London 1931) pp. 12–13;

later in the post which he considered most demanding, he was zealous neither to guard departmental prerogatives nor to immerse himself in departmental duties. Routine diplomatic business was generally left to his deputy, Cecil, and Permanent Under-Secretary, Hardinge, whose advice on high policy was not much sought. Balfour had formed his working relationship with the Foreign Office in the days when top civil servants were still regarded primarily as clerks. He expected his subordinates to perform their work with minimal supervision and to provide instant information. Otherwise he did not pay them very much attention. One official recalled: 'If he was not interested – and how often he was not! – it was hard indeed to break through his indifference and procrastination'.[26] Arnold-Forster, Secretary of State for War 1903–5, once complained that briefing Balfour was a waste of time anyway: 'nothing will remain but the purely fancy picture which he has evolved out of his own consciousness, and from a variety of tags of conversation, scraps of speeches, and mis-applied general propositions, which are the materials with which he works'.[27]

US Secretary Lansing noticed that he 'had no desire or intention of mastering details if they were at all complex or confused'. The man himself maintained: 'You may know very little, and not be superficial; you may know a great deal, and be thoroughly superficial.' A modicum of knowledge combined with a grasp of general principles was not to be despised. He may generally be reckoned to escape Enoch Powell's stricture that more politicians err through refusal to see simplicities than through unwillingness to grapple with complexities.[28]

Balfour formed opinions distinct from the governmental or departmental view. He did not speak much in Cabinet (relative to his status) and often spoke only for himself. Austen Chamberlain recalled that, even when Balfour thought the same as everyone

---

R. Meinertzhagen *Middle East Diary 1917–1956* (London 1959) p. 23; Balfour to Asquith, 19 May 1915, BP 49692 f. 148.

[26] R.M. Warman 'The Erosion of Foreign Office Influence in the Making of Foreign Policy, 1916–1918' *Historical Journal* vol. 15 no. 1 (1972) p. 155; Salter *Personality in Politics* p. 26.

[27] Diary, 17 June 1908, Arnold-Forster Papers 50353 f. 131.

[28] R. Lansing *The War Memoirs of Robert Lansing* (London 1935) p. 351; W.M. Short (ed.) *Arthur James Balfour as Philosopher and Thinker* (London 1912) p. 182; R. Lewis *Enoch Powell* (London 1979) p. 205.

else, he usually had his own reasons.[29] This disinclination to stand squarely behind a commonplace argument both exasperated and impressed: it marked him as a politician outside the common run. His prestige and authority were largely independent of his office. It is notable that although he held Cabinet rank for a total of twenty-seven years, he was a regular departmental Minister for only nine. As First Lord of the Treasury, as Lord President of the Council latterly, even as Prime Minister, he had freedom to choose issues in which to interest himself. The tendency was fairly much fixed and perennial. He observed in 1924 that membership of the Committee of Imperial Defence without Government office 'exactly suits me, – no pay and no responsibility, except for the work I actually do and the advice I actually give'.[30] It was ever his way to ponder a problem alone, offer his opinion, accept the decision, and – if he did not like it – shrug and head for the golf-links. This was often the measure of his alleged pragmatism. When the War Cabinet, for example, elected against his advice to send Smuts to secret peace talks with Austria in December 1917, Balfour simply recorded his fears, telling Lloyd George: 'I bore you with this note only to liberate my soul!'.[31] His post-war success as an 'Elder Statesman' came after years of rehearsal.

When he left the Foreign Office in October 1919 and became Lord President, his involvement in foreign policy did not end. He was principal British representative at the League of Nations 1920–3, and chief negotiator at the Washington Conference (1921–2). An Earldom followed this popular triumph. He also occasionally acted as Foreign Secretary when Curzon was stricken with back pain. In this capacity in 1922 he penned the 'Balfour Note' on war debt.

As an unrepentant Coalitionist, who supported Lloyd George's stand against Turkey at Chanak, Balfour was excluded from Bonar Law's Ministry in October 1922, although he did not immediately leave the League Council and his connection with the Committee of Imperial Defence continued under Baldwin in 1923. He rejoined the Committee in November 1924 to consider the Geneva Protocol (his memorandum being adopted as the British

---

[29] Chamberlain to Balfour, 20 Apr. 1916, BP 49736 f. 214; Notes by Selborne, Selborne Papers 80 f. 288; Chamberlain *Down the Years* p. 214.
[30] Balfour to Alice Balfour, 26 Nov. 1924, SRO GD 433/2/76 no. 8.
[31] Balfour to Lloyd George, 10 Dec. 1917, PRO FO 800/199 f. 51.

response), and in March 1925 returned to the Cabinet as Lord President. Continuing to contribute to defence and foreign policy discussions, he was prominent at the 1926 Imperial Conference, when the 'Balfour Definition' expressed the relationship between Britain and the Dominions.

His health declined after 1928, and with the resignation of the Baldwin Government in 1929, his career came to a close.

Lord Balfour died on 19 March 1930.

CHAPTER 2

Race, progress, patriotism

His politics were a philosophy.
Ramsay MacDonald on Balfour 1930[1]

Understanding of the actions of statesmen is enhanced by appreciation of the 'philosophies of life' which lie at the back of their minds.[2] These beliefs, which reflect the psychology of the individual and his knowledge of the external world, are both very personal and a product of the times. Say that Balfour called himself an Imperialist and spoke of the 'mission' of the 'co-heirs of Anglo-Saxon freedom and civilisation', for example, and most listeners are today straightway alienated.[3] To his contemporaries these utterances were unsurprising, and there was not much call for him to justify them in depth. Nor perhaps would it have been wise for him to try too explicitly. A philosophical argument between Balfour, Curzon, and Joseph Chamberlain on the ultimate nature of the British Empire could easily have become acrimonious if pursued with rigour. Such questions were generally buried beneath the rhetoric of the platform and the pragmatism of the Cabinet room.

Balfour certainly did not leave his fundamental assumptions about international politics entirely unspoken, however, although he never presented them as a coherently justified whole. This chapter traces his thought from the philosophical bases of his conservatism to his vision of Britain's world-role. The first part introduces Balfourian philosophy against the background of contemporary debate, which was suffused with the implications of the theory of evolution. Attention is drawn to his scepticism of evol-

[1] 20 Mar. 1930, *HCD* vol. 236 col. 2162.
[2] J. Joll *1914* (London 1968) p. 7 and *passim*.
[3] Balfour to Choate, 1 June 1905, BP 49742 ff. 122-3.

20

utionary progress and his emphasis on non-rational forces. Part II shows how these ideas led him to deny that Europeans had a duty to 'civilise' non-Europeans. Part III examines his conception of patriotism and an international system in which widening loyalties would sustain the world leadership of the English-speaking peoples.

PART I: THE DARWINIAN IMBROGLIO

Wrote the Imperial administrator, Alfred Milner, in his self-styled 'Credo': 'this is the law of human progress, that the competition between nations each seeking its maximum development, is the Divine Order of the World, the law of Life and Progress'.[4] The tone of Balfour in Parliament in 1898 was rather different:

Observe that as the world is constituted there is a struggle – sometimes industrial, sometimes military, sometimes diplomatic – going on between the leading nations of the world. I am glad to think that is not the only way in which we can contemplate a display of civilised forces, but that is the way we have to keep in view.[5]

Social Darwinism – the application of biological theories of natural selection to human affairs – was a major influence on the ideology of imperialism in the late nineteenth and early twentieth centuries. Though best remembered for its more extreme manifestations (militarism, racism, eugenics), Darwinian theory had a wider impact on political thought in an age when speculation on the future of mankind was highly fashionable, not least in Britain. To Herbert Asquith, for example, territorial expansion appeared 'as normal, as necessary, as inescapable and unmistakeable a sign of vitality in a nation as the corresponding processes in the growing human body'.[6] By 1900, white English-speakers had succeeded in colonising most of the available temperate regions of the world, and the question arose: would the British Empire endure, or was its zenith the prelude to decline and displacement? The theory of evolution seemed highly relevant. Were 'Anglo-Saxons' of all peoples the fittest, as their measure of global dominion seemed

---

[4] A.M. Gollin *Proconsul in Politics* (London 1964) p. 129.
[5] 29 Apr. 1898, *PDeb* 4th Series vol. 56 col. 1590.
[6] H.C.G. Matthew *The Liberal Imperialists* (Oxford 1973) p. 153. See D.R. Oldroyd *Darwinian Impacts* (Milton Keynes 1980) ch. 17.

to suggest? If so, how could they preserve themselves in the contest with other nationalities?

As 'an outstanding figure of intellectual culture'[7] – President of the British Sociological Society indeed – Balfour was conversant with these questions and took part in the debate. It is perhaps predictable that he did not see eye to eye with stern advocates of perpetual struggle. The bachelor who rose at noon could not easily be regarded, even by his admirers, as the ideal representative of 'this vigorous and virile race'.[8] The more pugnacious type of Edwardian right-winger thought 'the Philosophic Doubter' sadly deficient in fighting spirit.[9] Despite his concern for the armed forces, Balfour shunned the use of Darwinian rhetoric to help promote defensive militarisation. Great international struggles, he said in 1904, always retarded human progress.[10] He was no militarist.

There were yet plenty of unwarlike people who imagined that evolution disclosed the whole plan of life, and they expected politicians to devise policy in the spirit of the new holistic science of society.

Balfour was old enough to have experienced the 'Darwinist Revolution' from early days. Raised in a home 'saturated' with orthodox religion and educated at Cambridge in the 1860s (where he knew Charles Darwin), he was much affected by the contemporary intellectual agonizing over risen apes and fallen angels.[11] A 'curious relic of an older generation' to the Cambridge liberal agnostic set, Balfour found that he could not endure 'complacent acquiescence in the loss of all the fairest provinces of our spiritual inheritance'.[12] Consequently, the bulk of his non-political publications relate to 'the so-called "conflict between religion and science"'. Although dismissed by some as 'outright reactionism', his

---

[7] Malcolm *Balfour* p. 30.
[8] Benjamin Kidd *Social Evolution* new edn (London 1895) p. 48.
[9] E.g. A. Wilson *The Strange Ride of Rudyard Kipling* (London 1977) p. 239. Balfour was a particular target of Kipling's attack on British complacency about invasion in *The Islanders*:
Arid, aloof, incurious, unthinking, unthanking, gelt,
Will ye loose your schools to flout them till
Their brow-beat columns melt?
[10] 'Mr. Balfour on the Crisis' *Times* 29 Oct. 1904 p. 11.
[11] Balfour *Chapters of Autobiography* p. 17; 'The Darwin Centenary' *Times* 24 June 1909 p. 10.
[12] Brett and Brett *Journals and Letters of Esher* vol. 1 p. 182; A.J. Balfour *The Foundations of Belief* 9th impression (London 1906) p. 97.

contribution was not made lightly. He said in 1894 that he felt he had a message to give which was of far greater importance than anything he could do in politics.[13]

Balfour advocated a theistic view of the universe. He argued that ethics, aesthetics, and science itself, are more intelligible when framed in a theological setting, and he attacked the tendency to elevate scientific methods and conclusions into the test and measure of universal truth. Drawing on the philosophy of Hume, he rejected empiricism as a theory of knowledge. Since the uniformity of nature cannot be ascertained, 'the exceedingly thin fare which has so often been served out to us under the imposing title of Inductive Theory' provides no rational justification for belief: 'If scepticism proves anything, it proves that experience proves nothing.' Reasons usually figure among the immediate causes of belief, but 'it is always possible to trace back the causal series to a point where every trace of rationality vanishes'. Religion and science are unproved systems of belief standing side by side, and humanity has a practical need for both. He admitted that this was purely destructive criticism, but 'speculation seems sadly in want of destructive criticism just at the present time'.[14]

It may be objected that consideration of Balfour the metaphysician can reveal nothing about Balfour the politician. A given theory of knowledge can co-exist with all manner of practical belief. Psychologically, however, the human mind is not so cleanly divisible. Nor was Balfour himself convinced of the distinctness of metaphysics. His criticism of the epistemology of scientific materialism easily merged with criticism of evolutionary theory. It is with a certain glee that he approves Berkeley's refutation of the independent existence of matter, challenges the reader to explain evolution in the language of philosophic idealism, and then cites the realist evolutionist Herbert Spencer: 'if idealism be true, Evolution is a dream'.[15] Even a sympathetic reviewer felt concern at the way in which Balfour's causal explanation of belief burgeoned into a glorification of 'Authority' as contrasted with Reason[16]:

[13] R. Bannister *Social Darwinism* (Philadelphia 1979) p. 140; Rayleigh *Balfour* p. 20.
[14] Balfour *Foundations of Belief* p. xviii; A.J. Balfour *Reflections Suggested by the New Theory of Matter* (London 1904) p. 20; A.J. Balfour *A Defence of Philosophic Doubt* (London 1879) pp. 146, 320, and 293; A.J. Balfour *Theism and Humanism* (London 1915) p. 46.
[15] A. and E.M. Sidgwick: *Henry Sidgwick* (London 1906) p. 537; Balfour *Defence of Philosophic Doubt* pp. 303, 50, and 183.
[16] Seth Pringle-Pattison, Dugdale: *Balfour* vol. II pp. 426–7.

we must not forget that it is Authority rather than Reason to which, in the main, we owe, not religion only, but ethics and politics; that it is Authority that supplies us with essential elements in the premises of science; that it is Authority rather that Reason that lays deep the foundations of social life: that it is Authority rather than Reason which cements its superstructure.[17]

Authority was the name given by him to non-rational causes of belief which have their origin in the social environment: 'custom, education, public opinion, the contagious convictions of country-men, family, party, or Church'. Balfour sympathised with the grander efforts of Bergson (probably his favourite contemporary philosopher) to appraise instinct as distinguished from intelli-gence.[18] Whether it was 'the new bigotry' or 'the immemorial association of religious obscurantism and political reaction', lib-eral intellectuals predicted that the legacy of Balfourian irrationalism would be national disaster.[19]

Although he liked to claim that he joined the Conservatives because J.S. Mill called them 'the stupid party', Balfour never eschewed reason within the sphere of its validity. It was the 'piti-less' application of rationalising methods to the whole circle of belief which he found unacceptable.[20] He took a very keen interest in the physical sciences and was President of the British Associ-ation for the Advancement of Science in 1904. Epistemological inadequacy notwithstanding, he came indeed to grant provisional acceptance to evolution as a *biological* theory. Efforts were then directed towards demonstrating the limits of its plausible application.

'Romantic love goes far beyond race requirements', he told his audience. Did communities rich in artistic accomplishments necessarily breed more freely? If not, the evolutionist must rate aesthetic sensibility a purposeless accident – so why did civilised people think it important? Above all, he refused to accept popu-lation increase as the standard of morality. The qualities which secured the 'fitness' of the race were determined merely by

---

[17] Balfour *Foundations of Belief* p. 243.
[18] Balfour *Foundations of Belief* pp. 390 and 226; A.J. Balfour 'Creative Evolution and Philo-sophic Doubt' *Hibbert Journal* vol. 10 (1911) pp. 14–15.
[19] Karl Pearson *Reaction!* (London 1895) pp. 3 and 38–40; 'Hugh Cecil' *Pseudo-Philosophy at the End of the Nineteenth Century* (London 1897) pp. 2 and 304.
[20] Balfour *Chapters of Autobiography* p. 85; Balfour *Foundations of Belief* pp. 179 and 183.

environment. 'In Britain we have so managed matters that con-
genital idiots increase faster than any other class of the population', he remarked: 'If so, they must be deemed the 'fittest' of
our countrymen.' Such 'fitness' was far removed from excellence.
Balfour was not interested in attempts to establish British ethical
superiority through population statistics. Evolution appeared to
him to leave no room for compassion, generosity, or peace. If it
were truly the universal law, Nietzsche was right to denounce the
perverted 'slave morality' of the civilised world. Altruism could
not be based upon egoism: ' "Why" [it is asked] "should we do
anything for posterity, seeing that posterity will do nothing for
us?" The implication is infamous, but the statement is true'.[21]

Religion was the indispensable fount of ethical conduct. All cos-
mologies which excluded the supernatural – variously labelled
Naturalism, Positivism, Materialism, Agnosticism, or Humanism –
were powerless in themselves to promote good behaviour. Super-
naturalism was the only system 'under which we may share the
millennium to which we are invited to contribute'. 'God, freedom,
and immortality,' declared Balfour, 'I believe in them all.' There
was no inevitable incongruity between organic evolution and
Divine design, but as development proceeded the role of evolution
diminished: 'the whole machinery of selection and elimination has
been weakened, if not paralysed, by civilisation itself'.[22] As people
grew more sensitive, they would increasingly turn to Christian
morality and faith in the after-life. Without religion, there was
only a chilling scepticism, which Balfour was eloquent in
expounding:

Famine, Disease, and Mutual Slaughter, fit nurses for the future lord of
creation, have gradually evolved, after infinite travail, a race with conscience enough to know that it is vile, and intelligence enough to know
that it is insignificant. We survey the past and see that its history is of
blood and tears, of helpless blundering, of wild revolt, of stupid acquiescence, of empty aspirations. We sound the future, and learn that after a
period . . . the energies of our system will decay, the glory of the sun will
be dimmed, and the earth, tideless and inert, will no longer tolerate the
race which has for a moment disturbed its solitude . . . Nor will anything
that remains be better or worse for all that the labour, genius, devotion,

[21] Balfour *Theism and Humanism* pp. 71, 60, 109, 118, and 115.
[22] A.J. Balfour *The Religion of Humanity* (Edinburgh 1888) p. 33; Balfour *Theism and Humanism* pp. ix, 35 and 110; Balfour *Foundations of Belief* p. 256.

and suffering of man have striven through countless generations to effect.[23]

Ernest Newman commented that Balfour 'implores us not to believe in naturalism, not because it is false, but because it is horrid'.[24]

Balfour unequivocally rejected the claim of natural selection to be the guiding principle of human society.[25] There was 'no close or necessary connection between biological "fitness" and military or political success'. Natural selection could play no important part in the future development of civilised man – and that was good. Far from being a benevolent social reformer, Nature had no intelligible meaning or purpose.[26]

He was by no means alone in finding pure Darwinism unacceptable. The late nineteenth century spawned numerous theories claiming to harmonise morality and science. One of the most politically influential in Britain was that of Benjamin Kidd, whose *Social Evolution* was a best-seller in the mid-1890s. Kidd was a protégé of Milner, and his work was hailed as a rationale for Empire. Joseph Chamberlain acknowledged its impact on him. Moreover, certain similarities between the thought of Kidd and Balfour were noted.[27]

Kidd sought to include the conflict between religion and reason within the evolutionary dynamic. Rational self-interest would lead men to ease competition by limiting population growth, regardless of subsequent degeneration. Only religion subordinated the present interests of the individual to the future interests of society and promoted the qualities which allowed peaceful competitive progress. The Anglo-Saxon was 'deeply affected, more deeply than many others' by Christian altruism, and the result was superior

[23] Balfour *Religion of Humanity* pp. 44–6.
[24] 'Cecil' *Pseudo-Philosophy* p. 192.
[25] Cf. Mackay *Balfour* p. 17, which uncritically accepts the view of Wilfrid Scawen Blunt that Balfour was a convinced Social Darwinist who found moral sanction for hard-line Imperialism in the rule of survival of the fittest. Blunt, though acquainted with Balfour, was an impassioned anti-Imperialist agitator, who had been imprisoned in Ireland in 1887.
[26] Balfour *Theism and Humanism* p. 111; A.J. Balfour *A Fragment on Progress* (Edinburgh 1892) p. 17; A.J. Balfour *Theism and Thought* (London 1923) p. 32.
[27] D.P. Crook *Benjamin Kidd* (Cambridge 1984) p. 3; Pearson: *Reaction!* p. 6; 'Cecil' *Pseudo-Philosophy* pp. 1–5.

'social efficiency', victory in the struggle for existence, and global preponderance.[28]

Kidd and Balfour were one in their estimate of the beneficence of religion. Kidd's defence of the spiritual was utterly mundane and consequentialist, but Balfour too was given to recommending Christianity on the ground of its efficacy as a 'moralising agent'. They agreed that mankind was escaping violent primal influences and coming under the sway of emotional altruism. Balfour deemed continuity the boast of the British, who, harmonising progress with stability, were ready 'to lead the very van of civilisation'. Though not necessarily the cleverest people in Europe, they were still the most reasonable. Kidd would not have demurred: the accomplishments of civilisation were primarily the measure of social efficiency rather than of intellectual pre-eminence.[29]

The superficial unanimity between the sceptical conservative and the popular philosopher of Imperialism begins to crumble, however, when attention is turned to the nature and function of the British Empire. As a 'religious evolutionist', Kidd believed that progress was universal and desirable. Balfour remained wary of 'the optimism that is always apt to lurk in the word "evolution" '.[30] The difference was not purely academic. It led Balfour and Radical Imperialism to part company over the question of the so-called 'lower races' – no small matter, given that it encompassed the destinies of maybe 800 million inhabitants of Africa, Asia, South America, and the Pacific.

PART II: THE 'LOWER RACES'

'Looking to the world at no very distant date', wrote Darwin, 'what an endless number of the lower races will have been eliminated by the higher civilised races throughout the world.' Hard-line evolutionists could believe that difficulties connected with the existence of non-European peoples would diminish through the effects of mere contact. Kidd predicted that the temperate zones would become the preserve of the white man – the race problem in South

---

[28] Kidd *Social Evolution* pp. 48, 67, 264, 299–301, and 321.
[29] Balfour *Religion of Humanity* p. 50; Crook *Kidd* p. 96; Balfour *Opinions and Argument* pp. 106, 85, and 83; Kidd *Social Evolution* pp. 285 and 349–53.
[30] Kidd *Social Evolution* pp. vii and 37; Balfour *Theism and Humanism* pp. 31–2.

Africa and the USA would vanish.[31]

Balfour agreed that Australian aborigines were dying out, but he doubted that natural law alone would generally sustain the higher races. Inter-marriage rather than extinction was often the legacy of racial domination. This led him to hold 'very decided and advanced views as to the absolute necessity' of keeping white and coloured races apart.[32]

The British Empire contained a greater number of different races than any other State in history. The vast majority of its people were non-whites. What should Britain aim to do with them?

Kidd argued that ethically advanced races had a duty to educate their subject peoples as they would children. British 'trusteeship' could accelerate the evolution of tropical society, which would in time reach a level of social efficiency compatible with self-government within an Imperial federation.[33] This educative justification of colonialism became a kind of orthodoxy.

It was an ideal to which Balfour found it difficult to pay even lip-service. He warned Parliament not to over-rate the chances of reforming Egyptian society:

The time may come when they will adopt, not merely our superficial philosophy, but our genuine practice. But after 3,000, 4,000, or 5,000 years of known history, and unlimited centuries of unknown history have been passed by these nations under a different system, it is not thirty years of British rule which is going to alter the character bred into them by this immemorial tradition.[34]

He was wholly out of sympathy with those to whom the elevation of the lower races seemed an inevitable feature of the march of progress. Kidd said democracy was a stage of human evolution – non-Western peoples (who survived) would attain social organisation of the European type. Balfour refused to accept any 'law' of human progress derived from 'a merely empirical survey of the surface lessons of history'. Given that there was still 'a vast number of savage communities, apparently at a stage of culture

---

[31] F. Darwin (ed.) *The Life and Letters of Charles Darwin* (London 1887) vol. 1 p. 316; Kidd *Social Evolution* pp. 49–54.

[32] 21 Mar. 1904, *PDeb* 4th Series vol. 132 col. 352; Balfour *Theism and Humanism* p. 111; D. Burton 'Theodore Roosevelt and his English Correspondents' *Transactions of the American Philosophical Society* vol. 63 pt 2 (1973) p. 33.

[33] Benjamin Kidd *The Control of the Tropics* (New York 1898) pp. 43–56.

[34] 13 June 1910, *HCD* vol. 17 col. 1142.

not profoundly different from that which prevailed among prehistoric man', history could equally be read as proof that progress was the exception rather than the rule. 'Progress is with the West', said Balfour. Where were the untried races competent to construct a new and better habitation for the spirit of man? 'They do not exist.'[35]

Progressive civilisation was 'a plant of tender habit, difficult to propagate, not difficult to destroy, that refuses to flourish except in a soil which is not to be found everywhere'. Most races were capable of creating and sustaining some level of civilisation, but apparently that level could not permanently be overpassed:[36]

They have emerged from the dim workshop where the rough machinery of nature has, in remotest ages, wrought in to each its inalienable heritage of natural gifts and aptitudes; – and in these must the character and limits of their development in part be determined.[37]

I at least find it quite impossible to believe that any attempt to provide widely differing races with an identical environment, political, religious, what you will, can ever make them alike. They have been different and unequal since history began; different and unequal they are destined to remain through future periods of comparable duration.[38]

The inherited constitution of a race set a limit to its capacity for civilisation, and any forced advance beyond that limit would soon be nullified by decadence. Balfour did not assume that the lower races had already achieved all of which they were capable. It was unlikely that any community had ever reached its limit by its own unaided efforts. He might not believe what he chose to tell Parliament – that British rule was of 'infinite benefit to the races with whom we deal' – but his biological assumptions alone did not preclude their limited advancement.[39]

In contemporary usage, the word 'race' subsumed both physiological and cultural characteristics, but this did not lead Balfour into the trap of attributing all important traits to an immutable 'germ-plasm'. History provided examples of races which passed from barbarism to civilisation and back again. The varying shades

---

[35] Kidd *Control of the Tropics* pp. 43–4; Balfour *Fragment on Progress* pp. 6 & 4; A.J. Balfour *Decadence* (Cambridge 1908) p. 42.
[36] Balfour *Fragment on Progress* p. 6; Balfour *Decadence* pp. 38–9.
[37] Balfour *Fragment on Progress* p. 18.
[38] Balfour *Decadence* pp. 46–7.
[39] Balfour *Decadence* p. 47; 13 June 1910, *HCD* vol. 17 col. 1143.

of national character could not, therefore, simply be put down to variations in national descent. Two factors made each generation what it was: the 'raw material' produced by genetic inheritance and the 'process of manufacture'.[40] Could the colonial apostles of Western civilisation, albeit constrained by the quality of the raw material, yet manufacture an improved type of Asian or African?

In effect, Balfour's answer was the one for which he was notorious: 'Theoretically: YES . . . Practically: NO.'[41] The process of human manufacture, which largely determined the level of the social system, was the inheritance of environment, beliefs, traditions, sentiments, customs, laws, and organisation. These were the forces of Authority, which produced a 'Psychological Climate' – an atmosphere favourable to certain modes of belief, unfavourable, or even fatal, to others. One could talk of the Psychological Climate of an individual, a family, a sect, a generation, a nation, an epoch, or a whole civilisation.[42]

Psychological Climate could prove very resilient. The use of reasoned argument to persuade a man to give up barbaric practices (which were in tune with his Psychological Climate) would most likely prove futile. This was not because he was necessarily unintelligent, but because Reason played so small a part in belief. Balfour thought it obvious that:

a man's beliefs are very much the results of antecedents and surroundings with which they have no proper logical connection. That the sons of Christians are much more often Christians, and the sons of Mahommedans much more often Mahommedans, that a man more commonly holds the opinions of those with whom he lives, and more commonly trusts the policy of the party with whom he acts, than on the theory of probability could happen supposing that conviction was in all cases the result of an impartial comparison of evidence, must always have been plain to the most careless observer.[43]

Since 'the beliefs, the affections, the passions, and the prejudices of Mankind' were not grounded in Reason, Reason by itself was powerless to uproot them. Any appearance to the contrary stemmed from the use of Reason to clear superannuated beliefs

[40] Balfour *Fragment on Progress* pp. 19–21, 12, and 17–18.
[41] P. Brendon: *Eminent Edwardians* (London 1979) p. 77.
[42] Balfour *Decadence* pp. 43–4; Balfour *Foundations of Belief* pp. 218–19.
[43] A.J. Balfour 'A Speculation on Evolution' *Fortnightly Review* vol. 28 no. 131 (Nov. 1877) p. 698.

out of the way, when the sentiments supporting them were already in decay.[44] Where Western notions of morality did find favour with other races, it was in consequence of their association with Western armaments and science. The real reason for European dominance was the singular ability of Western nations 'to cultivate *in the same class* both the love of commerce and the love of fighting'.[45]

Idealistic Imperialists could still argue that the mere presence of powerful foreigners in a society must alter the forces of Authority. This, coupled with social reform, would create a new environment, with new laws, new institutions, new customs, and new sentiments, and thus, over generations, transform the Psychological Climate of the race. The nature of society was more potent to determine the nature of the people, than was the nature of the people to determine the nature of society. This was pure Radicalism – meet for Joseph Chamberlain maybe, but quite unacceptable to Balfour, whose conservatism ruled out deliberate reconstruction of the social fabric on rational principles. Mankind had not sufficient knowledge to employ political action to great effect, he maintained. There was not yet anything deserving the name of political science, and attempts to create one were unlikely to prove fruitful: 'a sociologist so coldly independent of the social forces among which he lived as thoroughly to understand them, would, in all probability, be as impotent to guide the evolution of a community as an astronomer to modify the orbit of a planet'.[46]

In promoting the social sciences, Balfour stressed the need to prevent well-meaning but stupid people rushing to the first quack remedy for social evils that presented itself.[47] It was inadvisable to tamper with the customs and codes that fixed and rendered stable those feelings and beliefs on which society was founded. The primary role of government was not to transform society, but to provide the conditions under which the world might be advanced by the scientific and artistic fruits of individual genius. Scientists were the motive power of progress, with politicians 'but

[44] Balfour *Fragment on Progress* pp. 53–4; Balfour *Foundations of Belief* pp. 219–21 and pt 3 ch. 2 *passim*.
[45] Balfour *Theism and Humanism* p. 116; Balfour to Ronaldshay, 3 Nov. 1906, BP 49859 f. 107.
[46] Balfour *Fragment on Progress* pp. 51–2.
[47] Balfour *Religion of Humanity* pp. 18–19; A.J. Balfour 'Politics and Political Economy' *National Review* vol. 5 (1885) p. 367.

the fly on the wheel':[48] 'It is only the thinnest surface layer of law and custom, belief and sentiment, which can either be subjected to destructive treatment, or become the nucleus of any new growth . . . so many of our most famous advances in political wisdom are nothing more than the formal recognition of our political impotence'.[49]

By this standard, Balfour took a prudent view of colonial government. While Kidd predicted that within a century the British Empire would consist of 'four hundred million people speaking one language and inheriting one law and one ethos', Balfour thought British values would remain essentially alien to most Imperial subjects. Even where a different race accepted an imperial system with contentment and pride, disharmony persisted undetected by those who suffered from it. This was Balfour's explanation of the collapse of Roman civilisation. Traditional social organisation was deeply ingrained in all races. Western peoples displayed the capacity for self-government as soon as they emerged into history.[50] For much of Asia and Africa absolutism was the inherent order of things:

We may crystallise and re-crystallise a soluble salt as often as we please, the new crystals will always resemble the old ones . . . So it is, or seems to be, with these oriental states . . . always either autocracies or aggregations of autocracies; and no differences of race, of creed, or of language seem sufficient to vary the violent monotony of their internal history.[51]

He told Parliament not to approach the troubles of Egypt as if they were problems affecting the Isle of Wight. Orientals had different values:

a true Eastern sage would say that the working government which we have taken upon ourselves in Egypt and elsewhere is not a work worthy of a philosopher – that it is the dirty work, the inferior work, of carrying on the necessary labour. Do let us put this question of superiority and inferiority out of our minds. It is wholly out of place.[52]

Balfour's philosophy was strongly relativistic: a man's beliefs

[48] Balfour *Fragment on Progress* pp. 57, 39, 25 and 33; Balfour *Decadence* pp. 55 and 60; Rayleigh *Balfour* p. 31.
[49] Balfour *Fragment on Progress* pp. 59–60.
[50] Benjamin Kidd *Individualism and After* (Oxford 1908) pp. 35–6; Balfour *Decadence* pp. 40–1; 13 June 1910, *HCD* vol. 17 col. 1141.
[51] Balfour *Decadence* pp. 35–6.
[52] 13 June 1910, *HCD* vol. 17 cols. 1140–1.

were the results of his time and circumstances. He endorsed Christianity because it met his 'ethical needs'.[53] Critics thought it odd that a champion of orthodox religion should have no means of showing that the ethical needs of a Hindu mystic were any less good than his own. A Brahman even thanked him for supplying arguments which could be used against Christian missionaries.[54] Relativism did not prevent Balfour from passing judgments – it was a matter of coherence that any known ethical system which differed from one's own must be regarded as an inferior ethical system. He nevertheless believed that all great religions were inspired of God, and that every human being, whatever his race or creed, spelt out something of the message of 'the One Reality'.[55]

On hearing the problems of the world in 1925 attributed to the decline of European prestige, Balfour disagreed: 'I sometimes regret that European civilisation, or what passes for such, retains as much prestige as it does.'[56] He feared that the sudden invasion of modern Western culture into ancient societies must have catastrophic effects, which would endanger some of the highest interests of Oriental peoples, and he was sorry that the impact could not be slowed to permit gradual adaptation. No community could ever flourish if it was faithless to its own past.[57] Deliberate re-education of the lower races seemed to him a massive undertaking of doubtful feasibility, offering little lasting reward:

the influence which a superior civilisation ... may have in advancing an inferior one, though often beneficent, is not likely to be self-supporting; its withdrawal will be followed by decadence, unless the character of the civilisation be in harmony both with the acquired temperament and the innate capacities of those who have been induced to accept it.[58]

Even more decisively, he lacked belief in the universal applicability of Anglo-Saxon values. Without that, an Imperial crusade for civilisation made no sense.

---

[53] Balfour *Defence of Philosophic Doubt* p. 268; Balfour *Foundations of Belief* pp. 332–3 and 344.
[54] Sir Frederick Pollock 'A.J. Balfour, the Foundations of Belief', *Mind* vol. 4 (1895) p. 380; Frederic Harrison *The Philosophy of Common Sense* (London 1907) pp. 56–9; Vamadeo Shastri 'Brahmanism and the Foundations of Belief' *Fortnightly Review* vol. 64 no. 347 (Nov. 1895) pp. 690 and 697.
[55] A.J. Balfour 'The Philosophy of Ethics' *Mind* vol. 3 (1878) pp. 85–6; Balfour *Foundations of Belief* pp. 320–1 and 375.
[56] 6 July 1925, *HLD* vol. 61 col. 1042.
[57] Short *Balfour* pp. 195–6; 'L.C.C. Election Campaign' *Times* 24 Feb. 1925 p. 14.
[58] Balfour *Decadence* pp. 58–9.

Such thinking seemed almost amoral to the idealistic Imperialists of 1900. It had been more widespread thirty or forty years earlier in the wake of the Indian Mutiny. The President of the London Anthropological Society in 1866 had emphasised the impossibility of applying the civilisation of one race to another race essentially distinct: 'Statesmen may ignore the existence of race-antagonism; but it exists nevertheless.'[59] Of this Balfour seldom needed to be reminded.

PART III: THE ANGLO-SAXON PEACE

It is true that Balfour tended to 'strip humanity down to ruthless cultural and racial essences'.[60] Different racial and cultural essences gave rise to different social and political systems. This created a gulf between dissimilar peoples. It also united kindred ones.

'The days are for great Empires and not for little States', said Chamberlain, encapsulating an opinion widely held. The sociological theory of Radical Imperialism predicted that the larger political aggregates would consist of semi-civilised and savage communities under the protection of civilised nations.[61] Balfour accepted the aphorism, but he rejected the sociology.

The basis of any stable polity, he believed, was loyalty. It lay at the root of all effective co-operation, acting 'like those alloys which add strength and elasticity even to steel'. It empowered social institutions to command disinterested service and uncalculating devotion. Like all great social forces, loyalty was constantly perverted, but it was no less vital for that.[62] His recognised sources of loyalty come as no surprise: 'Think of the thousand ties most subtly woven out of common sentiments, common tastes, common beliefs, nay, common prejudices, by which from our very earliest

---

[59] C. Bolt *Victorian Attitudes to Race* (London 1971) p. 4.

[60] E.W. Said *Orientalism* (London 1978) p. 36. Said was ill-advised, however, to select Balfour as his archetypal British Imperialist for purposes of argument. Not all his conclusions are true of the man to whom he specifically relates them.

[61] 'Mr. Chamberlain in Birmingham' *Times* 17 May 1902 p. 12; Franklin Giddings *Democracy and Empire* (New York 1900) p. v.

[62] Balfour *Foundations of Belief* p. 229; Balfour *Theism and Humanism* pp. 104–7; Balfour *Decadence* p. 50.

childhood we are all bound unconsciously but indissolubly together into a compacted whole.'[63]

There was no reliable substitute for Authority. To think otherwise was a great delusion.[64] Coercion could not forge a durable nation where no fundamental accord existed. If economic considerations had been paramount, nations in their present form would have disappeared in the attempt to maximise the fluidity of capital and labour. Custom and sentiment, and not economic self-interest, largely ruled mankind. A community founded on rational argument would soon be a community no longer: 'imagine nicely adjusting our loyalty and our patriotism to the standard of a calculated utility'.[65]

The Britain that commanded loyalty was not so much a land as a Psychological Climate, which transcended time and space. The nation was more than the sum of its individuals. Its corporate reality was not a fiction.[66] 'Britishness' existed wherever men were predominantly subject to the Authority of a particular set of habits, customs, and traditions. 'A common method of dealing with all problems, a common outlook upon the world', Balfour explained, 'these are things which we did not acquire for ourselves, but which we inherited and which we cannot dissipate.'[67] The bonds of sentiment and understanding which joined these people made armed conflict between them almost unthinkable. They would, moreover, stand together in defence of their common way of life against any external attempt to impose on them a regime alien to their temperament. The British communities of the world constituted a truly natural alliance – an ideal coalition for mutual service and protection – which owed its enduring cohesiveness, not primarily to legal ties or to self-interest, but to an inherent sense of loyalty. Similarity of language, literature, law, religion, and constitution 'ought surely to produce a fundamental harmony, – a permanent sympathy – compared to which all merely political alliances with other States should prove to be the evanescent

---

[63] Balfour *Fragment on Progress* pp. 55–6.
[64] Balfour *Fragment on Progress* p. 55; Balfour *Theism and Humanism* p. 106.
[65] A.J. Balfour *Economic Notes on Insular Free Trade* (London 1903) pp. 4–5; Balfour *Fragment on Progress* p. 56.
[66] Balfour to Esher, 12 Oct. 1912, BP 49719 f. 234.
[67] E.S. Martin *The Life of Joseph Hodges Choate* (London 1920) vol. II pp. 292–3.

result of diplomatic convenience'.[68]

Balfour cast his net wide: the United States of America was 'not in any sense' a foreign community. Americans were 'our own flesh and blood, speaking our own language, sharing our own civilisation':[69]

Churches, Universities, Schools, Representative Assemblies, Debating Societies, Games, Sport, Charitable Institutions, Religion, Irreligion, Modes of philosophic thought, Quality of moral judgments, Political aptitudes, National ambitions, Individualistic preferences.

These are but samples: but does not each one of them suggest points on which, for good or evil, the English-speaking peoples instinctively resemble each other, and instinctively differ from the rest of the world?[70]

Such resemblances might defy verbal analysis, but they were nonetheless real. Britain and the USA 'cannot help being considered as one nation', for from common inheritance sprang common sentiments, which would result 'in not inconceivable eventualities, in common action'. He proclaimed 'that our pride in the race to which we belong is a pride which includes every English-speaking community in the world' – Britain, the United States, Canada, Australia, and New Zealand were united in 'an Anglo-Saxon patriotism'.[71]

This did not imply a doctrine of racial purity: 'There is no such thing in these islands as a man of pure descent from any race whatever.' Anglo-Saxon was a useful generalisation which gave way to 'English-speaking' when racial terminology became unfashionable. Anglo-Saxon patriotism was not highly exclusive. Balfour told an American correspondent that it might well be professed by all who elected to become citizens of Britain or the USA, whatever their origin – though this was an overstatement, given his racial views. He did believe that each Briton possessed 'that trace of inherited aptitude of blood' – an inheritance not indeed from the Anglo-Saxons of the Dark Ages, or their Celtic predecessors, but from the prehistoric people of the British Isles. A trace of the

[68] Balfour to White, 12 Dec. 1900, BP 49742 f. 69.
[69] Balfour to Carnegie, 28 July 1903, BP 49742 f. 244; 'Mr. Balfour's Challenge' *Times* 2 Dec. 1910 p. 9; A.J. Marder (ed.) *Fear God and Dread Nought* (London 1952) vol. II p. 350 n. 1; 'Mr. Balfour on Foreign Affairs' *Times* 16 Jan. 1896 p. 10.
[70] 'English Speaking Patriotism' by Balfour, Apr. 1923, BP 49959 f. 312.
[71] Short *Balfour* p. 294; Balfour to Kerr, 18 Mar. 1911, BP 49797 f. 13; 'Mr. Balfour on Foreign Affairs' *Times* 16 Jan. 1896 p. 10.

ancient blood being enough, however, he condoned absorption of a certain number of European immigrants. Anglo-American civilisation could learn from other nationalities, though it 'must through all time maintain a separate individuality of its own'.[72]

Anglo-Saxon patriotism did not demand the destruction of more localised loyalties. Variation was a necessary part of full and healthy national life. Balfour was ever ready to praise 'the intense and ardent patriotism for a part, which yet reinforces and strengthens the larger patriotism for the whole'.[73] That patriotism need have no exclusive application was a Balfourian article of faith:

some combination of different patriotisms is almost universal among thinking persons. If I consider the case I know best (namely my own), I find that within a general regard for mankind, which I hope is not absent or weak, I am moved by a feeling, especially patriotic in character, for the group of nations who are the authors and the guardians of western civilisation, for the sub-group that speaks the English language, and whose laws and institutions are rooted in British history, for the communities which compose the British Empire, for the United Kingdom of which I am a citizen, and for Scotland, where I was born.[74]

Statesmanship could have no higher aim than to make harmony between the various patriotisms easy and conflict impossible. Imbalanced loyalties lay at the root of many national and international difficulties. In a well-constructed community, noble patriotisms did not clash – they strengthened each other. To be a Scotsman was a privilege, the greater because it entailed membership of Britain, the British Empire, and the English-speaking world.[75]

The broadening of effective sympathies was a gradual process, in which political action could not run far in advance of the development of the Psychological Climate. Balfour concentrated on promoting it at the level which was currently appropriate – by consolidating the common patriotism of the British Empire and integrating it with the United States of America. 'I am nothing

---

[72] A.J. Balfour 'Race and Nationality', *Transactions of the Honourable Society of Cymmrodorian* (1908–9) pp. 238–9; Balfour to White, 12 Dec. 1900, BP 49742 f. 69; Martin *Life* p. 293.
[73] 'Mr. Balfour at Haddington' *Times* 22 Sept. 1902 p. 5; Balfour *Opinions and Argument* p. 60.
[74] Balfour *Opinions and Argument* pp. 66–7.
[75] Balfour *Opinions and Argument* p. 67; 'Mr. Balfour at Haddington' *Times* 22 Sept. 1902 p. 5; Intro. by Balfour, J.V. Bates *Sir Edward Carson* (London 1921) p. xi.

if not an apostle of the English-speaking world', he said.[76]

It was commitment to principles, and not lack of them, which led him to oppose Irish nationalism and champion Zionism. He believed that the doctrine of nationality had played a valuable part in the construction of the modern world. Insofar as it was a centripetal principle, it helped people to work easily and naturally together, but nationality was only 'one of the methods by which humanity avails itself in the gradual evolution of civilisation, in order to act in some corporate capacity'. It was not an eternal measure but one step in the hierarchy of patriotisms. Nationalism was pernicious when used as an artificial barrier to the extension of loyalty, but those who would so pervert it had to contend with scientific progress. Modern transport was reducing the importance of natural geographical barriers.[77] Mass communications were diminishing linguistic divisions. Balfour was not interested in preserving minority languages and dialects: 'The legacy of the Tower of Babel is sufficiently burdensome already!' More important was 'the maintenance of the Anglo-Saxon language [*sic*] in a single undifferentiated form'.[78]

It was not only among English-speakers that loyalties were expanding. Awareness of the wider community of race and culture was resulting in a global trend towards unification. This great movement to bind peoples together had already produced the United States of America, Italy, and Germany. Believing that great empires generally made for peace, Balfour thought this ultimately to the good.[79]

He also looked beyond 'race patriotism' to the gradual strengthening of patriotic feeling for Western civilisation as a whole. Co-operation between Powers with similar Psychological Climates was realisable, but not too much was to be expected from the Concert of Europe yet, and it would not do to force the pace. The various peoples of the world had never been in closer contact, but they still bore the stamp of 'a different upbringing, a different history, a different psychology from ourselves'.[80] Indeed it was a blessing

---

[76] Dugdale *Balfour* vol. II p. 401.
[77] Balfour *Opinions and Argument* pp. 60 and 88; 'Nationality and Frontiers' *Times* 28 Sept. 1920 p. 12.
[78] Balfour to Bruce, 8 Sept. 1925, SRO GD 433/2/25 no. 203; Balfour to Le Maistre, 6 July 1911, BP 49861 f. 250.
[79] 29 Mar. 1895, *PDeb* 4th Series vol. 32 col. 557–8; Short *Balfour* p. 204.
[80] Balfour *Opinions and Argument* pp. 83–4.

that Britain stood 'on the outskirts of the European system, morally, as well as physically'. Never wholly absorbed, never wholly independent, 'she has developed after a fashion of her own; catching every continental disease – religious, political, or social, – but usually catching it in its least virulent form'.[81]

He nevertheless appreciated the contribution of the leading European nations to the common stock of civilisation. 'I am an immense believer in these separate nationalities', he said: 'I think they give a quality, a tone, a variety to the common work of Western culture which can never be got in any other way.'[82] A regular visitor to Cannes and Bad Gastein, he knew French and some German. Cultural diversity was all important to the future of mankind. He trusted that no one would accuse him of being insensible to the genius of other nations – or of his own:

I do think that among the English-speaking peoples is especially and peculiarly to be found a certain political moderation in all classes which gives one the surest hope of dealing in a reasonable progressive spirit with social and political difficulties. And without that reasonable moderation interchanges are violent, and ... reactions are violent also, and the smooth advance of humanity is seriously interfered with.[83]

The English-speaking peoples were 'the political light bearers for the rest of the civilized world'. Their distinctive contribution to mankind was 'the cause of ordered freedom'.[84] From the distant past the Anglo-Saxon inherited exceptional political aptitudes: 'a passion for independence not inconsistent with a capacity for co-operation, an instinctive liking for Law and Order, and a deep-seated aversion to what seems arbitrary'.[85] Britain had developed the first modern free state, and every great free self-governing community in existence had imitated British institutions. Even now, representative government was rarely very successful except in English-speaking lands, where it was a natural growth.[86] When

[81] Balfour to Aldenham, 18 Mar. 1920, SRO GD 433/2/1 no. 35; Balfour to Younghusband, 21 Nov. 1905, BP 49858 f. 42.
[82] Balfour to White, 12 Dec. 1900, BP 49742 f. 69; Balfour 'Race and Nationality' pp. 240–1.
[83] 'Balfour Realizes Dream of his Life' *New York Times* 13 May 1917 p. 3.
[84] 'Balfour Sees us as Liberty's Leader' *New York Times* 6 Dec. 1921 pp. 1–2.
[85] Foreword by Balfour, L.S. Amery: *The Empire in the New Era* (London 1928) p. viii.
[86] Balfour *Opinions and Argument* pp. 183–4; 'Balfour Sees us as Liberty's Leader' *New York Times* 6 Dec. 1921 p. 2; 'A Note on Indian Reform' by Balfour, 7 Aug. 1917, War Cabinet 214 Appendix I, PRO CAB 21/68.

the Anglo-Saxon turned from domestic to foreign politics he
retained his disposition to peace, freedom, and order. English-
speakers were uniquely qualified to exercise benevolent world
leadership: they had the skill derived from centuries of constitutional government and they had the power derived from possession of territory on every continent. An Anglo-American
alliance need fear no external foes.[87] Here then was the mission
of the 'co-heirs of Anglo-Saxon freedom and civilisation'. It was
not to educate the world but to police it. Balfour urged idealists
to forget 'the impossible aspirations of fanatical peace-at-any-price
persons' and recognise that Britain and the USA were ordained
by Providence to carry out the ideals of self-government, order,
and liberty as a great duty to the world:

we are for peace – peace – peace above all! We are pre-destined to pray
and work together for the great aim of civilisation and progress ... It
is no dream: it is reality. It is not a fantastic representation of what
might be if the world only were constructed on different lines from what
it is. Such dreams are useless. The vision that I am calling up before
you is based on the realities of history – the realities of the past, the
realities of the present, and the common burden thrown upon the two
great nations in the future.[88]

On first thought, peace can appear to be a justification of
hegemony, but a moment's reflection reveals that it is not rated
the one ultimate desideratum. Those in the West who believed
that potentially peaceful Soviet hegemony was on offer after 1945
did not generally rush to accept it. Balfour was at pains to emphasise that so tolerant was Anglo-American hegemony that it hardly
warranted the name:

the fruit of that union will not be the domination over the world of any
special type of civilization, of any particular world power, but rather that
opportunities will be given for each race, for each nation, to develop that
which is best in its own character, that which its own history suggests
is the true line of its development, and that under the aegis of a world
peace, which it will be the business of the Allied nations to guard, all
the family of man may find a higher, a freer, and a safer development
than they ever yet found in the history of the world.[89]

[87] 'Mr. Balfour at Bristol' *Times* 4 Feb. 1896 p. 7.
[88] 28 June 1911, Short *Balfour* p. 295.
[89] 'America's Decision' *Times* 8 May 1918 p. 5.

The crucial assumption was that Anglo-Saxons had acquired a habit of self-mastery which enabled them to use force with wisdom and justice. Believing there to be 'some natural moderation in our British blood',[90] Balfour could claim that his Pan-Anglican vision promised not only a more peaceful world, but a world in which people would be left to live in stable communities where the social system would be broadly in harmony with their deepest natures. The critic may retort that peace is the policy of those who are satisfied. Purely on the basis of his own conservative philosophy, Balfour might have replied that maybe everyone would have been.

[90] 'Mr. Balfour at Haddington' *Times* 22 Sept. 1902 p. 5.

CHAPTER 3

Imperialism

We are not less capable of sustaining the burden of Empire than were our fathers before us. The task is now one of great difficulty. Problems of which in our youth and even in our maturity we never dreamt seem to multiply upon us, until those who endeavour to see the way through the immediate future are almost overwhelmed.

Balfour 1922[1]

'He is now, as he has always been, an Imperialist to the core.' Thus was Balfour commended to his people on assuming the Premiership. A few months before, a distant relative had supplied Elgar with famous stanzas extolling British greatness: 'Wider still and wider shall thy bounds be set; God who made thee mighty, make thee mightier yet.'[2]

In this atmosphere, Balfour could usually be confident that a speech about 'that great colonial Empire which is our boast and pride' would be punctuated with cheers.[3] He did not eschew the standard Conservative claim that Imperial interests were safe in the hands of one party only (at least while Campbell-Bannerman led the Liberals), but his commitment to Empire unquestionably transcended partisan considerations.[4] He could hardly doubt that it was in the interest of mankind that 'the most solid, the most conservative, the most secure State in all Western civilisation' should retain global dominance. The British Empire was 'an influence for the peace of the world and

[1] Balfour *Opinions and Argument* p. 35.
[2] B. Alderson *Arthur James Balfour* (London 1903) p. 357; A.C. Benson *Land of Hope and Glory* (London 1902). Benson's uncle, Henry Sidgwick, was Balfour's brother-in-law.
[3] 'Mr. Balfour in Glasgow' *Times* 15 Jan. 1896 p. 7.
[4] 'Mr. Balfour on the Situation' *Times* 7 June 1902 p. 8; Balfour to Macdonald, 17 July 1908, BP 49859 f. 256.

for the progress of civilisation which yields precedence to no other'.[5]

When Balfour headed the Imperial Government, British world power meant ruling 397 million people and 11 million square miles on five continents, and patrolling the sea-ways between them.[6] This chapter examines his views on three fundamental features of this domain. Naval supremacy is the subject of Part I. Part II is concerned with territorial expansion. Colonial government and the future of British rule are considered in Part III.

PART I: 'RULE BRITANNIA!'

Balfour was ever adamant that the most essential element in Imperial strategy was the British Fleet. He avowed no subject nearer his heart. The Empire could not live a day without the Navy: 'It is the absolute foundation of everything – of all our liberties, of all our greatness.'[7]

He judged Britain unique in this regard. The naval requirements of an island kingdom, reliant on sea-borne trade and responsible for widely scattered colonies, could not be likened to those of France, Germany, or Russia, because their shores were comparatively unassailable and they could trade by land. 'We stand alone', he declared, 'in the fact that our Navy is substantially and essentially a defensive force.'[8]

A defensive force, he insisted – but if the defence were to be effective, the force had to be supreme. Localised naval defence might postpone invasion, but it was powerless to prevent an island being starved into submission: 'England can be brought to her knees ... without a single foreign soldier landing upon these shores. If ... any foreign Power or combination of foreign Powers was to wrest from Great Britain the command of the seas, that day would see the downfall of the British Empire.'[9]

While virtually all British political leaders adhered to the 'Blue

[5] Austen Chamberlain and A.J. Balfour *The Unionist Party and Future Policy* (London 1922) p. 14; 24 July 1924, *HLD* vol. 58 col. 1001.
[6] *The Statesman's Year-Book 1903* (London 1903) p. xxviii.
[7] 24 Feb. 1903, *PDeb* 4th Series vol. 118 col. 777; M. Arnold-Forster *The Rt. Hon. Hugh Oakeley Arnold-Forster* (London 1910) p. 110; 'Mr. Balfour and the Crisis' *Times* 18 Nov. 1910 p. 9.
[8] 1 Mar. 1904, *PDeb* 4th Series vol. 130 cols. 1411–12.
[9] 'Mr. Balfour at Bristol' *Times* 23 Jan. 1894 p. 8.

Water' School of strategy, few were so active in its cause. It was the Balfour Government which scrapped 150 small vessels in 1904, and concentrated on building capital ships which could drive enemy fleets from the oceans. Hailed as the 'Godfather of the Dreadnought', Balfour trusted that Britain would always retain 'that maritime preponderance which is the very condition of our being.'[10]

He could not imagine anyone who read history supposing that the liberties of the world had anything to fear from British naval supremacy. By interest and by tradition, his was of all nations the most desirous of peace. Quite simply: 'I do not think this country will ever indulge in a war of aggression.' In any case, continental Powers (unlike Britain) had large land armies which would make invasion by a maritime Power 'absolutely ludicrous and futile'.[11]

This pointed to even higher considerations than the defence of Britain. The Royal Navy was 'one of the great securities for the peace of the world'.[12] Balfour did not expect other nations merely to tolerate British naval supremacy; he thought they should be grateful for it. In a 1919 memorandum, he explained:

it is land Powers not sea Powers which constitute the most formidable menace to the free development of civilized communities ... In spite of the example of Athens in antiquity, of the Norsemen in the dark ages, of Venice in the late mediaeval period, I think this statement is, broadly speaking, true; and is probably ... at least as true now as it ever has been before. Certainly the Great War that ended in 1815, and the yet greater War whose last act is still unfinished, give ample support to the contention.[13]

History would recognise that Britain had ministered to the freedom of the world by preventing any one Power possessing both sea and land supremacy. If a great military Power had secured dominance at sea, international tyranny would have been the result. How unlike the era of unchallenged British naval mastery, which saw the creation of Belgium, Greece, and the South

[10] H. d'Egville *Imperial Defence and Closer Union* (London 1913) pp. 59 and 64; Fisher to Balfour, 30 Dec. 1907, BP 49712 f. 28; 'The Press Conference' *Times* 10 June 1909 p. 6.
[11] 24 Dec. 1921, *Conference* (Washington 1922) p. 544; 'Mr. Balfour at Norwich' *Times* 5 Nov. 1897 p. 6; 27 July 1906, *PDeb* 4th Series vol. 162 col. 111; 9 May 1906, *PDeb* 4th Series vol. 156 col. 1410.
[12] 14 July 1924, *HLD* vol. 58 col. 510.
[13] Memo. by Balfour, 11 Jan. 1919, BP 49750 f. 215.

American republics, the unification of Italy, and the promulgation of the Monroe Doctrine![14]

Given that 'the freedom of the *Land* is due in no small measure to British ships', Balfour was very wary of the doctrine of 'The Freedom of the Seas'. The vision of a neutral sea untouched by the horrors of war was superficially alluring – and the word 'freedom' was 'naturally, attractive to British and American ears' – but putting an end to blockade and search rights would simply render the ocean a base of hostile operations, where military concentration could be effected without interception. Absolute freedom of the seas would be disastrous: 'To paralyse naval power and leave military power uncontrolled is surely the worst injury which international law can inflict upon mankind.' It would shift the global balance of armed force in favour of the land Powers of Europe, to the detriment of the sea Powers, Britain and the USA. Even if free transportation of troops were forbidden, what about weapons, material for making weapons, food for those who fired the weapons, or any of these bound for transit via neutral ports? Maritime practice had to settle on some fairly arbitrary intermediate position, and Balfour always wanted Britain to retain substantial blockade rights.[15] Do not be misled by his support in 1898 for American proposals to make all private cargoes free from capture. He wanted to limit the change to relief of commerce not attempting to run an *effective* blockade (such as Britain was singularly well equipped to mount).[16] More straightforward was his condemnation of the Declaration of London (an abortive 1911 international agreement on belligerent rights at sea) as favouring the military Powers: 'You do not promote peace by making it easy, or a relatively cheap and a relatively innocuous operation, to go to war with the British Empire.'[17]

Balfour preached that 'gigantic sacrifices' would be worthwhile to ensure that 'whatever happens, whatever comes, whatever be the policy of this or that great military country, the supremacy of Great Britain on the seas shall be undisputed and indisputable'.

---

[14] 'Patriotism and Empire' *Times* 5 Aug. 1915 p. 8; A.J. Balfour *The Freedom of the Seas* (London 1916) pp. 10–11.

[15] 'Mr. Balfour on German Submarines' *Times* 6 Sept. 1915 p. 10; Balfour *Freedom of the Seas* pp. 1 and 4–5; Memo. by Balfour, 11 Jan. 1919, BP 49750 ff. 203–19.

[16] J.W. Coogan *The End of Neutrality* (New York 1981) p. 26.

[17] 3 July 1911, *HCD* vol. 27 cols. 854–6; 'The Declaration of London' *Times* 28 June 1911 p. 9.

It was good for the world. It was essential for the defence of the Empire – and for the defence of the British Isles. The naval estimates would not be reduced by a farthing, even if the principal colonies were lost tomorrow.[18] Was naval supremacy needed to support the Empire, or the Empire needed to support naval supremacy?

PART II: 'WIDER STILL AND WIDER'

Balfour told Parliament in 1906: 'I believe it to be undesirable that we should ever add another square mile to the territories we already possess. For my part, the last thing I want to see is any extension of the British Empire. I want to see its strengthening and consolidation.'[19]

During his political career (1874–1929), the British Empire expanded in northern India, Cyprus, Egypt, the Sudan, the Gold Coast, Nigeria, Kenya, Uganda, Somaliland, the Transvaal, the Orange Free State, Rhodesia, Burma, Malaya, Borneo, New Guinea, Palestine, Jordan, Iraq, Tanganyika, Togoland, Cameroon, South-West Africa, and several Pacific archipelagos. Since Balfour was a Cabinet minister for half this time, to him may reasonably be attributed a share of the responsibility. That he should have denied 'the greedy appetite of John Bull' is predictable,[20] but how did he justify himself?

Publicly he employed the standard formula – and probably recognised it as such. The vaunted desire to confer 'the blessings of peace and civilisation' was inoffensive to foreign Powers and morally acceptable to the British public.[21] Although it has been said that there is no need to question his paternalistic desire for native welfare,[22] the philanthropic motive should not be overstressed. Balfour found any association with physical suffering repugnant, but in his general attitude to human life there was something less of compassion than might have been looked for in a man of his perception and gentility. In 1900, for example, he

---

[18] 'Mr. Balfour on the Navy and the Budget' *Times* 8 May 1909 p. 10; 'Mr. Balfour on the Navy and Tariff Reform' *Times* 31 Mar. 1909 p. 9; 15 Feb. 1907, *PDeb* 4th Series vol. 169 col. 465.
[19] 9 May 1906, *PDeb* 4th Series vol. 156 col. 1409.
[20] 16 Feb. 1900, *PDeb* 4th Series vol. 79 cols. 253.
[21] 5 June 1899, *PDeb* 4th Series vol. 72 col. 349.
[22] Judd *Balfour* p. 294.

strongly deprecated British subsidies to India in famine. Asked if the likely death of 20 million Indians was not a case of extreme necessity, he replied, 'It is not financial necessity.' He admitted that Australian aborigines were 'predestined for extinction' for reasons not always creditable to the white races, but 'the fact is there, and, even if I am charged with inhumanity, I cannot find it in my heart to regret it'. Balfour boasted that Britain could dispense good government to other peoples – but if he was not overmuch concerned whether they lived or died, he was hardly going to be eager to take the trouble.[23] In 1918, Curzon wanted Britain to assume responsibility for the nascent Caucasian republics:

BALFOUR: Why should there be a mandatory? . . . Of course the Caucasus would be much better governed under our aegis . . . But why should it not be misgoverned?
CURZON: That is the other alternative – let them cut each other's throats.
BALFOUR: I am in favour of that.[24]

He added: 'I should say we are not going to spend all our money and men in civilising a few people who do not want to be civilised.' When a Conservative peer sympathised with the view that it would have been better for Africans to have been left in their 'native barbarism', Balfour, responding for the Government, was less than convincing:

I am not going to argue it; it would be folly to argue it. We are committed to the policy. We believe in it. Whether we have been assailed by such doubts as those which have troubled the peace of Lord Howard de Walden, we must all assume that our mission, which we have deliberately undertaken, is that of benefiting the natives by civilising the country and by making them sharers in that civilisation.[25]

In truth, he did not believe that Imperial rule could civilise 'lower races' in any real sense. Nor was he impatient to evangelise them. Opening a Nonconformist bazaar, he said that Christianity ought to be the world religion, but other races would develop their own types of Church.[26]

---

[23] 26 July 1900, *PDeb* 4th Series vol. 86 col. 1434; 16 Aug. 1909, *HCD* vol. 9 col. 1001; 21 Mar. 1904, *PDeb* 4th Series vol. 132 col. 352; 13 June 1910, *HCD* vol. 17 col. 1143.
[24] Eastern Committee, 9 and 16 Dec. 1918, Milner Papers dep.137 ff. 199–200 & 209.
[25] 20 May 1925, *HLD* vol. 61 cols. 398 and 409.
[26] 'Mr. Balfour at the City Temple' *Times* 20 June 1906 p. 10. See above pp. 27–34.

In the absence of a compelling interest in the welfare of non-European peoples, cynics might expect to find a keener interest in their exploitation. The economic side of imperialism, however, was not at all prominent in Balfour's thought. His personal business acumen was slight,[27] and in public life he seldom mentioned colonial commercial opportunities. If a possession could be made to pay, that was all to the good, but he feared that the Colonial Office was expensively administering territories from which the tax-payer would 'never get a sixpence of advantage'. The opening up of markets was to him an occasionally useful argument, rather than a prime political motive. When British involvement in Africa was criticised, he replied that it was important to protect part of that continent from hostile tariffs.[28] He advanced this to justify the cost of keeping order in Somaliland in 1903. In Opposition six years later, he dilated on the burden of Somaliland, which would never be a great outlet for British enterprise. Extraction of colonial raw materials did not excite him either. Assenting to Chamberlain's proposal to spend the 1895 Suez Canal Company dividend on developing Crown Colonies, he yet canvassed the merits of railway construction in Scotland and Ireland.[29]

While not regarding economic expansionism as his direct concern, Balfour appreciated that private sector activities were a dynamic for the extension of British influence. On the fringes of the Empire it was 'practically impossible – human nature being what it is that you will not have the immigration of the civilised people into the territory of the uncivilised in search of working concessions, and so on'. Businessmen then sought protection for their investment, philanthropists demanded regulation to protect the local population, and calls would mount for official British intervention, which might clash with foreign interests (actual or potential) and create international tension. Discussing the Middle East in 1918, he complained that all the trouble with 'these half-civilised States' essentially arose from the struggle for commercial concessions. He had earlier favoured assigning peripheral territories in Africa to chartered companies in order to obviate the need

---

[27] Young *Balfour* pp. xx and 321–2; Egremont *Balfour* pp. 311–2.
[28] 9 Nov. 1893, *PDeb* 4th Series vol. 18 col. 592; 24 Feb. 1899, *PDeb* 4th Series vol. 67 col. 517.
[29] 10 Aug. 1903, *PDeb* 4th Series vol. 127 col. 717; 15 Mar. 1909, *HCD* vol. 2 col. 773; Judd *Balfour* pp. 279–80.

for Government intervention (before the Boer War showed that the British South Africa Company did the reverse). He wished somebody would come up with an answer to the problem.[30]

Recognising that other imperial Powers were subject to similar pressures, Balfour counselled tolerance of rival empires. All commercial States could ultimately benefit from the spread of good order in Africa, so each should be allowed to develop its own sphere.[31] He was anxious that colonial partition be peaceful and clear-cut. When the Allies came to divide the spoils of the Great War, he recommended a generous all-embracing settlement: 'if we could really leave the French and Italians in their own areas, without ever interfering with them, and bring about reciprocity, I believe the greatest British interests would be satisfied. I would much rather have that than some of the colonies we possess or are likely to get.'[32]

If the Balfour who condoned Imperialism was neither a missionary nor a merchant, what was he?

First, he was a guardian of British world leadership, the twin pillars of which were maritime supremacy and Imperial prestige. Other countries were welcome to their 'place in the sun', but he had no intention of allowing them certain places by the sea. Nor could he tolerate their threatening any British possession with impunity. Wherever uncertainty arose concerning the future of territory which could menace an Imperial sea-way or an existing British colony if occupied by a hostile Power, Balfour discerned a *prima facie* case for occupying it first.

Secondly, he was a politician with more pressing matters on his mind than details of frontiers far from Britain – and usually correspondingly remote from British politics. His attitude to the request of the High Commissioner of Northern Nigeria for a military expedition in 1902 is illustrative: 'I think we have been rather ill-used in the matter of information by Lugard, and I am very sorry to think that we seem likely to have another little war upon our hands. But it can't be helped.'[33]

Delegation of frontier policy was practically unavoidable.

---

[30] 9 Nov. 1893, *PDeb* 4th Series vol. 18 cols. 590–5; Eastern Committee, 18 Dec. 1918, Milner Papers dep.137 f. 224.
[31] 'Mr. Balfour at Bristol' *Times* 4 Feb. 1896 p. 7 and 30 Nov. 1898 p. 10.
[32] Eastern Committee, 18 and 26 Dec. 1918, Milner Papers dep. 137 ff. 222 and 253.
[33] Judd *Balfour* p. 271.

Balfour appreciated the result. Commercial pressure for piece-meal expansion was compounded by an inherent institutional tendency:

The perennial difficulty of governing the empire lies in the fact that the rulers in its outlying portions have great local knowledge, but no responsibility & little thought for the general situation; and we at home are naturally reluctant to over-rule people on the spot who say, & often with truth, that their policy is the only one that will save bloodshed & money in the long run.[34]

Faulty perspective characterised 'the terrible breed of those who have been there'.[35]

When Balfour countenanced British expansion, he saw two basic categories. There was (i) strategic expansion on defensive grounds, which he might be willing to support, and there was (ii) peripheral growth, in which he might be prepared to acquiesce.

He explained in 1900 that recent territorial gains were subsidiary to three great responsibilities 'based deep upon incidents in the history of the Empire': Egypt, the Cape of Good Hope, and India.[36] His policies on expansion in each region will be considered in turn. The first two were of strategic value to the maritime Power. Dominance in the region of the Suez Canal ensured access from the Mediterranean to the Indian Ocean. The Simon's Bay naval base facilitated control of passage to the Indian Ocean from the Atlantic. The Indian Empire was a focus of Imperial prestige.

Egypt

Balfour brooked no equivocation here. 'British supremacy exists, British supremacy is going to be maintained', he stated in 1919: 'let nobody either in Egypt or out of Egypt make any mistake upon that cardinal principle.' The unrealisable expectations of Egyptian nationalists, if indulged, would damage Britain and the world – and 'damage most of all the Egyptian population itself'.[37]

He generally spoke as if no people benefited more from British

---

[34] Balfour to Brodrick, 28 Oct. 1903, Midleton Papers 50072 ff. 103–4.
[35] Count Carlo Sforza *Europe and the Europeans* (London 1936) p. 126.
[36] 16 Feb. 1900, *PDeb* 4th Series vol. 79 cols. 251–3; 'Mr. Balfour in Derbyshire' *Times* 12 Oct. 1900 p. 9.
[37] 17 Nov. 1919, *HCD* vol. 121 col. 771.

rule than Egyptians. In the early years of the occupation, he had urged the Government to resist pressure for internationalisation: 'It might suit other Powers to grind down the unhappy people, but it would not suit us.' He did acknowledge strategic considerations: any limitation of British power in Egypt was a thing to be avoided at all hazards.[38]

Believing that the Suez Canal should be open permanently to all shipping, Balfour could argue that the British were its appropriate custodians, for they had the greatest incentive to preserve free passage. Suez was 'the wasp waist of our Empire'. Other Powers would value it less as a means of communication, and more as a tourniquet. British occupation of Egypt was thus a service to the civilised world. Foreign criticism was not prompted by justified concern about command of a waterway: 'they dislike our occupation of Egypt because they dislike *us*'.[39]

Suez, Egypt, and the Sudan formed 'an organic and indissoluble whole'. Dominion over the Sudan gave control of the water-supply of Egypt, so extension of permanent British administration was a defensive corollary. The Sudan question 'had to be settled sooner or later'. Military intervention saved the Sudanese from the 'cruel grasp of the Mahdi' and precluded the 'possibility of any Power other than Egypt occupying a position in the Nile Valley'.[40]

At the other end of the Red Sea, the story was much the same. Somaliland was the colony 'on which our fortress of Aden in a large measure depends'. Contending with 'the Mad Mullah' was an ungrateful task, however, and Britain could not 'go on indefinitely pouring money into the Somali sands'. In 1904, the Cabinet decided to accept minimal responsibility for Somaliland beyond safeguarding the coast-line. 'We have got it and we must keep it', Balfour told Parliament − for the sake of the loyal natives 'if for no other reason.'[41]

---

[38] 30 July 1907, *PDeb* 4th Series vol. 179 col. 841; 26 Mar. 1885, *PDeb* 3rd Series vol. 296 col. 729; 27 May 1884, *PDeb* 3rd Series vol. 288 col. 1484.

[39] 18 Apr. 1919, S. Bonsal *Suitors and Suppliants* (New York 1946) p. 61; Balfour to Goschen, 5 Apr. 1900, BP 49706 ff. 251–3.

[40] 17 Nov. 1919, *HCD* vol. 121 col. 771; 24 Feb. 1899, *PDeb* 4th Series vol. 67 col. 518; 'Mr. Balfour at Rochdale' *Times* 18 Nov. 1896 p. 6.

[41] 17 Feb. 1903, *PDeb* 4th Series vol. 118 col. 95; Balfour to the King, 23 Mar. 1904, PRO CAB 41/28 no. 9; CID, 17 June 1904, Sandars Papers c. 748 ff. 111–12; 15 Mar. 1909, *HCD* vol. 2 col. 773.

Balfour and foreign policy

The Cape

Glib references to native welfare could not vindicate the conquest of the Boer republics of the Transvaal and the Orange Free State. In South Africa 1899–1902, Britain was subjugating free white men by force. Balfour had to face the hard facts of Imperialism, uncushioned by cliches about civilisation and prejudices about non-Europeans. He was decidedly uncomfortable. There is something to be said for the intuition that, if Balfour (rather than Chamberlain) had directed policy towards South Africa, there might have been no Boer War.[42]

'Our object in absorbing these colonies is not to curtail freedom, but to spread it', Balfour insisted. The conflict directly arose from official efforts to secure civil rights for the 'Uitlanders' (English-speaking immigrants whom the Transvaal Boers effectively barred from public life) – but British motives were mixed. The Rand gold and diamond companies wanted more political influence. Milner, the Governor of Cape Colony, wanted uniform administration throughout South Africa. Chamberlain maintained: 'our supremacy in S. Africa and our existence as a great Power in the world are involved'.[43]

Balfour did not fundamentally disagree. He himself believed in the questionable British claim to suzerainty over the Transvaal. In January 1896, after the Jameson Raid tried to overthrow the Transvaal Government, he told his family that, had he lived there, he should probably have joined Jameson, 'though he ought to be hung all the same'.[44]

The Boer republics were not in themselves a serious threat. Balfour saw little future for small backward States. They would probably be drawn into a greater conglomerate – and there was the crux. The Boers, who formed the majority of whites in South Africa (as a whole), had greater affinity with the Germans than with the British. Germany already possessed South-West Africa, and pro-German tendencies among the Boers made Balfour nervous.[45]

---

[42] 'Raymond' *Balfour* p. 87.
[43] 6 Dec. 1900, *PDeb* 4th Series vol. 88 col. 138; J.S. Marais *The Fall of Kruger's Republic* (Oxford 1961) pp. 70 and 268.
[44] Frances Balfour to Betty Balfour, 2 Jan. 1896, SRO GD 433/2/477.
[45] Lady Selborne to Selborne, 16 Sept. 1908, Selborne Papers Adds.3 f. 12.

As Acting Foreign Secretary in August 1898, he sought to reduce this danger with the Anglo-German Agreement on Portuguese Colonies (a contingent partition of Portuguese territory in Africa). Chamberlain thought German claims excessive, and Salisbury said he would never have signed the Treaty, but Balfour attached great value to German recognition of British rights of pre-emption over southern Mozambique. It was 'a public advertisement to the Transvaal Government that they had nothing more to hope for from Germany, . . . by which our task in South Africa would be greatly lightened'. If the Germans expected a lot in return, it was because they realised that the Agreement dealt 'a final and conclusive blow to their S. African aspirations'.[46]

Balfour thus pursued the encirclement of the Boer States. He supported the Imperialist end of British policy in South Africa: unchallengeable hegemony. He felt qualms, however, about Imperialist means: coercion of the Boers and destruction of their traditional society.

The Transvaal was a community in which the (supposed) Uitlander majority was 'alien in blood, different in language, superior in cultivation and wealth, to a minority which constitutes the original national stock to whom the country politically belongs'. This problem was unprecedented, and 'equitable principles, in accordance with which the practical solution should be attempted, are by no means easy to discover'. International law would justify Britain in asking for concessions to the Uitlanders, but the Boers were certain to disregard a request not accompanied by menace. If menace failed, however, there did not seem to be anything like a *casus belli* established.[47] Britain would not think of using force 'if it did not happen that the oppressed majority consisted of our own countrymen', but the Boers had an equally patriotic justification for oppressing immigrant aliens. What Englishmen described as electoral reform, Boers might describe as a transfer of nationality – 'and can any one say that they are wrong?'. As a conservative and a patriot, Balfour could sympathise: 'Were I a Boer, brought up in Boer traditions, nothing but necessity would

---

[46] Chamberlain to Balfour, 17 Aug. 1898, BP 49773 ff. 146–7; N. Rich and M. Fisher (eds.) *The Holstein Papers* (Cambridge 1955–63) vol. IV p. 141; Judd *Balfour* p. 163; Memo. by Balfour, 17 Aug. 1898, BP 49773 f. 153.

[47] Memo. by Balfour, 1 May 1899, PRO CAB 37/49 no. 29; Balfour to Chamberlain, 6 May 1899, BP 49773 ff. 163–4.

induce me to adopt a constitution which would turn my country into an English Republic, or a system of education which would reduce my language to the *patois* of a small and helpless minority.'[48]

If Britain were to insist on anything 'at the point of a bayonet', Balfour suggested that it should be municipal reform. The Uitlanders should have the right to serve on juries and to levy a rate for English-speaking schools. If this failed to satisfy them, then they were unreasonable. The Uitlander leader Percy FitzPatrick thought Balfour completely misunderstood South Africa.[49]

When the Cabinet decided in May 1899 to demand full Uitlander enfranchisement, Balfour did not press his objections. His criticism seemed insufficiently constructive. Instead he prevaricated. When Chamberlain sent more troops to the Cape, Balfour had earlier remarked: 'His favourite method of dealing with the South African sore is by the free application of irritants; and although it does not easily commend itself to me, this method may possibly be the best.'[50]

During the summer of 1899, Balfour proclaimed his hopes for a settlement, while mentioning that, if diplomacy proved ineffectual, 'other means must inevitably be found'. At the same time, he advised Chamberlain to soften the tone of his dispatches. In August, he still thought war would be avoided somehow – 'though whether this will in the long run be for the good of mankind is another question'.[51]

The pre-emptive Transvaal attack on Cape Colony in October 1899 simplified the whole matter. The Boers had forced the Empire into 'a war simply of self-defence'. For righteousness and civilisation, Britain was 'fighting those who owe their very existence as separate communities to our forbearance, our carelessness, or our charity' to ensure that 'the *Pax Britannica* shall be supreme'.[52] His commitment to victory was complete.

What had disrupted the consolidation of Anglo-Saxon

---

[48] Memo. by Balfour, 1 May 1899, PRO CAB 37/49 no. 29.
[49] Balfour to Chamberlain, 6 May 1899, BP 49773 ff. 164–5; J.P.R. Wallis *Fitz* (London 1955) p. 82.
[50] Balfour to Chamberlain, 6 May 1899, BP 49773 ff. 162–5; Balfour to Salisbury, 10 Apr. 1897, Hatfield 3M/E f. 168.
[51] 'Mr. Balfour on the Transvaal' *Times* 28 July 1899 p. 8; Balfour to Chamberlain, 21 July 1899, BP 49773 ff. 167–72; Young *Balfour* p. 185.
[52] 17 Oct. 1899, *PDeb* 4th Series vol. 77 col. 79; 'Mr. Balfour on the War' *Times* 9 Jan. 1900 p. 7 and 29 Nov. 1899 p. 10.

supremacy in South Africa? A Pan-Afrikaner conspiracy was the stock Conservative explanation: the Boers were making 'a bold bid for Empire'.[53] Balfour also blamed the Rand gold for the war. It was that which made the sudden irruption of the Uitlander population so enormous. It was that which made the corrupt Boer oligarchy cling so obstinately to power. Had he spoken frankly, he might also have singled out British impatience. He knew that wanting to go too fast was Chamberlain's peculiarity.[54] Balfour had written in May 1899:

No doubt the Boers are engaged in fighting a hopeless cause. The South African Republic may last forever, but it cannot for very long be a Boer Republic. In the nature of things, Boer supremacy means a condition of political equilibrium, which gets day by day more unstable. But I do not think we can complain of the Boers not taking this view, nor (if they do take it) of their struggling to the last in favour of a lost cause.[55]

When two divergent ideals of civilisation collided, he lamented, it was almost beyond human power to secure that it should be without 'the destructive results which are, unfortunately, exhibited in the present case'.[56]

India

Curzon railed unfairly at the 'Blue Water' Premier who left India to look after itself. Balfour was deeply concerned about Indian defence, precisely because it did not fit his grand strategy. 'In India, and in India alone', he told Parliament, 'we have a great dependency with a land frontier' – only there was the British Empire adjacent to a first-class military Power. Indian defence was therefore the dominant purpose of the British Army. He estimated in 1904 that the Empire required 209,000 troops: 27,000 for home defence, 30,000 for the colonies, and 152,000 to garrison and reinforce India.[57]

---

[53] 'Mr. Balfour on the War' *Times* 29 Nov. 1899 p. 10; 1 Feb. 1900, *PDeb* 4th Series vol. 78 col. 257; 'Mr. Balfour at Bingley' *Times* 10 Oct. 1900 p. 4; Balfour to Mahan, 20 Dec. 1899, BP 49742 ff. 254–5.

[54] 19 Oct. 1899, *PDeb* 4th Series vol. 77 col. 360–1; Hatzfeldt to Foreign Ministry, 5 Apr. 1898, *Grosse Politik* vol. 14 no. 3786.

[55] Memo. by Balfour, 1 May 1899, PRO CAB 37/49 no. 29.

[56] 'Mr. Balfour on the War' *Times* 29 Nov. 1899 p. 10.

[57] Lord Newton *Retrospection* (London 1941) pp. 142–3; 15 Mar. 1906, *PDeb* 4th Series vol. 153 col. 1459; 24 Feb. 1903, *PDeb* 4th Series vol. 118 col. 783; Memo. by Balfour, 19 Dec. 1904, PRO CAB 3/1 no. 28A. For Canada, see below, pp. 184–5.

Could strategic expansion ease this burden? Back in 1881, Balfour condemned the Liberal decision to withdraw from Kandahar after the Afghan War, contending that Indian official opinion had generally, if not always, been right in recommending annexations. In 1895 he rejoiced that the Conservatives took office in time to prevent the evacuation of Chitral. It was to be far otherwise in later years. As Prime Minister, Balfour strove to restrain a Viceroy whom he believed to entertain 'schemes of territorial expansion, or, at least, of extending responsibilities, which would be equally detrimental to Indian interests, and to the international relations of the Empire'.[58]

In truth, Balfour had never so much advocated advance as opposed retreat. Respecting Kandahar and Chitral, his primary concern was prestige, which, far from being 'a word of shame', was equivalent to many battleships and army corps. Its loss would presage the demise of the Empire. To enter a territory and then abandon it was detrimental to prestige.[59] The moral to be drawn was that Britain should think carefully before entering. Balfour genuinely wished to preserve the independence of Afghanistan, Persia, and Tibet as buffer States.

In 1903, he was fearful about Curzon's military mission to Tibet. It could easily lead to a British protectorate, which would be a very great misfortune.[60] He rejected Curzon's plan to secure British dominance over Seistan Province in south-east Persia by controlling the River Helmund. Not only might it cause serious complications in Persia, but it required leasing territory from Afghanistan.[61]

Britain already subsidised and guaranteed Afghanistan. Balfour observed that it was hard to imagine closer relations between independent States – on paper. In reality, relations were so bad that 'they become almost comic if they are regarded as normal between allies'. Although determined to defend Afghanistan, his instinct was to withdraw the formal guarantee. Foreign Powers might then

[58] 25 Mar. 1881, *PDeb* 3rd Series vol. 259 col. 1988; 'Mr. Balfour in Glasgow' *Times* 15 Nov. 1895 p. 6; Balfour to the King, 6 Nov. 1903, Sandars Papers c. 715 f. 165.
[59] 'Mr. Balfour in Glasgow' *Times* 15 Nov. 1895 p. 6; Mr. Balfour at Norwich' *Times* 5 Nov. 1897 p. 6; 25 Mar. 1881, *PDeb* 3rd Series vol. 259 col. 1987; 15 Aug. 1895, *PDeb* 4th Series vol. 36 col. 89.
[60] Balfour to the King, 19 Feb. 1903, PRO CAB 41/28 no. 2; 13 Apr. 1904, *PDeb* 4th Series vol. 133 col. 130.
[61] Balfour to Curzon, 3 Nov. 1904, BP 49732 ff. 175–8.

be more inclined to respect Afghan independence, and the Amir would be more malleable if less secure. He realised, however, that a sudden reversal of policy would be destabilising. His Government reluctantly renewed the existing arrangement, unsatisfactory though it was.[62]

The Government of India also disliked the Anglo-Afghan Treaty: they wanted a *closer* alliance, which would compel the Amir to accept British military advisers and build strategic railways. This was the latest manifestation of the 'forward policy'. Balfour countered it strongly. First, to create a powerful Afghan *ally* was to risk a powerful Afghan *enemy*. Secondly, interference with Afghan independence could make the Amir more anti-British. Thirdly, British railway building might encourage Russian railway building, and a Russian line in Afghanistan would be the heaviest conceivable blow to the Indian Empire.[63] It was vital to retain the 'non-conducting' qualities of the territory between India and Russia:

The safety of India lies in the fact that before India can be touched any invading force has to go through a region of extraordinary natural difficulty, largely devoid of food, and defended by the most formidable natural barriers. And so long as we can prevent those natural difficulties being surmounted in time of peace, so long in time of war we shall be relatively secure.[64]

Invaders would have to advance through this region under guerrilla attack while constructing roads and railways as they went. This would give Britain time to enlarge the Army and ship it East. To promote railways, commerce, and irrigation in Afghanistan and Persia would be to improve them as bases of operation *against* India. Even at the cost of forgone trade, Balfour favoured sterilisation. Expansion in Asia 'would leave us in a much worse strategical position than that which we presently occupy'.[65]

This debate resumed towards the end of the Great War. Curzon proposed an Anglo-Persian alliance, revision of the Afghan-

---

[62] Memo. by Balfour, 30 Apr. 1903, PRO CAB 38/2 no. 26; Memo. by Balfour, 16 Dec. 1902, PRO CAB 38/1 no. 12; Balfour to Brodrick, 17 Dec. 1903, BP 49720 f. 263.

[63] Memo. by Balfour, 23 July 1904, PRO CAB 38/5 no. 78; Balfour to Brodrick, 17 Dec. 1903, BP 49720 f. 265; 11 May 1905, *PDeb* 4th Series vol. 146 col. 83.

[64] 17 Feb. 1908, *PDeb* 4th Series vol. 184 col. 552.

[65] 11 May 1905, *PDeb* 4th Series vol. 146 cols. 81–4; 'Mr. Balfour on Army Reform' *Times* 28 Nov. 1903 p. 12; Draft by Balfour, 24 Nov. 1903, PRO CAB 38/3 no. 73; Memo. by Balfour, 20 May 1903, PRO CAB 38/2 no.35; Balfour to Lansdowne, 21 Dec. 1903, BP 49728 ff. 122–3.

Russian border, and a British mandate over the Caucasus. Balfour opposed all these, and complained:

> Every time I come to a discussion – at intervals of, say, five years – I find there is a new sphere which we have got to guard, which is supposed to protect the gateways of India. Those gateways are getting further and further from India, and I do not know how far west they are going to be brought.[66]

By now, indeed, he viewed all Imperial enlargement with misgiving. Although aware that his credit as a guardian of Empire might 'suffer serious eclipse', he advised the Cabinet in 1918 against retaining any conquered colonies. Commercial equality and demilitarisation were all that British interests demanded. Those secured, he would give the captured colonies 'to anybody except the Germans'. With a clear conscience, he could tell the US Ambassador: 'Heaven knows I do not care to add to the British Empire.'[67] Balfour was not interested in accumulating territory. It was always necessary to defend existing possessions in order to uphold prestige. It had sometimes been necessary to acquire new ones in order to ensure control of sea-ways. Beyond this, he tended to regard colonies as a burden rather than a blessing. Looking to the post-war settlement, he said:

> I am very much afraid of some of the things we are proposing to do at this Conference. The Colonial Office would like to take up as many colonies as they could get. We talk of huge protectorates all over the place. I am really frightened at the responsibilities we are taking upon ourselves ... Where are they going to find the men and money for these things? I do not know.[68]

PART III: 'THE WHITE MAN'S BURDEN'

Balfour declared that Imperialism should broaden the outlook of 'perhaps the most insular nationality that has ever been known'. It had fallen to the British to direct an Empire 'which, in the multifariousness and complexity of interests it embraces, demands

---

[66] Eastern Committee, 24 June, 9 and 16 Dec. 1918, Milner Papers dep. 137 ff. 48–51, 199–201, and 208–9.
[67] Memo. by Balfour, 2 May 1918, PRO CAB 24/53 GT 4774; P. Gifford and W.R. Louis *Britain and Germany in Africa* (New Haven 1967) p. 290.
[68] Eastern Committee, 16 Dec. 1918, Milner Papers dep. 137 f. 208.

the highest qualities of sympathetic imagination from everyone of its citizens'.[69]

It cannot be pretended that his own sympathetic imagination extended evenly across the Imperial domain. The Psychological Climates of some races were repugnant: 'we can hardly comprehend them with sympathetic understanding'.[70]

'As long as we rule India we are the greatest power in the world', Curzon once told him; India was 'part of the inalienable heritage of Englishmen and the lasting glory of the British race'.[71] For all that his family fortune had been made in the sub-continent, Balfour never felt this way. India was to him 'the strange responsibility which the events of 150 years have thrown upon our shoulders'.[72] White English-speaking colonies ever held first place in Balfour's affections – he had no qualms about *their* Psychological Climate. Extolling the uniqueness of the Dominions in the history of Imperialism in 1915, he simply acknowledged that there was another type of colonisation – 'using a colony as a source of wealth for the mother-country, making them commercial plantations . . . ; that also has been practised, sometimes with success, very often with failure'.[73]

The direct rule of non-white colonies was not a subject on which he cared to dwell. Although both his first Parliamentary speech and his first publication related to India, they signified no deep interest.[74] The speech about the rupee reflected his desire to address a depleted House on a topic 'intrinsically dull', while the article about the Indian Civil Service concentrated exclusively on the relation of the entrance examination to university education.[75]

---

[69] 'Mr. Balfour on Commercial Education' *Times* 24 Apr. 1902 p. 8; 'Mr. Balfour on the Opposition' *Times* 13 May 1896 p. 10.

[70] Balfour *Foundations of Belief* p. 222.

[71] Curzon to Balfour, 31 Mar. 1901, BP 49732 f. 75; 'Mr. Balfour and Lord Curzon' *Times* 2 Aug. 1904 p. 11.

[72] G. Elers *The Memoirs of George Elers, Captain in the 12th Regiment of Foot (1777–1842)* (London 1903) p. 177; 'The Prince and Princess in the City' *Times* 18 May 1906 p. 11. His grandfather, James Balfour, supplied the Navy in Madras, c. 1805, and made £300,000 in four years.

[73] 'A Builder of Empire' *Times* 9 July 1915 p. 3.

[74] Cf. Mackay *Balfour* p. 22: 'India itself continued to be a major focus of Balfour's attention throughout his political career.' Mackay conflates attention to India with fear of an Anglo-Russian war fought mainly on the North-West Frontier.

[75] 10 Aug. 1876, *PDeb* 3rd Series vol. 231 cols. 1033–4; Balfour *Chapters of Autobiography* p. 91; A.J. Balfour 'The Indian Civil Service' *Fortnightly Review* vol. 28 no. 128 (Aug. 1877) pp. 244–58.

He continued to urge reform of Indian silver currency, both to advance international bimetallism and to improve Indian finances. The position of India towards Britain was that of a country paying tribute to another. Every new Indian tax went 'to the very root of our rule', but no subsidy should ever come from British revenue. Talk of amending the Government of India Act in 1905 humoured the Viceroy.[76]

This meagre record (and he said far less about Africa) is not altogether surprising. Balfour acquired his direct experience of the non-white Empire when in his twenties. Calls at Singapore, Colombo, and Aden, and a trip to Egypt were the sum of it. In an Empire embracing 'almost every form of government which the mind of man can conceive', subject populations could only be ruled 'with the slightest prospect of success' by specialists versed in their needs and wants.[77] On questions of colonial administration, Balfour deferred to the likes of Cromer, Curzon, and Milner.

It was widely accepted that Britain should gradually extend to subject peoples facilities for acquiring the power to govern themselves. Milner, for example, envisaged black colonies enjoying self-government in the future, albeit not as independently as white Dominions.[78] Balfour spoke in favour of reform only in the very long term. He thought in favour of reform not at all. He said that he failed to see the point of the Indian Councils Act (1909):

Although at one time there were doctrines fashionable that no Government could be good Government unless it was based upon the rights of man, and that the rights of man carried with them the right of representation and with them an apparatus of a highly abstract and abstruse theory once so fashionable, yet I think that view of the world has vanished or is vanishing, even from democratic debating societies in provincial towns.[79]

Balfour was a conservative. 'What on the continent are called Liberal principles' were indeed the precious heritage of every British citizen, but liberal political theory was 'ostentatious futility'.

---

[76] Memo. by Balfour, 12 Oct. 1897, PRO CAB 37/45 no. 35; 10 Aug. 1876, *PDeb* 3rd Series vol. 231 col. 1033; A.J. Balfour *British Industries and International Bimetallism* (London 1892) p. 33; 26 July 1900, *PDeb* 4th Series vol. 86 col. 1433; Judd *Balfour* p. 237; Balfour to Curzon, 1 Jan. 1905, BP 49733 ff. 1–2.

[77] 'Mr. Balfour at Bristol' *Times* 4 Feb. 1896 p. 7; 'Mr. Balfour on the Politics of the Future' *Times* 22 June 1894 p. 11.

[78] V. Halperin *Lord Milner and the Empire* (London 1952) p. 181.

[79] 1 Apr. 1909, *HCD* vol. 3 cols. 552–3.

Support for government based on public opinion stemmed from Authority and not from Reason. The democratic movement arose from changes in the social environment (and hence Psychological Climate) of certain countries, and liberal ideology had merely served a function in nursing it 'through its infant maladies'.[80]

Liberalism had no universal application. Anglo-American politics advanced along narrow and specialised lines. Successful representative government required 'national character trained in that particular kind of work' and depended on 'qualities the very origin of which is lost in the prehistoric period of human development'. Balfour did not believe that non-Europeans possessed those qualities. That all men were born equal was an eighteenth-century fallacy refuted by the advance of science. He maintained that black races were endowed with a wholly different potentiality of culture, and it was 'folly to suppose that your petty educational regulations, be they what they may, can obliterate distinctions deep-seated under the laws of nature'. Parliamentary institutions in Liberia and San Domingo had inevitably proved 'disastrous and almost ludicrous failures'.[81]

He declined to predicate inferiority indiscriminately to Indians. Some belonged to 'the most distinguished human breeds'. By implication others did not, and that precluded effective parliamentary institutions. Representative government was only suitable where people were essentially homogeneous and equal, 'all alike in the traditions in which they are brought up, in their general outlook upon the world'. India was subject to every sort of religious and social division. Only fundamental social reconstruction could make it fit for constitutional government, but 'there never was a vast body of mankind who were more the creatures of their antecedents'. Absolutism was the natural organisation of that part of the world. Indian loyalty might crystallise around a great Emperor, but never around abstract institutions. Direct British rule was ideal, since 'we have been able to combine something that is good in the system of free institutions with all that can

[80] 4 June 1908, *PDeb* 4th Series vol. 190 col. 248; Balfour *Foundations of Belief* p. 231; Balfour *Fragment on Progress* pp. 57–8.
[81] 27 Feb. 1924, *HLD* vol. 56 col. 418; Intro. by Balfour, W. Bagehot *The English Constitution* (Oxford 1928) p. xxii; 21 Mar. 1904, *PDeb* 4th Series vol. 132 col. 354; 16 Aug. 1909, *HCD* vol. 9 col. 1008; 'Note on Indian Reform', 7 Aug. 1917, PRO CAB 21/68.

be found of good in absolute government'.[82] The Viceroyalty was despotism tempered by criticism in the British Parliament and press.

Parliamentary government would be equally alien to Egyptians, who had never desired it until indoctrinated with shallow English political philosophy.[83] Balfour lamented: 'It's partly the fault of the British nation – and of the Americans; we can't exonerate them from blame either – that this idea of "representative government" has got into the heads of nations who haven't the smallest notion of what its basis must be.'[84] If only Britain could have left Egyptians to rule Egypt in Egyptian fashion and concentrated on protecting Suez! That was alas impracticable in this most 'international' country. Egypt was 'abnormal and like nothing else under heaven'.[85]

Denis Judd suggests that Balfour moved unwillingly with the times on colonial government.[86] It is more accurate to say that he exercised discretion. His two main Parliamentary speeches on India were given in Opposition – in 1909 and 1924 – and in them he tempered stern arguments for the failure of reform with airy hopes for its success: 'It may prove – please Heaven it will not so prove, but it may prove that the thing is impossible ... I hope better things'.[87] In 1929, a last political letter praised Baldwin's speech accepting the Irwin Declaration, but this was no death-bed conversion. Baldwin had consulted him in advance and was striving to reconcile the die-hards. Balfour thought Dominion status impossible for India.[88] It was always vital, however, to preserve cross-party consensus. Once subject populations sensed that the Imperial official was not backed by undivided British might, they would 'lose all that sense of order which is the very basis of their

---

[82] 'Note on Indian Reform', 7 Aug. 1917, PRO CAB 21/68; 1 Apr. 1909 *HCD* vol. 3 cols. 553–4; 27 Feb. 1924, *HLD* vol. 56 cols. 421–2; 'The Prince and Princess in the City' *Times* 18 May 1906 p. 11.

[83] 13 June 1910, *HCD* vol. 17 col. 1142.

[84] Dugdale *Balfour* vol. II p. 363.

[85] Imperial Conference, 6 July 1921, PRO CAB 32/2 f. 113.

[86] Judd *Balfour* p. 267.

[87] 27 Feb. 1924, *HLD* vol. 56 col. 422.

[88] Dugdale *Balfour* vol II pp. 403–4; Baldwin, 7 Nov. 1929, *HCD* vol. 231 cols. 1303–13; K. Middlemas and J. Barnes *Baldwin* (London 1969) p. 537; Balfour to Hankey, 19 Sept. 1928, SRO GD 433/2/6.

civilisation'.[89] Only in a note to Cabinet colleagues in 1917 had he baldly stated his position: Indian constitutional self-government was a hybrid, certainly worthless, and probably dangerous. Britain should not promise what it neither could nor ought to give:

Now everybody admits that for India, as it is, this form of Government is totally unsuitable. Where I differ with some misgiving, from high Indian authorities, is in holding the view that in all probability neither the lapse of time nor the development of education will ever make it suitable. East is East and West is West.[90]

Feasibility was not the only consideration. Balfour doubted that self-governing non-English-speaking communities could be held within the Empire. True cohesion was impossible without deep-lying likeness in tastes, opinions, and habits. Political societies were bound together by feeling, which coalesced around identity of race, language, and country (with 'mere material interest' a poor fourth).[91] What loyalty would politically-minded Indians feel to Britain? The importance which Balfour assigned to racial and cultural differences within the Empire is exemplified by his views on South Africa.

Balfour admitted that Briton and Boer did not differ greatly in blood or religion, and he publicly predicted an intimate union. 'Race jealousies' would die down (as he supposed they had in Canada) once British supremacy was indisputable, but he never expected easy integration.[92] In 1900, he suggested dividing South Africa into colonies, either definitely Boer or definitely British. Special constitutions for the Boer colonies should grant basic internal self-government, while forbidding all things military. An Imperial garrison would be financed from local revenue, and the Lieutenant-Governor would be free to suspend the constitution whenever Britain pleased.[93] This scheme respected Boer society, but it was also permanent military occupation thinly disguised.

[89] 'The Prince and Princess in the City' *Times* 18 May 1906 p. 11; 13 June 1910, *HCD* vol. 17 col. 1144.
[90] 'A Note on Indian Reform', 7 Aug. 1917, PRO CAB 21/68.
[91] Balfour *Foundations of Belief* pp. 56–7 and 358.
[92] 'Mr. Balfour at Dundee' *Times* 29 Sept. 1899 p. 6; Balfour to Bryce, 2 Oct. 1899, BP 49853 f. 121.
[93] Memo. by Balfour, 24 Jan. 1900, PRO CAB 37/52 no. 6.

Instead the new colonies were to be prepared for responsible government on the model of English-speaking communities, with Balfour emphasising slowness. Milner hoped to postpone self-government until large British settlements had been created, and Balfour supported him. In 1905, the Orange River Colony and the Transvaal were still under direct rule. He then proposed to introduce 'representative government as a stage, and a very long stage, on the road to that final form of responsible government which is the goal'.[94]

When his Liberal successor decided to grant responsible government to the Transvaal immediately, Balfour denounced a reckless experiment, which was 'bound to carry disaster in its train'.[95] There was nothing to prevent a self-governing Transvaal preparing for a new war. To trust the Boers was to ignore human nature:

What is it that animates them? It cannot be yet what it would be if you would only wait – it cannot yet be that natural in-born loyalty to the British Throne and the British people ... How can it be that? I believe it will come in time. But you are asking the Dutch to do what you would not do in their place.[96]

In 1907, he dismissed the idea of South African confederation within five years as incredible. The Union of South Africa Act (1909) was therefore 'a unique historic phenomenon'. He trusted that now 'all agreed with the idea of having in South Africa one European race dominating'.[97]

Anglo-Boer tension, however, was not 'the real ultimate problem'. Balfour realised that South Africa could never be 'a white man's colony' in the true sense. In addition to 750,000 whites south of the Zambesi were 6–8 million blacks. Where a white aristocracy ruled over a black proletariat, unparalleled social problems were a certainty. Racial integration was out of the question. The sentiment of white superiority was 'so strong in the breasts of every man of British origin and birth that it was quite hopeless and, he thought, frankly undesirable, to attempt to get over it'. He disliked the 1907 Transvaal Constitution, because white *manhood* suffrage implied a theory of natural rights which left no logical

[94] Balfour to Milner, Oct. 1904, BP 49697 f. 118; 6 Mar. 1905, *PDeb* 4th Series vol. 142 col. 498.
[95] 'The Primrose League' *Times* 3 May 1906 p. 4.
[96] 31 July 1906, *PDeb* 4th Series vol. 162 cols. 802–4.
[97] Lord Shaw *Letters to Isabel* (London 1921) p. 200; 16 Aug. 1909, *HCD* vol. 9 cols. 1006–7.

ground for excluding blacks. South Africa was 'extraordinarily embarrassing', but how could a race, determined to have constitutional freedom for itself, extend justice and equity to other races within the framework of *any* constitution?[98]

Where racial differences are clear cut and profound, where a race obviously superior is mixed with a race obviously inferior, the superior race may be constituted as a democracy, but into that democracy the inferior race will never be admitted. It may be kept out by law, as in South Africa, or it may be kept out by practice, as in the Southern States of America; but kept out it will be.[99]

Judd has criticised Balfour's 'blind faith that goodwill would eventually resolve fundamental racial antagonisms'. He had no such faith at all. To be sure, he told Louis Botha in 1909 that he looked forward with great hope to the future of South Africa. Eighteen days earlier, however, he had declared: 'Darkness hangs over that problem. I do not look forward to it with any assurance, and I doubt whether anybody has a right to look forward to it with any assurance.'[100] The explanation is not complicated. To Fitz-Patrick, Balfour had written: 'I am glad you take no despairing view of the South African future. I do not believe in pessimists. Whatever be their moral virtues or their intellectual capacities, in the long run they do more harm than good.'[101] This is typical of the man who so dwelt on the horrors of a God-less universe, that he recommended Christianity as the surest practical alleviation to pessimism.[102] Balfour often told people how optimistic he was – just when they would never have guessed. The more explicit his assertion, as a rule, the greater his desperation.

'The Kaiser conjured up a yellow nightmare', Balfour mused in 1929: 'It's quite easy to conjure up a black one'. The race problem was global and intensifying: 'Honestly I don't see what the future of South Africa is to be. And India – though I know absolutely nothing about India.' It was another of the most embarrassing

[98] 31 July 1906, *PDeb* 4th Series vol. 162 cols. 799–800; 21 Mar. 1904, *PDeb* 4th Series vol. 132 cols. 352–4; James Bryce *Impressions of South Africa* 3rd edn (London 1899) p. 45; 'Mr. Balfour in East Manchester' *Times* 13 Jan. 1906 p. 14; 16 Aug. 1909, *HCD* vol. 9 cols. 1001–3.
[99] 'A Note on Indian Reform', 7 Aug. 1917, PRO CAB 21/68.
[100] Judd *Balfour* p. 219; Balfour to Botha, 3 Sept. 1909, BP 49697 f. 195; 16 Aug. 1909, *HCD* vol. 9 col. 1008.
[101] Balfour to FitzPatrick, 12 Nov. 1908, BP 49697 f. 211.
[102] Balfour *Foundations of Belief* p. 399.

problems ever, and he knew of no solution. Colonial rule was becoming increasingly awkward everywhere. The 'oratorical trash' talked by British MPs gave encouragement to nationalists, who valued democracy purely as a weapon against existing authorities.[103] In Balfour's eyes, the driving force behind demands for self-government was antipathy to the white man.

'You have never served your country in foreign parts', Curzon once told him: 'For your own sake I hope you never may.'[104] Sheltered from the practicalities of colonialism, Balfour could remain intransigent and unconstructive. Yet he was not blind to the danger. His equanimity stemmed from resigned acceptance of the inevitable. He could no more see a future for a multi-racial British Empire than he could for a multi-racial South Africa. It was not the destiny of Great Britain to be an Asian Power. In India there would be a transition of free institutions, and then reversion to traditional absolutism. Egypt was the same. About black Africa he did not know what to think. To cloak British withdrawal with self-government would not be credible. In 1895, he had endorsed investment in tropical Crown Colonies, since they were held in perpetuity so far as he could foresee.[105]

The eventual loss of great non-Anglo-Saxon populations seemed to Balfour natural and even desirable. The British Empire had in the main to 'be composed on the ideas of a common civilization'. He was anxious to prevent the 'phenomenon of, I will not necessarily say inferior, but, at all events, a wholly different culture gradually percolating into society'.[106] It was wiser to let widely dissimilar peoples go their own way than to attempt to integrate them. In ancient times, 'the most conservative nation in the world' had tried to create 'the political organisation, by which men of different races, different religions, of widely divergent history were to be bound together under one system of laws and one administrative polity ... and Rome lost its very character in the process of making its empire'.[107]

[103] Dugdale *Balfour* vol. II pp. 401 and 363; 16 Aug. 1909, *HCD* vol. 9 cols. 1000–4; 27 Feb. 1924, *HLD* vol. 56 cols. 416 and 421; C.C. Repington *The First World War* (London 1920) vol. II p. 52; Balfour to Lansdowne, 10 Sept. 1908, BP 49729 f. 317.

[104] Curzon to Balfour, 20 Nov. 1902, BP 49732 f. 95.

[105] 27 Feb. 1924, *HLD* vol. 56 col. 422; Judd *Balfour* p. 280.

[106] 'Empire's Future' *Times* 30 Nov. 1923 p. 7; 31 July 1906, *PDeb* 4th Series vol. 162 col. 799.

[107] 'The Colonial Premiers and the 1900 Club' *Times* 19 Apr. 1907 p. 12.

CONCLUSION

An Imperialist to the core? It depends on what is meant by Imperialism. On Balfour's own definition, Imperialists were those who 'recognised themselves as part of a great Empire spread over the world which had great responsibilities and duties; and, further, that this was not a burden to be grumbled at and thrown off at the first opportunity, but one that had great privileges'.[108]

Balfour thought it good that British influence stretch far beyond the British Isles, and, if that influence was to be beneficial, it had to be strong. Maritime supremacy required the possession of territory at strategic points around the world. With the territory often came non-British populations, but for this sort of Imperialism he felt no enthusiasm. It did not fit into his political philosophy. Belief in virtually immutable racial and cultural differences sustained his faith in the Empire: Anglo-Saxons were uniquely qualified for world leadership. That same belief excluded 350 million other Imperial subjects from playing any active part in the enterprise. They were something of an embarrassment.

He could not employ the educative justification of colonialism with much sincerity. The first duty of any State was to defend from alien influences the social system which was the natural outgrowth of the temperament of its citizens. Balfour had to convince himself that the concept of the State was inapplicable to Indians and Africans. They were just masses of people bound to be ruled by somebody or other – and they could think themselves lucky if it were the British, whose political aptitudes ensured them 'far better government than in the whole history of the world they ever had before'.[109]

He had no time for the idea of the British Empire as a bridge between East and West. Between very different races and cultures he saw an 'unbridgable abyss' which time was unlikely to narrow.[110] Such links as presently existed were unlikely to be permanent, and the tool which would be used to sever them was the British export of liberal philosophy.

Exactly how Britain was to withdraw from alien climes with power and prestige intact he could not say. India and Africa were

[108] 17 Dec. 1878, *PDeb* 3rd Series vol. 243 col. 997.
[109] 13 June 1910, *HCD* vol. 17 cols. 1140 and 1143.
[110] 24 Mar. 1904, *PDeb* 4th Series vol. 132 col. 354.

a worry for the future – but he did not despair. The younger English-speaking communities of the world were approaching maturity. Might not Anglo-Saxondom one day stand on its own solid foundations?

CHAPTER 4

Greater Britain

But, in truth, the Dominions are much the simplest part of
the Imperial problem.

Balfour 1928[1]

'Colonies of white men which can be permanently made and
retained as colonies of white men' – these were 'the glory and the
security and the greatness of the Empire'.[2] In his enthusiasm for
them, Balfour often spoke as if the Imperial realm consisted of
little else. It was 'naturally an outgrowth of the British character
and of the British Constitution' by virtue of 'the fact that our
children across the seas share our beliefs and our affections'.
Quite simply: 'We British believe that the British Empire is synonymous in the extension of liberty and self-government in every
part of the world which the men of our race and our language
occupy.'[3]

Aborigines, Red Indians, and Maoris were mercifully dwindling,
he thought, and the Dominions were quite right to restrict alien
immigration.[4] He did his bit in 1919 to prevent the International
Labour Organisation proscribing discrimination against immigrant workers and to oppose the inclusion of a racial equality
clause in the League Covenant. Asked to assist in devising a formula, he read the first phrase of the draft – 'all men were created
equal' – and answered that it was not true.[5]

[1] Balfour to Hankey, 19 Sept. 1928, SRO GD 433/2/6.
[2] 21 Mar. 1904, *PDeb* 4th Series vol. 132 col. 352; 'Patriotism and Empire' *Times* 5 Aug.
1915 p. 8.
[3] 'The Colonial Premiers and the 1900 Club' *Times* 19 Apr. 1907 p. 12; Short *Balfour*
p. 295.
[4] 21 Mar. 1904, *PDeb* 4th Series vol. 132 cols. 351–2; 16 Aug. 1909, *HCD* vol. 9 col.
1001.
[5] H. Borden (ed.) *Robert Laird Borden* (London 1938) pp. 933, 940, and 958; D.H. Miller
Drafting the Covenant (New York 1928) vol. 1 p. 183.

69

When Balfour entered politics, Canada, Newfoundland, New Zealand, and the Australian colonies were already established communities, very largely self-governing with regard to internal affairs, and he was confident that they would prove themselves 'to be possessed of the Anglo-Saxon gift of "muddling through" '.[6] They therefore exercised his mind almost exclusively in the context of the quest for closer union. Balfour claimed to have been a Pan-Anglican even before he went 'hurrying around the English-speaking world' in 1875–6 – on a route very similar to that described in Dilke's popular Imperialist travelogue *Greater Britain* (1868).[7] He remained a Pan-Anglican all his life. The self-governing colonies were natural pillars of Anglo-Saxon power: 'the very sinews of the Empire that is to be'.[8] He declared in 1905:

> I would rather fail with those who hold to the great ideal . . . than succeed with the purblind and narrow-minded and unimaginative persons, . . . who are incapable of picturing what our great Colonies are to become or, . . . of framing an idea of what the British Empire might be, what it might do in the cause of peace, of freedom, and civilization, if these great and growing communities, when they reach the full plenitude of their strength, should find themselves not loosely connected to the mother country, but bound to it by organical ties, which on stress of war or difficulty, no danger from within or threats from without, could either shake or for an instant imperil.[9]

It may seem ironic that this seer of Imperial unity is best remembered in this context for the 'Balfour Definition' (1926) – generally reckoned a step towards nationhood for the Dominions. In formally recognising that the self-governing communities of the Empire were all of equal status, the Definition provided the basis for increased constitutional autonomy. It was perhaps the ease with which Balfour reconciled such apparent contradictions that won him acclaim as a model Imperial statesman.

Relations between Britain and the Dominions changed gradually and subtly, but the Great War was something of a watershed. Before 1914, discussion of the Imperial relationship in Britain focused on schemes for closer integration. Balfour's thoughts on

---

[6] Balfour to Northcote, 14 June 1904, BP 49697 f. 45.
[7] Balfour to Choate, 1 June 1905, BP 49742 f. 122; Balfour *Chapters of Autobiography* p. 91; Sir Charles Dilke *Greater Britain* (London 1868).
[8] 'Mr. Balfour at Sheffield' *Times* 2 Oct. 1903 p. 4.
[9] 'Mr. Balfour in Glasgow' *Times* 13 Jan. 1905 p. 8.

these are examined in Part I of this chapter, and his attitude to the Dominions is compared with his views on Ireland. Part II is concerned with his reaction to the growing assertiveness of the Dominions after the War. Tariff Reform receives detailed consideration in a separate annexe at the end of the chapter – detailed because Balfour said so much about it, separate because it was not an integral part of his Imperial thought.

PART I: BEFORE THE WAR

'Whatever the present Premier can do to strengthen the bonds of Empire and draw still closer the ties that unite us to our kinsmen across the sea ... he may be relied upon to support.' So wrote Balfour's first biographer in 1903.[10] Interest in the unification of the Empire had just been stimulated by the participation of 50,000 colonial troops in the Boer War – a ray of hope which Balfour himself had chosen to magnify. Did not the blood tingle to read such feats as had been performed by colonial squadrons? No one could henceforth regard the self-governing communities as 'merely so much paper glory'. For the first time, they had come forward and thrown in their lot with the Mother Country. Imperial patriotism had been shown to be a reality, and Balfour proclaimed 'a new chapter in our Imperial history'. The conclusion he drew is perhaps as revealing a remark as ever he made on the subject: 'This being so, this evidence of the spirit being there, it matters relatively little – I do not say it does not matter – but it matters relatively little, in what particular form these great sentiments of Empire are embodied.'[11]

Not everyone shared this insouciance. 'Social Imperialists' like Chamberlain and Milner desired Imperial reorganisation to marshal the resources of the Empire with maximum efficiency. Insofar as this meant closer union with the self-governing colonies, Balfour was *in principle* all for it. Unification seemed a global trend, he observed in 1895. If Britain were to keep its international position, it must do as other nations and bind together elements

---

[10] Alderson *Balfour* p. 357.
[11] 'Mr. Balfour on the War' *Times* 9 Jan. 1900 p. 7; 'The Guildhall Banquet' *Times* 11 Nov. 1902 p. 11; 5 June 1902, *PDeb* 4th Series vol. 108 cols. 1587–9; 'The Prime Minister at Fulham' *Times* 21 July 1902 p. 10.

which might otherwise tend to separate.[12] Political expediency did not preclude sincerity when he praised the work of Chamberlain as Colonial Secretary (1895–1903). No man had done more to bring the Empire to 'full and corporate consciousness' of itself. There was yet that unfortunate peculiarity of his: wanting to go too fast. Regardless of twelve calendar years to the contrary, Balfour explained: 'The difference between Joe and me is the difference between youth and age: I am age.'[13]

At the Colonial Conferences of 1897 and 1902, Chamberlain pushed for Imperial Federation, Imperial military union, or, at the least, a consultative Council of the Empire. The Colonial Premiers were at best ambivalent. They required assurance that any demand for closer union would have to come from them.[14] Balfour accepted this and sought to subdue precipitate integrationist zeal:

The universal desire in this country, and, I think, in the colonies, to bind us more closely together is one which it is extremely difficult to carry out by any means; but it seems impossible at this moment to carry it out by political or constitutional means – I mean by having colonial representation on a large scale or by a Federal Parliament or machinery of that kind. That may some day be possible, but I do not see my way to it now.[15]

The goal was noble. What would he not have sacrificed to see the Empire draw as close together as the United Kingdom? There was simply no prospect of an executive Imperial Council – certainly for the present generation, perhaps for all time. The colonies would not hear of it. Nor would the people of Britain when they realised that independent power would have to be surrendered. Public opinion was not ripe.[16]

In practice, Balfour was wary of introducing even consultative Imperial institutions. In 1904, the Colonial Secretary, Alfred Lyttelton, suggested reforming the Colonial Conference as an

---

[12] 29 Mar. 1895, *PDeb* 4th Series vol. 32 col. 558; 6 Feb. 1900, *PDeb* 4th Series vol. 78 col. 817.

[13] 6 July 1914, *HCD* vol. 64 cols. 853–4; 'A Builder of Empire' *Times* 9 July 1915 p. 3; Balfour *Opinions and Argument* pp. 179–85; J. Amery *The Life of Joseph Chamberlain* vol. IV (London 1951) p. 463.

[14] J.E. Kendle *The Colonial and Imperial Conferences 1887–1911* (London 1967) pp. 20–56.

[15] A.J. Balfour *Fiscal Reform* (London 1906) p. 28.

[16] 29 Mar. 1895, *PDeb* 4th Series vol. 32 col. 559; 20 and 15 Feb. 1907, *PDeb* 4th Series vol. 169 cols. 868–9 and 468.

'Imperial Council' in which representation would reflect population (easing the way to majority voting). Additionally, a permanent Imperial Commission might be created to investigate questions referred by the Council (or any two colonies). While assuring Lyttelton that these ideas were on the right lines, Balfour was inclined to water them down. Apart from the considerable organisational difficulties, he feared that the Commission might come into direct collision with the Government – say over Tariff Reform.[17]

He yet made one 'modest but substantial' constitutional innovation – and trumpeted its Imperial potential. The Committee of Imperial Defence was 'the first, the most practical and perhaps even the best model' for formal co-operation:[18]

If a Colony desires to discuss its position in a general scheme of Imperial Defence, its Delegate would, of course, be asked to join the Committee. He would attend its deliberations so long as the questions in which his Government had a direct interest were under discussion: and he would attend as a full member. The value of such consultations in producing co-operation between the different parts of the Empire, is, I believe, beyond our present power of estimation. And they would have no drawbacks. They could not excite jealousy or suspicion. They would interfere with no rights of self-government: and the advice which they issued, though it might guide, could never coerce either the Colonies or the Mother Country.[19]

He greeted 'a new precedent of great imperial significance' when the Canadian Minister of Militia attended in December 1903. ('Unfortunately, it appears that this particular gentleman is of rather inferior quality – but we shall be careful what we say before him!') For their part, colonial politicians remained dubious of a body primarily advisory to the British Cabinet.

Beyond this, Balfour was discouraging about formal military union. The colonies would never have appeared at the CID if it had the slightest power to impose an obligation. Unified command of colonial armies was unlikely: 'They are, I think, rightly

[17] Balfour to Lyttelton, 13 Jan. 1905, BP 49775 ff. 22–6; Lyttelton to Balfour, 1 Feb. 1905, BP 49775 ff. 31–40; Kendle *Colonial and Imperial Conferences* pp. 61–8.
[18] 20 Feb. 1907, *PDeb* 4th Series vol. 169 col. 869; 11 May 1905, *PDeb* 4th Series vol. 146 col. 64; Balfour *Fiscal Reform* pp. 142–4; Balfour to Hankey, 14 Oct. 1926, BP 49704 f. 114.
[19] Memo. by Balfour, 29 Feb. 1904, PRO CAB 37/69 no. 33.

intolerant of anything which says, "You raise a force and you maintain a force, and we will tell you what to do with it".'[20]

Naval union was a more delicate matter. The sea defence of the Empire was undertaken by the Royal Navy, which was funded almost entirely by the United Kingdom. In 1904, the colonies voluntarily donated just £876,665 to total British defence spending of £66 million. A Liberal MP protested that they should pay 25% on the basis of relative population, or 50% on the basis of relative revenue.[21] Balfour consistently deprecated this 'debtor and creditor' thinking:

> It is quite true that the Colonies get from us for nothing a great strength and a great security. But ... the British Empire touches world-politics at a very large number of points .... We may at any moment be involved in a conflict with some first-class Power, which does not obviously concern the interests of Canada, New Zealand, or Australia ... they have to run dangers which, were they self-contained, small, and isolated communities they would, for that reason escape. If that be true, I think the case is not so clear, is not so simple.[22]

Pecuniary calculation of colonial defence needs encouraged a piece-meal approach which was inimical to unity. In Parliament in 1907, he opposed compulsory schemes for fixed naval subsidies, saying it was impossible to ask the legislatures of Canada, Australia, New Zealand, and the Cape to vote monies which somebody else was going to spend. Taking this for outright rejection of the subsidy system, advocates of separate Dominion fleets claimed Balfour for their cause.[23] The Canadian and Australian navies were founded in 1909.

His position was in fact rather equivocal. As a 'Blue Water' strategist who desired 'constant consciousness in each part of the Empire that it is but part of a greater whole', he cannot have been altogether pleased by a change which might undermine commitment to common defence. He later summarised the message to the Dominions concerning subsidies as: 'We do not ask you to

---

[20] Balfour to the King, 4 Dec. 1903, PRO CAB 41/28 no. 26; 2 Aug. 1904, *PDeb* 4th Series vol. 139 cols. 618–19; 29 July 1909, *HCD* vol. 8 col. 1395.

[21] Churchill, 27 Mar. 1906, *PDeb* 4th Series vol. 154 col. 1060; Harold Cox, 15 Feb. 1907, *PDeb* 4th Series vol. 169 cols. 455–6. See P. O'Brien 'The Costs and Benefits of British Imperialism' *Past and Present* no. 120 (1988) pp. 186–95.

[22] 15 Feb. 1907, *PDeb* 4th Series vol. 169 col. 466.

[23] 15 Feb. 1907, *PDeb* 4th Series vol. 169 cols. 467–8; R. Jebb *The Imperial Conference* (London 1911) vol. II p. 60; d'Egville *Imperial Defence* pp. 161–2.

contribute ... unless your conscience and your belief in the Empire suggest to you to do so.' When New Zealand gave Britain a battleship he extolled a magnificent tribute to the Imperial ideal. The fate of the Dominions, he declared in 1909, would not be decided in the Pacific or Indian Oceans, but in the Channel, the North Sea, and the Mediterranean. Here was a doctrine for the Imperial press to preach: 'local security must fundamentally and in the end depend upon Imperial security'.[24]

He nevertheless recognised that, failing unforeseeable constitutional developments, creating local navies was the only practical way of extending colonial co-operation. These squadrons should in time grow into fleets capable of assisting Britain on the high seas. 'There is no use kicking against the pricks', he said generally: 'We must adapt our military system to what is the ultimate constitutional necessity of the Empire'. Britain could not take sole control of truly Imperial forces: 'Put what you like on paper, if the Colonies objected, if they thought we were wrongly engaged in the quarrel with another great Power, you would not get that assistance you thought you had a right to count upon.' Until the Imperial communities were united in a systematic organisation the only method was to trust to voluntary patriotic enthusiasm.[25]

A delegation to Balfour from the Imperial Federation (Defence) Committee was told that the colonies were Britain's children. In Imperial life as in domestic life, as children grew up they assumed a larger share of the common support of the household. It had to be a gradual process. The colonies would become more and more sensible of their obligation – 'by the force of their own public opinion, not of ours'.[26]

Frustrated in their constitutional and defensive schemes, apostles of closer union turned to Chamberlain's commercial strategy: Imperial Preference. Balfour basically gave them the same old tale (see annexe). Imperial Preference 'ought to stir a responsive fibre in the heart of every citizen of the Empire' – but the time for it was not yet:

---

[24] 20 Feb. 1907, *PDeb* 4th Series vol. 169 col. 870; 'Mr. Balfour in the City' *Times* 4 Dec. 1912 p. 6; 'Mr. Balfour on the Navy and Tariff Reform' *Times* 31 Mar. 1909 p. 9; 'The Press Conference' *Times* 10 and 11 June 1909 p. 6.
[25] CID, 13 July 1905, PRO CAB 38/9 no. 60; 15 Feb. 1907, *PDeb* 4th Series vol. 169 col. 469; 2 Aug. 1906, *PDeb* 4th Series vol. 162 col. 1393.
[26] Balfour *Fiscal Reform* p. 210.

you should not endeavour in a rush of enthusiasm, in a moment of lofty, it may be of mistaken, inspiration, to effect a change which will not stand the test of time, not because it is intrinsically wrong, not because it is based on unsafe principles, but because it has not behind it that body of fixed sentiment and conviction which is the only sure basis of any great reform.[27]

Do nothing and wait – yet he admitted that there was a great Imperial problem. How were freedom and unity to be reconciled? A plan was wanted whereby the growing self-consciousness of young communities might be combined with a sense of higher communion with the Mother Country. 'That is a problem which we have only half solved', he said in 1907, 'and of which the half-solution we have given deals only with the negative.' Britain was not to interfere with the free development of the self-governing colonies. Centrifugal forces could not be neutralised by jurisdiction from London.[28]

Balfour made this point frequently. He spoke in 1904 of 'those self-governing Colonies of the Empire over which no office in this country has any control at all'. When Canada considered drawing closer to the USA in 1911, he politely suggested that the Empire offered far better prospects for autonomous development. Everyone realised that each Dominion was 'to manage its own affairs – carry out its own life, make its own experiments as freely as if it were an independent political entity'. (When Canadians rejected US trade reciprocity, he hailed an epoch-making victory for the Imperial ideal). The British Empire had reached a point at which Britain was simply first among equals. In 1914, he told Parliament 'that absolute equality as between these great self-governing communities and ourselves was and must remain an essential element of this Empire'.[29]

He maintained that this development was inevitable. Free institutions were a natural outgrowth of British characteristics. Britons in the Dominions did not differ in race, temperament, or political capacity from Britons in the Mother Country. Therefore self-

---

[27] Balfour *Fiscal Reform* pp. 248 and 140.
[28] 20 Feb. 1907, *PDeb* 4th Series vol. 169 cols. 867–70; 'The Colonial Premiers and the 1900 Club' *Times* 19 Apr. 1907 p. 12.
[29] 2 Aug. 1904, *PDeb* 4th Series vol. 139 col. 618; 'Tariff Reform and the Empire' *Times* 24 May 1911 p. 9; 'The Speech in Glasgow' *Times* 23 Oct. 1911 p. 10; 6 July 1914, *HCD* vol. 64 col. 853; 6 Feb. 1911, *HCD* vol. 21 col. 57.

governing British colonies would be just that. 'You cannot call into being great representative Assemblies and put one under the control of, and in subordination to, another', he insisted; 'we learned that lesson, and it was a sharp lesson, in dealing with America'. Although the British Parliament was technically supreme, the Empire had to be framed on the co-operation of absolutely independent Parliaments.[30]

This early recognition of Dominion autonomy was accompanied by equally prescient emphasis on common allegiance to the Crown, the Sovereign being the focus of the patriotic sentiment which made such an Empire possible.[31] Fundamental to this whole vision was the grading of loyalties. It was right that Canadians, Australians, and New Zealanders should have their own feeling of separate nationality. It was also right that they should have a common feeling for the British Empire. Complex loyalties were not necessarily weakened loyalties: 'Imperial patriotism may be supported and enriched by Dominion patriotism, but never need impair it'.[32]

Balfour conceded that an Empire of free co-operation through Imperial sentiment was, of all political experiments, the most audacious. To its credit, however, the British Empire was also, of all political facts, one of the most natural. It was not to be compared to an alliance or a commercial partnership: 'the parallel is poverty stricken and falls far below the reality at which we should aim'. It was a family – and a family did not cease to exist when the children reached their majority. He declared the parental stage to be over in 1909. Henceforward the self-governing communities of the Empire should be like 'members of a family all of whom have reached the years of discretion, but yet feel how much they gain by the mutual interchange of services, by mutual affection, by regarding each other as in some respects nearer than the outside world'.[33]

This all sounded very easy-going. 'We have to deal with young,

[30] Amery *Empire in the New Era* p. viii; 20 Feb. 1907, *PDeb* 4th Series vol. 169 col. 868; A.J. Balfour *Aspects of Home Rule* ed. L. Magnus (London 1912) p. 17.
[31] 25 Jan. 1901, *PDeb* 4th Series vol. 89 col. 20; Harold Nicolson *King George the Fifth* (London 1952) pp. 67–8.
[32] 'Mr. Balfour on the Larger Patriotism' *Times* 2 Dec. 1912 p. 8; 'Mr. Balfour at Haddington' 22 Sept. 1902 p. 5; Amery *Empire in the New Era* p. xi.
[33] 'The Colonial Premiers and the 1900 Club' *Times* 19 Apr. 1907 p. 12; 'The Press Conference' *Times* 11 June 1909 p. 6.

growing nations conscious of their destiny', he said. Tact and
mutual consideration were indispensable. In empire-building, the
British were 'pioneers of enlightenment which the world may well
be content to follow'.[34]

What about 'Bloody Balfour' the scourge of Irish nationalism?
The broad-minded sympathiser with colonial aspirations appears
far removed from the unswerving defender of the Union. Did he
have one law for Canadians, Australians, and New Zealanders, and
another for the Irish?

In opposing Home Rule for Ireland, Balfour employed all
manner of argument save generalised anti-Catholicism. (Despite
a marked distaste for Roman Catholic doctrine, he ridiculed
alleged plots against Protestant supremacy and doubted ultramon-
tane influence in European diplomacy).[35] He always held 'that
rather than submit to Nationalist rule Ulster would fight – and
Ulster would be right'. Home Rule was 'atrocious political wicked-
ness'. It would be absolutely destructive to the United Kingdom,
ruinous to Ireland, and would shatter the Empire to its
foundations.[36]

Balfour was warned that his uncompromising attitude could
alienate Dominion opinion. That signified to him that Dominion
opinion misperceived the Irish Question – a widespread failing.
The Liberal view of Home Rule as a one-off measure of devolution
sprang from a fundamental misunderstanding of the working of
human institutions. Any movement towards a federal United
Kingdom would certainly not facilitate the ultimate federalisation
of the Empire – it would rather destroy the centre around which
the colonies should crystallise.[37] The success of federal government in the USA and Germany was irrelevant. It was all too easy
to miss the point:

If you find two trains at Grantham, trains similarly constituted in the

---

[34] 20 and 12 Feb. 1907, *PDeb* 4th Series vol. 169 cols. 867 and 75; Balfour *Fiscal Reform*
p. 212.
[35] Lady Selborne to Selborne, 16 Sept. 1908, Selborne Papers Adds. 3 f. 12; Dugdale *Balfour*
vol. 1 p. 276; Balfour to Amery, 14 July 1904, BP 49775 f. 115–16.
[36] Memo. by Balfour, 24 June 1916, PRO CAB 37/150 no. 17; 'Mr. Balfour on the Opposition' *Times* 13 May 1896 p. 10; 'Mr. Balfour in East Manchester' *Times* 10 Jan. 1906
p. 10.
[37] Garvin to Balfour, 17 Oct. 1910, BP 49795 ff. 86–93; Earl Grey to Balfour, 23 Feb.
1910, BP 49697 ff. 1–9; Balfour to Ware, 30 Nov. 1910, BP 49861 f. 81; 29 Mar. 1895,
PDeb 4th Series vol. 32 cols. 558–9.

same place, is it to be a matter of indifference into which you get? Not at all. One lands you at York, the other in London. So if you go from unity to federalism you are on the way to separation. If you go from separation to federalism you are on the way to unity. That really makes the whole difference. These things are dynamic, they are not static.[38]

Provincial powers, once granted, only increased the appetites they were intended to satisfy. Home Rule was a rotten compromise. Irishmen would soon regard the Westminster Parliament as foreign and defy it. Then the only sanction left to the British Government would be force: 'An Irish Parliament controlling an Irish Executive cannot itself be controlled by an Imperial Parliament.'[39]

But why should not Ireland have an independent Parliament? Balfour seemed happy enough with independent Dominion Parliaments. Happy enough, yes; but not perfectly satisfied. His ideal would have been one Chamber in which everyone of British blood could consult, through his immediate representatives, with regard to all things Imperial. Geography rendered that impractical so far as the Dominions were concerned, but Ireland had no such excuse. Then there was the Irish character. Celts were a valuable element in the United Kingdom, but a purely Irish Parliament was unlikely to be very successful. Irishmen were clever and voluble, he thought, but they lacked drive and were not trustworthy in business.[40]

More serious was the problem of Irish loyalties. Balfour denied that Ireland possessed a truly distinct national identity on racial, linguistic, historical, religious, institutional, economic, or cultural grounds. The Irish sense of nationality had been produced by English persecution of the Catholics. Consequently, 'the sincerity of their love for Ireland is measured by the intensity of their hatred of England'. The Irish were handicapped by this outmoded negative sentiment. The Union was in their highest interests. A small nation could achieve nothing nowadays except indirectly, when attached to a Great Power. Balfour said that he would have liked to go to the Irish as a missionary and show the real position

---

[38] Balfour *Aspects of Home Rule* pp. 5–6.
[39] Balfour to Garvin, 22 Oct. 1910, BP 49795 ff. 103–6; Balfour *Aspects of Home Rule* p. 197; Alderson *Balfour* p. 112.
[40] Balfour *Opinions and Argument* p. 197; Balfour *Aspects of Home Rule* p. 197; M. Digby *Horace Plunkett* (Oxford 1949) p. 171.

they might occupy with a great moral influence over a vast civilisation. Narrow and destructive Irish nationalism was best consigned to history and replaced with a positive feeling consistent
with wider loyalties. He expressed the hope in 1899 that he would
see in his life-time the full promise, if not the full fruition, of this
'cardinal article' of his political faith.[41]

Home Rule of any kind would be fatal. Meeting a difference of
sentiment with separate organisation made the original distinction ineffaceable.[42] Either the Irish changed their sentiments and
took their place as Irish Britons, or the old exclusivism would
triumph.

The Easter Rising of 1916 was decisive. 'When the liberties of
the world depended upon the strength of the British Empire, and
the strength of the British Empire depended upon its unity, a
section of the Irish people allied themselves with the common
enemy.'[43] It was deeply depressing, but perfectly clear: southern
Ireland had no place in the British Empire. Balfour henceforth
supported partition. The traitorous South was best abandoned.[44]
It was unlikely to play 'a satisfactory part in the world's history'.[45]

The loyal North should be a homogeneous community with no
Hibernia irredenta and no devolution.[46] 'United Ireland' was a fatu-
ous notion. If the Nationalists could not perceive sufficient community of sentiment to make union with Britain tolerable, how
could they desire union with Ulster, or expect Ulster to desire it
with them? The Dominion status of the Irish Free State meant
almost nothing to Balfour. 'The Irish had owed their success to
crime', he said: 'How could such a state of things be said to fit in
with the scheme of the Empire?'[47]

---

[41] A.J. Balfour *Nationality and Home Rule* (London 1913); draft article by Balfour, *c.*1920,
BP 49959 ff. 245–51; Digby: *Plunkett* pp. 171 and 167; Bates *Carson* p. xi; 'Mr. Balfour
in Manchester' *Times* 31 Jan. 1899 p. 10.
[42] 29 Mar. 1895, *PDeb* 4th Series vol. 32 col. 558.
[43] Bates *Carson* p. x.
[44] Memo. by Balfour, 24 June 1916, PRO CAB 37/150 no. 17; F.S.L. Lyons *John Dillon*
(London 1968) pp. 398–9; Augustine Birrell *Things Past Redress* (London 1937) pp. 135
and 206; Balfour to Carson, Feb. 1918, BP 49709 f. 166; Memo. by Balfour, 25 Nov.
1919, PRO CAB 24/93 CP 193.
[45] Balfour to Bonar Law, 8 Nov. 1913, BP 49693 f. 113.
[46] Balfour to Lloyd George, 10 Feb. 1920, Lloyd George Papers F/3/5/2; H.A.L. Fisher *An
Unfinished Autobiography* (London 1940) pp. 125–6.
[47] Bates *Carson* p. xiv; W.S. Churchill *Great Contemporaries* (London 1937) p. 254; Dugdale
Balfour vol. II p. 337.

Ireland was a special case. Other English-speaking communities could reconcile patriotism for the part with patriotism for the whole: 'the Canadian for the Canadians, the Australian for the Australians, but all for the British Empire'.[48]

PART II: AFTER THE WAR

Balfour saw proof of the moral bond of Empire in the 'political miracle' of 1914. When the Dominions sent troops to Europe, men of British blood were shown to be all one in heart: 'the community of ideals which could come only through a common sacrifice for a common cause was the common end of the whole Empire'.[49] He declared himself profoundly moved.

There remained, however, the abiding difficulty of finding some organisation which would enhance unity of action and sentiment without interfering with autonomy. He had realised before 1914, that, as the Dominions gave more support to the Empire, they would demand an increasing share in guiding its destinies. The Great War so accelerated the pace of change that a few years saw Imperial developments which might normally have taken a quarter of a century.[50] Defence *per se* was not troublesome. A freely co-operating Empire had proved itself 'as powerful for purposes of Imperial defence as the most highly organised military despotism'. Balfour knew that foreign policy was the crux.[51] Back in 1912, he had assured the Canadian Premier that he recognised the need for Dominion involvement in foreign policy-making, but told him, 'We must not hurry it too much.' At the Imperial War Conference of 1917 the Dominions insisted on their right to an adequate voice.[52]

Balfour readily conceded that 'if the united strength of the Empire was to be put forward for any external purpose, the Dominions would have to exercise a share in the control of a single

[48] 'Mr. Balfour on the Larger Patriotism' *Times* 2 Dec. 1912 p. 8.
[49] 'On the Side of Democracy' *Times* 30 May 1917 p. 6; 'Mr. Balfour and the German Colonies' *Daily Telegraph* 24 Oct. 1918 p. 8; 'The Middle Stage' *Times* 19 Oct. 1916 p. 11; 12 June 1918, *Imperial War Conference 1918* (1918) Cd 9177 p. 19.
[50] 'Mr. Balfour on Empire Constitution' *Times* 16 Dec. 1919 p. 9; 22 July 1912, *HCD* vol. 41 col. 860; Inter-Imperial Relations Committee, 27 Oct. 1926, PRO CAB 32/56.
[51] Balfour *Opinions and Argument* p. 192; Imperial War Cabinet 26, 23 July 1918, PRO CAB 23/41.
[52] Borden *Memoirs* p. 367; *Imperial War Conference 1917* (1917) Cd 8566 p. 5.

Foreign Office'. How that was to be achieved he did not know. After stating that the matter would have to be faced, he gave himself over fully to the stop-gaps and compromises which were all that was available. More direct communication between Prime Ministers might help. He even rather lamely brought the Brazilian Arbitration Treaty before the Imperial War Cabinet: 'in the ordinary course he would have dealt with it as a matter of Foreign Office routine', but in view of the rights of the Dominions, 'he thought it better to clear his conscience'.[53] He accepted that the Dominions could not be ordered to give up colonies they had taken from Germany, though he found their annexationist opposition to the mandate system rather trying. No objection was raised by him to separate Dominion representation at the Paris Peace Conference and the League of Nations. Their sense of nationhood was natural, 'and it would be foolish to deplore it'.[54] While apparently content to fudge the constitutional implications, he realised that individual signature of treaties was an unsettling portent. Speaking of Imperial relations in December 1919, he struck a cautious note: 'in national life as well as in individual life moments of prodigious strain are always followed by some discouragement and reaction'.[55]

It did not prey on his mind. When concern was expressed about disagreement between the Dominions and Britain at the League of Nations, he merely laughed: if five different points of view were possible on any question, he should not be surprised to find them advocated by the five components of the Empire.[56] He was satisfied that they were all agreed on plain Imperial interests. Foreigners were probably right to complain about separate Dominion representation.[57]

In the absence of equal control over Imperial foreign policy, however, the Dominions grew wary of European entanglements.

[53] Imperial War Cabinets 26, 27 and 29, 23 and 25 July and 2 Aug. 1918, PRO CAB 23/41.
[54] Digby *Plunkett* p. 182; Diary, 29 Jan. 1919, Cecil Papers 51131 f. 28; Empire Delegation, 13 Jan. 1919, *BDFA* vol. 3 no. 43.
[55] Balfour to Milner, 23 July 1919, Milner Papers dep. 390 ff. 76–7; Milner to Balfour, 26 July 1919, Milner Papers Adds. c. 705 ff. 192–4; Borden to Blanche Dugdale, 16 Apr. 1932, BP 49833 f. 314; W.A.S. Hewins *The Apologia of an Imperialist* (London 1929) vol. II pp. 321–2; 'Mr. Balfour on Empire Constitution' *Times* 16 Dec. 1919 p. 9.
[56] Sir Almeric Fitzroy *Memoirs* (London 1925) pp. 741–2. There were in fact six. Did Balfour discount India?
[57] Balfour to Blanche Dugdale, 2 Feb. 1921, SRO GD 433/2/227.

The call to help defend Constantinople in 1922 received an unenthusiastic response, and Canada and Ireland distanced themselves from the Turkish settlement. In 1925, Britain made little effort to commit the Dominions to the Locarno guarantee of the Franco-German frontier, such was their antipathy to the scheme. When called to explain in the Lords, Balfour floundered embarrassingly. He could only suggest that the Locarno Treaty did 'not show the British Empire as the unity which, practically, it undoubtedly is'. He admitted that this was unsatisfactory but rallied himself for the peroration:

let nobody tell me that, so long as the British Empire exists, it will not act as a single body when that great moment comes and that we shall not see in the future, as we have seen in the past, an absolutely united Empire, joined together, working with a single purpose for a single end in the cause of peace.[58]

This formed the (more or less discreet) secondary strand of many a Balfour speech on Imperial relations in the 1920s. In the main, he carried on talking about an Empire of free communities 'united by something which was certainly much greater and much more sublime than control'. There was rather more emphasis on the insuperability of geographical barriers to closer union, but otherwise his pre-war thoughts on Imperial sentiment were as serviceable as ever. Underlying them, however, was a hint of uneasiness. 'It would be an almost fatal blow to the very idea of the British Empire', he wrote in 1922, 'that we should assume its various parts to take upon themselves different shares of responsibility in connection with the same great international emergencies.'[59] He described the Empire as an arrangement for unlimited mutual protection:

Every member of this great Commonwealth of free communities knows that if it is attacked, every other member of the British Empire, without question, without delay, without raising any problems, national or international, will spend its last shilling in its defence. No mutual arrangement ... or treaty under the League of Nations can equal that in strength.[60]

---

[58] 24 Nov. 1925, *HLD* vol. 62 cols. 844–6.
[59] 'Lord Balfour on the Empire' *Times* 22 Nov. 1926 p. 9; Memo. by Balfour, 15 Sept. 1922, Cecil Papers 51071A f. 82.
[60] 24 July 1924, *HLD* vol. 58 col. 1001.

That was how Imperial sentiment should show itself. In recommending construction of the Singapore naval base, he emphasised that the 'whole scheme of political thought' of Australians and New Zealanders depended on the idea that they were bound to Britain, not only by constitutional ties, but by the knowledge that Britain would 'throw every ounce of strength' into defending them. The 'sentiment of security based upon the British Fleet' was one of the strongest bonds of Empire. In Opposition in 1924, he put it plainly: in war, 'the British Empire goes together, or it ceases to go at all'.[61] In Government two years later, he felt obliged to be less categorical:

so far as this country is concerned we are bound to go to war to defend any part of the Empire which is in danger. Personally I think the duties of all the other members of the Empire to us are not less than our duties to them, but, as to the particular conditions under which that great duty is to be exercised, I do not believe anything is to be gained by inventing hard cases before hand.[62]

The post-war 'nationalism' of the Dominions signified their desire to make commitments to Britain optional rather than obligatory.[63] Balfour could appear very tolerant. He had long understood that Britain could not *compel* them to act, and technical supremacy was trivial: 'I do not believe in wooden guns.'[64] At the same time, he had no wish to dwell on this 'optional' aspect of Empire, lest it undermine that sense of community which inspired voluntary co-operation.

His personal perspective on the Balfour Definition thus becomes apparent. Denis Judd creates a false impression when he writes that 'the Imperial Conference afforded Balfour the opportunity of putting his convictions into practice', and that Balfour 'relished the process' of matching constitutional theory with reality. In truth, Balfour did not much want the Balfour Definition. He cared little for constitutional theory and hoped that the Imperial Constitution could always remain unwritten. Letting a committee of lawyers loose on it would be a disaster. Discussing documents was

---

[61] 13 Mar. 1924, *HLD* vol. 56 cols. 767 and 770; 24 July 1924, *HLD* vol. 58 col. 1002.

[62] 27 July 1926, *HLD* vol. 65 col. 286.

[63] R.F. Holland *Britain and the Commonwealth Alliance 1918–1939* (London 1981) p. 68 and *passim*.

[64] Cited by Churchill, 20 Nov. 1931, *HCD* vol. 259 col. 1190.

the surest way of dividing people who ought to be friends.[65] Opening the Inter-Imperial Relations Committee in October 1926, he affirmed that, however much it might perplex students of comparative politics, the British Empire rested on a solid base of patriotic sentiment. The co-existence of seven autonomous communities gave rise to some secondary difficulties, 'but in dealing with them it is vital to remember that they *are* secondary, and that the fundamental truth to which they are subordinate is the equality of status which is the essential foundation of this part of our imperial fabric'.[66]

When Hertzog, the Prime Minister of South Africa, contended that it was imperative to state that the Dominions were not subordinate to Britain, Balfour replied that he *had* just stated that most explicitly and would deprecate going into the nuances of independence under any circumstances. Was it not enough to know that in the view of every British statesman whatever rights and status Britain had the Dominions had too? It was a commonplace. Hertzog persisted. He wanted Britain and the Dominions formally defined as 'independent states, equal in status and separately entitled to international recognition, with governments and parliaments independent of one another, united through a common bond of loyalty to the King and freely associated as members of the British Commonwealth of Nations'.[67] Balfour devised a counter-draft:

Great Britain and the Dominions are autonomous communities of equal status, united by a common bond of allegiance to the Crown, but in no sort of subordination one to another.

All their inhabitants though under many governments are citizens of one Empire under one Crown. To that Empire and Crown they have duties and obligations, but each is (through its own Parliament) the sole judges in its own case of the manner in which those duties and obligations may best be fulfilled.[68]

'Duties and obligations' – he was not going to let collective defence slip. Hertzog expostulated that Balfour apparently wanted

---

[65] Judd *Balfour* pp. 332 and 339; 'Empire's Future' *Times* 30 Nov. 1923 p. 7; 8 Dec. 1926, *HLD* vol. 65 cols. 1331–6; CID, 19 Feb. 1925, PRO CAB 2/4.
[66] Inter-Imperial Relations Committee, 27 Oct. 1926, PRO CAB 32/56 f. 9.
[67] Inter-Imperial Relations Committee, 27 Oct. 1926, PRO CAB 32/56 ff. 11–12; C.M. van den Heever *General J.B.M. Hertzog* (Johannesburg 1946) p. 213.
[68] Draft by Balfour [Oct. 1926], BP 49704 f. 153.

some sort of super-state. Five unminuted meetings of vigorous word-play ensued. New Zealand, Newfoundland, Australia, Canada, Ireland, and South Africa (roughly in that order) presented the spectrum of views from greater emphasis on unity to greater emphasis on independence. Britain desired emphasis on unity, but primarily wanted agreement. Balfour frequently dozed off, but stirred himself to defend 'duties and obligations' and attack 'freely associated', because it implied freedom to disassociate. He also insisted on 'Empire'.[69]

On 9 November the final compromise evolved, and he could write in the Committee report that the position of Great Britain and the Dominions 'may be readily defined': 'They are autonomous Communities within the British Empire, equal in status, in no way subordinate one to another in any aspect of their domestic or external affairs, though united by a common allegiance to the Crown, and freely associated as members of the British Commonwealth of Nations.'[70]

He was less than happy with this 'series of negations'. Where was mutual co-operation? The formula did not capture the true character of the Empire. He would have to 'set it in a framework which would place it in better perspective'. On his own, Balfour wrote a preamble around the Definition, explaining that while every self-governing member of the Empire was now master of its destiny, an account of the negative relations between them only expressed a portion of the truth. The British Empire was founded on positive ideals. Peace, security, and progress were its objects. Dominion autonomy would imperil no common cause. Immutable dogmas were inappropriate to questions of diplomacy and defence, moreover, so equality of status could not be extended to function.[71] This 'setting' worked just as he hoped. Witness the editorial of *The Times*: 'The preamble . . . includes a description of the British Empire in language . . . which has long been common coin and is only saved by its italics from being almost incidental. It may have

[69] Heever *Hertzog* pp. 214–17; L.S. Amery *My Political Life* (London 1953) vol. II p. 392; Amery to Balfour, 1 Nov. 1926, BP 49775 f. 236; H. Duncan Hall 'The Genesis of the Balfour Declaration of 1926' *Journal of Commonwealth Political Studies* (1962) p. 189.
[70] *Imperial Conference 1926* (1926) Cmd 2768 p. 14.
[71] Notes on Dominion status [Nov. 1926], BP 49736 f. 260; Cabinet 59, 17 Nov. 1926, PRO CAB 23/53; Amery *My Political Life* vol. II p. 390; *Imperial Conference 1926* Cmd 2768 pp. 14–15.

its uses for quotation to suspicious nationalists, but that is all.'[72] (The italics were a printer's error, which the Dominions Office had dared not correct lest South Africa object.[73])

Hertzog went home to tell the Boers that the old British Empire was no more, leaving Balfour to write privately: 'As regards the Imperial Conference, you are perfectly right; – nothing *new* has been done.'[74] He had proclaimed 'the stage of formal equality' nearly twenty years before. His preamble tactics were now carried over to his speeches, which cleverly played down the significance of the actual Definition while seeming not to. (It was 'very easy to say the wrong thing' about Imperial relations.)[75] All the troubles had been due to 'the difficulties of the various Prime Ministers in their own Dominions', where some people had not understood the reality of Imperial relations.[76] The 'new truth' was that the Dominions 'now explicitly regarded themselves as elements in a great unity which did not depend upon control, but did depend upon common ideals and common beliefs' – a unity, he added, to which 'they owed, as he was sure they would be ready to pay, free service whenever a great world necessity should arise'. The Empire did not end with the maturity of the communities to which it had given birth; it began there: 'It is only now that the British Empire is going to be what it was pre-destined to be.'[77]

More Balfourian sham optimism? When he hoped for voluntary co-operation between English-speaking peoples, his hopes were at least grounded in his beliefs (unlike his 'hopes' for racial harmony in South Africa). He truly did not regard the absence of a central Imperial authority 'with the kind of fears that assail those who are brought up upon legal considerations, and who put emotional considerations on one side'.[78] That the positive half of the Imperial problem remained unsolved cannot have surprised him. The evolution of the Empire might one day supply a constitutional remedy,

---

[72] 'The Empire As It Is' *Times* 22 Nov. 1926 p. 15.

[73] Amery *My Political Life* vol. II p. 392.

[74] L.E. Neame *General Hertzog* (London 1930) pp. 252–3; Balfour to Foster, 27 May 1927, BP 49697 f. 40.

[75] 'The Press Conference' *Times* 11 June 1909 p. 6; Balfour to Hankey, 19 Sept. 1928, SRO GD 433/2/6.

[76] Balfour *Opinions and Argument* pp. 190 and 194; Cabinet 59, 17 Nov. 1926, PRO CAB 23/53; Balfour to Esher, 24 Nov. 1926, BP 49719 f. 298.

[77] 'Lord Balfour on the Empire' *Times* 2 Dec. 1926 p. 9.

[78] Balfour *Opinions and Argument* p. 197.

but he never pretended to know what it was. To imagine that he felt any personal failure, moreover, would be to forget his conservatism. He always said that it would take many generations of statesmen to perfect Imperial co-ordination.[79] Political movements were symptoms of change, and not causes. Until the Empire was ready to be unified, there was no use 'in asking people to do that which they are not as yet prepared to do'.[80]

'A common interest in loyalty, in freedom, in ideals – that is the bond of Empire', he declared in 1926: 'If that is not enough, nothing else is enough.' He had once previously conceded that idealism *on its own* did not sustain a community,[81] but where was the motive for separation?

That it would diminish national wealth and impair national security seems to me obvious; that it would hamper any form of productive co-operation between the scattered fragments of what had once been the British Empire will hardly be denied; that it would increase the liberty of autonomous development registered in 1926 will hardly be affirmed; that it would weaken the influence for peace of the English-speaking peoples is much to be feared.[82]

Some may see this as evidence that his belief in Imperial solidarity really rested on the knowledge that the Dominions were too weak, economically and militarily, to risk independence. To this it can only be replied that he never stepped any further off his moral pedestal. Speaking of Anglo-Saxon patriotism, Balfour once remarked: 'According to observation of the world, the cynics are always wrong.' He had seen colonies become Dominions and Dominions become nations, 'and these daughter nations have fought gloriously beside their Mother Country through the greatest war in history'.[83] He remained sanguine enough that 'the political instincts, identical in character, identical in aim, which spring from the fact that we have all been brought up under common traditions and with common political instincts, will carry through all the difficulties of discussion and, when the occasion arises, through all the perils and perplexities of action'.[84]

---

[79] 24 Nov. 1925, *HLD* vol. 62 col. 844; 'Mr. Balfour in Glasgow' *Times* 13 Jan. 1905 p. 8; 'Mr. Balfour at Hanley' 5 Jan. 1910 *Times* p. 7; 'Mr. Balfour on American Ideals and Progress' *Times* 5 July 1917 p. 8.
[80] Balfour *Fragment on Progress* p. 38; 29 July 1909, *HCD* vol. 8 col. 1396.
[81] 8 Dec. 1926, *HLD* vol. 65 col. 1334; 'Empire's Future' *Times* 30 Nov. 1923 p. 7.
[82] Amery *Empire in the New Era* p. xii.
[83] 'Mr. Balfour in Manchester' *Times* 31 Jan. 1899 p. 10; Amery *Empire in the New Era* p. xi.
[84] 27 July 1926, *HLD* vol. 65 cols. 286–7.

CONCLUSION

It is fitting that Balfour should be associated with the 1926 Imperial Conference. Though he did not rejoice in the letter of the Definition, he was very much at home with the prevailing spirit. The Balfour Report has been labelled a piece of political romanticism – with some justification.[85] Balfour plainly had his doubts (especially about Ireland and South Africa), but thought it damaging to voice them. Transcendant was the ideal:

Whence comes the cohesion of the Brit. Emp?
1) Patriotism. Loyalty. Custom.
2) Religion. Race. Pride in various manifestations. Habit. Language. *Mere* law is among the weakest of bonds.[86]

The Empire of his vision was a white Anglo-Saxon community – a stable social organism which would naturally act as a unity when vital interests were at stake. It existed as an entity primarily because it regarded itself as such.

Within this framework, his Imperial thought was flexible. While desiring the closest possible union, he recognised that only perpetual contiguity can secure perfect interchange of ideas and sentiments. 8,000 miles of ocean could not be ignored. His aims were not restricted to keeping Britain and the Dominions together as one nation. Indeed the ordinary nation – the centralised State – belonged 'rather to an older order of things' than the British Empire. Once more the Anglo-Saxon peoples were at the forefront of political advance and typically they scarcely realised it. The free Empire was a unique experiment in human co-operation – the first supra-national community. The USA might have prior claim to the title, said Balfour in 1918, but in truth 'the British Empire is more an Empire of united States than the United States itself'.[87]

Some people would perceive the arrangement of 1926 as indistinguishable from separation.[88] In dismissing the 'Empire of the New Era' as an empty form, they failed to understand the importance of form as the sustaining focus of ideas. The Empire was a wider loyalty. Among those who shared it, petty bargaining would

---

[85] Holland *Britain and the Commonwealth Alliance* p. 58.
[86] Note by Balfour [Feb.–Mar. 1930], cited in 'The Empire and the Crisis' *Times* 14 Dec. 1936 p. 15.
[87] 'Mr. Balfour on Empire Constitution' *Times* 16 Dec. 1919 p. 9; 24 Nov. 1925, *HLD* vol. 62 cols. 844–5; 'Mr. Balfour and the German Colonies' *Daily Telegraph* 24 Oct. 1918 p. 7.
[88] Amery *Empire in the New Era* p. xi.

give way to mutual service without too close a calculation. It was 'a higher ideal, and one that may some day be imitated from the British Empire by all civilized countries'. To abandon the Imperial idea would be to deprive the English-speaking people of all the ennobling influences which attached 'to the consciousness of citizenship in a community on whose proper conduct depends so much of the felicity and the progress of the whole civilized world'.[89]

This was the Imperialism which Balfour embraced. This was why he was proud to be rated an Imperialist to the core.

ANNEXE: TARIFF REFORM

Free Trade or Tariff Reform? 'That infinite and never ending controversy I put on one side', said Balfour in 1896: 'I leave it to others bolder than myself to express an opinion on it.'[90] He was not to be so lucky.

To help meet the cost of the Boer War, the Budget of 1902 imposed a small duty on imported corn. That autumn the Cabinet favourably received a suggestion from Joseph Chamberlain that corn from the colonies be exempted. In April 1903, Ritchie, the Free Trade Chancellor of the Exchequer, insisted on abolishing the corn duty. In May, Chamberlain publicly renewed his call for preferential tariffs. Soon, Free Traders and Tariff Reformers were locked in vehement argument over Imperial relations, the world trading order, prices and employment, manufacturing and finance, agriculture, the distribution of wealth, the funding of social reform, and the whole nature of British politics.

The debate had long been simmering. British trade policy was based on Free Trade doctrines which stipulated that only revenue requirements excused tariffs – any wider use would degenerate into a conspiracy of vested interests. Heightened industrial and agricultural competition from abroad, however, inevitably swelled the protectionist lobby, which sought justification in the 'unfairness' of foreign trade barriers. Super-added to this was the Imperial factor: tariffs which altered the relative prices of Imperial and foreign imports could induce citizens of the Empire

---

[89] 'Tariff Reform and the Empire' *Times* 24 May 1911 p. 9; 'The Colonial Premiers and the 1900 Club' *Times* 19 Apr. 1907 p. 12.
[90] 'The Cutlers' Feast' *Times* 20 Nov. 1896 p. 7.

to buy more Empire-made goods. Furthermore, common commercial interests could warrant common commercial legislation by a common institution. Chamberlain became convinced that increasing economic interdependence presented an alternative route to Imperial federation. In 1903 he set out to transform the British Empire into a (more) exclusive trading bloc. Imperial and economic considerations were thus intertwined in the crusade for Tariff Reform.

Was the Prime Minister in favour? Who could tell? Incapable of giving a straight answer, he was derided as 'the incarnation of all that is ambiguous, tortuous and pusillanimous in politics'. He was not just sitting on the fence; he was working on both sides of it.[91]

Balfour wrily dismissed these aspersions as testimony to the disappointing level of intelligence of large numbers of educated adults. In fairness, less subtle minds might have been perplexed to read in his own book such statements as: 'I am not a Free Trader nor a Protectionist' and 'I am a Free Trader. I have always been a Free Trader'.[92]

One cause of his terminological inconsistency was the inherent sophistication of the issue. Practical trade policy is not a simple dichotomy. Balfour possessed a sound understanding of positive economics. That every major trading nation except Britain was protectionist suggested to him that the majority of the civilised world advocated economic theories which were false. The prosperity of one nation usually conduced to the prosperity of all nations, and to be alarmed at the inevitable growth of foreign manufactures was really unreasonable. It was 'certainly impossible, and probably not wholly desirable' that Britain should ever regain overwhelming manufacturing supremacy[93]: 'He did not think we had any right to complain of that. We must take our chance in this competitive universe, and if we had not the energy or capital or brains or muscles to enable us to do that which other countries could do, we must acquiesce in our inferiority.'[94]

[91] H. Morgan-Brown *Balfourism* (London 1907) p. 2; W.S. Robson *et al. The Premier's Fiscal Doctrines* (London 1905) p. 11.

[92] Balfour *Fiscal Reform* pp. viii, 5, and 189.

[93] A.J. Balfour 'Morley's *Life of Cobden*' *Nineteenth Century* vol. 11 no. 59 (1882) p. 46; 'Mr. Balfour on Technical Education' *Times* 13 Dec. 1901 p. 4; 'The Cutlers' Feast' *Times* 20 Nov. 1896 p. 7; Balfour *Opinions and Argument* p. 133.

[94] 'Mr. Balfour in East Manchester' *Times* 13 Jan. 1906 p. 14.

Balfour appreciated, however, that classical economics was not the last word in practical wisdom. There was no guarantee that what was good for the wealth-producing capacity of the world was best for each particular State. Protection might be warranted on patriotic or social grounds.[95] All this was perfect reasoning, but it did not help people decide whether their Prime Minister was a Free Trader or not.

The confusion was also due to the exigencies of party politics. While Liberals rallied behind Free Trade, there were Unionists maintaining every shade of fiscal opinion. To preserve party unity, Balfour needed room to manoeuvre. This he secured by developing two lines of fiscal argument, mutually consistent but logically distinct. When necessary, he mixed them together or emphasised whichever best suited the political requirements of the situation.

Balfour's arguments for his first policy – retaliatory tariffs – were firmly grounded in Free Trade theory. As foreign tariffs rose and open markets disappeared, a protectionist contagion threatened 'the strangulation of our development as a great commercial nation'.[96] In past centuries, Britain had fought wars for external markets. There was clearly a better way, but subservience to an extreme form of *laissez-faire* deprived Britain of all bargaining power in tariff negotiations. It was necessary to abandon the doctrine that import duties should only be for revenue. The selective use of tariffs in order to promote Free Trade was 'one of the greatest of the modern weapons of diplomacy'.[97]

Liberals accused Balfour of cynically advancing retaliation as a protectionist Trojan Horse. That was unfair. He did believe his case. He had advanced it as far back as 1880. On the other hand, he knew (just as well as the economists who criticised him did) that the scope for retaliatory tariffs would never be wide. They were 'full of difficulty'. A retaliatory tariff might be in place for years before it corrected foreign trade policy. The costs of over-investment in the temporarily protected domestic industry might easily exceed the ultimate gain. His repeated pleas for 'fiscal free-

[95] Balfour *Economic Notes on Insular Free Trade* pp. 4–9.
[96] 28 May 1903, *PDeb* 4th Series vol. 123 cols. 158–9; 20 Feb. 1907, *PDeb* 4th Series vol. 169 col. 874.
[97] 'Mr. Balfour and the Unionist Party' *Times* 13 Feb. 1906 p. 6; Balfour *Fiscal Reform* pp. vii and 111; A.J. Balfour *Negotiation and Imperial Trade* (London 1904) p. 13.

dom' were above all superfluous – nothing was *stopping* Britain retaliating.[98] Balfour's motive for giving retaliatory tariffs such prominence after 1903 was tactical. Tariff Reform in the cause of Free Trade was a formula to which he hoped all Unionists might adhere.

Zealous Chamberlainites were impatient of these diversions. Their man had declared Imperial Preference 'the decisive step towards the realization of the most inspiring ideal that has ever entered into the minds of British statesmen'.[99] The self-governing colonies were willing, so how could the Prime Minister allow a clique of Unionist Free Traders to stand in the way?

Balfour conceded that Imperial Preference would be advantageous. Closer commercial integration with the self-governing colonies was his second fiscal policy. Fiscal union had often been 'the prelude to that closer and more intimate union which is the basis of national strength'. He swept aside Liberal warnings that the intrusion of material interests would sully the Imperial bond with venal bickering. Did interdependence inevitably breed disharmony? Quarrels between husband and wife were more possible if they lived together than if they lived apart, but no one put his ideal of marriage in perpetual separation![100]

Balfour said that any difference between Chamberlain and himself related only to the practicability of preference.[101] He keenly apprehended the fundamental obstacle: 'I question whether the people of *this* country will be sufficiently tolerant of the protective side of the scheme, or the people *of the colonies* sufficiently tolerant of the Free Trade side, to permit them to accept the compromise in which it essentially consists.'[102] Colonial exports were mainly foodstuffs. Britain could not grant significant preference to the colonies without taxing food. British consumers would suffer. British exports were mainly manufactures. The colonies could not grant significant preference to Britain without exposing their

---

[98] 24 June 1880, *PDeb* 3rd Series vol. 253 cols. 772–3; 9 June 1881, *PDeb* 3rd Series vol. 262 cols. 131–2; A.C. Pigou *The Great Inquest* (London 1903) pp. 10–12; Balfour to Pilditch, 10 Oct. 1904, BP 49857 f. 86; Balfour to Crease, 30 Aug. 1894, SRO GD 433/2/70 no. 16; H. Cox *Mr. Balfour's Pamphlet: A Reply* (London 1903) pp. 4–5.
[99] 'Congress of Chambers of Commerce of the Empire' *Times* 10 June 1896 p. 4.
[100] 1 Aug. 1904, *PDeb* 4th Series vol. 139 col. 379; Balfour *Fiscal Reform* pp. 107 and 132.
[101] Balfour *Fiscal Reform* pp. 69–70.
[102] Balfour to Devonshire, 4 June 1903, BP 49770 f. 13.

nascent industries to British competition. Colonial industrial interests would suffer. Both sides would have to weigh the costs.[103]

Balfour hoped that untaxed colonial imports would increase so rapidly that price rises would not be appreciable, but his standard response was a call to patriotism: 'I have always found the working classes of this country open to the loftiest ideals of British citizenship.' Was it so certain that they would repudiate a food tax as part of a larger policy to place the Empire on a better footing?[104]

He rather thought it was. Fear of a corn duty had eaten into the historical imagination of the British people. Neither the most conclusive reasoning nor the most eloquent speeches could eliminate it. Other nations might tax food imports (since history had given other nationalities different prejudices), but in Britain a food tax was outside practical politics. It was to be hoped that Imperial Preference would ultimately claim 'the heart and the conscience and the intellect of the great body and mass of the people', but Balfour was acutely conscious that premature commitment to Tariff Reform could have disastrous political consequences. Even if it did not split his party, it was almost certain to lose it votes. He did not want to rebuff the colonies, however, for that would have been inimical to the cause of Imperial Union.[105] Nor did he want to rebuff Chamberlain, for that would have been inimical to the continuance of the Unionist Party under his leadership.

His solution was to advocate Imperial Preference while keeping it nebulous and remote. First another Colonial Conference was needed. Then two General Elections, perhaps, or a referendum. Only when the people were thoroughly committed to Imperial Union could a food tax be welcomed as a real step towards federalising the Empire.[106]

Thus he proposed retaliatory tariffs for the short term (to please the Free Traders), proclaimed the merits of preferential tariffs for the long term (to please the Chamberlainites), and procrastinated with a will. In the eyes of his critics, Balfour 'callously

---

[103] 28 May 1903, *PDeb* 4th Series vol. 123 col. 161.
[104] Balfour to Palgrave, 18 Oct. 1911, BP 49861 f. 358; 'Mr. Balfour in Manchester' *Times* 28 Jan. 1905 p. 10; 28 May 1903, *PDeb* 4th Series vol. 123 cols. 161–2.
[105] Balfour *Fiscal Reform* pp. 109 and 28; Balfour to Devonshire, 27 Aug. 1903, BP 49770 ff. 131–2.
[106] Balfour *Fiscal Reform* pp. 216, 137, and 220.

subordinated true patriotism to party tactics'. He saw his patriotic duty rather differently.[107] What would it profit the British Empire if it gained Imperial Preference and lost the Unionist Party?

This prompts a second question: did Balfour save his party and sacrifice his soul? He *did* favour retaliation. He *did* favour Imperial Preference. He did *not* favour supporting home industries by raising import prices. But the preservation of integrity was difficult. 'British markets for British labour – Free Trade all round', declared his 1906 election leaflet. Balfour valued the economics of Free Trade, but he wanted people to prize the politics of Imperial Preference. He argued that a duty on foodstuffs, which might incidentally be protective, but whose object was to provide an instrument for Imperial Union, was a very different thing from protection.[108] This delicate distinction between intention and consequence was not widely observed, for reasons he understood:

It is hard enough to induce people to take a broad and unselfish view of Imperial questions even in the Mother Country. It is, I suppose, in consequence of this particular difficulty, that Joe has run a policy which his enemies describe as 'protection', and which certainly is of the nature of an appeal to particular interests, in double harness with his Imperial propaganda. Personally, I think it a mistake; and, so far as I am concerned, I play for the big ideal in its simplicity, and nothing else.[109]

This purity was constantly at risk. Balfour would say, for instance, that if Tariff Reform allowed the British Empire to equal 'the magnificent economic position of the United States then I think we should have done well'. The USA was protectionist. He could then explain that the greatest triumph of Free Trade was the banning of inter-state tariffs *within* the USA. The British Empire had unfortunately failed to imitate this example – the self-governing colonies succumbed to protectionism – but might not Imperial Preference result in *freer* trade within the Empire?[110]

The ascendency of Tariff Reformers within the party after 1905 compelled him to shift his stance. He was soon arguing that social reform and naval supremacy necessitated a broader basis of taxation – only tariffs could avert ruinous rates of direct tax. More

[107] Morgan-Brown *Balfourism* p. 2; Balfour to Devonshire, 27 Aug. 1903, BP 49770 f. 127.
[108] 'The General Election' *Times* 3 Jan. 1906 p. 6; Balfour to Churchill, 26 May 1903, BP 49694 ff. 41–2.
[109] Balfour to Northcote, 1 Jan. 1905, BP 49697 ff. 51–2.
[110] 28 May 1903, *PDeb* 4th Series vol. 123 col. 165; Balfour *Fiscal Reform* pp. 101 and 216.

suspect was his discovery (in time for the next General Election) that tariffs would increase industrial productivity and employment. He was none too clear about how. They would apparently boost business confidence and encourage domestic investment.[111]

Tariff Reform elicited a multitude of carefully chosen words from Balfour, but a reading of them ultimately supports the conclusion that he took little real interest in the economics of the fiscal problem.[112] Did he take much *real* interest in its Imperial aspect?

Balfour was predisposed to support all modes of Imperial Union. Looking back in his final year, he observed: 'Joe was becoming an Imperialist, and he saw that Imperialism was impossible on the bare naked Free Trade basis, – or at any rate that it would lose half its strength.' Asked if he agreed, he replied, 'Yes, I did – I should say I certainly did.' He had indeed worried that British failure to grant preference would impel Canada towards fiscal alliance (or 'something even more unsatisfactory') with the USA. His public advocacy of Imperial Preference was never more ardent than in 1911, when US–Canadian reciprocity nearly came about. He then declared that Free Trade was imperilling the unity of the Empire – but his argument was oddly technical. The Dominions were permitted to negotiate their own tariff deals with foreign countries. The British Empire, as a whole, however, was bound by international treaties conferring most-favoured-nation status. In bilateral trade negotiations, therefore, a Dominion was unable to offer exclusive advantages to a foreign nation. Balfour predicted that the Dominions would object to this limit on their bargaining powers and demand full fiscal freedom. Britain would then face a dilemma. Refusal would provoke a crisis in Imperial relations. Acceptance, entailing denunciation of all Imperial most-favoured-nation treaties, would leave Britain defenceless against hostile tariffs.[113]

Was the most-favoured-nation clause the seed of Imperial dissolution? Balfour never advanced a more urgent argument for

---

[111] 'Mr. Balfour on Preference' *Times* 4 May 1907 p. 7; 'Mr. Balfour in Birmingham' *Times* 15 Nov. 1907 p. 8; 'Mr. Balfour at Hanley' *Times* 5 Jan. 1910 p. 7; 'Mr. Balfour at Haddington' *Times* 25 Jan. 1910 p. 7.

[112] Lord Birkenhead *Contemporary Personalities* (London 1924) p. 19.

[113] Dugdale *Balfour* vol. 1 p. 345; Memo. by Balfour, 1 Aug. 1903, PRO CAB 37/65 no. 47; 'Mr. Balfour on Unionist Policy' *Times* 9 Oct. 1911 p. 8.

Imperial Preference (as distinct from closer union generally). Indeed, he hardly advanced arguments for Tariff Reform at all once he resigned the party leadership. He considered Baldwin a fool to fight an election on the issue in 1923 (when his own speeches were as ambiguous as ever).[114]

Balfour never thought Imperial Preference crucial. If Imperial sentiment could be reinforced by economic ties, that was good – but the introduction of Imperial Preference waited on the growth of Imperial sentiment, and not the other way around.

The broader question of the relationship between the international trade system and world order seemed to him academic. He wanted to see the threads of commerce and finance 'bind all civilised nations together, and bind in a yet closer and more organic whole the separate parts of this great Empire'. Autarky did not appeal to him. It was simplistic to say that the economic dependence of a State destroyed its political independence. Had it done so, Britain would have been 'the least independent country in the world'.[115] The Free Trade vision of an interdependent cosmopolitan community did not much inspire him either. Free Trade had the admitted virtue of increasing the indirect costs of war. Was it not then absurd that its famous proponent, Richard Cobden, had simultaneously demanded the Freedom of the Seas – the very reform that would diminish those costs? Cobden's design for perpetual peace was not without nobility, but it was rooted in a philosophy of selfish individualism which provided no enduring basis for co-operation. Since the 1840s, moreover, the sentiment of nationality had received an unprecedented accretion of strength.[116] Balfour expected lasting peace to stem from the further expansion of human loyalties – not from the narrow self-interest of 'economic man'.

---

[114] Balfour to Birkenhead, 11 Dec. 1923, SRO GD 433/2/1 no. 2; Alice Balfour's diary, 15 Mar. 1924, SRO GD 433/2/136 p. 53; 'Security and Trade' *Times* 21 Nov. 1923 p. 17.
[115] 'The Franchise Bill' *Times* 22 Jan. 1913 p. 7; League Council, 25 Oct. 1920, *Procès-Verbal of the Council of the League of Nations* 20/29/16 p. 31.
[116] Balfour 'Morley's *Life of Cobden*' pp. 54–5; Balfour to Esher, 12 Oct. 1912, *BP* 49719 ff. 233–4; Balfour *Fiscal Reform* p. 100.

CHAPTER 5

The Franco-Russian challenge

> A quarrel with Russia anywhere, or about anything, means the invasion of India.
>
> Balfour 1901[1]

When Balfour exchanged the duties of Irish Secretary for the wider remit of Leader of the Commons in 1891, international politics were just entering the post-Bismarckian era. Germany let the Russo-German Reinsurance Treaty lapse, while renewing the Triple Alliance with Austria and Italy. In response, Russia and France came to a political understanding in 1891 and formed the Dual Alliance in 1893.

Britons were meanwhile tempted to think that a peace-loving island without continental entanglement was free from the risk of war. That, declared Balfour in 1894, was sheer ignorance. European Powers were now inter-continental empires, and the greatest dangers to peace lay in the struggle for dominance over distant countries on a lower plane of civilisation. Britain could not possibly 'turn back the tide of events or prevent the natural and legitimate development of other great commercial and military Powers', but 'the general movement of the world's history' was increasing the Imperial burden. Continental Powers were magnifying their armed forces to an unprecedented degree.[2] Britain retained naval supremacy, but the maintenance of an explicit Two Power Standard from 1889 was itself symptomatic.

Defence was a preoccupation of Balfour's political life from the 1890s onwards. He was acutely conscious that geography and history had made the British singularly unmindful of military pre-

---

[1] Balfour to Lansdowne, 12 Dec. 1901, BP 49727 f. 172.
[2] 'Mr. Balfour in Manchester' *Times* 23 Jan. 1894 p. 8; 'Mr. Balfour in Liverpool' *Times* 14 Feb. 1903 p. 9; 10 Aug. 1898, *PDeb* 4th Series vol. 64 col. 823; 14 Mar. 1901, *PDeb* 4th Series vol. 90 col. 1653.

paredness. The Boer War laid the problem bare. Balfour confessed in 1901 to viewing the whole of Imperial policy – military, financial, and diplomatic – with the greatest anxiety. Immense additional taxation was necessitated not only by the War, but by 'increases in the Army and Navy, which are quite independent of the war'. A great growth in military spending, however, 'would never be tolerated by the country, and might lead to a dangerous reaction, and *this* is a [matter of] Imperial importance'.[3]

The task of British statesmanship was therefore to defend with limited resources the position of the leading World Power against mounting competition. Great exertions were required to ensure that, whatever 'the arrangements and rearrangements among the nations of the world', Britain would continue 'to stand secure in the van of civilization, showing its desire for peace'.[4]

This chapter considers how Balfour directed his exertions to this end in the first half of his ministerial career – essentially from the 1890s to 1905. During this period he was convinced that the Dual Alliance constituted the principal challenge. Part I examines his perception of the threat and its manifestations in the Near East, Central Asia, and the Far East. The last of these gives rise to questions of the wider British response. Part II is accordingly concerned with his views on the acquisition of allies, entente with Russia and France, and the Russo-Japanese War.

PART I: THE CHALLENGE

In December 1891, Balfour saw some tables comparing the navies of the Great Powers. To the First Lord of the Admiralty he wrote anxiously: 'a war against France and Russia combined might end in our losing the command of the sea, and with the command of the sea our national existence'. In Opposition two years later, he took to the public platform:

Foreign nations are accustomed to plainer speaking than has been customary in England ... Foreign nations contemplate, and are obliged to contemplate, the possibility of war. We habitually shut our eyes to it; and yet at this moment there is shipbuilding going on in French and

---

[3] 'Mr Balfour in Manchester' *Times* 23 Jan. 1894 p. 8; Balfour to Selborne, 25 Oct. 1901, Selborne Papers 26 f. 12; Balfour to Knollys, 9 Feb. 1901, Sanders Papers c. 718 f. 19; Balfour to the King, 29 Dec. 1904, Sanders Papers c. 716 f. 159.
[4] 'The Guildhall Banquet' *Times* 10 Nov. 1905 p. 10.

Russian dockyards; there are movements which are being made ... in Asia which, so far as I can see, can be directed against no Power in the world at this moment except England ... Are we to be blindfolded, and we alone among the nations of Europe?[5]

It had to be realised that France and Russia were increasing their navies to a degree which could only mean 'that a time may come when, either separately or together, it may be their business, their duty, to go to war with Britain'. He immediately followed this with generalised compliments to the French, who played 'a part in the European family for which we could certainly ill spare them':

But while we have these friendly feelings as a nation to the French, I must frankly say that I do not believe the French have these feelings towards us ... my conviction ... is that, at the present moment the French are, as a nation, hostile to us, and that in the lower ranks of their Diplomatic and Civil Service you will find French officials constantly animated by a desire which you will not find in any official of any other country, to embarrass and humiliate the English Government.

The French Ambassador was appalled.[6]

Balfour denied that party polemics played any part in this 'naval scare', which followed the visit of the Russian fleet to Toulon in October 1893. The future of the Empire was at stake. Was it not criminal to delay new ships when, by 1897, Britain would be inferior by eight battleships to the combined forces of France and Russia?[7]

With land access to markets, and nearly self-supporting in food, France was not susceptible to maritime blockade. Russia was aiming for complete self-sufficiency and was virtually free from attack by sea. Balfour thought the Russian and French navies had to be regarded as aggressive. The agitation of 1893–4 was effective: Gladstone retired, naval building was accelerated, and British superiority over the navies of the Dual Alliance was preserved – at considerable cost.[8]

[5] Balfour to Hamilton, 29 Dec. 1891 (and reply), BP 49778 ff. 13–18; 'Mr. Balfour in Manchester' *Times* 23 Jan. 1894 p. 8.
[6] Decrais to Casimir-Périer, 29 Jan. 1894, *Documents Diplomatiques Français 1871–1914* 1st and 2nd Series (Paris 1929–59) 1st Series vol. 11 no. 33.
[7] 19 Dec. 1893, *PDeb* 4th Series vol. 19 cols 1805–6, 1811, and 1809; 'Mr. Balfour in Manchester' *Times* 23 Jan. 1894 p. 8.
[8] 23 Dec. 1921, *Conference* p. 524; 28 May 1903, *PDeb* 4th Series vol. 123 col. 158; 1 Mar. 1904, *PDeb* 4th Series vol. 130 col. 1411. See P.M. Kennedy *The Rise and Fall of British Naval Mastery* (London 1976) p. 209.

Russia, Balfour later admitted, was almost a traditional enemy. Given British interests in Asia, tension seemed unavoidable. Russia had been progressively absorbing territory for two centuries, externally guided by 'a sort of mechanical law'. On the rim of the Russian Empire there was always unrest, and Russian power extended over districts so disturbed. He told Parliament that he did not hold the Russian Government responsible.[9] Never did he accuse Russia of *desiring* war with Britain. Internal conditions discouraged it. Tsar Nicholas II seemed committed to peaceful development, and reliance on foreign loans inclined his ministers in the same direction. Russian expansion, however, did not require war. It was an incremental process of extending and consolidating exclusive economic and political influence. The Russian commercial agent, said Balfour, was indistinguishable from a Russian political agent.[10] The growth of the Russian Empire was insidious:

Petty acts of bad faith, taken each by themselves, supply very poor reasons for plunging the world into war, yet if they are condoned they mount up to what is, in its cumulative effect, a serious menace to the British Empire, and in the meanwhile it seems extremely difficult to erect any diplomatic barrier in front of this slowly-creeping tide.[11]

The most evident menace was to India, but the extension of Russia towards the periphery of Asia, coupled with the growth of the Russian navy, suggested a potential challenge for global supremacy.

Balfour admitted that British diplomatic endeavours to halt Russian expansion had historically been 'quite in vain'. The contest, he realised, was not fought on equal terms. The British Government had to contend with public opinion, indignant at apparent reverses and sometimes belligerent. Secrecy and the absence of criticism allowed the Russian Government far greater freedom to manoeuvre. Balfour perceived the result: Russia tended to suffer from 'the delusion that a *conciliatory* attitude is a *weak* attitude; and that Great Britain is prepared to make any concession rather than defend her rights by force'. Resistance

[9] Statement by Balfour [22 Mar. 1917], *The Lansing Papers 1914–1920* (Washington 1939–40) vol. II p. 21; 1 Aug. 1878, *PDeb* 3rd Series vol. 242 cols. 945–6.
[10] Balfour to Ridgeway, 4 Jan. 1899, BP 49812 f. 296; 17 Feb. 1908, *PDeb* 4th Series vol. 184 col. 555.
[11] Balfour to Lansdowne, 21 Dec. 1903, BP 49728 ff. 121–2.

could only be effective if the Russians were convinced that diplomacy might be backed by military action.[12]

But how could Britain strike at Russia? Sending the Fleet into the Black Sea, bombarding Kronstadt, advancing through Persia – all seemed imprudent. Examining frontiers from the Baltic to Vladivostok, Balfour wrote: 'I do not personally believe that Russia is vulnerable in any mortal spot except her Exchequer.' Russia had to be feared as an expansive Power in Asia, the possible disturber of European peace, and the ally of France.[13]

'He has always been pre-eminent among the statesmen of the United Kingdom in his friendship, nay, his affection and sympathy for France'[14] – this much was later assumed from the simple fact of *Entente Cordiale* (1904). It was not a misperception Balfour cared to rectify.

Much as he admired French literature, he was probably sincere when in 1899 he spoke of the French *nation* in a tone of pitying disparagement. The decadence of 'atheistic' France was then almost a by-word. Balfour believed 'Romanism' to be incapable of retaining its hold upon the educated classes '– a result which must penetrate in course of time more deeply into the social organism' of Catholic countries. Humanism could not be an effective stimulus to high endeavour. Its greatest flourishing in Italy had been 'synchronous or immediately precedent to a period of national decay'.[15] In the contest for world leadership, the French had lost to the English. The American colonies had stayed within the British Empire long enough to foil French conquest of the New World. Then, with the defeat of 1870, France had lost its leading position in Europe – irrevocably, as Balfour saw it. (The impact on him of a visit to Paris immediately after the fall of the Commune may be

---

[12] 11 May 1905, *PDeb* 4th Series vol. 146 col. 78; 29 Apr. 1898, *PDeb* 4th Series vol. 56 cols. 1591–2; Balfour to the King, 11 Aug. 1904 PRO CAB 41/29 no. 31; Note by Balfour [1903], BP 49698 f. 115.

[13] Balfour to Selborne, 6 Apr. 1904, Selborne Papers 1 ff. 50–1; Memo. by Balfour, 3 Mar. 1892, SRO GD 433/2/68 no. 19; D. Dilks *Curzon in India* (London 1969–70) vol. II p. 59; Memo. by Balfour, 29 Dec. 1903, PRO CAB 37/67 no. 97.

[14] 'Balfour as Staunch Friend of France' by F. Cunliffe-Owen *New York Times* 1 Jan. 1922 II p. 3.

[15] Balfour to Sarolea, 14 Nov. 1896, BP 49851 ff. 151–4; Memo. by Bülow, 24 Nov. 1899, *Grosse Politik* vol. 15, no. 4398; Balfour to Shaw, 16 May 1899, BP 49853 f. 89; Balfour *Religion of Humanity* p. 49; Balfour to unnamed, 27 Dec. 1898, BP 49853 ff. 16–17.

conjectured.)[16] The French were nevertheless acquiring overseas territories which they could not hope to colonise with Frenchmen. Balfour did not involve himself in specific colonial disputes, but he criticised selfish aggression in Tunis and encroachments on Siam. After British and French forces confronted each other in the Sudan in 1898, he complained that the French Colonial Party were again 'prepared apparently to embark on any enterprise, however useless to themselves, which would be annoying to us, and this without any regard of the consequences either to France or to Europe'.[17]

Publicly, he spoke of Anglo-French friendship. Privately, he speculated that 'those who really govern the destinies of France' would probably have liked to indulge in the luxury of war in the relatively cheap form of fighting a maritime Power. The Psychological Climate of the French was not averse to it. Englishmen, Protestants, and Jews were what they traditionally hated, and parts of the French press were extraordinarily hostile. France, he wrote in 1899, was 'the incalculable quantity and the most obvious danger to European peace'.[18] The French did not currently feel safe to go to war alone with the British, whose naval supremacy promised immunity from invasion and superior communications with colonial theatres of war. Whether France sought war or peace depended on Russia. The Dual Alliance was directed against Germany, but Franco-Russian co-operation had no prescribed limits. If Britain ever found itself at war with Russia and France simultaneously, Balfour warned: 'Our position would then be perilous.'[19]

This then, on a Balfourian analysis, was the current requirement of continuing British world leadership: to contain an invulnerable military empire, while braving any crises which the petulant jealousy of an allied declining Power might provoke, and all

---

[16] Amery *Empire in the New Era* p. viii; Metternich to Bülow, 31 Jan. 1907, *Grosse Politik* vol. 25 no. 7206; Balfour *Opinions and Argument* p. 34.
[17] 24 June 1881, *PDeb* 3rd Series vol. 262 col. 1318; 2 Aug. 1893, *PDeb* 4th Series vol. 15 cols. 1141–3; Balfour to Maxse, 5 Dec. 1898, BP 49853 f. 14.
[18] 'Mr Balfour at Bristol' *Times* 30 Nov. 1898 p. 10; Balfour to Maxse, 5 Dec. 1898, BP 49853 f. 13; Balfour to Amery, 14 July 1904, BP 49775 f. 116; Balfour to Ridgeway, 4 Jan. 1899, BP 49812 f. 296.
[19] Balfour to Maxse, 5 Dec. 1898, BP 49853 ff. 13–14; Balfour to Lansdowne, 12 Dec. 1901, BP 49727 ff. 172–3.

without war or loss of prestige. Given his knowledge of regional problems, he cannot have expected this to be easy.

The Near East

Throughout the nineteenth century the struggle had been waged to prevent Russia profiting from the weakness of the Turkish Empire. Balfour was present at the Congress of Berlin, where Britain succeeded in mitigating the consequences of the Russo-Turkish War by reducing the size of the new Bulgaria. He never claimed to have been more than 'a humble follower' of this policy, but it so polarised British opinion that it was long his duty to defend it. The Anglo-Turkish Convention (1878) was the 'most tangible inducement ever held out to the Turkish Empire to reform itself'. It would be incumbent on any British Government to prevent the extension of Russian influence through Asia Minor, 'supposing that Asiatic Turkey were well governed'. Come the Armenian massacres of 1895–6, Balfour was admitting that hopes for speedy reform had been bitterly disappointed. The Crimean War and the Treaty of Berlin had still not been mistakes. Russia was certainly not the proper reforming authority in the Balkans.[20]

The British had done their best to preserve the Ottoman Empire, but the Turks had almost deliberately alienated them. Like Salisbury, Balfour had none of the Turcophil sentiments of the thorough-going 'Jingo'. Asked if he would mind going to war with Turkey in 1895, he replied, 'Not in the least.'[21] Turkey in Europe was doomed. An analysis written after the event encapsulates his fundamental stance throughout:

What permanence could a political system possess which depended on the domination of a militant minority over peoples differing fundamentally from it in race and religion, superior to it in economic efficiency, in capacity for modern culture, and in aptitude for modern science and modern administration? Such a system . . . is sure to be unstable as long as its elements refuse to mingle. If it does not break up at the centre it will gradually contract from the periphery. One alien element after

[20] 24 June 1881, *PDeb* 3rd Series vol. 262 col. 1318; 11 Feb. 1896, *PDeb* 4th Series vol. 37 col. 117; 27 Feb. 1905, *PDeb* 4th Series vol. 141 col. 1392.
[21] 11 Feb. 1896, *PDeb*, 4th Series vol. 37 col. 118; Balfour to Ashmead Bartlett, 30 Aug. 1898, BP 49746 ff. 116–7; Frances Balfour to Betty Balfour, 8 Sept. 1895, SRO GD 433/2/314.

another will be torn from it, till its diminished territories are no more than sufficient to accommodate a population in which the majority now belong to what was once a dominant minority.[22]

The liberation of the Balkans was great civilising work. Turkish rule rendered every place sterile, and, in 1918, he urged that expulsion be complete. Europe was not the place for Mohammedanism: an Oriental race ought to go back to an Oriental country. 'You may think the Serbians, Bulgarians, Greeks and the Roumanians are not the highest specimens of the Aryan race', he said: 'I don't argue that, but they are people who will improve their own country as soon as you relieve them of Turkish domination.' To his mind, racial and religious heterogeneity was the inherent reason why the Near East was the despair of European statesmanship. He could not imagine how Constantinople was to be governed, with its 'mixture of Turks, Greeks, Armenians, Jews, and odds and ends'. Even so, he viewed British withdrawal from Chanak in 1922 with regret: Britain could not prevent the return of the Turks to Europe single-handed, but history would probably condemn their failure.[23]

He also viewed with distaste any settlement entrenching Europeans in Asia Minor. In 1919, he supported the Greek ethnographical claim to Smyrna, but Hellenism had 'never really been much more than skin-deep' in central Anatolia. Perhaps Greece would accept Cyprus instead. (He had some premonition of the problems Britain would face in that ethnically divided colony.)[24] As for Italian claims in Turkey, looked at 'in the light of reason, justice or anything else, except the price given for necessary assistance', they were outrageous. The Agreement of St Jean de Maurienne (1917), which allotted southern Anatolia to Italy, had been signed in opposition to his views while he was in the USA.[25] When Lloyd George tried to rush through a partition scheme at Paris

[22] Balfour *Chapters of Autobiography* pp. 96–7.
[23] 27 Feb. 1918, *HCD* vol. 103 col. 1470; Memo. by Balfour, 9 Oct. 1917, PRO FO 800/200 f. 173; Eastern Committee, 23 Dec. 1918, Milner Papers dep. 137 f. 244; Imperial Conference, 27 July 1921; PRO CAB 32/2 ff. 50–1; 'Mr. Balfour at the Albert Hall' *Times* 7 May 1904 p. 14; Vincent *Crawford Papers* p. 445.
[24] Meinertzhagen *Middle East Diary* p. 23; Memo. by Balfour, 9 Oct. 1917, PRO FO 800/200 ff. 173–4; Eastern Committee, 16 Dec. 1918, Milner Papers dep. 137 f. 212; 1 June 1880, *PDeb* 3rd Series vol. 252 cols. 918–19.
[25] Eastern Committee, 5 Dec. 1918, Milner Papers dep. 137 f. 188; Warman 'Erosion of Foreign Office Influence' p. 136.

in 1919, he threatened resignation. Balfour wanted a community 'made up of Turks governed by Turks for Turks in a manner which suits the Turks'.[26]

As he saw it, the aim of British Near Eastern policy was never maintenance of Turkey in Europe. The dual objective before 1914 was (i) peaceful contraction of the Ottoman Empire and (ii) limitation of Russian gains therefrom. 'Practical autonomy with the technical maintenance of Turkish sovereignty' was what Macedonia needed.[27] (Home Rule was just the thing to destroy an empire!) Balfour reacted strongly to the suggestion that Russia should simply be allowed to take over the Balkans:

For *our* time it is nothing to me. But what of our children? ... What kind of world will it be when Russia, which has already a hundred and twenty million inhabitants, exercises an enormously dominating influence over the whole of south-east Europe? What kind of Europe will it be, dominated by the Slavs – with a Hungary barely able to hold her own, with a strong Germany, I suppose, but what else?[28]

A Pan-Anglican could not wholly discount Pan-Slavism, but linguistic and religious divisions consigned *voluntary* Slav union to the distant future[29] – and the more distant the better. Though it is unlikely that Balfour would ever have gone to war to prevent 'Russianisation' of the Balkans, he had absolutely no desire to expedite it. Russian policy was to be resisted – but the priority had to be peace. With Russian support for the Slavs, Austrian fear of Russia, German support for Austria, and French support for Russia, any attempt by the Balkan peoples to expel the Turks by force could easily escalate into a great war. At worst that war might end with Russia dominating not just the Balkans, but the whole Eastern Mediterranean. The Russians always ensured they were 'extremely well paid' when they came to the defence of Eastern Christians.[30]

Balfour saw no alternative to co-operation with the Great Powers to preserve the *status quo*. This meant leaving Christian

[26] R. Albrecht-Carrie *Italy at the Paris Peace Conference* (Hamden 1966) pp. 220–3; Harold Nicolson *Peacemaking 1919* new edn (London 1945) p. 280; 6 Nov. 1917, *HCD* vol. 98 col. 2041. Also Memo. by Balfour, 16 May 1919, *FRUS* PPC 1919 vol. v pp. 669–72; Memo. by Balfour, 26 June 1919, *DBFP* vol. IV no. 211.
[27] Balfour to Lansdowne, 22 Feb. 1904, BP 49728 f. 182.
[28] Spring 1898, F. Whyte *The Life of W.T. Stead* (London 1925) p. 126.
[29] Memo. by Balfour, 4 Oct. 1916, PRO CAB 37/157 no. 7.
[30] 25 Mar. 1881, *PDeb* 3rd Series vol. 259 col. 1985.

populations to suffer Turkish oppression, but it was a question of choosing the lesser evil. In 1897, he suppressed his Hellenist sentiments, declared that Greek seizure of Crete would mean European war, and praised the international occupation. There could be no 'insane policy of philanthropic adventure', despite 'the harrowing horrors which undoubtedly take place'.[31]

Balkans nationalities were themselves 'stained by mutual crimes'. Their division was responsible for the Turk being in Europe at all, and for his staying ever since. As Foreign Secretary in 1917, he dutifully presented proposals to sanitise 'the plague spot of Europe' with clear ethnographical frontiers, but he concluded that, unfortunately, Balkan peoples 'would much rather injure a rival than benefit themselves'. At the Peace Conference, he thought the attainment of lasting peace in the region beyond human powers. Back in 1903, he had offended all sides by saying that 'the balance of criminality' in Macedonia lay not with Turkey, but with the insurgents. Balkan Christians might have a greater capacity for civilisation, but, as things stood, they were really no better than Turks.[32]

It was usually politic to burke the issue with faint praise for the Concert of Europe.[33] Back in 1879 he had argued that experience and common sense alike showed the Concert to be 'a perfectly worthless instrument' for solving the Balkan problem. Twenty-five years on, he reflected that its very success in averting war had reduced the chances of constitutional reform. So long as the Powers desired to maintain the territorial *status quo*, they were capable of doing so. Russia and Austria could intimidate Romania, Bulgaria, and Serbia, while Anglo-French naval action restrained Greece and Turkey. Crisis over, however, the Powers lost interest in good order and resumed their intrigues till next time.[34]

---

[31] 'The Guildhall Banquet' *Times* 10 Nov. 1903 p. 10; Hatzfeldt to Foreign Ministry, 17 Mar. 1897, *Grosse Politik* vol. 12 no. 3192; 2 and 5 Apr. 1897, *PDeb* 4th Series vol. 48 cols. 471 and 518; Balfour to Waldstein, 8 Apr. 1897, BP 49852 f. 87; 'Mr. Balfour at Norwich' *Times* 5 Nov. 1897 p. 6; 'Mr Balfour in Manchester' *Times* 11 Jan. 1898 p. 8; 27 Feb. 1905, *PDeb* 4th Series vol. 141 cols. 1394–5.

[32] 27 Feb. 1905, *PDeb* 4th Series vol. 141 cols. 1393–4; Memo. by Balfour, 9 Oct. 1917, PRO FO 800/200 ff. 173–4; Balfour to Bryce, 15 Aug. 1919, BP 49749 ff. 168–70; 10 Aug. 1903, *PDeb* 4th Series vol. 127 col. 696; F.R. Bridge *Great Britain and Austria-Hungary 1906–1914* (London 1972) p. 6.

[33] E.g. 'The Guildhall Banquet' *Times* 10 Nov. 1903 p. 10.

[34] A.J. Balfour *Mr. Gladstone's Scotch Speeches* (Edinburgh 1880) pp. 6–7; Balfour to Lansdowne, 28 Feb. 1904, BP 49728 f. 184–5.

'Russia in her dealings with the Balkan Peninsula, as elsewhere', Balfour did not doubt, 'is moved much more by territorial aspirations than by philanthropy.' He thought the Russians wished to avoid war, but weak leadership and Pan-Slavist agitation rendered their policy unreliable.[35] Austria, equally short of humanitarian instincts, was indecisive and timorous. What was the Austrian game? Surely they would not be so stupid as to add to their existing diversity of populations? Either they were pursuing a far-reaching design so subtle that he failed to perceive it, or else they had no design at all. He suspected the latter. Austro-Hungarian statesmen were content merely to defer the ultimate conflagration. Germany (since 1895) was ever 'anxious to make Turkey think her her only friend'. One relatively disinterested Power might have helped bring order to Macedonia – but France was bound to Russia. 'It is unfortunate', Balfour observed.[36]

The Franco-Russian Alliance undermined British influence in the Eastern Mediterranean. When Turkey let Russian torpedo-boats through the Dardanelles in 1902, no foreign Power would join Britain in protesting at a breach of the Rule of the Straits. Balfour acknowledged that French naval support would allow Russia to defy the Royal Navy and seize Constantinople at the start of any conflict. He seems as early as 1895 to have accepted that to pretend otherwise was merely to antagonise the Dual Alliance. In 1903, he stated plainly: 'the maintenance of the *status quo* as regards Constantinople is not one of the primary naval or military interests of this country'. The essential tenet of Jingoism – 'The Russians shall not have Constantinople' – was jettisoned. He told his colleagues not to worry. The defence of Egypt would be simplified. A vast amount of territory would have to be Russianised before Suez was threatened. 'Turkish patriotism, concentrated upon the defence of what are truly Turkish territories' would give the Russians endless trouble. German and French interests in Asia Minor and Syria would have to be challenged, and the Turks were less likely to be fighting alone when 'unembarrassed by the complications which have made Euro-

---

[35] Balfour to the King, 16 Dec. 1904, PRO CAB 41/29 no. 43; Balfour to Lansdowne, 10 Sept. 1903, BP 49728 f. 53.
[36] Balfour to Lansdowne, 28 Feb. 1904 and 10 Sept. 1903, BP 49728 ff. 184–5 and 53; Balfour to Lansdowne, 6 Jan. 1905, BP 49729 ff. 39–40; Balfour to the King, 16 Dec. 1904, PRO CAB 41/29 no. 43.

pean Turkey for centuries a common enemy of Christendom'.[37]

When Turco-Bulgarian war threatened in 1904, he suggested that traditional British support for the territorial *status quo* should be revised. If the Turks seemed likely to win, they should be informed that Britain would not acquiesce in the extension of their territory: 'If on the other hand, the *Bulgarians* seem likely to get the best of it, we should refrain from making any corresponding statement to them.' 'Big Bulgaria' (so strenuously opposed in 1878) should not now be an *aim* of British diplomacy, but it would be 'impolitic' to protect European Turkey against Bulgarian invasion. The Bulgarians had proved surprisingly independent — 'the only Nationality in the Balkans with the makings of a nation in them' — and they would be much more efficient guardians of the Straits than the Turks.[38]

The Near East hardly gave ground for satisfaction, but there was little to do but wait and hope. Though British leverage had diminished, the shaky peace was holding, and Russia was getting nowhere fast. Balfour saw more pressing problems elsewhere. He once wrote: 'The more Russia is made a European rather than an Asiatic Power the better for everybody'.[39]

Central Asia

The annexations of Chitral and Pamir in 1895 brought British India and the Russian Empire closer than ever before. Balfour's assurances that this delimitation of frontiers was totally free from mutual suspicion were for public consumption. Admiral Fisher, for one, was to consider the future Prime Minister 'stupefied by the Indian Frontier Bogey'.[40]

In 1881, Balfour depicted Russia in Asia as an investor who had laid out money on unremunerative work and, after acquiring barren deserts, would then be tempted by prospects for profit in adjoining lands. Twenty-two years later, he still maintained:

[37] G. Monger *The End of Isolation* (London 1963) pp. 84–7; Hamilton to Balfour, 12 Jan. 1896, BP 49778 ff. 31–4; Balfour to Salisbury, 16 Dec. 1895, Hatfield 3M/E f. 57; Memo. by Balfour, 14 Feb. 1903, PRO CAB 38/2 no. 6; Balfour to Selborne, 10 Jan. 1905, Selborne Papers 46 ff. 7–8.
[38] Memo. by Balfour, Feb. 1904, BP 49698 ff. 136–44; Balfour to Lansdowne, 22 Feb. 1904, BP 49728 f. 183.
[39] Memo. by Balfour, 4 Oct. 1916, PRO CAB 37/157 no. 7.
[40] 'Mr Balfour in Glasgow' *Times* 15 Nov. 1895 p. 6; Marder *Fear God* vol. I pp. 320–1.

We possess a good deal that she would like to have and even if India is too big a mouthful for her to swallow, her statesmen believe that if she could secure a position of strategical superiority along our Indian frontier we should be so much afraid of her in Asia as to be her very humble servant in Europe.[41]

The Indian frontier was the weakest spot in the Empire. Balfour's defensive strategy was to preserve a sterilised buffer zone. While communications in Afghanistan and Persia remained primitive, the overwhelming numerical superiority of the Russian army could not be brought to bear on the North-West Frontier.[42] If Russia absorbed Afghanistan south of the Hindu Kush, India would become indefensible. If Russia gained control of Persia, 'our Eastern possessions would no longer be a strength to the Empire, but a burden and a weakness'. If Russia secured dominance in Tibet, it would be disastrous. He was adamant: 'this country cannot allow the limit of countries which lie between us and Russia to be eaten up'. Therefore: 'until Russia moves we remain still'.[43]

This was a difficult policy to execute. While not advancing beyond the southern limit of the buffer zone, Britain had to display credible determination to fight if Russia violated the northern limit. Balfour sought to postulate 'as regards all the essentials of our Eastern position, certain well-defined principles, ... which, if broken, we should regard as a *casus belli*'. The defence of Afghanistan was clear-cut: Britain guaranteed it. Britain would also, it was announced in 1903, regard the construction of any foreign naval base in the Persian Gulf as a hostile act.[44]

Persia as a whole, however, presented almost impossible perplexities. Balfour was certainly anxious to support 'the tottering fabric of the Persian monarchy'. If Russia invaded, Britain should retaliate – but the military feasibility of this was doubtful, and it

---

[41] 25 Mar. 1881, *PDeb* 3rd Series vol. 259 col. 1987; Balfour to Lansdowne, 21 Dec. 1903, BP 49728 f. 121.

[42] Balfour to Lansdowne, 12 Dec. 1901, BP 49727 f. 173; Memo. by Balfour, 30 Apr. 1903, PRO CAB 38/2 no. 26. See above, pp. 55–7.

[43] Note by Balfour [1903], B 49698 f. 115; Memo. by Balfour, 22 Apr. 1904, PRO CAB 37/70 no. 57; Balfour to the King, 19 Feb. 1903, PRO CAB 41/28 no. 2; 2 Aug. 1904, *PDeb* 4th Series vol. 139 col. 621; Monger *End of Isolation* p. 89.

[44] Balfour to Lansdowne, 21 Dec. 1903, BP 49728 ff. 123–4; Lansdowne, 5 May 1903, *PDeb* 4th Series vol. 121 col. 1348.

scarcely met the case anyway. The peaceful Russianisation of Persia was already in progress. In the struggle for influence, 'evidently the combatants will not fight on equal terms'. Constrained by parliamentary scrutiny, the British Exchequer could hardly compete with the Russian Finance Ministry in the matter of bribes. (Balfour had to hint at resignation merely to persuade Edward VII to give the Shah the Order of the Garter). Since the Russian army could be in Teheran within a fortnight, Russia could master Persia and harvest 'the fruits of conquest' simply by menace.[45]

Russia possessed indefeasible geographical advantages: it abutted Central Asia and its land communications were impregnable. British sea communications were open to attack by the French navy (assuming the Dual Alliance operated). Balfour saw that progress only worsened this strategic imbalance. Russian invasion of India had once been a mere bugbear, but no longer – and the reason? Railways. The great threat to British India was the development of transport. The Orenburg–Tashkent railway, built 1899–1904 with French assistance, linked the Turkestan network to European Russia. More such links could be expected. Balfour explained that this placed the British Empire in the position of a continental Power with land frontiers vulnerable to military attack. The standard continental response was conscription, but he did not think Britain would tolerate 'a compulsory levy *en masse* to defend possessions far off across the seas in distant and tropical climes'.[46] To be effective, principles of policy in Central Asia needed to be of such obvious importance to Imperial interests that the British people would regard their infraction 'as a sufficient ground for putting forward their whole strength'.[47]

It was not with *public* opinion, however, that he had primarily to contend. Curzon, the Viceroy (1899–1905), scorned 'a moribund government with fear of Russia on the brain' and persistently favoured a more 'forward' policy. Balfour felt that India under

---

[45] Memo. by Balfour, 22 Apr. 1904, PRO CAB 37/70 no. 57; Monger *End of Isolation* pp. 87–92.
[46] Memo. by Balfour, 30 Apr. 1903, PRO CAB 38/2 no. 26; 2 Aug. 1904, *PDeb* 4th Series vol. 139 col. 621; 11 May 1905, *PDeb* 4th Series vol. 146 cols 78–9; 'Mr. Balfour on Army Reform' *Times* 28 Nov. 1903 p. 12.
[47] Balfour to Lansdowne, 21 Dec. 1903, BP 49728 f. 124.

Curzon was becoming 'an independent and not always friendly power'.[48] One incident stands out. The closed kingdom of Tibet refused to acknowledge the existence of Britain. Rumours of a Russian agent at Lhasa convinced Curzon that a military mission was required to open the Dalai Lama's eyes. Balfour worried about irritating Russia, but gave his reluctant assent. Justifying the Younghusband mission to Parliament with pretended indignation at the failure of Tibetan herdsmen to observe the frontier with Sikkim, he assured Russia that Britain had no territorial ambitions.[49] A three-year indemnity would punish Tibet for its imperviousness. The Lhasa Convention of 7 September 1904, negotiated by Younghusband and approved by Curzon, set a *seventy-five*-year indemnity with British occupation of the strategic Chumbi Valley as security. Balfour was furious. He denounced Younghusband, who had 'touched the honour of his country', but:

whatever we do now will be too late to prevent hostile critics saying we have taken a leaf out of Russian books; have made promises in Europe, have encouraged the breach of them in Asia in the hopes that the matter will be passed over, and when it is *not* passed over have disavowed our agent.[50]

He increasingly supervised policy in Central Asia personally, lest Curzon's overbearing diplomacy provoke 'a calamity the magnitude of which it would not be easy to measure'.[51]

Though critics accused him of timidity, Balfour was convinced that his 'backward' policy was the right one. Russia had the edge in Central Asia, and a war there could only weaken Britain. If military reverses tempted other Powers to attack elsewhere – and he feared France would find it irresistible[52] – it could even destroy British world power. Imagine India, a strategic and cultural anomaly, bringing down the great Anglo-Saxon sea-empire! The risk

---

[48] Balfour to Curzon, 23 Aug. 1905, BP 49733 f. 75; Memo. by Balfour, 6 Sept. 1905, PRO CAB 37/79 no. 154; Lord Midleton *Records and Reactions 1856–1939* (London 1939) p. 198.

[49] Balfour to the King, 19 Feb. 1903, PRO CAB 41/28 no. 2; Balfour to Brodrick, 28 Oct. 1903, Midleton Papers 50072 ff. 101–4; 13 Apr. 1904, *PDeb* 4th Series vol. 133 cols. 126–32.

[50] Balfour to Lansdowne, 4 Oct. 1904, BP 49729 f. 1.

[51] E. David (ed.) *Inside Asquith's Cabinet* (London 1977) p. 102; Balfour to the King, 8 Aug. 1905, PRO CAB 41/30 no. 32.

[52] Memo. by Balfour, 30 Apr. 1903, PRO CAB 38/2 no. 26; Balfour to Lansdowne, 12 Dec. 1901, BP 49727 ff. 172–3.

could not be eliminated. A sterilised buffer zone to limit the scale of hostilities was the best he could suggest.

The Far East

Beyond the security problem of Central Asia lay the diplomatic problem of the Far East. China emerged as an area of Great Power rivalry after the Sino-Japanese War (1894–5). French interests extended north from the ominously named Empire of Indo-China. The Trans-Siberian Railway brought Russian power to the northern border of China – and beyond it: the connected Chinese Eastern Railway was being built through Manchuria by a subsidiary of the Russian Finance Ministry. In 1897, Germany occupied and leased Tsingtao in Shantung. In 1898, Russia followed suit, taking Port Arthur in Kwantung and linking it to the railway. The Boxer Rebellion of 1900 supplied a pretext for multiplying the Russian garrisons which guarded the line. Russianisation of Manchuria was progressing apace.

This increased Russian influence in the Pacific and challenged British economic predominance in China. Protectionist Powers could be expected to seek exclusive spheres of influence. Partition of China seemed a distinct possibility; Russia taking the north, France the south, and Germany the east, with the Yangtsze Valley left to Britain.

Few in Britain failed to oppose this and align themselves with what Balfour called 'the forces of commerce and freedom'. With reference to China, he extolled Free Trade as a policy conducive to prosperity, international understanding, and perpetual peace.[53]

Any move towards partition would signal British weakness. Balfour commented on competition for the Newchwang Railway concession: 'we are really fighting a battle for prestige rather than for material gain'. It was not easy. The British might proclaim the 'Open Door' – which in its fullest expression meant the maintenance of a united and independent China with equal opportunity for the commerce of all nations – but they were in no position to guarantee China. The Triple Intervention of Russian, French, and German fleets to force Japan to evacuate the main-

---

[53] 29 Apr. 1898, *PDeb* 4th Series vol. 56 col. 1596; 'Mr. Balfour in Manchester' *Times* 11 Jan. 1898 p. 8.

land in 1895 had ended undisputed British supremacy in the
Yellow Sea. With France allied to Russia, a Far Eastern dispute
could mean conflict in the English Channel. Balfour would not
risk war over Port Arthur.[54] Was it worth risking war over China
at all? 'We should be fighting because we want Manchuria and
the Yangtsze to be a common field for English and Russian con-
cessionaires. *They* would be fighting because they preferred dividing the field into two portions . . . A small matter about which to
set the world on fire.'[55]

Acquiescence in Russian encroachments was inadmissible, but,
if Britain did successfully call Russia's bluff, the utility of a diplomatic victory would only be temporary. Britain could alternatively
threaten (and even use) force against the Chinese to compel them
to resist Russian pressure – but would that do any good? 'We want
no more fragments of China ourselves', he noted; 'we do not desire
to give other people a fresh excuse for piracy.' It might hasten the
break-up. Partition was 'a counsel of despair only to be accepted in
the last resort'. The British might not be left secure even in their
own portion.[56] This raised a dilemma. If the Russian share in any
partition was to be minimised, it was necessary to lose no time in
defining a British sphere of influence. The very mention of spheres
of influence, however, suggested capitulation to Russian pressure.
MPs laughed when Balfour struggled to distinguish self-evident
spheres of *interest* from unthinkable spheres of *influence*. The Open
Door was being preserved, he argued unconvincingly – even if the
Russians were possibly 'half-shutting' it in Manchuria.[57]

The Government meanwhile equivocated, mixing Open Door
declarations with intimations of zones of influence, tacking
between resistance to Russia and conciliation. Balfour was as
equivocal as any of them, torn between loyalty to Salisbury, the
advocate of conciliation, and sympathy with Chamberlain, the
advocate of resistance in alliance with other Powers.

Most unfortunate was his speech of 3 February 1896. Lauding

---

[54] Memo. by Balfour, 15 Aug. 1898, PRO CAB 37/47 no. 62; Balfour to the Queen, 26
Mar. 1898, PRO CAB 41/24 no. 34.
[55] Memo. by Balfour, 15 Aug. 1898, PRO CAB 37/47 no. 62.
[56] Memo. by Balfour, 15 Aug. 1898, PRO CAB 37/47 no. 62; Balfour to Chamberlain, 10
Aug. 1900, BP 49773 ff. 198–204.
[57] 29 Apr. 1898, *PDeb* 4th Series vol. 56 cols. 1582–3; Geoffrey to Hanotaux, 30 Apr.
1898, *Documents Diplomatiques Français* 1st Series vol. 14 no. 176; 10 Aug. 1898, *PDeb*
4th Series vol. 64 cols. 827–9.

British unselfishness, he stated 'that so far, for example, from regarding with fear and jealousy a commercial outlet for Russia in the Pacific Ocean which would not be ice-bound half the year, I should welcome such a result'. He was not allowed to forget this two years later, when he denounced Russian seizure of Port Arthur as a menace to Peking which had to be countered by British occupation of Wei-hai-wei.[58] Accused of having given away Britain's whole position, he insisted that his words had referred only to – *commercial* privileges, while Port Arthur was a naval base.[59]

His embarrassment reflected more general discomfiture. Critics scorned a 'halting, drifting, ineffective policy' which always lost against Russia. Balfour resorted to his 'I am an optimist' device and protested: 'The Government are not responsible for the fact that, as Russia borders China by land, for these thousands of miles she had military power closer to Peking than any other nation.'[60]

British Far Eastern policy drifted on. At the Foreign Office in August 1898, Balfour worked for a spheres of interest deal with Russia respecting railway concessions, but he was not very satisfied with the way Salisbury was handling things.[61] Deputising earlier in the year, he had shown that he did not share his uncle's disinclination to look for allies.

PART II: THE RESPONSE

The search for alliance

His first choice was characteristic. A friendly agreement with Russia, a defensive arrangement with the USA – 'there seems no reason why the two policies should not properly be run together'. The Americans favoured the Open Door in China, because they shrank from creating a sphere of influence. Balfour on 7 March

---

[58] 'Mr. Balfour at Bristol', *Times* 4 Feb. 1896 p. 7; 8 Feb., 24 Mar., 5 Apr., 29 Apr. and 16 June 1898, *PDeb* 4th Series vol. 53 cols 126, vol. 55 col. 782, vol. 56 cols. 263, 277 and 1600, and vol. 59 col. 424; Lord Hardinge *Old Diplomacy* (London 1947) p. 102.

[59] Satow to Seymour, 28 Mar. 1898, *British Documents on the Origins of the War* (London 1926–38) vol. I p. 41; 5 and 29 Apr. 1898, *PDeb* 4th Series vol. 56 cols. 233–4 and 1600.

[60] 29 Apr. 1898, *PDeb* 4th Series vol. 56 cols. 1644 and 1665; 10 Aug. 1898, *PDeb* 4th Series vol. 64 col. 824.

[61] Balfour to Salisbury, 30 Aug. 1898, Hatfield 3M/E ff. 280–1; Alice Balfour's diary, 11 Aug. 1898, SRO GD 433/2/224.

1898 instructed the Ambassador in Washington to ascertain whether Britain 'could count on the co-operation of the United States in opposing action by foreign Powers which could restrict the opening of China to the commerce of all nations'. He would have liked an Anglo-American treaty 'having for its object to prevent the littoral of China being ceded piecemeal to other Powers'. President McKinley refused to depart from traditional American policy.[62]

At the end of March 1898, Balfour sanctioned Chamberlain to conduct informal alliance talks with the German Ambassador, Hatzfeldt, and told Parliament that in China ' – I do not limit the statement to that, but certainly in China – British interests and German interests are absolutely identical.' The two countries should be able without difficulty to work hand in hand. A political understanding appeared to be in the interests of both. While avoiding specific proposals, he did not shirk the embarrassing prerequisite of collaboration – virtual recognition of German predominance in Shantung.[63] (He might have acted differently had he known that the Kaiser had encouraged the Tsar to acquire Port Arthur.) In the event, Hatzfeldt soon withdrew from talks, and Balfour made light of the affair to the disapproving Salisbury:

> altho' I am inclined to favour an Anglo-German agreement, it must, if possible, be made at the worst on equal terms. Of this loving couple I should wish to be the one who lent the cheek, not that imprinted the kiss. This I take it is not the German view; and they prefer, I imagine, reserving their offers until they are sure of being well paid for them.[64]

To the Germans, Balfour's guarded interest had in fact seemed more promising than Chamberlain's rash enthusiasm. Balfour was the Conservative they most wanted to see Foreign Secretary. In August 1898, it was he who sealed the Anglo-German Agreement on Portuguese Colonies. Then, during prolonged Anglo-German-American negotiations about Samoa in 1899, it was heard that

---

[62] Balfour to Goschen, 26 Feb. 1898, BP 49706 f. 173; A. Nevins *Henry White* (New York 1930) p. 162; C.S. Campbell *Anglo-American Understanding 1898–1903* (Baltimore 1957) pp. 19–20. Cf. G.F. Kennan *American Diplomacy 1900–1950* (Chicago 1951) p. 26. Kennan imagines that Balfour acted solely to appease Chamberlain. In fact, Balfour himself repeatedly anticipated the end of American isolationism. See below, pp. 123–5.

[63] 5 Apr. 1898, *PDeb* 4th Series vol. 56 vol. 232; Hatzfeldt to Hohenlohe, 7 Apr. 1898, *Grosse Politik* vol. 14 no. 3788; Hatzfeldt to Foreign Ministry, 5 Apr. 1898, *Grosse Politik* vol. 14 no. 3763; Harcourt, 29 Apr. 1898, *PDeb* 4th Series vol. 56 cols. 1563–5.

[64] Balfour to Salisbury, 14 Apr. 1898, Hatfield 3M/E ff. 225–6.

he thought British claims should have been given over to Germany in the first place.[65] Balfour *did* take the idea of Anglo-German alliance seriously:

The real fact is that the Emperor of Germany, in spite of his air of universal domination, is in a mortal fright of Russia; and especially of a *maritime* (as well as military) combination of France and Russia. From the effects of the maritime combination we could save him – and he is prepared to buy us. If we are not for sale, he will go elsewhere – to our detriment.[66]

During the Kaiser's visit in 1899, Balfour again spoke of Anglo-German collaboration, though adding that he did not think Anglo-Russian differences unbridgeable (Britain must not appear too desperate). Next year he joined Chamberlain and Lansdowne in pushing Salisbury into the Anglo-German Convention on China, whereby the signatories pledged to act together to preserve the Open Door 'as far as they can exercise influence'. When Russia sent more troops to Manchuria, however, the Germans decided that their influence did not stretch that far.[67]

While other Powers endorsed the principles of this dud Convention, Japan had adhered to it in full. Balfour recognised that the Japanese might help thwart Russian ambitions.[68] He was not happy, however, when the Cabinet in November 1901 authorised Lansdowne to negotiate an alliance with them.

To abandon the traditional policy of isolation was a momentous step, Balfour warned, and Britain was taking it in the wrong company. A Far Eastern pact with Japan was inherently one-sided. The parties promised to defend each other's interests in China and Korea against attack by any two Powers. These places might pose questions of life and death for Japan, but British interests there were not vital: 'we may find ourselves fighting for our existence in every part of the Globe against Russia and France, because France has joined forces with her ally over some obscure Russo-Japanese quarrel in Corea'. Japan, meanwhile, was under no

---

[65] Bülow to the Kaiser, 9 Apr. 1898, *Grosse Politik* vol. 14 no. 3769 (also nos. 3768 and 3789); Metternich to Bülow, 15 June 1900, *Grosse Politik* vol. 17 no. 4977; Bülow to Hatzfeldt, 16 May 1899, *Grosse Politik* vol. 14 no. 4073.
[66] Balfour to Salisbury, 22 Apr. 1898, Hatfield 3M/E ff. 236–7.
[67] Memo. by Bülow, 24 Nov. 1899, *Grosse Politik* vol. 15 no. 4398; I. Nish *The Anglo-Japanese Alliance* (London 1966) pp. 104 and 120.
[68] Memo. by Balfour, 14 Mar. 1898, BP 49746 ff. 67–8; Memo. by Balfour, P.S., 15 Aug. 1898, PRO CAB 37/47 no. 62; Balfour to Chamberlain, 10 Aug. 1900, BP 49773 f. 200.

obligation to act if the Dual Alliance attacked British interests in India, the Mediterranean, or the Channel. Policy had to be viewed in global terms, and 'the Japanese Treaty, if it ends in war, brings us into collision with the same opponents as a German alliance, but with a much weaker partner'.[69]

Eckardstein, the German First Secretary in London, had earlier floated the idea of an Anglo-German-Japanese alliance, only to be rebuked from Berlin for suggesting a scheme which left no inducement for Britain to join the Triple Alliance. The Germans could not have complained of Balfour, who argued that 'the dangers are less and the gains are greater from joining the Triple Alliance than would follow from pursuing a similar course with regard to Japan'. Big alliances promoted peace, by making war 'so great an undertaking that even the most adventurous statesmanship would shrink from it'. An arrangement with the Triplice would probably deter France from entering an Anglo-Russian war. If not, Germany, Austria, and Italy would be efficient allies. 'If . . . we had to fight for the central European Powers', Balfour asserted, 'we should be fighting for our own interests, and for those of civilisation, to an extent which cannot be alleged with regard to Japan.'[70]

These views met little response. Lansdowne assured him that there was much less chance of a *casus foederis* arising from a regional Anglo-Japanese agreement than from a general Anglo-German one.[71] The Anglo-Japanese Alliance was signed in January 1902, and Balfour had to swallow his fears. In Parliament, he declared British and Japanese interests in the Far East identical and let significant omission say the rest:

there can be no greater blow to the policy which not only Japan and Great Britain, but also America, Germany, all the commercial nations, I believe, have – their interest is also the *status quo* – there can be no greater blow to the *status quo* in the Far East than that two Powers should coalesce to crush either us or Japan.[72]

'A Treaty of this kind makes strongly for peace', he averred. The Alliance was indeed conceived as diplomatic support for

---

[69] Balfour to Lansdowne, 12 Dec. 1901, BP 49727 ff. 159–74.
[70] Hermann von Eckardstein *Ten Years at the Court of St. James 1895–1905*, transl. G. Young (London 1921) p. 219; Balfour to Lansdowne, 12 Dec. 1901, BP 49727 ff. 170–4; 13 Feb. 1902, *PDeb* 4th Series vol. 102 col. 1296.
[71] Lansdowne to Balfour, 12 Dec. 1901, BP 49727 ff. 180–1.
[72] 13 Feb. 1902, *PDeb* 4th Series vol. 102 cols. 1294–8.

Japan. Some people thought Japan wanted 'to have it out with Russia', Lansdowne admitted: 'I do not believe a word of it.'[73]

The search for entente

The disagreement over the Anglo-Japanese Alliance reflected an underlying difference of perception between Balfour and Lansdowne. Lansdowne was less resigned to the inevitability of Anglo-Russian antagonism. His patient efforts to reach an agreement with Russia on spheres of influence enjoyed Prime Ministerial approval after 1902, but inspired little Prime Ministerial optimism. Balfour figured that any British Government would have liked a permanent arrangement with Russia in Central and Eastern Asia – so why had an entente never yet been found practicable?[74]

He perceived three reasons. The first was institutional. The uncoordinated nature of the St Petersburg Government allowed Russia to pursue one foreign policy in the East and another in the West. It was all very well to negotiate with Westward-looking diplomats, but the Tsar was the only link between the Foreign Minister and the Ministers directing eastern expansion. Who could tell what decision would be taken 'when everything depends upon the feeble will of one unhappy man, struggling with perplexities which the most resolute genius might find it difficult to resolve?'.[75]

The second obstacle was diplomatic. Little reliance could be placed on Russian assurances, for 'Russia always thinks herself absolved from them if she can show, or assert without showing, that circumstances have changed since they were made.' On Balfour's orders, the Foreign Office kept a list of instances of Russian bad faith.[76]

The third and greatest difficulty was the essential nature of the case. A satisfactory permanent arrangement with Russia was unlikely, because:

[73] Lansdowne to Macdonald, 31 Mar. 1902, PRO FO 800/134 ff. 102–3.
[74] Monger *End of Isolation* pp. 117 and 143; Balfour to Lansdowne, 21 Dec. 1903, BP 49728 f. 118.
[75] Balfour to Lansdowne, 21 Dec. 1903, BP 49728 f. 118; Balfour to Lodge, 11 Apr. 1905, BP 49742 f. 176.
[76] Balfour to Lansdowne, 21 Dec. 1903, BP 49728 f. 120; Norton to Sandars, 27 May 1903, BP 49747 f. 38.

There is really nothing in the way of territory that Russia possesses and we desire. In the Far East we are not an expansive Power. We want no territory we have not already got, and our one object is to make that secure. Russia, on the other hand, whether wisely or unwisely in her own interests, is still pressing forward Eastward and Southward ... The situation, therefore, hardly supplies the elements of a bargain. We cannot, for instance, say to Russia 'It is not worth your while appropriating a portion of China, because if you do we will appropriate another portion,' and it is no use, because Russia does want a portion of China and we do not.[77]

The basic Anglo-Russian problem could not be solved by diplomatic bargaining. 'Temporary arrangements, however, are better than nothing', Balfour concluded; they smoothed things over and much might happen in the meantime.

The position respecting the other party to the Dual Alliance was fundamentally different, and it was perhaps with this comparison in mind that Balfour declared in May 1904:

There are arrangements – Heaven forbid that I should decry their utility – which put off the evil day, and an evil day put off may perhaps never come, but which do nothing in themselves to prevent the hostile forces even gathering strength during the currency of these agreements, and which do nothing ... to establish a solid basis upon which international friendship ... may perpetually rest. Such is not the nature of the Anglo-French understanding.[78]

While thinking the French more belligerent than the Russians, he had also thought them more foolish. There was a certain honesty in his telling Parliament in 1899 that he could see no valid or substantial reason for antagonism between Britain and France. Outstanding questions between the two countries were 'centres of infection, from which some warlike disease or germ is always liable to spread'. He wanted to see them all brought to an amicable settlement.[79]

Accordingly, when the French Parliamentary Group for International Arbitration visited Westminster in 1903, he fully endorsed their search for means by which 'small diseases may not develop into fatal maladies'. Anglo-French arbitration was a step in the right direction. (Significantly, his speech contained nothing

[77] Balfour to Lansdowne, 21 Dec. 1903, BP 49728 ff. 121–3.
[78] 'Mr. Balfour at the Albert Hall' *Times* 7 May 1904 p. 14.
[79] 7 Feb. 1899, *PDeb* 4th Series vol. 66 col. 107.

comparable to Chamberlain's evocation of *Entente Cordiale* and alliance in the Crimean War.)[80] By the time the Arbitration Treaty was signed in October 1903, Anglo-French negotiations were addressing a range of long-standing disputes respecting Morocco, Egypt, Newfoundland, West Africa, Siam, and the New Hebrides. Balfour thought it most desirable to remove these causes of friction. Leaving details to Lansdowne, he interested himself primarily in the key *quid pro quo*: British Egypt for French Morocco. He insisted that France formally recognise the British occupation of Egypt, diminish international financial control, and help gain the assent of the other Great Powers.[81]

Balfour called the Anglo-French Entente of 8 April 1904 a perfect bargain. Each side was simply giving up 'the power of hampering the natural and free development of the other'. A 'bulwark against the invading tide of war', which time would strengthen, it lifted a load of anxiety from his mind. (Significantly, he did not echo the statement of Earl Percy that Britain and France would 'give to one another as friends, advantages which are ordinarily given only to allies'.) Balfour celebrated the end of rivalry after 800 years of conflict, but he had not become a Francophile. Acknowledging that mutual influence had benefited both national cultures, he attributed this to 'the very difference of temperament which separates these closest of neighbours.'[82]

The Russo-Japanese War

While relations between Britain and France improved, relations between their respective allies sharply deteriorated. Russia and Japan were heading for war, having failed to agree spheres of influence in Manchuria and Korea.

'If Japan goes to war, who is going to lay long odds that we are not at loggerheads with Russia within six months?' asked Balfour in October 1903. Having studied form, however, by December he was inclined to gamble. 'I detest all war' he wrote, but 'if any war

---

[80] 'France and England' *Daily Telegraph* 23 July 1903 p. 10; Balfour to the King, 21 July 1903, PRO CAB 41/28 no. 15.

[81] Balfour to the King, 4 Aug. 1903, PRO CAB 41/28 no. 17; Cambon to Delcassé, 25 Mar. 1904, *Documents Diplomatiques Français* 2nd Series vol. 4 no. 364.

[82] 1 June 1904, *PDeb* 4th Series vol. 135 cols. 573, 575, and 515; 'Mr. Balfour at the Albert Hall' *Times* 7 May 1904 p. 14; 'The Visit of the French Fleet' *Times* 14 Aug. 1905 p. 8.

could be conceived as being advantageous to us, this is one.' British diplomatic efforts to defend the *status quo* in northern China were plainly failing, and he was not eager to see a 'Manchuria for Korea' entente between Russia and Japan.[83] What would Britain gain from that? It was still 'impossible to contemplate anything at once so horrible and so absurd as a general war brought on by Russia's impracticable attitude in Manchuria', but the Anglo-Japanese Alliance should 'keep the ring' – France would not join Russia unless Britain first joined Japan. Therefore he opposed putting any pressure on the Japanese to abate their demands.[84]

In this he differed from Lansdowne, who wanted no stone left unturned in the effort to preserve peace, lest Russia succeed in reducing Japan to an almost negligible factor in Far Eastern politics. Balfour retorted that Japan would not be crushed unless Russia successfully invaded – and that was impossible; 'doubly impossible if we had a large force of ships in the East watching events'.[85] If the British exhorted the Japanese to reduce their demands, they would be regarded as false friends: 'We should lose Japan in trying to save it.' Did not the original policy of the Alliance assume that Japan was a match for Russia (though not for Russia and another Power combined)? The whole Treaty was otherwise open to serious criticism.[86]

He did not expect the Japanese to be victorious. They were not to receive any encouragement to fight, lest they turn and say, 'you must help us, for it was following your lead that we find ourselves in this mess!'. He maintained, nevertheless, that a Russo-Japanese war, in which Britain was not actively concerned, and in which Japan did not suffer serious defeat, 'would not be an unmixed curse'.[87] Japan would be driven from Korea, which was regrettable

---

[83] Balfour to Brodrick, 28 Oct. 1903, Midleton Papers 50072 f. 102; Balfour to Selborne, 23 Dec. 1903, Selborne Papers 34 ff. 51–2; Balfour to the King, 14 July 1903, PRO CAB 41/28 no. 14.

[84] Balfour to the King, 11 and 28 Dec. 1903, PRO CAB 41/28 no. 26 and BP 49683 ff. 254–5; Memo. by Balfour, 22 Dec. 1903, PRO CAB 37/67 no. 92.

[85] Lansdowne to Balfour, 22 and 24 Dec. 1903, BP 49728 ff. 109 and 130–2; Memo. by Balfour, 22 Dec. 1903, PRO CAB 37/67 no. 92; Balfour to Lansdowne, 26 and 31 Dec. 1903, BP 49728 ff. 133 and 144–5; Balfour to Selborne, 23 Dec. 1903, Selborne Papers 34 ff. 49–50.

[86] Balfour to the King, 28 Dec. 1903, BP 49683 ff. 256–7; Memo. by Balfour, 29 Dec. 1903, PRO CAB 37/67 no. 97.

[87] Balfour to Lansdowne, 22 Dec. 1903, BP 49728 ff. 116–17; Balfour to Selborne, 23 Dec. 1903, Selborne Papers 34 f. 51; Balfour to the King, 28 Dec. 1903, BP 49863 ff. 257–8.

insofar as it weakened Japan, but:

From every other point of view (except that) there could be nothing better for us than that Russia should involve herself in the expense and trouble of Korean adventure – with the result that at the best she would have become possessed of a useless province, which would cost more than it brought in, which could only be retained so long as she kept a great fleet in the Far East, and a large army thousands of miles from her Home base, and which would be a perpetual guarantee that whenever she went to war with another Power, no matter where or about what, Japan would be upon her back.[88]

In consequence: 'her value to France in a war with us would be greatly reduced and her whole diplomacy, from the Black Sea to the Oxus, might be weakened into something distantly resembling sweet reasonableness'.[89] Given that the Russian tide seemed unstoppable in the Far East, Balfour preferred to see it advance controversially and dearly than slyly and cheaply.

The day after war was declared found him scheming to pare down the fruits of Russian victory. Not content with preserving their present position in Manchuria, the Russians would surely accuse China of breaking neutrality as a pretext for annexation. Could this be prevented? Balfour saw only one possibility: 'If the Americans would so far violate their traditions as to make any suggestion of an alliance for the purpose of preserving by arms, if necessary, the integrity of China, it would open a new era in the history of the world.' Britain would have to induce the USA to make the proposal, he realised, but there was no hurry. This time he did not consider approaching the Germans for help: they were ingratiating themselves with Russia, in the hope of a Russian Pyrrhic victory, which would leave them comparatively stronger in both the Far East and Europe. Germany overvalued Shantung, when 'her true interest would be to throw herself into line with the United States and ourselves, and play for the "open door." '[90]

The eighteen months of Russo-Japanese War were not without anxiety. The French, Balfour complained, 'to please their Russian allies, have stretched the laws of neutrality to breaking point'. It was the Dogger Bank incident, however, which brought Britain to

---

[88] Memo. by Balfour, 22 Dec. 1903, PRO CAB 37/67 no. 92.
[89] Memo. by Balfour, 29 Dec. 1903, PRO CAB 37/67 no. 97.
[90] Balfour to Lansdowne, 11 Feb. 1904, BP 49728 ff. 172–4; Balfour to Clarke, 20 Sept. 1904, BP 49700 f. 145.

'the very edge of war'. On 21 October 1904, the Russian Baltic fleet *en route* to Eastern waters attacked British fishing-boats in the North Sea in the belief that they were Japanese torpedo-boats. Britain demanded an international enquiry, and Balfour found the wait for a reply from St Petersburg nerve-wracking.[91] Subsequent negotiations confirmed his opinion that the Russians were 'extraordinarily difficult to deal with' by 'destroying any confidence we might otherwise have felt in the honesty of their diplomacy'.[92]

By January 1905, Balfour thought a decisive Russian victory improbable. Revolutionary unrest in Russia raised the question of a compromise peace, whereby Japan would gain Port Arthur, while Russia took northern Manchuria.[93] He told the Archbishop of Canterbury that the Government would welcome the termination of the war, but diplomatic intervention would be useless. Twelve days later he admitted to Lansdowne that he thought British interests better served by continued hostilities.[94]

Balfour wanted to see Japan in a strong position when fighting ceased, for the attitude of Germany might prompt Russia to attempt a repeat of the Triple Intervention. Balfour deemed it time to approach the USA, encouraged by a letter from President Roosevelt to Cecil Spring Rice, First Secretary at St Petersburg. Roosevelt invited 'Springy' to Washington to discuss the Far East, commended Japan, and wrote of Britain and America standing together against Russia, France, and Germany. He also referred to the impossibility of engaging with another Power to carry out a policy which was not part of 'the inherited tradition' of the USA. Overlooking this, Balfour prepared a letter for Spring Rice, stressing the peril of important fragments of China being dominated by more warlike Powers. Such aggression, he argued, would never be attempted if Britain and America were bound by treaty to resist it: 'Together we are too strong for any combination of Powers to fight us.'[95]

[91] Marder *Fear God* vol. II p. 57; 'Mr. Balfour in Glasgow' *Times* 13 Jan. 1905 p. 8; Dugdale *Balfour* vol. I p. 385.
[92] Balfour to the King, 8 and 19 Nov. 1904, PRO CAB 41/29 nos. 36 and 38.
[93] Balfour to Spring Rice, 17 Jan. 1905, BP 49729 ff. 74–5; Balfour to Lansdowne, 24 Jan. 1905, BP 49729 ff. 90–1.
[94] Balfour to Archbishop, 12 Jan. 1905, BP 49747 ff. 150–1; Balfour to Lansdowne, 24 Jan. 1905, BP 49727 ff. 90–1.
[95] S. Gwynne (ed.) *The Letters and Friendships of Sir Cecil Spring Rice* (London 1929) vol. I pp. 441–7; Balfour to Spring Rice, 17 Jan. 1905, BP 49729 ff. 61–75.

This letter does not appear to have been sent, but Gerald Balfour conveyed to Spring Rice his brother's desire for 'joint action at the end of the war in connection with possible terms of peace'. It was to no avail. The Anglo-American-Japanese treaty desired by Balfour was not to be.[96] He determined instead to strengthen the hand of Japan by renewing the Anglo-Japanese Alliance two years early. The Treaty signed on 12 August 1905 was new in significant aspects:

The really important changes are that it is a defensive alliance, not against any *two* Powers, but against any single Power, which attacks either us or Japan in the East: so that Japan can depend on *our* Fleet for defending Korea, etc., and we can depend on *her* Army to aid us on the north-west frontier if the security of India is imperilled in that quarter.[97]

Balfour was the driving force behind these changes. By guaranteeing Japan against a war of revenge, the revised Alliance entrenched the new balance of power in the Far East. The Treaty provided for the defence of territorial rights and special interests in 'the regions of Eastern Asia and of India'. Balfour wanted 'special interests' to cover Afghanistan, eastern Persia, and Tibet, but Japan would only agree to Afghanistan. This geographical extension reflected his original objection to the Alliance as one-sided. (In 1902, he had observed of the first Anglo-Japanese military talks: 'I agree with the general tenor: but I notice that while there seems to be a question of our landing troops in Manchuria the Japanese do not suggest aiding us in India.')[98]

Balfour's Japanese solution to the Indian defence problem was not popular with the General Staff, which doubted that Japanese troops would ever be sent, and feared what might happen if they were.[99] The Committee of Imperial Defence, chaired by Balfour, nevertheless proposed that 150,000 Japanese soldiers be sent to India in the event of an attack, although the number was later

---

[96] Dugdale *Balfour* vol. I p. 386; Gwyne *Spring Rice* vol. I p. 449; Balfour to Percy, 15 Jan. 1905, BP 49747 ff. 152–4.
[97] Balfour to Cooper, 11 Sept. 1905, BP 49747 ff. 192–3.
[98] Balfour to the King, 23 Mar. 1905, PRO CAB 41/30 no. 11; Nish *Anglo-Japanese Alliance* pp. 307, 313, 317 and 324; Balfour to Lansdowne, 30 Jan. 1905, BP 49729 f. 136; Minute by Balfour, Selborne to Lansdowne, 30 July 1902, Selborne Papers 30 f. 163.
[99] Grierson to Sanderson, 16 June 1905, *British Documents on the Origins of the War* vol. IV no. 127.

omitted, lest it tempt a Radical Government to cut military spending.[100]

'It is, of course, clear that the new alliance will be regarded by the Russians as directly aimed at them', Balfour observed, 'and, in a sense, they will be right.'[101] On the day he wrote that – 27 May 1905 – the Russian fleet was decimated at Tsushima in the decisive battle of the war.

Russia was rebuffed and weakened by revolution. By 11 October 1905, five weeks after the formal conclusion of the Russo-Japanese War, Balfour judged that the time was propitious for an Anglo-Russian understanding. The object was to enshrine the buffer zone in Central Asia: no partition of Persia, no recognition of British dominance in Afghanistan, no representatives in Afghanistan or Tibet, no commercial concessions in Tibet or Persia, and no railway building for ten years. Additionally, Britain would drop its opposition to the passage of warships through the Dardanelles.[102]

In so far as the Anglo-Russian Entente of 1907 deviated from this strategy, Balfour took a low view of it (though he tried to retain a semblance of cross-party consensus). All the giving seemed to be on the British side. In granting Russia commercial equality in Afghanistan, the Liberal Government had 'gone rather out of their way' to destroy the efficacy of the buffer State, and it was no comfort to him to be told that the division of Persia into spheres of influence put an end to the sterilisation of material progress in that country.[103]

Democratic progress in Russia after 1905 raised hopes that social change would diminish the power of the expansionists, but he warned that the greatest wars had been carried out by nations in the throes of social revolution. Britain should not let down its guard. He anticipated that the Anglo-Japanese Alliance would remain the foundation of peace in the East 'through the lifetime of every man I am now addressing'.[104]

---

[100] Balfour to the King, 9 June 1905, PRO CAB 41/30 no. 22.
[101] Memo. by Balfour, 27 May 1905, PRO CAB 37/77 no. 98.
[102] Balfour to Clarke, 11 Oct. 1905, and Draft Entente by Clarke, 20 Oct. 1905, BP 49702 ff. 96 and 128–30; Monger *End of Isolation* pp. 217–20.
[103] 29 Jan. 1908, *PDeb* 4th Series vol. 183 col. 126; 17 Feb. 1908, *PDeb* 4th Series vol. 184 cols. 555 and 563.
[104] 15 Mar. 1906, *PDeb* 4th Series vol. 153 cols. 1459–60; 9 May 1906, *PDeb* 4th Series vol. 156 col. 1409; 'Mr. Balfour in Manchester' *Times* 11 Dec. 1905 p. 6.

CONCLUSION

On leaving office in December 1905, Balfour declared it impossible to find a decade of more essentially successful British foreign policy than the preceding ten years.[105] It was not an entirely hollow boast, for even without the American *deus ex machina* or its German substitute, peace and prestige were being preserved. Britain had faced no reverse like that dealt to France in 1898 over the Sudan, or to Russia in 1878 over Bulgaria, and German diplomacy had been none too successful.[106]

As Imperial expansion reached its limit, great pacific work had been done to establish boundaries and spheres of influence. Outstanding questions between Britain and France were resolved. Diplomacy and arbitration had also removed causes of quarrel with Germany, Portugal, and the USA.[107] The omission of one particular empire from this list was not surprising, but even Russia was alright. The Near East remained a powder-keg, but the lid was on. In Central Asia, despite the Orenburg–Tashkent Railway, the basically unfavourable position was still holding up, and now Russia faced the added deterrent of Japanese intervention. In the Far East, Russian gains had been overturned by the Russo-Japanese War. Improved Anglo-French relations reduced the risk of conflict with the Dual Alliance, and the Russian push was being contained.

Alerting the nation to the Franco-Russian challenge in 1894, Balfour had said that he could not flatter himself with hopes of an indefinite era of international peace. In 1905, he dared to prophesy, 'so far as human foresight can go', a long peace for his country and for the world. By the criteria appropriate to his own perception of the situation, Balfour may have been justified in claiming public gratitude.[108] He was aware, however, that many people now believed in a new threat from quite another quarter. Perhaps it was this which prompted him to continue:

in future we shall not see wars, unless, indeed, we can conceive that

---

[105] Balfour *Fiscal Reform* p. 267.
[106] Balfour to Amery, 14 July 1904, BP 49775 f. 119.
[107] 'Mr. Balfour in Glasgow' and 'The Guildhall Banquet' *Times* 13 Jan. 1905 p. 8 and 10 Nov. 1905 p. 10.
[108] 'Mr. Balfour in Manchester' *Times* 23 Jan. 1894 p. 8; 'The Guildhall Banquet' *Times* 10 Nov. 1905 p. 10; 'Mr. Balfour in Glasgow' *Times* 13 Jan. 1905 p. 8.

either a nation or a ruler should arise who feel that they cannot carry out their schemes of national aggrandisement except by trampling on the rights of their neighbours. I see no prospect of any such calamity to Europe. It would indeed be a tragic reversion to ancient days if Europe had again to make a coalition against any too ambitious Power.[109]

[109] The Guildhall Banquet' *Times* 10 Nov. 1905 p. 10.

CHAPTER 6

Germany and the War

I have sorrowfully to admit that the world is not always
governed by enlightened self-interest.

Balfour 1902[1]

In August 1914, earlier twentieth-century international relations
were thrown into a particular perspective. They were henceforth
'the origins of the War'. The Anglo-French Entente, the Committee of Imperial Defence, and the Naval Scare were seen in a
designated context, and Balfour's reputation shone in the light of
retrospection. His first post-war biographer praised a statesman
quick to perceive the German menace. The fiscal obfuscator of
1903 had really been 'intent on the enormous European problem'
then shaping itself. Dalliance with Germany in 1898 could be dismissed as an indiscretion committed under the influence of that
impetuous Chamberlain – and even Joe had come round to *Entente
Cordiale* by 1902. Kenneth Young assures us that Balfour understood 'the necessity for the re-orientation of British policy' which
're-established the equilibrium of Europe'.[2]

Enough was said in the previous chapter to cast doubt on this
interpretation. Much more will be said in this, which deals with
Balfour's attitude to Germany from the turn of the century until
after the Great War. Part I follows him through the period of
mounting Anglo-German antagonism. It is largely chronological,
as he was reacting to events. In Opposition after 1905, moreover,
he was ignorant of detail and did not try to second guess policy.
This section ends with his efforts to explain the causes of the War
and what was at stake. War aims and the Paris Peace Conference

---

[1] Balfour to Selborne, 5 Apr. 1902, Selborne Papers 30 f. 6.
[2] 'Raymond' *Balfour* pp. 117–18 and 174–7; Young *Balfour* p. 248.

are covered in Part II, which concentrates on the European settlement.[3] A third part looks beyond 1919.

PART I: TOWARDS WAR

'Mr. Balfour replied that he had never been anti-German and was
not now. On the contrary, he harboured the greatest admiration
for the German people and their achievements. He did not believe
in an Anglo-German war.'[4] This was said in 1910 to Metternich,
the German Ambassador. Diplomacy demanded it. Probably sincerity did too. Long before professions of Anglo-German friendship became inseparable from denials of enmity, Balfour had intimated a predilection for Germany over other foreign Powers (USA
excepted). In 1899, the strengthening of bonds of amity between
Britain and Germany was 'an object which I regard as second only
in importance to that of drawing closer the English-speaking races
on the two sides of the Atlantic'. In July 1902, Metternich
reported that the new Prime Minister inclined towards Teutonic
solidarity.[5]

A natural corollary of antipathy for Russia and France, this sympathy for Germany was not impeded by any cultural aversion. Balfour thought Britain could learn much from Germany in matters
of social reform and schooling. The philosopher may not have been
enamoured of German Idealism, but the pianist deemed German
music utterly indispensable – 'a great thing to say of the work of
any nation' – and his interest extended to Wagner. The German
contribution to science and history was also prodigious.[6] Balfour
even rather liked Kaiser Wilhelm II, who, he assured Hatzfeldt,
was too great a man to be troubled by the rudeness of his uncle
(the future Edward VII).[7] 'The fact that he firmly believes that
he has a mission from Heaven', he observed to a friend in 1891,

---

[3] Related topics (US intervention, the Russian Revolution, the Middle Eastern settlement,
the League of Nations) receive attention in other chapters.
[4] Metternich to Bethmann Hollweg, 10 Feb. 1910, *Grosse Politik* vol. 28 no. 10371.
[5] Balfour to Holls, 13 Nov. 1899, BP 49853 ff. 130–1; Metternich to Bülow, 17 July 1902,
Grosse Politik vol. 17 no. 5089.
[6] 'British Workers' Visit to Germany' *Times* 26 Apr. 1910 p. 4; Short *Balfour* p. 321; Balfour to Pollock, 6 Feb. 1914, BP 49863 f. 130; Young: *Balfour* p. 118; Balfour to Devine,
17 Sept. 1910, BP 49860 f. 278.
[7] Hatzfeldt to Foreign Ministry, 18 Aug. 1898, *Grosse Politik* vol. 14 no. 3853; Hatzfeldt
to Hohenlohe, 2 Dec. 1899, *Grosse Politik* vol. 15 no. 4401.

'though this will very possibly send him and his country ultimately to Hell, may in the meanwhile make him do considerable deeds on the way there.'[8] Despite his oddity, Wilhelm was 'the only Royalty I ever met who was in the least interesting to talk to. He talks like we all do.'[9]

Little wonder that Berlin anticipated better relations when 'honest Balfour' replaced 'his fat uncle'. He had seemed unusually friendly during the preceding winter[10] – the time when he was recommending British adhesion to the Triple Alliance: 'It is a matter of supreme moment to us that Italy should not be crushed, that Austria should not be dismembered, and, as I think, that Germany should not be squeezed to death between the hammer of Russia and the anvil of France.'[11] To an Austrian diplomat in May 1902, he praised the Triplice as the keystone of continental peace.[12]

Tentative British moves towards the Triple Alliance were apparent in the first year of the Balfour Government. In autumn 1902, there were broad hints about possible Italian co-operation in Somaliland and the Near East.[13] Regarding Italy as a legitimate naval Power – 'she almost counts as an island' – Balfour long desired good Anglo-Italian understanding.[14] Then in December Britain and Germany jointly blockaded Venezuela,[15] and, in the spring, Balfour strongly favoured British commercial participation in the German-based Berlin–Baghdad Railway. He had expressed pleasure on hearing the Kaiser outline the scheme in 1899, because German ambitions in Asia Minor were a counterpoise to Russia.[16]

[8] J. Ridley and C. Percy (eds.) *The Letters of Arthur Balfour and Lady Elcho 1885–1917* (London 1992) p. 73.
[9] Balfour to Salisbury, 22 Apr. 1898, Hatfield 3M/E f. 235; Viscountess Milner *My Picture Gallery* (London 1951) p. 233; Lady Frances Balfour *Ne Obliviscaris* (London 1930) vol. II p. 345.
[10] Rich and Fisher *Holstein Papers* vol. IV pp. 185–6; Bülow to the Kaiser, 22 July 1902, *Grosse Politik* vol. 18 no. 5413 (IV); Metternich to Bülow, 17 July 1902, *Grosse Politik* vol. 17 no. 5089.
[11] Balfour to Lansdowne, 12 Dec. 1901, BP 49727 f. 170. See above, pp. 117–18.
[12] Bridge *Great Britain and Austria-Hungary* p. 2.
[13] 'The Guildhall Banquet' *Times* 11 Nov. 1902 p. 11; Balfour to the King, 15 Dec. 1902, PRO CAB 41/27 no. 38; Monger *End of Isolation* pp. 84–7.
[14] A. Macartney and P. Cremona *Italy's Foreign and Colonial Policy* (London 1938) p. 2; Balfour to Browning, 9 Mar. 1915, BP 49863 f. 302.
[15] See below pp. 183–4.
[16] Metternich to Bülow, 12 Apr. 1903, *Grosse Politik* vol. 17 no. 5259; Memo. by Balfour, 28 Nov. 1899, BP 49691 ff. 72–3; Note of Conversation between Kaiser and Balfour, 1 Dec. 1899, SRO GD 433/2/15 no. 20; Dilks *Curzon in India* vol. I p. 148.

Opposition to collaboration with Germany proved intense, however, not only in the press but also within the Foreign Office and the Cabinet. 'Everyone in the office and out talks as if we had but one enemy in the world', exaggerated Spring Rice.[17] Alarmed by extreme German nationalist propaganda, British right-wing publicists stridently denounced the perverse blindness of Balfour and Lansdowne. In *The National Review*, Leo Maxse declaimed that Britain was becoming a satellite of Germany, with Downing Street a mere annexe of the Wilhelmstrasse. The Prime Minister was obliged to deny that the Kaiser's visit and the Venezuelan affair augured an Anglo-German alliance.[18] Vainly did he argue the merits of internationalising the Berlin–Baghdad Railway. Chamberlain would have none of it, and Balfour had to back down. He did not change his opinion. It was not British participation in the Anatolian Railway which would give Germany commercial control over Asia Minor, but British inactivity.[19]

Balfour took the Germanophobes to task: 'I would, with all the earnestness in my power, remind my countrymen that these international animosities are a great source of international weakness.' Nations foolish enough to cherish grudges risked greatly aggravating any real controversy which might arise. German public opinion, however provocative, must not be allowed to warp British policy.[20]

He always denied (even after 1914) that the Anglo-French Entente signed in April 1904 was anti-German. He took it at facevalue. 'We must earnestly hope that these promising negotiations will not wholly break down', he wrote in January: 'it would be lamentable, especially from the Egyptian point of view.'[21] One Foreign Office official told another: '*Entre nous*, I do not think that Mr. Balfour at all realizes what may be expected from the Anglo-French understanding and would be ready to make an agreement

[17] A.J.A. Morris *The Scaremongers* (London 1984) pp. 53–5; P.M. Kennedy *The Rise of Anglo-German Antagonism 1860–1914* (London 1980) pp. 259–61; Gwynne *Spring Rice* vol. 1 p. 350.
[18] *National Review* vol. 41 (Mar.–May 1903) pp. 9–11, 165–7, and 342–6; 'The Guildhall Banquet' *Times* 11 Nov. 1902 p. 11; 'Mr. Balfour in Liverpool' *Times* 14 Feb. 1903 p. 9.
[19] 7 and 8 Apr. 1903, *PDeb* 4th Series vol. 120 cols. 1247 and 1373–4; 23 Apr. 1903, *PDeb* 4th Series vol. 121 col. 222; Balfour to the King, 23 May 1905, PRO CAB 41/30 no. 19.
[20] 'Mr. Balfour in Liverpool' *Times* 14 Feb. 1903 p. 9; 'The Guildhall Banquet' *Times* 10 Nov. 1903 p. 10.
[21] Balfour to Prothero, 7 and 10 Apr. 1916, BP 49864 ff. 266 and 268; Balfour to the King, 24 Jan. 1904, PRO CAB 41/29 no. 1.

with Germany tomorrow.'[22] The Premier did realise that the Germans would 'make things difficult' on hearing that Morocco was under negotiation, but he was equally concerned about Spanish reaction. Germany duly demanded compensation in return for assent to the Khedival Decree required to formalise increased British rights in Egypt. He deprecated this 'dog in the manger attitude': countries which attempted to drive a hard bargain should not gain advantages denied more generous nations, and German views 'savoured too much of blackmail!'.[23]

Balfour was never an admirer of the tactics of the Wilhelmstrasse. Negotiating the colonial agreement of 1898, he had perceived a German bribe to hasten the dismemberment of the Portuguese Empire. Berlin had been 'unusually reasonable' over Venezuela, but when Britain found itself in dispute with Uruguay in 1905, he was glad to be *'relieved of the incubus of German assistance!'*.[24] He tended to think that a poor understanding of the psychology of other nations was part of the German character. They had certainly shown themselves very stupid in recent years, persisting in ill-mannered behaviour despite poor results. What bad diplomats they were![25]

Tactless German diplomacy was one reason for the regrettable anti-German tone of the English press, initially provoked by the Kruger Telegram of 1896. At the time, Balfour had thought it hilarious that 'Shouting Billy' put his foot in it and brought 'real joy' to the Jameson Raid fiasco.[26] By 1898 he recognised that public sentiment was an obstacle to Anglo-German co-operation. In December 1901 he still thought it a transitory one.[27] By then, however, a second cause of antagonism had arisen. The German Naval Law of 1900 soon convinced even the Admiralty that

---

[22] Mallet to Bertie, 2 June 1904, Bertie Papers 63016 f. 104.

[23] Balfour to the King, 4 Aug. 1903, PRO CAB 41/28 no. 17; Balfour to the King, 1 Mar., 4 May, 14 June, & 14 May 1904, PRO CAB 41/29 nos. 6, 14, 19, and 16.

[24] Balfour to Lascelles, 22 Aug. 1898, PRO CAB 37/48 no. 69; Balfour to the King, 15 and 18 Dec. 1902, PRO CAB 41/27 nos. 38 and 39; Balfour to the King, 11 Apr. 1905, PRO CAB 41/30 no. 14.

[25] Bernhard von Bülow *Memoirs* (London 1932) vol. III p. 7; A.F. Pribram *England and the International Policy of the European Great Powers 1871–1914* (Oxford 1931) p. 100; Balfour to Amery, 14 July 1904, BP 49775 f. 119.

[26] Balfour to Lascelles, Jan. 1905, BP 49747 ff. 158–9; Frances Balfour to Betty Balfour, 2 and 9 Jan. 1896, SRO GD 433/2/477.

[27] Hatzfeldt to Hohenlohe, 7 Apr. 1898, *Grosse Politik* vol. 14 no. 3788; Balfour to Lansdowne, 12 Dec. 1901, BP 49727 f. 178.

Germany was the principal potential opponent of the Royal Navy.[28] In April 1902, Balfour concurred in the decision to build a North Sea base, but he told the First Lord of the Admiralty:

I find it extremely difficult to believe that we have, as you seem to suppose, much to fear from Germany, – in the immediate future at all events. It seems to me so clear that, broadly speaking, her interests and ours are identical. But I have sorrowfully to admit that the world is not always governed by enlightened self-interest.[29]

Germany was presumably improving its maritime defences against the Dual Alliance[30] – but no risks could be taken with naval supremacy. Rising estimates in 1904 were defended with the dictum that the Two Power Standard must always include 'something of the nature of a margin'. That year he admitted that the German navy was (in part) directed against England in the course of an argument with Maxse, who reported to a fellow journalist: 'we have not wholly laboured in vain, because a year ago he was laughing at this idea'.[31]

Balfour was aware that a school of German political thinkers denounced the role of Britain in history, demanded colonies for Germany, and argued that territory be wrenched from the British Empire. How criminal was their folly! Two nations were being infected with 'what physicians call a bad habit of body'. German writers had started it, but public opinion in England was just as stupid as in Germany.[32]

Germanophobia intensified in late 1904. The Dogger Bank incident was popularly attributed to a German plot to envenom Anglo-Russian relations. Balfour himself recognised that neutral Germany would be the chief beneficiary if Britain and France were drawn into the Russo-Japanese War. The German Government was informed both that he was occasionally suspicious, and that he posited a *Russian* plot to envenom Anglo-German relations.[33]

---

[28] A.J. Marder *From the Dreadnought to Scapa Flow* vol. 1 (London 1961) p. 40.
[29] Balfour to Selborne, 5 Apr. 1902, Selborne Papers 30 ff. 5–6.
[30] See above p. 117 and below p. 139.
[31] 1 Mar. 1904, *PDeb* 4th Series vol. 130 col. 1410; Maxse to Garvin, 30 June 1904, Morris *Scaremongers* p. 57.
[32] Balfour to Lascelles, Jan. 1905, BP 49747 ff. 155–62; Balfour to [Metternich], 22 June 1905, BP 49857 f. 247; 'The Guildhall Banquet' *Times* 10 Nov. 1903 p. 10; Pribram *International Policy* p. 100.
[33] Balfour to Wilkinson, 3 Jan. 1904, BP 49747 ff. 63–4; Memo. by Bülow, 4 Nov. 1904, *Grosse Politik* vol. 19 no. 6114; Bülow to Holstein, 25 Dec. 1904, Rich and Fisher *Holstein Papers* vol. IV p. 321.

Balfour assured the Austrian Ambassador at this time that he did not ascribe aggressive or Machiavellian plans to German leaders, and thought distrust of them unfounded. 'I have, as you know', he told a British diplomat, 'never at any time been anti-German.' Of the naval journalist who campaigned for a pre-emptive attack on the German fleet, he cried: 'Arnold White ought to be hanged!'[34]

Anglo-German war would be 'perfect lunacy', Balfour declared in June 1905, but by then he could not avoid contemplating it altogether. After the Kaiser visited Tangiers to challenge French preponderance in Morocco, he conceded that Wilhelm might mean 'serious mischief'. While judging German trouble-making abominable[35], he was also unimpressed by the French response:

Mr. Balfour pointed out that Mr. Delcassé's dismissal or resignation under pressure from the German Government displayed a weakness on the part of France which indicated that she could not at present be counted on as an effective force in international politics. She could no longer be trusted not to yield to threats at the critical moment of a negotiation. If Germany is really desirous of obtaining a port on the coast of Morocco, and if such a proceeding be a menace to our interests, it must be to other means than French assistance that we must look for our protection.[36]

At that Cabinet meeting, however, the 'all-important topic' was renewal of the Anglo-Japanese Alliance. Balfour did not appear agitated about the Moroccan ports: Britain should simply follow the French lead, offering strong diplomatic support 'in strict conformity with the principles of the "Entente Cordiale" '.[37] The Moroccan crisis made no great impact on his general outlook. He heeded advice to enquire about the likelihood of Belgian neutrality being violated in a Franco-German war and the time needed to despatch British troops.[38] On July 1905, he had inaugurated the Permanent Sub-Committee to Consider and Elaborate Schemes of Joint Naval and Military Action – specifically amphibious attacks on the German coast – but he never called a second

---

[34] Pribram *International Policy* p. 100; Balfour to Lascelles, Jan. 1905, BP 49747 f. 156; Memo. by Metternich, 18 Dec. 1904, *Grosse Politik* vol. 19 no. 6140.

[35] Metternich to Bülow, 9 June 1905, *Grosse Politik* vol. 20 no. 6855; Balfour to the King, 22 and 28 June 1905, PRO CAB 41/30 nos. 23 and 25; Marder *Fear God* vol. II p. 57.

[36] Balfour to the King, 8 June 1905, PRO CAB 41/30 no. 21.

[37] Marder *Fear God* vol. II p. 57; Balfour to the King, 22 June 1905, PRO CAB 41/30 no. 23.

[38] Clarke to Balfour, 17 and 25 Aug. 1905, BP 49702 ff. 19–20 and 30; Memo. by General Staff, 29 Sept. 1905, PRO CAB 38/10 no. 73.

meeting. Attention is sometimes drawn to his anxiety to see the eighteen-pounder gun come into service. 'These were the guns which were first fired in earnest in Flanders in August 1914', adds Mrs Dugdale. So they were, but Balfour intended them for India.[39] Commenting on Liberal plans for Army Reform the following year, he acknowledged that:

We might be asked to land 150,000 men on the coast of Europe, but I do not know that I should sacrifice much money or take enormous pains so to organise my force that that could be done straight away and immediately. What is required, so far as I am able to see, is the power of sending continuous reinforcements to India in a great emergency.[40]

The replacement of Balfour and Lansdowne by Campbell-Bannerman and Grey in December 1905 was welcomed in Germany. The new Premier was in fact a cultural Francophile, while the new Foreign Secretary rated Germany 'our worst enemy'.[41] Balfour (like Berlin) seemed unaware of this. He voiced no public criticism on principle: so long as the Opposition was 'fairly confident' that the general lines were alright, the less time given to foreign policy the better. When not avoiding the subject, he blandly affirmed that the traditions of Lansdowne and Salisbury were being continued. Grey had promised as much on taking office, although during the subsequent election campaign, Balfour had dared to doubt the success of the imitation: the diplomacy of a patriotic Foreign Secretary could not succeed in the absence of strong armed forces.[42]

When the new Government began to trim defence spending, Balfour declared that the Two Power Standard in 'Dreadnoughts' was in danger. He warned that this would not conduce to peace. He also stressed that it must not be assumed that Britain could build battleships faster than a highly industrialised country like Germany.[43] This set the tone for the next five years. After 1905,

[39] Mackay *Balfour* pp. 181–7 and 193; Dugdale *Balfour* vol. I pp. 424–8.
[40] 12 July 1906, *PDeb* 4th Series vol. 160 cols. 1161–3.
[41] Kennedy *Anglo-German Antagonism* p. 282; J. Wilson *C.B.* (London 1973) p. 130; 'E.T. Raymond' [E.R. Thompson] *Portraits of the New Century* (London 1928) pp. 26–7; K. Robbins *Sir Edward Grey* (London 1971) p. 131.
[42] *Report from the Select Committee on the House of Commons (Procedure)* (1914) vol. VII para. 1705; 'Mr. Balfour at Cardiff' *Times* 20 Nov. 1908 p. 11; 'The General Election' *Times* 3 Jan. 1906 p. 6.
[43] 27 July 1906, *PDeb* 4th Series vol. 162 cols. 108–13; 5 Mar. 1907, *PDeb* 4th Series vol. 170 cols. 676–82.

the German fleet was the third largest in the world and growing. Balfour thought it had to be considered essentially aggressive, since no maritime blockade could cut Germany off from external markets, and the idea of a British invasion of Germany was grotesque. At the same time, he perceived no fundamental clash of interests between Britain and Germany, and deep down he assumed that all responsible men in London and Berlin thought as he did. Anglo-German animosity seemed to him a morbid condition of public opinion.[44] It was only gradually that he came to credit that there was more to it. Prior to 1908, he did not regard the naval race as the product of substantive Anglo-German antagonism. His worry was that Anglo-German antagonism would be the product of the naval race.

In informal conversations with the German Ambassador in 1907 and 1908, Balfour emphasised that Britain was neither resentful of German economic strength nor opposed to German dominance in Europe. Asked why Anglo-German relations were no longer what they had been, Balfour replied: 'Yes, but then you had no fleet.'[45]

He consistently denied that commercial rivalry had much to do with Anglo-German friction. Germany was vigorous in its pursuit of material prosperity, but Britain was too far ahead to be jealous. (When Balfour remarked that it might be easier to have a war than to work harder, he was being flippant.) Britain and Germany were good reciprocal customers. The prosperity of one would ultimately help the other. Economic competition had not soured Anglo-American relations. The resentments felt by individual businessmen were in international terms a trifle.[46]

Respecting the continental situation, Balfour supported his assertions to Metternich with argument.[47] German strength in Europe caused him no anxiety. It was the natural consequence of

[44] 1 Mar. 1904, *PDeb* 4th Series vol. 130 cols. 1411–12; Balfour to Fisher, 20 May 1913, BP 49712 f. 100; 14 July 1910, *HCD* vol. 19 col. 648; Balfour to Lascelles, Jan. 1905, BP 49747 f. 162.
[45] Metternich to Bülow, 10 July 1908, *Grosse Politik* vol. 24 no. 8215.
[46] 'The Cutlers' Feast' *Times* 20 Nov. 1896 p. 7; Memo. by Bülow, 24 Nov. 1899, *Grosse Politik* vol. 15 no. 4398; Metternich to Bethmann Hollweg, 10 Feb. 1910, *Grosse Politik* vol. 28 no. 10371; Metternich to Bülow, 31 Jan. 1907, *Grosse Politik* vol. 21 no. 7206; Nevins *Henry White* pp. 257–8; Balfour to Lascelles, Jan. 1905, BP 49747 f. 158; 13 Mar. 1911, *HCD* vol. 22 col. 1972.
[47] Metternich to Bülow, 31 Jan. 1907 and 10 July 1908, *Grosse Politik* vol. 21 no. 7206 and vol. 24 no. 8215.

population size and efficiency. It also rested on a formidable army, but geography dictated that the army was to Germany as the Navy was to Britain.[48] There never was an absolute balance of power in Europe: one Power was always strongest, and he would rather it were the hitherto peaceable Germans than the restless French. British policy had in no sense taken an anti-German direction in 1904. He would never have consented to the Anglo-French Entente if he had thought war with Germany could arise from it. It stood to reason. A Franco-German war would be decided on land, where British military support for France would be insignificant. He pointed out that Britain continued to reject conscription.[49] This Balfour himself opposed (before 1916) as electorally unpopular, socially undesirable, and, above all, strategically unnecessary – 'because I happen to live in an island'.[50] Given that Britain could not help France to victory over Germany, British involvement would merely win the lasting enmity of the German people. Intervention on the side of France was only conceivable in the case of wholly groundless German aggression or the very strongest German provocation. Even then he would cry 'tears of blood' sooner than adopt such a calamitous course. The ententes were concluded without any hostile intent. Englishmen did not want continental alliances. They wanted the security of naval mastery.[51]

When Balfour denounced the 1906 naval estimates, Campbell-Bannerman replied that it was preposterous to base the Two Power Standard on the hypothesis of war against a Franco-German coalition. Balfour, however, was adamant that British security must not depend on 'a mere *entente*, however *cordiale* it might be'. To ground defence policy on current foreign relations was to build upon quicksands.[52] 'If I had thought that C.B. represented his Government in this matter', he told a correspondent, 'I should regard it as one of the gravest events in our history.'[53]

The Anglo-Russian Entente he valued even less. It might have

[48] 14 July 1910, *HCD* vol. 19 col. 649.
[49] *Grosse Politik* vol. 24 no. 8215 and vol. 21 no. 7206.
[50] 6 Jan. 1916, *HCD* vol. 77 col. 1244. Also Balfour to Thorburn, 14 Dec. 1912, BP 49862 ff. 213–21; CID, 7 Nov. 1905, PRO 38/10 nos. 81 and 82.
[51] *Grosse Politik* vol. 21 no. 7206 and vol. 24 no. 8215.
[52] 27 July 1906, *PDeb* 4th Series vol. 162 col. 116; CID, 29 May 1908, PRO CAB 38/14 no. 7; 13 Mar. 1911, *HCD* vol. 22 col. 1976.
[53] Dugdale *Balfour* vol. II p. 52.

reduced the probability of war in Asia, but it rendered India no safer if a quarrel did arise, so military expenditure had to be maintained.[54] He was confident that the Agreement was in no sense directed against Germany. The Foreign Secretary simply wanted to reduce Anglo-Russian tension – but 'I have great doubts as to whether his methods have been judicious.' Balfour was profoundly anxious about the Germans: 'I think they misunderstand Grey's policy, as is but natural: but this does not make things better.'[55] Discussion with the Russian Foreign Minister in 1908 left Balfour feeling that it was no use looking to St Petersburg for a lessening of international difficulties.[56]

Balfour did not wish to see an Anglo-Franco-Russian bloc, but he did regard the Anglo-German problem in an increasingly serious light. 1908 put paid to any hopes that it was a short-term difficulty which a few years of ship-building Conservative government could rectify.

At the CID Invasion Enquiry in May 1908, Balfour agreed that plans should be made to meet a German attack. He said, however, that the German fleet had been built up primarily 'for the purpose of protection against other Powers who are not superior to Germany on the sea'. There was a secondary purpose, yet he presupposed Britain at war with some other Power in the first instance:

Personally, I was one of those who was most reluctant ever to believe in the German scare. But I cannot now resist the conclusion that every German thinks that 'the enemy is England'; that while the more sober Germans probably admit to themselves that they will never be able to deal single-handed with the English navy, the German Staff and, what is much worse, the German nation, have ever before them the vision of a time when this country will find itself obliged to put out its utmost strength in some struggle with which Germany is not at all connected, and that then the opportunity will come for displacing the only Power which stands between it and the universal domination of Europe, or hinders the establishment of a colonial Empire.[57]

In September, Lady Selborne found him 'much pre-occupied with the German scare, having read an article in the Quarterly which has quite convinced him that the Germans are determined

[54] 2 Mar. 1908, *PDeb* 4th Series vol. 185 cols. 455–8.
[55] Balfour to Hewins, 17 June 1908, BP 49779 f. 173.
[56] Balfour to Asquith, 14 Oct. 1908, BP 49692 ff. 82–95.
[57] CID, 29 May 1908, PRO CAB 38/14 no. 7.

to sweep us out of the way'.[58] He was doubtless impressed by the anonymous article because its approach was akin to his own.[59] It advised that race patriotism could allow Germany to absorb Holland and Denmark. Balfour thought the Dutch still valued their independence – but a British guarantee might be warranted to prevent customs union with Germany. The independence of the Low Countries was clearly desirable, although he did not suppose their occupation by a Great Power would be fatal to Britain.[60] The article went on to warn that South Africa was in danger too, and that this could herald German global preponderance. Unchallenged British naval supremacy in the nineteenth century had been the exception rather than the rule. As Britain once struggled with Spanish and French sea-power, so it must again with German. Scorning English liberal politics and brimming with self-confidence born of economic success, the German people now believed themselves capable of displacing the British Empire.

Balfour had observed in 1907 that it was hard to find any other ground for German naval construction. Not valuing tropical dependencies much himself, he was predisposed to take a casual view of German colonialism. Back in 1885, indeed, he had joined Gladstone in wishing it 'God speed'. He was not opposed to Germany finding a 'place in the sun'.[61] When in 1913 Grey considered revising the Anglo-German Agreement on Portuguese Colonies, Balfour thought it excellent to do anything to convince Germany that Britain was not animated by enmity.[62] He later explained German envy of the British Empire in these terms:

We are all familiar with the stock character in fiction of the *nouveau riche*, who is at once justly proud of having made his own fortune, and bitterly contemptuous of those who have inherited theirs ... But in the very midst of his envious indignation, he cannot shake off the ambition to follow in their steps; he must imitate those whom he affects to despise.[63]

---

[58] Lady Selborne to Selborne, 16 Sept. 1908, Selborne Papers Adds. 3 f. 12.
[59] 'The German Peril' *The Quarterly Review* vol. 209 no. 416 (July 1908) pp. 264–98.
[60] CID, 6 July 1905, PRO CAB 38/9 no. 54; Balfour to Selborne, 29 Dec. 1903, Selborne Papers 34 f. 55.
[61] Metternich to Bülow, 31 Jan. 1907, *Grosse Politik* vol. 21 no. 7206; 12 Mar. 1885, *PDeb* 3rd Series vol. 295 col. 979; Metternich to Bethmann Hollweg, 9 Dec. 1911, *Grosse Politik* vol. 31 no. 11339; Memo. by Balfour, 2 May 1918, PRO CAB 24/53 GT 4774.
[62] Balfour to Grey, 16 Dec. 1913, BP 49731 ff. 17–19.
[63] Intro. by Balfour, G.H. von Treitschke *Politics* (New York 1916) pp. xix-xx.

Balfour would not have feared a German colonial empire *per se* any more than he feared the French colonial empire. He doubted that German leaders had definite plans of extra-European expansion or any desire 'to destroy the British Empire *simpliciter*'. It was the thought of German naval supremacy which appalled him. It would mean the end of the Anglo-Saxon vision. The great undeveloped continents which were the Dominions might ultimately become German lands. Balfour tried to console himself with the observation that increasing prosperity reduced the German birth rate and hence emigration, but that was not reassurance enough. He ardently campaigned for rearmament and warned of great national difficulties. The Empire would have to work in unity to preserve 'everything that we hold dear in common'.[64]

He did not dread a German invasion – he ridiculed the possibility while 'anything like a fleet' existed – but, if the German fleet were allowed to approach the strength of the Royal Navy, Britain might have to choose between humiliation and war. The crisis could be a German threat to forbid Imperial Preference. Submission would mean the end of diplomatic independence. Resistance would mean naval war in highly unfavourable circumstances: unfavourable because on the seas Britain would be fighting for its existence, while Germany would not.[65]

It was not from party motives that Balfour condemned the Liberal defence record. Much Anglo-German friction would have been avoided – British supremacy would never have been challenged – if the Government had not cut the naval programme 1906–8. Germany had seen its chance, and now gigantic expenditure was necessary.[66] His campaign unavoidably entailed 'saying things about Germany which hardly seem discreet'. In January 1910, he declared that all the lesser Powers foresaw an Anglo-German war – 'I do not agree with them, but that is their opinion.' Against the ensuing outcry, he protested that he would regard such a war

---

[64] Balfour to Horn, 4 Apr. 1911, BP 49861 ff. 170–1; 'Mr. Balfour on Tariff Reform' *Times* 22 May 1909 p. 6.

[65] Vincent *Crawford Papers* p. 287; 'Mr. Balfour at Hanley' *Times* 5 Jan. 1910 p. 7; Metternich to Bethmann Hollweg, 3 and 10 Feb. 1910, *Grosse Politik* vol. 28 nos. 10370 and 10371.

[66] R.H. Williams 'The Politics of National Defence 1904–1911' (Oxford DPhil 1986) p. 325 and *passim*.; 16 Mar. 1909, *HCD* vol. 2 cols. 944–54; 'Mr. Balfour at Haddington' *Times* 25 Jan. 1910 p. 7; 14 July 1910, *HCD* vol. 19 cols. 647–52.

'with peculiar horror'. He still ruled out a surprise attack on the German fleet as immoral and foolish.[67]

By 1909, Balfour was underlining his case for rearmament with warnings that the law of Europe – the treaties which sustained a civilised community of nations – was fading away.[68] Dual Alliance versus Triple Alliance had seemed imminent the previous autumn, when the Franco-German Casablanca Incident coincided with the Austro-Russian Bosnian Crisis. On 5 November 1908, Balfour was called in to hear that 'incredible as it might seem' the Government believed that Germany wanted war:

I observed that the almost incredible frivolity of the excuses for hostilities which the Germans had devised would shock the civilised world beyond expression, and that it was difficult to see what Germany expected to gain by a war in which she must lose so much morally and was by no means certain to gain anything materially. Asquith's only answer to this objection was that the internal conditions of Germany were so unsatisfactory that they might be driven to the wildest adventures . . . I said that, quite apart from the Entente, we should, as I understood it, be involved under treaty obligations if Germany violated Belgian territory.[69]

Opposition support was duly pledged. Looking 'the picture of despair', Balfour complained that the Near Eastern policy of the Government had completely gone to pieces and they were in a fright about defence.[70] His next public speech contained a line of argument not previously heard from him: history demonstrated that the security of the British Empire depended on the equilibrium of Europe. Overwhelming naval strength was not enough. The British had found themselves:

again and again forced to take part in struggles in which the interests of this country, though remotely, were yet so closely and indissolubly involved that we could not stand aside and see the battle fought without our assistance except by the sacrifice of our most vital national interests. Look, then, to your Army and Navy.[71]

He did not return to the theme. The apparent readiness of

---

[67] Morris *Scaremongers* p. 215; 'Mr. Balfour at Hanley' *Times* 5 Jan. 1910 p. 7; Balfour to Miss Whiting, 4 Feb. 1910, BP 49860 f. 211; Metternich to Bethmann Hollweg, 10 Feb. 1910, *Grosse Politik* vol. 28 no. 10371; Metternich to Bülow, 10 July 1908, *Grosse Politik* vol. 24 no. 8215.
[68] 29 Mar. 1909, *HCD* vol. 3 cols. 144–5.
[69] Lord Newton *Lord Lansdowne* (London 1929) pp. 371–2.
[70] Hewins *Apologia* p. 225.
[71] 'Mr. Balfour at Cardiff' *Times* 20 Nov. 1908 p. 11.

Germany to resort to force had troubled him, but he was still not much interested in the Triple Entente. In this respect, the Agadir Crisis three years later – and the revelations arising from it – proved decisive.

Once again Germany menaced France on the pretext of lost rights in Morocco. Britain stood by France. At Balmoral in September 1911, Balfour was shocked to hear Lloyd George say that war was inevitable and the time to fight was now. 'For my own part', he replied, 'I earnestly hope there will *not* be war, but, if come it must, the Opposition will certainly not cause you any embarrassment.'[72] It has been written that Conservatives, thus committed to the 'militant policy', were happy to endorse continuity in foreign affairs at this time, because it was *their* policy which was being continued.[73] Balfour regarded cross-party support as a patriotic duty, and his reaction to what he now learnt about Anglo-French relations since 1905 suggests that he did not personally feel that it was *his* foreign policy which was being continued. Balfour confided in Lord Balcarres, who noted their conversation. (Lest the views expressed be attributed to Balcarres rather than Balfour, it may be pointed out that the former from the first supported *Entente Cordiale* on the ground that Germany was Britain's 'inveterate and unrelenting foe').[74]

The Anglo-French entente was embodied in a treaty. There were no secret [military] articles.

All we guaranteed was to give diplomatic support – and we dealt with Egypt, Morocco, Newfoundland.

Morocco had dropped out under Algeciras and so far as our Treaty is concerned that obligation is now concluded.

How does it come about that during the autumn we were apparently under obligations which amount to an offensive and defensive alliance? Has there been a further treaty?

At Balmoral Sir Edward Grey told A.J.B. what had occurred.

In January 1906 after Grey had been several weeks in office, Cambon asked for an extension of the Treaty. Grey said ... the proposal could not be entertained at that juncture.

Cambon then pressed Grey to allow our general staff to meet the French general staff ... and to talk over strategic questions. Grey

---

[72] Balfour to Sandars, 21 Sept. 1911, Sandars Papers c. 764 ff. 57–8a; Sir Austen Chamberlain *Politics from Inside* (London 1936) p. 363.
[73] K. Wilson *Empire and Continent* (London 1987) p. 114.
[74] Vincent *Crawford Papers* p. 74.

concurred in many ways more concrete than what any secret clause might have involved. In short he took covert steps towards participation in overt hostilities.

A.J.B. made no comment beyond saying that he questioned if at the time Grey realised what a tremendous step he had taken.

Gradually acting upon this initial concession, France had worked us to the point which we reached in September last, when we very nearly had to place 100,000 men on the French frontier. What have we gained? Newfoundland, Hebrides, Egypt are settled. Morocco is a country where our interests have been whittled away. Half Persia had gone to Russia. Next week half Manchuria will likely enough go to Russia, the other half to Japan, we being ousted.

A.J.B. says that on the old theory, discredited since the Crimean War, that our duty is to maintain the balance of power, Grey may be justified.[75]

This gives absolutely no support to Grey's questionable later claim that the Anglo-French Military Conversations began while Balfour was still Prime Minister.[76]

October found Balfour very gloomy about the state of Europe, and domestic politics were anything but a solace. That winter, the whole moral, social, and political outlook dismayed him. Foreseeing the end of British naval supremacy, he said that his optimism had fled.[77]

Out of this depression emerged in 1912 a new and hardened attitude. He had seen Germany threaten France with a recklessness which gave food for thought. In March 1912, he told Churchill:

A war entered upon for no other object than to restore the Germanic Empire of Charlemagne in a modern form appears to me at once so wicked and so stupid as to be almost incredible. And yet it is almost impossible to make sense of modern German policy without crediting them with this intention ... But imagine it being possible to talk about war as inevitable when there is no quarrel and nothing to fight for! We live in strange times![78]

He had also learnt the current state of *Entente Cordiale*. Balfour recognised that Britain was effectively aligned with France and

[75] 'Conversation with AJB, 21 Nov. 1911', Vincent *Crawford Papers* pp. 255–6.
[76] Viscount Grey *Twenty-Five Years 1892–1916* (London 1925) vol. 1 pp. 74–6. See Monger *End of Isolation* pp. 236–48, and S.R. Williamson *The Politics of Grand Strategy* 2nd edn (London 1990) pp. 61–3.
[77] 1 Oct. 1911, Vincent *Crawford Papers* p. 227; Memo. by Sandars, Nov. 1911, Sandars Papers c. 764 f. 162; Digby *Plunkett* p. 172.
[78] Balfour to Churchill, 22 Mar. 1912, BP 49694 ff. 75–6.

Russia against the Triple Alliance. He decided to embrace the fact, saying: 'it came to me as a shock of surprise – I am far from saying of disapproval – when I found how rapidly after I left Office the Entente had, under the German menace, developed into something resembling a defensive understanding.'[79]

In July 1912, Balfour delivered a Parliamentary speech of unprecedented grimness. He held out at best the prospect of an extended arms-race. Germany was 'moving steadily and remorselessly' to menace the Royal Navy. Even Austria was becoming a great Naval Power. Britain had to imitate the 'insanity' of foreign naval construction, for only preparation for war could secure peace. Therefore he welcomed the division of the Great Powers into two blocs. It was to be assumed: (i) that no Power would be so stupid as to involve itself in an offensive war in a cause in which it had no quarrel, and (ii) that sufficient sanity was still left among mankind to ensure that the alliances were on a defensive basis. If the theory worked in practice, any Power which committed an act of aggression would find itself without allies in a conflict with an overwhelming enemy. Were the war to spread at all, it would explode into 'universal Armageddon', destructive not only of human life, but of accumulated wealth, industrial organisation, social order, and 'everything that makes civilised life desirable or bearable':

That alone is surely a guarantee of peace, even if it be a costly peace, which you could not have if there was no organisation at all in these two camps. At any rate, in my sanguine moments, I believe that the very fact that the organisation will make war impossible unless it is universal is a reason why war cannot take place. It is too appalling.[80]

Anxious that the Triple Entente conform to his model of deterrence, Balfour had the previous month urged Grey to replace *Entente Cordiale* with a formal alliance. Force of circumstances had widened the scope of the Anglo-French Entente, and public opinion would now make it impossible 'for either Power to remain indifferent to any serious, – certainly to any gratuitous, – attack

---

[79] Balfour to Spender, 30 May 1912, BP 49862 f. 169; (misquoted as 'defensive Alliance' by Dugdale *Balfour* vol. 1 p. 374). This letter endorses the account of the Entente given by J.A. Spender *The Foundations of British Policy* (London 1912) p. 11, which argues that Britain 'slipped absent-mindedly' into the European complication via a purely colonial transaction.

[80] 22 July 1912, *HCD* vol. 41 cols. 860–8.

upon the other'. The Entente was the natural prey of diplomatic intrigue: 'It must (for example) be the object of every German Foreign Minister to drive a wedge between France and England, to aggravate every misunderstanding, to foster every suspicion.' An explicit Anglo-French alliance would reduce international strain. It would also mean assured French naval co-operation in the Mediterranean. Balfour was acutely conscious that the deployment of the Royal Navy in northern waters to confront concentrated German sea-power weakened control over Imperial seaways.[81] He did not, however, seek simply to strengthen Anglo-French commitments. He explained:

There are many people in this country, (I am one of them) who would do everything in their power to save France from destruction; but have no mind to be dragged at her heels into a war for the recovery of Alsace and Lorraine. Such persons want to be assured that the France for which they are asked to fight is France defending her own independence, and the independence of Europe, not the France of Louis XIV, of Napoleon, or even of the Second Empire.[82]

To ensure that a French alliance would be 'defensive in fact as well as in words', the treaty should stipulate that the Power which called for assistance must first have expressed readiness to submit its dispute to arbitration. Then the French 'would always have to bear in mind that in no course of action which brought them into collision with the Triple Alliance could they be sure of our support, *unless* they were prepared to argue their case, in the light of day, before an impartial tribunal:- a reflexion not favourable to "chauvinism"'. Balfour conceded that France 'might at the first glance think the new arrangement less favourable to her than the old', but, from a broader vantage-point, it would be almost wholly beneficial. It would show the Triple Alliance that British policy was purely defensive – a conclusive reply to the Anglophobe propaganda which led Germans to fear British attack.

The scheme came to nothing, and to Lichnowsky, who became German Ambassador in November 1912, Balfour merely seemed decidedly pro-French.[83] The peroration of his 1912 speech was now his precept. He had told the Government:

---

[81] Memo. by Balfour, 12 June 1912, BP 49731 ff. 1–6; 26 July 1909, *HCD* vol. 8 col. 895; 16 Mar. 1911 *HCD* vol. 22 cols. 2499–500; 22 July 1912 *HCD* vol. 41 cols. 862–3.
[82] Memo. by Balfour, 12 June 1912, BP 49731 f. 4.
[83] J. Rohl (ed.) *1914* (London 1973) p. 108.

If war occurs, and finds you unprepared – if it finds the defensive Powers of Europe without your support, and your adequate, instantaneous and immediate support – you and all of us who are dragged into your responsibilities will be guilty of the gravest crime against peace and humanity of which this country or any country has ever yet been guilty.[84]

When deterrence failed in 1914, there was nothing for it but to fight. In retrospect, Balfour said that he realised on 29 July that war was coming. Austria had attacked Serbia, Russia was mobilising, and, given general European conflict, Britain was bound to become involved sooner or later. He thought Grey should have taken it on himself to tell Germany as much. Balfour yet seemed so detached that the Permanent Under-Secretary of the Foreign Office assumed him to be indifferent about British intervention. This impression corrected, he joined Conservative calls for war and urged the immediate despatch of the Expeditionary Force. His reasoning was simple: 'as regards Germany, we have burnt our boats. We have chosen our side, and must bide by the result'.[85]

In public, Balfour said very little. On the night of 3 August he tried to silence anti-war Radicals in Parliament. Four sentences on the spy danger form the remainder of his contribution to *Hansard* that session. Elsewhere a few laments for Belgium, a pledge to fight to the end, and a turgid toast to 'Our Allies' served. It was not until December that he addressed the question: 'What is civilization, what is morality, what is Christianity coming to if such things can be?'[86] By then his thoughts had crystallised.

On 29 July 1914, Maxse had told 'an eminent statesman who was neither a Progressive nor a Pacifist' that Germany plainly wanted war. This 'man of light and leading outside the Government, of immense experience of public affairs and acute intellect' thought Maxse a lunatic to suggest such a thing. Balfour was certain that the Germans would have been quite content to destroy Serbia and humiliate Russia without war.[87] German diplomacy

---

[84]   22 July 1912, *HCD* vol. 41 col. 868.
[85]   Dugdale *Balfour* vol. II pp. 113, 119, and 116; Chamberlain *Down the Years* pp. 97–8; Nicolson to Balfour, 2 Aug. 1914, BP 49748 ff. 3–4.
[86]   3 Aug. 1914, *HCD* vol. 65 cols. 1880–3; 12 Nov. 1914, *HCD* vol. 68 col. 105; 'Mr. Asquith's Call to the Nation' *Times* 5 Sept. 1914 p. 10; 'Ministers on the War' *Times* 10 Nov. 1914 pp. 9–10; 'The "Superstate" ' *Times* 14 Dec. 1914 p. 12.
[87]   L.J. Maxse *Politicians on the War-Path* (London 1920) p. 48; Note by Balfour, 12 Jan. 1916, PRO CAB 42/7 no. 5 (Annex).

appeared to have been 'idiotic beyond all belief':[88]

they seem to have made five big mistakes – they thought Russia would not fight; they thought France would not support Russia; they thought we should not support France; they thought that Belgium would offer no resistance; and that Italy would remain in the Triple Alliance. One would have thought so many mistakes would have destroyed any cause, but the German military machine is a tremendous instrument.[89]

Germany had taken a 'desperate sort of "double or quits" gamble'.[90] Why? Austrian control of the Balkans was not in itself a sufficiently tempting prize. Balfour became convinced that the demise of Serbia was one step in a German design for world power. Thwarted elsewhere, Germany sought to extend south-eastwards, via Austria–Hungary and the Balkans, to win control over Turkey, Egypt, Arabia, Persia, India, and the Far East. On the basis of an unbroken avenue of influence from the North Sea to the Indian Ocean, Germany would make its bid for global supremacy. The British Empire would then face a severe struggle for existence, with Australasia especially at risk. Balfour accordingly saw political merit in military operations in the East, where the Allies had to preserve their prestige.[91]

Thus, while granting that the War arose from miscalculation, Balfour argued that it was not the accident of a day which made the Germans 'drench the world in blood'. It was an established plan rooted in established doctrine. Serbia and Belgium were but episodes. The deeper tragedy was that the war of 1870 and subsequent prosperity had turned the heads and polluted the consciences of a mighty people. Intellectual Germany was now intent on using all means 'to give to their country that dominating position which they think is its right, and they cannot understand why the rest of the world does not agree with them'.[92] This combination of cultural arrogance and ruthless amorality had made war almost inevitable. The Germanophobes had been right: Treitschke and Bernhardi did speak for Germany, which was now practising

[88] Balfour to Alice Balfour, 8 Aug. 1914, BP 49832 f. 221.
[89] Balfour to Lady Elcho, 7 Aug. 1914, BP 49863 ff. 197–8.
[90] 22 May 1915, Lady Cynthia Asquith *Diaries 1915–1918* (London 1968) p. 28.
[91] 'German War Aims' *Times* 14 July 1917 p. 4; 17 Aug. 1917, *HCD* vol. 97 col. 1665; Statement by Balfour, [Mar. 1917], *The Lansing Papers* vol. II pp. 30–1; Memo. by Balfour, 27 Dec. 1915, PRO CAB 42/7 no. 5 (Annex).
[92] 27 Feb. 1918, *HCD* vol. 103 cols. 1471–2; 'The "Superstate" ' *Times* 14 Dec. 1914 p. 12.

exactly what it preached. Any suggestion that German policies were no more pernicious than other imperialisms was vigorously countered. Had the critic never discovered that nations had a character?[93] German growth was peculiarly unacceptable in its means and in its ends.

Germany owed its political nationhood to the unscrupulous genius of one man, with the Prussian army as his instrument; and although Bismarck had sought only unity and prosperity, his success had given practical endorsement to profane theories.[94] *Realpolitik* had consequently been the doctrine of every German statesman, soldier, and thinker for two generations. The State was beyond morality, force was the only imperative, and war the mechanism of progress – and in Germany those who *disagreed* were the cranks.[95] Perhaps Balfour perceived in the Great War confirmation of his philosophical prediction that the discord resulting from the rise of the Naturalistic Psychological Climate – ultimately Nietzschean in its ethics – would 'at no distant date most unpleasantly translate itself into practice'.[96] He seemed genuinely astounded by the German view of treaties and the conduct of war: 'Morals after all do pay. No nation can do without them.' If German military terrorism were seen to succeed, what hope for international morality then?[97]

The Allies were fighting for not only world order and peace. They were also defending cultural identity, the harmony between man and society which fostered progress. Germany was more deliberately set on universal domination than any Power since ancient times ('leaving out certain episodes in the history of France'). German tyranny would be especially merciless, for, while Germany had no shortage of self-esteem, it lacked the self-confidence which permits kindly tolerance of perceived inferiors.[98] The British Empire did not seek to squeeze out the individual life

---

[93] 20 June 1918, *HCD* vol. 107 col. 568; 8 Aug. 1918, *HCD* vol. 109 cols. 1627 and 1633.
[94] Treitschke *Politics* vol. 1 pp. viii–ix; Asquith *Diaries 1915–1918* p. 28.
[95] 27 Feb. 1918, *HCD* vol. 103 col. 1470; 'German Ambitions' *Times* 11 Jan. 1918, p. 7; Hall Caine (ed.) *King Albert's Book* (London 1914) p. 15; 6 Nov. 1917, *HCD* vol. 98 cols. 2046–7.
[96] Balfour *Foundations of Belief* p. 91.
[97] Digby *Plunkett* p. 181; Balfour to Mrs. Gardner, 7 Sept. 1914, BP 49863 f. 203; 'Mr. Balfour on German Crimes' *Daily Telegraph* 12 Oct. 1918 p. 7; A.J. Balfour *Essays Speculative and Political* (London 1920) pp. 252–3.
[98] 6 Nov. 1917, *HCD* vol. 98 col. 2046; 27 Feb. 1918, *HCD* vol. 103 col. 1473; 8 Aug. 1918, *HCD* vol. 109 col. 1630; Treitschke *Politics* vol. 1 pp. xiii–iv.

of the nations it embraced: 'We have not tried – I think we are incapable of it – to force our own culture upon India or upon Egypt.' Germany pursued a different path, not for selfish reasons, but because German culture was deemed so superior that domination by a German was the highest privilege which an inferior race could hope to enjoy. A great effort, half military, half missionary, was being made to contrive that 'true culture' flourish the world over, even in those States to which it was abhorrent. Were we to have ' "Kultur" rammed down our throats by German bayonets'? No, every stout-hearted Briton would gladly die to save humanity from alien subjugation.[99]

Thus did Balfour convince himself and others that the World War was an epoch-making moral struggle for the highest spiritual advantages of mankind. Just as society would require police protection from the Nietzschean superman (if he ever materialised), so did the world require Allied protection from the Hegelian super-state. Anglo-American ideals and German ideals could not co-exist: either heaven or hell must prevail in 'this great battle between darkness and light'.[100]

PART II: TOWARDS PEACE

Balfour did not care to consider peace without victory. He was not insensible of the horror and carnage of war – after visiting a nephew at Blackdown army camp in August 1914 he had unexpectedly broken down in tears[101] – but he was fortified by his consistent belief in a future life:

The unbalanced evil of death is *separation*. There is no other. We have no reason to mourn because those who die young lose so much of life's fresh joys: – for we have no reason to doubt their change of State may be a gain. We *have* reason, I admit, to lament the loss which the world suffers from the early loss of those who would have done so much for mankind had they been given the opportunity. But according to my creed the loss is suffered by the world – not by the universe.[102]

[99] 27 Feb. 1918, *HCD* vol. 103 cols. 1472–3; 'Patriotism and Empire' *Times* 5 Aug. 1915 p. 8; 'German War Aims' *Times* 14 July 1917 p. 4; 'The "Superstate" ' *Times* 14 Dec. 1914 p. 12.

[100] E.H. Carr *The Twenty Years' Crisis 1919–1939* (London 1942) p. 98; 'The "Superstate" ' *Times* 14 Dec. 1914 p. 12; 'America Day' *Times* 8 Apr. 1918 p. 3; 'An End to Austrian Tyranny' *Times* 26 July 1918 p. 5.

[101] Dugdale *Balfour* vol. II p. 123.

[102] Balfour to Lady Elcho, 28 Dec. 1915, Ridley and Percy *Letters* p. 333.

The duty of the Foreign Secretary to sweep aside pacific talk with exhortations to fight on was well performed by him. He deprecated any return to the *status quo ante*, and such countenance as he gave to publication of the Lansdowne Letter was due to confusion rather than to sympathy.[103] In 1918, enemy propaganda ran the theme 'Balfour or Peace'. Hankey, the Cabinet Secretary, thought this not far wrong.[104] Balfour was very wary of peace overtures from the Central Powers. How could one trust shameless *Realpolitiker*? After all that had been sacrificed, only a lasting peace would do, but it was a frail settlement which rested on a solemn pact with Germany. Secret peace talks should be avoided where there was little prospect of success:[105]

If we make proposals fully satisfactory to our Allies, they will be regarded as utterly unreasonable by all our enemies. If, on the other hand, we make tentative qualifications in their extreme demands, and the negotiations nevertheless break down (as I rather think they will) then we shall have given a most powerful instrument into the hands of our foes for making mischief between us and our friends.[106]

The War had given him a profound contempt for all nations except the Germans and the English, and he dreaded the thought of formulating a list of joint Allied war aims.[107] Save in its Anglo-American extension, he regarded the Entente as an extraordinary combination born of extraordinary circumstances. While the aims of the Central Powers naturally converged, the Allies were separated by geography, temperament, tradition, and history. Twelve years earlier, Britain had viewed France and Russia as likely enemies, and Japan and Russia had been at war; while France and Italy were curiously incapable of getting on together. It had taken

[103] Draft Reply to Wilson, Dec. 1916, PRO CAB 37/162 no. 31; Egremont *Balfour* pp. 296–9; Hardinge *Old Diplomacy* pp. 223–4; Alice Balfour's diary, Dec. 1917, SRO GD 433/2/136 p. 9.
[104] 'Balfour or Peace' *Times* 3 July 1918 p. 5; S. Roskill *Hankey* (London 1970–2) vol. 1 p. 503.
[105] 6 Nov. 1917, *HCD* vol. 98 cols. 2047–8; 'Our Financial Mobilisation' *Times* 1 Feb. 1917 p. 8; 'Martyrdom of Belgium' *Times* 22 July 1918 p. 4; 16 May 1918, *HCD* vol. 106 col. 580; 'Mr. Balfour's Reply' *Times* 17 Sept. 1918 p. 7; Balfour to Milner, 12 Oct. 1917, PRO FO 800/200 f. 289.
[106] Memo. by Balfour, 15 Dec. 1917, BP 49697 f. 203.
[107] Digby *Plunkett* p. 192; Balfour to House, 21 Aug. 1917, BP 49687 f. 90.

insane German ambition and inept German diplomacy to weld these nations into one coalition, and 'we have to accept that residues of the old condition of things must to a certain extent remain'.[108]

Since his first duty was to say nothing which might split the Allies, Balfour tried to restrict his public utterances to broad phrases about destruction of militarism, national self-determination, and enforcement of international law. He told his deputy at the Foreign Office that definition of war aims was 'a problem in which I take no very great interest'. The War had set loose complex forces, the inter-play of which could not be prophesied. Basic objectives were clear, but the extent of their attainment would be determined by the circumstances of the victory.[109]

Given his caution, it is understandable that he was less than jubilant when informed on 13 October 1918 that Germany accepted President Wilson's Fourteen Points for Peace.[110] Earlier that day he had advised that Britain could not possibly assent to the Points.

For a start, Wilson failed to mention punishment of Germany. Balfour feared the eagerness of the US President 'to be kind to all nations', and initially hoped he would stay away from the Peace Conference. Germany ought to suffer.[111] It was true that the policy of ambitious domination was the real enemy, but German militarism did not mean the rule of a military caste in isolation. It was 'an affair of the heart, of the disposition of a nation'. The replacement of the German monarchy by democratic government was superficial. Balfour had previously explained: 'The spirit of their people has produced its institutions, and it is not its institutions which have produced the spirit of their people.'[112] If Germany were to become a peaceful member of international society, immoral heresies which permeated the whole nation had to be eradicated. They had been driven into the wider German population by Bismarck's victories. If experience taught that militarism ulti-

[108] Statement by Balfour [22 Mar. 1917], *The Lansing Papers* vol. II pp. 20–2.
[109] 16 May 1918, *HCD* vol. 106 cols. 584–5; Balfour to Cecil, 29 Dec. 1917, BP 49738 f. 184; 30 July 1917, *HCD* vol. 96 cols. 1847–52.
[110] A. Clark (ed.) *'A Good Innings'* (London 1974) p. 182.
[111] Conference, 13 Oct. 1918, PRO CAB 24/66 GT 5967; 11 Nov. 1918, Egremont *Balfour* p. 303; Empire Delegation, 1 June 1919, *BDFA* vol. 4 no. 20.
[112] 27 Feb. 1918, *HCD* vol. 103 cols. 1469 and 1472; 6 Jan. 1916, *HCD* vol. 77 cols. 1248–9; Jones *Whitehall Diary* vol. I pp. 68–9.

mately led to disaster, perhaps the liberalism of an earlier generation of German political thinkers – the men of 1848 – would
revive.[113] It had to be made plain 'that the wages of sin, after all,
is death'.[114]

In the last month of the War, Balfour recommended bombing
German towns, and he approved prosecution of war criminals
(while doubting its feasibility).[115] He did not, however, think it
essential to invade. 'I don't want to go beyond making Germany
impotent to renew the war, and obtaining compensation', he maintained: 'I don't want to trample her in the mud.' The armistice
was very humiliating, and the main test of victory was territory.
If the Germans were stripped of their colonies, their principal ally,
and European provinces which they had vowed never to surrender,
the War could not be represented in Germany as anything but a
complete defeat.[116] It was then to be hoped that reflection would
give rise to a higher conception of international relations. It would
take time: 'Too often do unsuccessful wrong-doers remain
embittered and unrepentant.' Pending spiritual conversion, Germany would remain 'an enemy strong enough to be dangerous',
so an anti-German coalition would have to continue.[117]

Here again, the Fourteen Points were a hindrance. Balfour
hoped that they would not be mentioned at the Peace Conference
more than could be helped. Ranging from territorial proposals to
sweeping declarations about open diplomacy and the Freedom of
the Seas, they were badly conceived and open to interpretation
even after revision. He later dismissed the charge of divagation
from them as excessively legalistic.[118] A plentiful crop of
ambitions, fears, and hatreds was springing up in the sunshine of
approaching peace. Continental Allies were already 'log-rolling'

[113] 'America's Decision' *Times* 8 May 1918 p. 5; 6 Nov. 1917, *HCD* vol. 98 col. 2046; 8
Aug. 1918, *HCD* vol. 109 col. 1627; 30 July 1917, *HCD* vol. 96 cols. 1853–5.
[114] 'Mr. Balfour on the New Epoch' *Daily Telegraph* 13 Nov. 1918 p. 7.
[115] Memo. by Balfour, 8 Oct. 1918, PRO CAB 24/66 GT 5931; Imperial War Cabinet 37
and 40, 20 Nov. and 3 Dec. 1918, PRO CAB 23/42; Council of Ten, 10 Feb. 1919,
FRUS PPC 1919 vol. III p. 953; Notes by Balfour, 10 Feb. 1919, BP 49751 ff. 268–72.
[116] Jones *Whitehall Diary* vol. I p. 69; G. Barnes *From Workshop to War Cabinet* (London 1924)
p. 216; Conference, 13 Oct. 1918, PRO CAB 24/66 GT 5967.
[117] 30 July 1917, *HCD* vol. 96 col. 1854; H. Elcock *Portrait of a Decision* (London 1972)
p. 251; Memo. by Balfour, 4 Oct. 1916, PRO CAB 37/157 no. 7.
[118] Imperial War Cabinet 43, 18 Dec. 1918, PRO CAB 23/42; Meinertzhagen *Middle East
Diary* p. 25; Conference, 13 Oct. 1918, PRO CAB 24/66 GT 5967; Empire Delegation,
1 June 1919, *BDFA* vol. 4 no. 20; Young *Balfour* p. 412.

and making utterly unreasonable demands.[119] In this environment, claims of justice and morality were 'pure aesthetics'. The Conference was going to be 'a rough and tumble affair', and it was better not to bind negotiators in advance.[120]

Before leaving for Paris, Balfour said, 'It is not so much the War as the Peace that I have always dreaded.' None of the delegates would come back with a shred of reputation.[121] His own performance over the following eight months prompted two sorts of reaction (beyond the obligatory perfunctory praise). Lord Selborne spoke for the majority when he remarked: 'I never could make out that he took any important part at all.' The dissenting minority voiced still harsher criticism, encapsulated by Lady Robert Cecil's comment that Balfour chose Clemenceau instead of Wilson.[122] The idealist critique of 1919 may be right or wrong, but examination of Balfour's opinions about the European settlement does not reveal the malign influence which these idealists supposed. (Of his sins of *omission*, however, more must be said later.)

The idealist attack was spear-headed by one of the first documented studies of the Peace Conference. In an attempt to vindicate the US President, Ray Stannard Baker's *Woodrow Wilson and World Settlement* argued that Balfour, the embodiment of old diplomacy, conspired with the French to squeeze out American idealism and secure a reactionary treaty while Wilson and Lloyd George were away in February and March. Balfour was angry at being charged with 'these crimes'.[123] Worried when Wilson left Paris, and suspicious of French intentions, he had reminded the Council of Ten that major questions could not be settled without the US President. Genuine fear of the dangers of delay prompted his efforts to accelerate the treaty-making.[124]

---

[119] Balfour to House, 17 Dec. 1918, BP 49687 f. 237; Imperial War Cabinet 43, 18 Dec. 1918, PRO CAB 23/42; Alice Balfour's diary, 4–5 Dec. 1918, SRO GD 433/2/136 p. 15.
[120] Nicolson *Peacemaking 1919* p. 277; Dugdale *Balfour* vol. II p. 264; Empire Delegation, 1 June 1919, *BDFA* vol. 4 no. 19.
[121] Dugdale *Balfour* vol. II p. 263; Alice Balfour's diary, 4–5 Dec. 1918, SRO GD 433/2/136 p. 15.
[122] Private memoirs, Selborne Papers 191 f. 70; Rose *The Later Cecils* p. 161.
[123] Ray Stannard Baker *Woodrow Wilson and World Settlement* (London 1923) vol. I pp. 295–303 and vol. II pp. 196–7; Balfour to House, 17 July 1922, BP 49687 ff. 244–8.
[124] Nicolson *Peacemaking* p. 199; Betty Balfour to Alice Balfour, 28 Feb. 1919, SRO GD 433/2/277; Notes by Balfour, 25 Feb. 1919, BP 49750 f. 112; Council of Ten, 25 and 22 Feb. 1919, *FRUS* PPC 1919 vol. IV pp. 123 and 85.

The French, he knew, wanted to exclude the Americans from any effective share in the world settlement. That was not even in the best interest of France, and British collusion would have been 'little short of insanity'.[125] When the Allied leaders – Lloyd George, Clemenceau, and Orlando – met in London in December 1918, it was Balfour who insisted 'in face of considerable opposition and annoyance' that their conclusions be subject to discussion with the Associated Power. Having 'entered the War for great world objects', Wilson deserved a say even about Turkey and Bulgaria (against whom the USA had not fought).[126]

Balfour believed that the nations best fitted to guide the peace-making were those who expected least for themselves from the collision of opposing interests. America inevitably stood first in this respect: 'We ought to stand second, and as near her as may be.' Therefore, while it would be madness to return conquered colonies to the Germans (who would use them for submarine bases and recruiting), Britain should not seek territorial gains.[127] By contrast, France was frankly imperialistic and certain to get a great deal out of the war. Told that the French were no more wicked than the British, he retorted, 'Oh, yes they are.'[128] Every morning, he said in December 1918, he was afraid that he might read that a free fight had happened between France and Italy. The Italians considered themselves the heirs of ancient Rome and conducted foreign relations as if it was better to have enemies than friends. The question was how to mollify them at the smallest cost to mankind.[129] He hated the Secret Treaties which promised Italy territorial spoils. Britain could not break its word, but he prayed that the USA would intervene.[130] There can be no doubt that Balfour

[125] Balfour to Lloyd George, 29 Nov. 1918, PRO FO 800/199 ff. 64–5.
[126] Miller to House, 5 Dec. 1918, *FRUS* PPC 1919 vol. 1 p. 339; Imperial War Cabinet, 3 Dec. 1918, PRO CAB 23/42; Roskill *Hankey* vol. 1 p. 606 and vol. 11 p. 30; War Cabinet 482A, 3 Oct. 1918, PRO CAB 23/14.
[127] Memo. by Balfour, 2 May 1918, PRO CAB 24/53 GT 4774.
[128] Eastern Committee, 18 Dec. 1918, Milner Papers dep. 137 ff. 224 and 221; Balfour to Lloyd George, 29 Nov. 1918, PRO FO 800/199 ff. 64–5; Balfour to Curzon, 14 Mar. 1919, *BDFA* vol. 6 no. 49.
[129] Imperial War Cabinet 45, 23 Dec. 1918, PRO CAB 23/42; Balfour to Rodd, 14 Mar. 1919, BP 49745 f. 15; Memo. by Balfour, 16 May 1919, *FRUS* PPC 1919 vol. v p. 670.
[130] H. Wickham Steed *Through Thirty Years 1892–1922* (London 1924) vol. 11 p. 268; Balfour to Murray, 29 Mar. 1918, Gilbert Murray Papers 36 ff. 63–4; Statement by Balfour [22 Mar. 1917], *The Lansing Papers* vol. 11 p. 24; Nicolson *Peacemaking* p. 199; Eastern Committee, 5 Dec. 1918, Milner Papers dep. 137 f. 188; Imperial War Cabinet 43, 18 Dec. 1918, PRO CAB 23/42.

wanted peace on Anglo-American lines. If France, Italy, and Belgium raised objections, they might be bought off with ex-German land in Africa, since they were 'all bitten with the mania for colonial expansion'.[131]

Why did Lloyd George say he wanted to deal with the Americans himself? Because Balfour was too much inclined to agree with Wilson.[132]

Faint echoes of Ray Stannard Baker are yet to be heard. On slender evidence, Harold Nelson's *Land and Power* presents Balfour as an upholder of balance of power theories opposed to Wilsonian national self-determination. It is true that Balfour did not think national self-determination, pure and simple, was the prescription for perpetual peace. The principle would have to be modified by geographical and economic factors, and therefore excessive emphasis on it was dangerous. A plebiscite supplied 'no sufficient evidence of those lasting sentiments on which alone stable States are founded', but how could the result be over-ruled? And if self-determination were hailed supreme, where would the Allies stand if Germany in future championed the claims of German minorities?[133] Balfour said (and believed) that the balance of power was a 'more or less antiquated doctrine', but until an ideal International Court dawned, 'it will never be possible to ignore the principle of action which underlies the struggle for the balance of power in which our forefathers engaged'. It was desirable to reduce the area from which the Central Powers could draw the resources required for aggression. It was also desirable to render aggression less attractive by rearranging the map in closer agreement with nationality. Germany and Austria included large non-German areas, so 'the double method' was the answer.[134]

Any preconception that notoriously conservative Balfour and notoriously liberal Wilson must have been fundamentally opposed stems from a misunderstanding. Balfourian conservatism in inter-

[131] 30 July 1917, *HCD* vol. 96 cols. 1849 and 1854; Memo. by Balfour, 2 May 1918, PRO CAB 24/53 GT 4774.
[132] Borden *Memoirs* p. 872.
[133] Nelson *Land and Power* pp. 4, 8, 18, 45, 50, 66, 199, 367, and 375; Note by Balfour, 18 Oct. 1918, PRO CAB 24/70 GT 6353; Council of Foreign Ministers, 28 Mar. 1919, *FRUS* PPC 1919 vol. IV p. 530; Imperial War Cabinet 46, 24 Dec. 1918, PRO CAB 23/42.
[134] 27 Feb. 1918, *HCD* vol. 103 cols. 1468–9; Memo. by Balfour, 4 Oct. 1916, PRO CAB 37/157 no. 7.

national affairs did *not* primarily mean adherence to the old ways. It meant attaching great importance to non-rational racial, cultural, linguistic, and historical loyalties – and the clearest manifestation of these was nationalism. Balfour did not admire the European settlement of 1815. The Congress of Vienna, in making arrangements to prevent wars, forgot that 'there were some things for which you had to fight, and you ought to fight' – namely, liberty and nationality – so the 'reactionary folly' of the Holy Alliance had inevitably broken down. A German peace in 1918 would have been no peace, for the imposition of German culture on alien peoples was a recipe for revolt and war. An Allied peace would allow each nation to develop in accordance with the 'cultural necessity' of its individual genius. It would be a permanent peace, since 'based on the permanent instincts, beliefs, traditions, and loyalties of mankind'.[135] Balfour easily acquired the language of the new era of national self-determination, because he had been speaking a conservative dialect of it all along.

If Germany was the acid test of self-determination, Balfour passed with the motto: 'Germany for the Germans – but only Germany.' He ruled out partition or reconstitution of German lands, and hoped that no attempt would be made to control or modify internal policy. Revision of frontiers would free Germany from the inconvenience of discordant French, Danish, and Polish minorities.[136] Heligoland and the Kiel Canal were matters of justifiable international concern,[137] but he doubted the wisdom of permanent disarmament. Unless guaranteed against invasion, Germany had just cause for complaint if its army were confined to 100,000 men, while France, Poland, and Czechoslovakia could raise unlimited forces. Drastic Allied restrictions might prove as counterproductive as Napoleon's efforts to destroy the Prussian army after Jena.[138]

---

[135] 'German Ambitions' *Times* 11 Jan. 1918 p. 8; 'America Day' *Times* 8 Apr. 1918 p. 3; 'Our Financial Mobilisation' *Times* 1 Feb. 1917 p. 8; 6 Nov. 1917, *HCD* vol. 98 col. 2040; 'German War Aims' *Times* 14 July 1917 p. 4.

[136] Memo. by Balfour, 4 Oct. 1916, PRO CAB 37/157 no. 7; Memo. by Balfour, 19 Jan. 1916, PRO CAB 37/141 no. 11.

[137] Memo. by Balfour, 16 Sept. 1916, PRO CAB 37/155 no. 21; Memo. by Balfour, 14 Apr. 1919, BP 49751 ff. 2–7; Council of Ten, 6 Mar. 1919, *FRUS* PPC 1919 vol. IV p. 225.

[138] Council of Ten, 17 and 10 Mar. 1919, *FRUS* PPC 1919 vol. IV pp. 375 and 298; Empire Delegation, 30 May 1919, *BDFA* vol. 4 no. 18; Betty Balfour to Alice Balfour, 25 Apr.

Concerning the western frontier, Nelson lays stress on Balfour's recommendation that Alsace-Lorraine be returned to France without a plebiscite in order to deprive Germany of population and iron reserves and thus improve 'the equilibrium of Europe'. It should be recognised, however, that Balfour was allowing these considerations to tip the scales where the national sentiments of the people seemed evenly balanced.[139] Even wider of the mark is the suggestion that he sympathised with the Foch Plan for an integrated security bloc of France, Belgium, Luxembourg, and an independent Rhineland.[140] When Balfour first heard the French propose a Rhineland State, he was not disposed to take 'this rather wild project' seriously. It was inconsistent with national self-determination.[141] No fear of French domination of Europe troubled him: Germany would remain more than a match for France, however much was given to France, and however much was taken from the Central Powers. The French plan was purely defensive and intelligible in view of 1870 and 1914.[142] It was also basically futile:

If Germany is again going to be a great armed camp, filled with a population about twice the size of that of any State in Europe, if she is going again to pursue a policy of world domination, it will no doubt tax all the statesmanship of the rest of the world to prevent a repetition of the calamities from which we have been suffering. But the only radical cure for this is a change in the international system of the world – a change which French statesmen are doing nothing to promote, and the very possibility of which many of them regard with ill-concealed derision. They may be right; but if they are, it is quite certain that no manipulation of the Rhine frontier is going to make France anything more than a second rate Power, trembling at the nod of its great neighbours in the East, and depending from day to day on the changes and chances of a shifting diplomacy and uncertain alliances.[143]

1929, SRO GD 433/2/136; Memo. by Balfour, 4 Oct. 1916, PRO CAB 37/157 no. 7; Minute by Balfour, Mar. 1919, PRO FO 608/128 f. 491.

[139] Nelson *Land and Power* p. 18; Statement by Balfour, [22 Mar. 1917], *The Lansing Papers* vol. II p. 31; Note by Balfour, 18 Oct. 1918, PRO CAB 24/70 GT 6357.

[140] Nelson *Land and Power* pp. 375 and 199.

[141] Balfour to Bertie, 2 July 1917, *Papers Respecting Negotiations for an Anglo-French Pact* (1924) Cmd 2169 no. 3; 6 Nov. 1917, *HCD* vol. 98 col. 2040; 19 Dec. 1917, *HCD* vol. 100 col. 2017.

[142] Memo. by Balfour, 4 Oct. 1916, PRO CAB 37/157 no. 7; Balfour to Curzon, 1 Mar. 1919, BP 49734 f. 65; Elcock *Portrait of a Decision* p. 108.

[143] Notes by Balfour, 18 Mar. 1919, BP 49749 f. 39.

Even Nelson admits that, if Balfour was a balance of power theorist, he was a gloomy one. When France persisted, Balfour reconciled himself to temporary occupation of the Rhineland 'which would only last so long as Germany remained suspect among the peoples of the world and was not permitted to enter the League'. (He had himself once suggested occupying some German territory until final payment of the indemnity – before the amount of reparations was discussed).[144] He also went along with the Anglo-American guarantee of France which was part of the bargain. Lloyd George offered this without consulting him, but Balfour revised the draft and inserted the provision making the coming into force of the British treaty conditional on ratification of the American treaty. He still disliked the Rhineland occupation and hoped that its size and duration would be reduced as far as possible. The less French soldiers were allowed to manage affairs in Germany the better.[145]

To the north, Balfour favoured return of the Danish portions of Schleswig-Holstein to Denmark with a guarantee.[146]

It was when he looked to the eastern frontier of Germany that he saw 'the greatest crux of European diplomacy'. He acknowledged the partition of Poland in the eighteenth century to have been a crime, and that unsatisfied Polish national aspirations were a nucleus of bitter discontent, but it was here that he found national self-determination hard to accept. He did not feel that an independent Poland was 'in the interests of Western civilisation'.[147] North-eastern Europe was not the place for a buffer State:

If Germany were relieved of all fear of pressure from Russia, and were at liberty to turn her whole strength towards developing her western ambitions, France and Britain might be the sufferers: and I am not by any means confident that cutting off Russia from her western neighbours might not divert her interests towards the Far East to an extent which British statesmen could not view without some misgivings.[148]

---

[144] Nelson *Land and Power* p. 50; P. Birdsall *Versailles Twenty Years After* (Hamden 1942) pp. 202–3; Empire Delegation, 10 June 1919, *BDFA* vol. 4 no. 21; Memo. by Balfour, 20 Oct. 1918, PRO CAB 24/67 GT 6045.

[145] Hardinge *Old Diplomacy* p. 241; W.M. Jordan *Great Britain, France, and the German Problem 1918–39* (London 1943) pp. 38–9; Empire Delegation, 1 June 1919, *BDFA* vol. 4 no. 20.

[146] Memo. by Balfour, 4 Oct. 1916, PRO CAB 37/157 no. 7.

[147] Statement by Balfour [22 Mar. 1917], *The Lansing Papers* vol. II pp. 26–8.

[148] Memo. by Balfour, 4 Oct. 1916, PRO CAB 37/157 no. 7.

Balfour doubted that Poland could survive. If Poles had understood the elements of reasonably good government, they would
never have been partitioned in the first place. He feared 'that the
new Poland would suffer from the diseases from which the old
Poland perished'. It would be a theatre of endless intrigues
between Germany and Russia and a perpetual occasion of European strife. Before the Bolshevik Revolution, he preferred, 'from
a selfish Western point of view', that reunified Poland be an autonomous part of the Russian Empire.[149] By 1918, Russia was in no
position to assert suzerainty over the insurgent Poles. In these
circumstances, Balfour wanted the principle of nationality to be
applied strictly. The best hope for stability was 'a Poland of the
Poles' – with as few Russians, Germans, and Lithuanians as
possible. French talk of restoring the Greater Poland of 1772
astonished him. Faced with a hard choice, he was more inclined
to leave Poles under German rule than place Germans under
Polish rule. Accordingly, he envisaged a land-locked Poland
(guaranteed free flow of commerce), with Germany retaining the
port of Danzig and territorial connection with East Prussia.[150] The
Conference compromise was a Polish Corridor to the sea and
Danzig as a Free City. (Two years later, it was the opposition of
Balfour which foiled a Franco-Polish attempt to slip a Polish
defensive mandate over Danzig through the League Council.)[151]

To the south lay Germany's ally, Austria–Hungary. Balfour had
long regarded this multi-racial Empire as unstable and artificial.
He had spoken of its impending dissolution in 1898.[152] The direct
Allied interest was simply to deprive the Germanic bloc of this
reservoir of non-German man-power. Either complete dissolution
or de-Germanisation under continuing Habsburg rule would serve.
Domination of Europe by Slavs was not to be feared, as they were
too divided to menace the Germans. During the War, Balfour was

[149] Statement by Balfour [22 Mar. 1917], *The Lansing Papers* vol. II pp. 26–8; Memo. by
Balfour, 4 Oct. 1916, PRO CAB 37/157 no. 7; Empire Delegation, 1 June 1919, *BDFA*
vol. 4 no. 20.
[150] Imperial War Cabinet 46, 24 Dec. 1918, PRO CAB 23/42; W.H. Dawson *Germany under
the Treaty* (London 1933) p. 60; Note by Balfour, 18 Oct. 1918, PRO CAB 24/70 GT
6354; Charles Seymour (ed.) *The Intimate Papers of Colonel House* (London 1928) vol. III
pp. 45–6.
[151] League Council, 12 Dec. 1920, *Procès-Verbal* 20/29/17 p. 29; Conference of Ministers,
16 Feb. 1921, PRO CAB 23/24.
[152] 14 Feb. 1893, *PDeb* 4th Series vol. 8 col. 1421; Bülow: *Memoirs* vol. II p. 317.

happy with the stated Allied aim of allowing the subject national-ities to determine their own development.[153] He did not want undue involvement in the internal affairs of Austria–Hungary, and he was not fussy about the outcome. An independent Bohemia was appealing, as the Czechs possessed national consciousness and Germanic civilisation was 'profoundly distasteful' to them. Trans-fers of territory should be made to Serbia, Romania, Poland, and Italy. The residue could remain the Dual Monarchy. Alternatively, a Quadruple Monarchy of Austrians, Hungarians, Bohemians, and Slavs would be alright. Such a federation was unlikely to last, but it would probably break up without doing any harm to mankind. When the Habsburg Empire actually fell apart during 1918, Bal-four simply endorsed this exercise in self-determination.[154] He appreciated, however, that sudden complete separation presented problems.

The future of Austria proper worried many, but Balfour always assumed that Germany and Austria would continue to co-operate closely even if they did not combine. Theirs was a natural alliance. To forbid the Germanic peoples the right of self-determination would be to 'violate one of the cardinal principles' of the Allies – to little effect. He did not consider *Anschluss* politically disadvan-tageous, for Austria would be a counterweight to Prussia. The only way to sustain an independent Austria would be to 'make terms such that she would be content to live apart', 'put in the way to earn money', he knew not how.[155] He did not negotiate this aspect of the Treaty of St Germain with much conviction.

He was personally more perplexed by Czechoslovakia: should its north-western border follow the natural frontier of the former Empire, or should it be redrawn to exclude ethnic Germans? He did nothing but equivocate. Partiality for the Czechs initially tempted him 'to throw ethnology to the winds', but political weak-ness might outweigh strategic strength. A quarter of the popu-

[153] Steed *Through Thirty Years* vol. II pp. 189–90; Memo. by Balfour, 4 Oct. 1916, PRO CAB 37/157 no. 7; 30 July 1917, *HCD* vol. 96 col. 1848.
[154] Memo. by Balfour, 4 Oct. 1916, PRO CAB 37/157 no. 7; Statement by Balfour [22 Mar. 1917], *The Lansing Papers* vol. II p. 25; Draft notes by Balfour, 15 Dec. 1917, BP 49697 f. 200; 'An End to Austrian Tyranny' *Times* 26 July 1918 p. 5; Imperial War Cabinet 30, 13 Aug. 1918, PRO CAB 23/42.
[155] Memo. by Balfour, 4 Oct. 1916, PRO CAB 37/157 no. 7; Balfour to Stamfordham, 11 Nov. 1918, PRO FO 800/200 ff. 164–5; Heads of Delegations, 25 Aug. and 17 July 1919, *DBFP* vol. I nos. 25 and 13.

lation would be Germans, 'bitterly hostile to their Slav neighbours, and in sympathy with the Saxons, Bavarians, and German-Austrians dwelling beyond their border'. When the Czechoslovak Commission recommended the natural frontier, Balfour acquiesced unhappily. There were too many Germans in Czechoslovakia, and allowing the Czechs the Sudetenland seemed inconsistent with denying the Poles Danzig.[156]

No one could look at Central and Eastern Europe without the deepest anxiety for the future for many years to come. Balfour emphasised that it was the War rather than the Peace which 'smashed up' Austria–Hungary and precipitated inescapable evils. Without economic union, the Succession States would be powerless and subject to German economic penetration on a larger scale than before the War.[157] If German ambition were renewed, it would be in the East that the storm would break. Scope for intrigue would be great, and resistance light. It was desirable therefore that the Balkan peoples should form a united force against external aggression.[158] But what could be done? The greed and jealousy of narrow nationalism, suddenly unchained (and spurred on by those 'positively harmful' Fourteen Points), condemned Eastern Europe to instability. These peoples were not trained in national self-government. 'Intoxicated with a perverted patriotism', they had not learnt to grade their loyalties.[159] The ultimate solution lay in their intellectual and moral development, but in the meantime:

Some critics say the changes being made in Eastern Europe will Balkanise Europe, but I look forward to something different. It would be intolerable if Europe and America made no provision against turning Europe into a cockpit ... I believe a League will be required to superintend and control not only the criminal ambitions of great autocracies, but to prevent any rash and inconsiderate countries going to war.[160]

[156] W. Fest *Peace or Partition* (London 1978) p. 250; Note by Balfour, 18 Oct. 1918, PRO CAB 24/70 GT 6355; Heads of Delegations, 25 Aug. 1919, *DBFP* vol. 1 no. 42; Note by Balfour, 1 Apr. 1919, BP 49734 ff. 69–74.
[157] 'Case for the Coalition' *Times* 12 Dec. 1919 p. 9; 12 Feb. 1920, *HCD* vol. 125 col. 304; Heads of Delegations, 23 Aug. 1919, *DBFP* vol. 1 no. 41.
[158] Notes by Balfour, 18 Mar. 1919, BP 49749 ff. 38–9; 30 Oct. 1917, *HCD* vol. 98 col. 1404.
[159] Meinertzhagen *Middle East Diary* p. 25; 12 Feb. 1920, *HCD* vol. 125 col. 305; Memo. by Balfour, 27 July 1919, PRO CAB 24/85 GT 7846.
[160] 'League of Nations' *Daily Telegraph* 9 Dec. 1918 p. 6.

Balfour added that the USA would have to bear a large share of the work. The Fourteen Points promised international guarantees for Poland and the Balkan States. The future American role would have to be like that of the European countries in the Middle East in the past (i.e. Great Power intervention in the Eastern Question).[161]

These were Balfour's views on the post-war settlement. In significant respects they were not followed. Britain weakened its bargaining position by seeking colonial gains. Germany was permanently disarmed. The Rhineland was occupied. Poland was enlarged. *Anschluss* was forbidden. On 21 May 1919, the South African delegate, Jan Smuts, met Balfour to express concern at these and other features of the German treaty. 'Poor innocent soul', exclaimed Smuts afterwards, 'he disclaimed all responsibility although I reminded him that he was Foreign Secretary'.[162] It was not as if Balfour had openly fought his corner and been defeated. Although dissatisfied, he acquiesced in whatever Lloyd George brought from the Council of Four. There is no end of testimony to Balfour's idle insouciance in Paris, and not all of it the perplexity of strangers unaccustomed to his personality. 'Everyone agrees to recognise that he is flattened, indifferent, and good for nothing', wrote Paul Cambon.[163] 'Even the Balliol boys who seek to keep him awake, and also informed, are inclined to throw up the sponge', noted Colonel Bonsol. 'He viewed events with the detachment of a choir-boy at a funeral service', recalled Robert Vansittart; while Harold Nicolson captured Balfour's usual performance in council: 'A.J.B., in the intervals of dialectics on secondary points, relapses into somnolence.'[164] It is customary to excuse him on grounds of age. He was seventy, the work was arduous, and he was often tired – but he found time for tennis, concerts, and parties. It was at the Supreme Council (observed Clemenceau) that he took his daily nap. His alertness at the Washington Conference (1921–2) was to be in sharp contrast with

[161] 'Mr. Balfour's Appeal to America' *Times* 3 Mar. 1919 p. 12.
[162] W.K. Hancock and J. van der Poel (eds.) *Selections from the Smuts Papers* (Cambridge 1966) vol. IV nos. 985 and 986.
[163] Diary, 1 May 1919, Cecil Papers 51131 f. 78; Paul Cambon *Correspondance 1870–1924* (Paris 1940) vol. III p. 321.
[164] S. Bonsol *Unfinished Business* (London 1944) p. 66; R. Vansittart *The Mist Procession* (London 1958) p. 218; Nicolson *Peacemaking* p. 269.

his Parisian torpor.[165] Smuts could only lament that Balfour was 'a tragedy, a mere dilettante, without force or guidance'. The verdict of British officials: 'Bonar Law cares but doesn't know; Balfour knows but doesn't care; Lloyd George neither knows nor cares'.[166]

Balfour's compliance in part reflected his conviction that speed was vital on three counts. First, the USA had to be made a party to the settlement: 'The situation now evolving in America was as important for the success of the labours of the Conference as what was taking place in Paris.' Secondly, delay meant more unrest in a Europe threatened by Bolshevism. Normality could not return until frontiers were drawn and troops demobilised.[167] Thirdly, it was increasingly difficult to conceal the military impotence of the Allies. Hungarians, Greeks, Romanians, Poles, Czechs, Jugoslavs, and even Italians were openly disobedient, but asking the War Office for troops was 'like asking a mendicant for a thousand pounds'. Economic sanctions were of limited value, because only the Americans had much worth withholding. In time, the authority of the Conference would be so diminished that it might be impossible even to bluff Bulgaria and Turkey into accepting unpleasant treaties.[168]

Mrs Dugdale admits: 'His judgment on the economic and financial provisions was formed less on their intrinsic soundness, and more in relation to the time factor.'[169] The reparations issue exemplifies Balfour's failure to assert himself. In 1916, he had advised against trying to reduce Germany to commercial subservience. Such treaties were needlessly humiliating, 'and when they are onerous they are sure – sooner or later – to be broken'. In the interests of international morality, the Central Powers should pay for damage done to Belgium, France, and Serbia, and surrender shipping equivalent to that sunk by their submarines. He did not mention cash reparation for Britain:

---

[165] Steed *Through Thirty Years* vol. II pp. 372–3; Lord Riddell *Lord Riddell's Intimate Diary of the Peace Conference and After* (London 1933) p. 337.

[166] A. Lentin *Guilt at Versailles* (London 1985) p. 126; Charles Seymour *Letters from the Paris Peace Conference* (New Haven 1965) p. 227.

[167] Balfour to Bryce, 15 Aug. 1919, BP 49749 f. 169; 'Mr. Balfour's Appeal to America' *Times* 3 Mar. 1919 pp. 11–12; Council of Ten, 13 Jan. and 22 Feb. 1919, *FRUS* PPC 1919 vol. III p. 536 and vol. IV p. 91.

[168] Memo. by Balfour, 27 July 1919, PRO CAB 24/85 GT 7846; Heads of Delegations, 26 July 1919, *DBFP* vol. I no. 19.

[169] Dugdale *Balfour* vol. II p. 267.

Whether more can or ought to be exacted is a point on which I feel incompetent to give an opinion; but it may be worth remembering that to take territories from the German or Austrian empires free of debt, is in effect to increase the burdens on the States from which they are taken and to relieve the burden on the States to which they are added.[170]

He contributed nothing to the 'Make Germany Pay' rhetoric of the 1918 General Election. He told a journalist that if the amount of reparations were to be determined according to the agreed formula – compensation for all damage to Allied civilians and their property – 'the narrowest interpretation of those points would call for payment which would strain German resources to the utmost'. In Paris, however, a broad interpretation went quite unchallenged by him. He said that he did not feel qualified to discuss the matter. His defence of the reparations clauses to the Empire Delegation was so feeble as to provoke howls of derision on all sides.[171] In December 1919, he circulated to the Cabinet a warning that Germany would collapse unless the Allies were more generous. He could not deny that the results of reparations were very bad, but he did deny responsibility: it had been a matter for experts, but the economists had given contradictory advice.[172]

His record on the wider economic aspects of the peace is much the same. He *talked* about interdependence. European recovery was inseparable from German industrial reconstruction. Trade was disordered by the universal need to export in order to pay war debts. He did not press his points, and, when the settlement failed to address these problems seriously, he resorted to easy phrases. It was a mistake to concentrate on German difficulties. Germany was responsible for all the trouble. Friendly countries had a prior claim to aid. Tragedy was universal.[173] The need for the economic union of the Succession States was apparent to him, but what could be done, when these peoples were too immature to perceive their own best interests? The Great Powers could hardly inaugurate the era of self-determination by dictating the fiscal

---

[170] Memo. by Balfour, 4 Oct. 1916, PRO CAB 37/157 no. 7.
[171] 'League of Nations' *Daily Telegraph* 9 Dec. 1918 p. 6; Empire Delegation, 1 June 1919, *BDFA* vol. 4 no. 20; S. Waley *Edwin Montagu* (London 1964) p. 212.
[172] Note by Hankey, 20 Dec. 1919, PRO CAB 24/95 CP 322; 12 Feb. 1920, *HCD* vol. 125 cols. 298–9; Dec. 1922, Dugdale *Balfour* vol. II pp. 285–6.
[173] Council of Ten, 27 Jan. 1919, *FRUS* PPC 1919 vol. III p. 731; Heads of Delegations, 28 July 1919, *DBFP* vol. I no. 20; Empire Delegation, 1 and 10 June 1919, *BDFA* vol. 4 nos. 20 and 21.

policies of the new nations. Balfour argued that the dire economic condition of Europe was not the fault of the peace-makers. It was the fault of the War: 'partly because, owing to the dislocation of credit, people can't work, partly, because, owing to the general demoralisation, they won't work'. The best Britain could do was to stabilise its own industrial system, and not attempt 'the impossible task of managing for other people the affairs which they seem incapable of managing for themselves'. Economic conditions did not much depend on conferences and treaties.[174]

This points to another underlying cause of his self-effacement. Balfour believed that the life and growth of States was determined by the undesigned co-operation of social and psychological processes. A proportion of the adaptations required by altered circumstances could only be effected by conscious decision-making, but the role played by political discourse was commonly much exaggerated.[175] The Conference was not so much determining the course of history as being swept along by the stream.

Moreover, the British were but one of four major delegations, and he could quite believe that critical colleagues 'had been driven into a peculiar state of mind by the greed of France, Belgium, and Italy'.[176] Then he was only one man in a Government which itself contained imperialistic anti-American elements. At the end of 1918 a friend had found him sunk in wretched pessimism, sick of being always in a minority of one.[177] Balfour was not by temperament a team-worker: either he led, or he stood apart. In Paris, it was noticed that, when left in charge, he rose to the occasion remarkably. His niece recalled that on walking expeditions if he did not carry the map, he followed without comment.[178] In 1919, the map-reading was left to Lloyd George.

At Versailles for the treaty ceremony on 28 June 1919, Balfour

---

[174] Heads of Delegations, 23 Aug. and 25 July 1919, *DBFP* vol. I nos. 41 and 17; 12 Feb. 1920, *HCD* vol. 125 cols. 304–6 and 309–14; Balfour to Mrs. Talbot, 28 Feb. 1920, SRO GD 433/2/26 no. 72.

[175] Balfour *Foundations of Belief* p. 217.

[176] Empire Delegation, 1 June 1919, *BDFA* vol. 4 no. 20.

[177] Cf. Curzon, Long, and Hughes, Imperial War Cabinet 47, 30 Dec. 1918, PRO CAB 23/42; Digby *Plunkett* p. 244.

[178] Sir J. Headlam-Morley *A Memoir of the Paris Peace Conference* (London 1972) p. 44; Lord Hankey *The Supreme Control at the Paris Peace Conference 1919* (London 1963) pp. 74–6; Dugdale *Balfour* vol. II pp. 266–7.

was 'smiling almost to the point of hilarity'. He used his gold pen ever after. In the hall of his home, the flag of a captured German submarine hung above the fire-place.[179] Right had triumphed in the moral drama of the Great War. He privately confessed, however, that he was not eager to defend a Peace Treaty which was not of his making.[180]

PART III: CODA

Balfour was pleased to leave the Foreign Office in October 1919. As Lord President, he yet made some encouraging remarks about the Paris Conference. The future historian would not think the Peace unworthy of the colossal sacrifices of the War – and he would appreciate that in 1919 human nature was still untamed, selfishness was not excluded, and the growth of nationality might have exacerbated international rivalries. Perhaps the results could never be properly estimated. He spoke of slow convalescence after a four-year disease which had left the world suffering psychological disturbances. The War had produced evils beyond measure, and the fact that the Americans 'could not see their way' to carrying through international reconstruction made things no easier.[181]

He was now more free to choose the international topics in which he interested himself. He did not choose the German problem. The Germans would likely 'try and make up to us', but how far this ought to be permitted he did not know. He favoured early German admission to the League of Nations.[182]

What did concern him was the 'grave menace' of French air power – especially when coupled with the nationalistic policies of Poincaré (1922–4). The possibility of France attacking Britain was remote, but Balfour was not prepared to tell a hysterical nation: 'We throw down our weapons; you can stab us in the back if you

---

[179] Lentin *Guilt at Versailles* p. 104; Young *Balfour* p. 407; P. Harris *Life in a Scottish Country House* (Whittingehame 1989) p. 76.

[180] 'Guildhall Banquet' *Daily Telegraph* 11 Nov. 1918 p. 3; *Dictionary of National Biography 1922–30* (London 1937) p. 54.

[181] 'Mr. Balfour on National Sympathy' *Times* 6 July 1920 p. 16; 'Case for the Coalition' *Times* 12 Dec. 1919 p. 9; Chamberlain and Balfour *The Unionist Party* pp. 11–14; Dugdale *Balfour* vol. II p. 313.

[182] Balfour to Curzon, 20 Sept. 1919, BP 49734 ff. 172–3; *Conference of Prime Ministers and Representatives of the United Kingdom, the Dominions, and India 1921* (1921) Cmd 1474 p. 40.

wish, but we are certain that you will not.'[183] It was difficult to induce 'those wretched politicians at Paris to behave like reasonable creatures', and, although Germans were very different from Frenchmen, they were not more scrupulous.[184] In 1923, the year of the Ruhr crisis, he could not see a single bright spot: 'Foreign politics are, thank Heaven, no longer my job.'[185]

Though he had earlier stated that defensive alliances would remain the basis of peace, he was not now anxious for Britain to enter any. In Washington in 1921 he tried vainly to reinterest the Americans in the unratified joint guarantee of France. When he suggested that Britain guarantee the *coast* of France against attack, he was out to undermine the French case for maintaining a substantial fleet.[186] The Draft Treaty of Mutual Assistance and the Geneva Protocol incurred his clear disapproval, and he opposed Austen Chamberlain's plans to guarantee the Franco-German border. 'What is the use of making pledges to fight?' he asked. In some continental dispute twenty years hence, the British people might think France in the wrong. They could not be driven to fight against their will. He confessed:

I am not sure that I am a fair judge of this, because I am so cross with the French. I think their obsession is so intolerably foolish . . .They are so dreadfully afraid of being swallowed up by the tiger, but yet they spend their time poking it . . .we are doing something which we do not approve of or see the immediate necessity for to please people who cannot manage their own affairs and which we should never do if they were not rather insane, if we were not dealing with people who are psychologically upset.[187]

Franco-German hostility was not rooted in any concrete dispute; it was an attitudinal problem. The French based their policy on the inevitability of war. That was absolute lunacy, and Britain should not encourage it. If history did repeat itself, and France

[183] CID, 14 and 31 Oct. 1921 and 24 May 1922, PRO CAB 2/3; Memo. by Balfour, 19 Oct. 1925, SRO GD 433/2/4 no. 6; CID Sub-committee, 16 May 1923, PRO CAB 16/46 p. 178.
[184] Balfour to Hankey, 29 Sept. 1922, SRO GD 433/2/2 no. 1; Balfour to Gerald Balfour, 9 June 1923, SRO GD 433/2/231 no. 66.
[185] Balfour to Fisher, 23 July 1923, Fisher Papers 65 f. 98; Balfour to Garvin, 22 Nov. 1923, SRO GD 433/2/22 no. 60; Balfour to Burt, 16 Nov. 1922, SRO GD 433/2/18 no. 83.
[186] Memo. by Balfour, 4 Oct. 1916, PRO CAB 37/157 no. 7; 21 Nov. 1921, *Conference* pp. 134–6; Balfour to Lloyd George, 18 Dec. 1921, Lloyd George Papers F/61/1/12.
[187] CID, 13 Feb. 1925, PRO CAB 2/4.

were aggressively attacked, Britain would again assist without delay. The French should be told as much, but no formal agreement should be made unless and until a German menace reemerged. In the meantime, perpetual contemplation of 'Armageddon No.2' harmed everybody.[188]

Balfour hoped 'with a certain confidence' that 'if we only in Europe managed our affairs without doing our best to irritate everybody all round – in England we do not do it – if the world went on that plan, there is not going to be a repetition of the Great War'. Therefore, despite his aversion to treaties which anticipated the worst, he could rejoice at the immense change in 'spiritual conditions' worked by Chamberlain, Briand, and Stresemann at Locarno in 1925. 'A great amelioration in the public feeling of Europe' was healing the moral bitterness left by war. A happier era was in sight.[189]

CONCLUSION

To those who mistakenly praised 'his great work in laying the foundations of the Entente', Balfour seemed 'the one British statesman of European mind'.[190] This he was not. He was a statesman of *global* mind. This distinction – between the European and the global – permeates his perception of the German problem and the Great War. His early complacency, his commitment to victory, and his later detachment are all attributable to it.

Balfour observed in 1903 that German unification was the greatest incident in modern European history. Germany had ousted France from continental leadership. The French found this as difficult to accept as their loss of world leadership to the British, but it was equally inevitable. 'The Franco-German problem appears insoluble', he remarked, 'for it is really a problem of making one Frenchman go as far as two Germans.'[191] The emergence of the German Empire was tribute to the power of race patriotism and the broadening of loyalties facilitated by modern

---

[188] CID, 13 and 19 Feb. 1925, PRO CAB 2/4; Draft letter to an imaginary American correspondent, Sept. 1922, SRO GD 433/2/11; Alice Balfour's diary, 14 Mar. 1925, SRO GD 433/2/136 pp. 59–60.
[189] CID, 19 Feb. 1925, PRO CAB 2/4; Balfour to Alice Balfour, 4 Dec. 1925, SRO GD 433/2/76 no. 33; 24 Nov. 1925, *HLD* vol. 62 cols. 836–9 and 847.
[190] 'E.T. Raymond' [E.R. Thompson] *Uncensored Celebrities* (London 1919) pp. 73–4 and 71.
[191] Balfour *Fiscal Reform* p. 107; Lord Swinton *Sixty Years of Power* (London 1966) p. 29.

communications. In the face of such forces, the eighteenth-century idea of the European balance of power seemed rather academic. It was not a concept much used by Balfour.

From a global point of view, there seemed even less cause for alarm. Germany was a continental Power. Geo-political rivalry with the British Empire seemed unlikely: what quarrel could arise between the whale and the elephant? Nor was historic prejudice a problem. English and German soldiers had often fought in the same cause.[192] The Powers which threatened German continental leadership were precisely those which might threaten British world leadership: France and Russia. Add to this that Germany was Teutonic and Britain partly Teutonic, and some sort of natural alliance seemed the result. He hoped so, although he did concede that the very similarity of the Englishman and the German might prove problematic: small difficulties and jealousies seemed to interfere with the close friendship of related nations 'because, being alike, they want the same things'.[193]

Within his world-view it was far from axiomatic that a strong Germany was dangerous. He never said it was. Well into the first decade of the century he eschewed opinions to the contrary. Even when war came, he did not repudiate his earlier analysis. Instead he added the missing factor: a malignant Psychological Climate. In December 1914 he explained:

He was not alone in believing up to 20 years ago [*sic*] that Germany, sated with glory and absolutely secure in her strength, would feel that her ideal should be that of a great peaceful, cultivated, and industrial nation ... That had not been the course of German thought ... Unhappily for herself, unhappily for mankind, she had apparently felt that it was not enough to be great, honoured, wealthy, and secure, but that no nation worthy of the name, having domination within its grasp, should fail by all means, fair or foul, to pursue domination until it was secured. He thought that was one of the greatest, if not the greatest tragedy in history.[194]

Germany, he added, had not been content to be 'first among equals' on the continent of Europe, but sought to reduce all others to servility. If so, Balfour had not been especially prompt in his concern. The first Moroccan Crisis failed to convince him of

[192] Balfour *Essays Speculative and Political* pp. 196–7.
[193] Alice Balfour's diary, 14 May 1898, SRO GD 433/2/224.
[194] 'The "Superstate"' *Times* 14 Dec. 1914 p. 12.

German designs, and he was *not* keen to build an anti-German coalition.[195] Historians have too often assumed that the reticent Unionist leader shared the views of his outspoken backbenchers. Before 1911, only ignorance of the facts and commitment to consensus seem to have prevented him from criticising the policy of Grey. Did he ever recall his 1908 fear about the impact of the Triple Entente on German minds? Perhaps not, for Germany did something far more worrying than menace France. It built a fleet. In retrospect, he rated the German Naval Law of 1900 a turning point in history.[196]

Only when he suspected that the Germans were aiming at global ascendancy did Balfour turn against them. 'Is it a question of right and wrong?' he wondered: 'Maybe it is just a question of keeping our supremacy.'[197] His readiness to entertain the doubt does not diminish the sincerity of his answer. In government lay the genius of the Anglo-Saxon race, which gave ordered freedom to the world. German genius was cultural: it contributed unsurpassed music and scholarship to civilisation. Germany had no pillars of world power comparable to the Dominions and the USA. It would have to rely on the direct domination of other races – a situation inherently unstable. Should one nation win supremacy on both land and sea, the danger of international tyranny would be great.[198] Bear in mind that the keenest advocates of *Weltmacht* were also whole-hearted militarists, and the prospect became intolerable.

When continental Europe stumbled into war in 1914, Balfour felt that Britain could not permit a German victory. The challenge to Anglo-Saxon preponderance had to be crushed lest it grow stronger. In his eyes, that was what the Great War was about. It was fought to preserve the vision of a peaceful Anglo-American world order and bring it nearer realisation.

The German bid for world power was foiled. Compared with that, the post-war rearrangement of Europe was a lesser matter.

[195] Cf. A.P. Ryan 'Arthur Balfour' *History Today* 2 (1952) p. 427: 'his energies were much engaged in re-adjusting the balance of Europe and cementing the Japanese and French alliances'. To support a similar interpretation, Kenneth Young resorts to presenting the anti-German pro-French opinions of Lord Esher and asserting that Balfour probably agreed with them (Young *Balfour* p. 228).
[196] Balfour to Hankey, 15 Mar. 1928, SRO GD 433/2/17 no. 26.
[197] Mar. 1907, Nevins *Henry White* p. 258.
[198] 'Patriotism and Empire' *Times* 5 Aug. 1915 p. 8.

Balfour was content to see coercive States cut up on national lines, but the priority was to put an end to traumatic war conditions and allow international convalescence to begin. He had a good idea of the weaknesses of the new Europe, but felt that little could be done. The continental turmoil of the early 1920s was a post-script to the catastrophe.

During the War, Balfour declared that peace could not be secure until Germany was either made powerless or made free. He knew that a rich and populous country could not long be kept powerless.[199] Therefore Germans had to be made free – free from a false set of beliefs, fostered by Frederick the Great, schematised by Hegel, demonstrated by Bismarck, and publicised by Treitschke. The first step towards emancipating them was defeating them. Beyond that he did not venture. The tide of intellectual and moral influence was unfathomable.

Balfour had been slow to perceive the clash of Anglo-German interests, and it was only with difficulty that he came to terms with it. His system of thought had not coped very well with the foremost international occurrence of his time, but he could at least fall back on scepticism. Mankind was borne along on an unexplored stream, he once mused: whether it hurried down perilous rapids or glided through fair scenes of peaceful cultivation would always be a matter of accident 'in relation to any laws which we are ever likely to discover'.[200]

---

[199] 30 July 1917, *HCD* vol. 96 col. 1854; Memo. by Balfour, 4 Oct. 1916, PRO CAB 37/157 no. 7.
[200] Balfour *Essays and Addresses* p. 26.

CHAPTER 7

Anglo-America

If you scratched the American you found the Briton.

Balfour 1917[1]

'It's a great day for the world', exclaimed Balfour on 3 April 1917: the US President had advised Congress to declare war on Germany. Dining off a Stars and Stripes table-cloth as the report came through, he hailed the greatest speech he had ever read.[2] Within three weeks, Balfour was in the United States as head of the British War Mission. Received by cheering thousands in Washington and New York with unprecedented displays of pro-British sentiment, he was at times speechless with emotion.[3] Apparently inexhaustible, even exuberant, he took to the hectic schedule 'like a duck to water'. The Balfour Mission symbolised to him a new departure in history.[4] For the first time the New World was taking an active role in global affairs. The USA was assuming its full and rightful place in the political community of Western nations. That it did so to fight in association with the British Empire for the principles of world order made this one of the most beneficent developments of international relations ever. In April 1917 'civilisation came to the full consciousness of itself'. Might not posterity judge that the best and most permanent consequence of the War was the coming together of the English-speaking race? Generation by

---

[1] Alice Balfour's diary, 17 June 1917, SRO GD 433/2/136 p. 2.
[2] B.J. Hendrick *The Life and Letters of Walter H. Page* (London 1924) pt II p. 228; Fisher: *Autobiography* p. 93.
[3] 'Cheering Thousands Greet Balfour' *New York Times* 23 Apr. 1917 pp. 1 and 8; 'City's Greetings to Mr. Balfour' *New York Times* 12 May 1917 pp. 1–3.
[4] Sir Tom Bridges *Alarms and Excursions* (London 1938) p. 171; Malcolm to Cecil, 6 May 1917, BP 49738 ff. 64–5; 'German War Aims' *Times* 14 July 1917 p. 4.

generation, a deep congruity of moral feeling should draw Britain and the USA into ever closer union:[5]

time shall have no grip upon it, decay shall never touch it, . . . it shall endure for all time, a monument not of the ingenuity or contrivance of this or that politician or body of politicians, but of spontaneous growth – spontaneous and natural – and therefore the eternal product of mutual goodwill, mutual comprehension, and the mutual pursuit of common ideals.[6]

'I pray God it may be for ever!', Balfour proclaimed. It had been the dream of his life to see the realisation of the spiritual unity of 'the English-speaking, freedom-loving branches of the human race' before he died. 'It is a theme which absorbs my thoughts day and night', he said, 'which moves me more, I think, than anything connected with public affairs in all my long experience.'[7]

These public utterances were extravagant, but they were not insincere. Few subjects roused Balfour to hyperbole. It is therefore all the more significant that Anglo-American co-operation almost invariably did. He asked New Yorkers in 1917 to recognise that his feelings, far from being the offspring of recent events, were based on convictions held with unalterable fidelity.[8] So true was this that a chapter on Balfour's view of relations with the USA is necessarily pervaded with 'Anglo-Saxonism'. Part I examines how he related his belief to America. Part II looks at how he responded to events in the light of his belief.

PART I: ELABORATING THE CREED

Balfour said that he could not remember the beginning of his belief in the solidarity of Anglo-Saxon civilisation: it dated from 'earliest youth', before his entering Parliament (and before his crossing America in 1875).[9] If so, he could count himself among

[5] 'German Ambitions' *Times* 11 Jan. 1918 p. 7; 'War Ideals of America' *Times* 21 June 1917 p. 4; 'America Day' *Times* 8 Apr. 1918 p. 3; 'Mr. Balfour on American Ideals and Progress' *Times* 5 July 1917 p. 8.
[6] 'German War Aims' *Times* 14 July 1917 p. 4.
[7] 'War Ideals of America' *Times* 21 June 1917 p. 4; 'Balfour Realizes the Dream of his Life' *New York Times* 13 May 1917 p. 3; 'Mr. Balfour on American Ideals and Progress' *Times* 5 July 1917 p. 8.
[8] 'Balfour Realizes the Dream of his Life' *New York Times* 13 May 1917 p. 3.
[9] 'The Bond of World Peace' *Times* 15 Nov. 1917 p. 6; Balfour to Choate, 1 June 1905, BP 49742 f. 122.

its early adherents. In the 1860s, Palmerston had worked on the assumption that the rise of the USA was a threat to British interests. Salisbury never viewed it with much satisfaction either. Traditional Tories often shrank from the populism of the Republic. Despite the odd jibe at American political immaturity, Balfour said that 'contemplation of the United States as it is, and even more, as its influence in the world will broaden' was long one of his intellectual pleasures.[10] The philosophical bases of his view have already been examined.[11] External influences are largely a matter of conjecture. Dilke's *Greater Britain* (1868) had suggested that America offered the English race 'the moral directorship of the world', while the notion of Anglo-Saxon freedom permeated Mill's *On Representative Government* (1861). By the age of eighteen, he had certainly read Tocqueville with interest, and although *Democracy in America* was no Pan-Anglican work, it did emphasise the importance of the USA.[12]

Balfour made no secret of his opinions. He said in November 1895 that, come the next General Election, he hoped to report:

that a deeper consciousness has begun to penetrate the convictions of the whole of the Anglo-Saxon race, whether subjects of the Queen or not, that they are all of one stock, that they speak one language, that they own one literature, that they live under institutions having a common origin, and that their mission throughout the world should be the same.[13]

Two months later, he capped his efforts to ease Anglo-American tension over Venezuela with an explicit appeal to the Anglo-Saxon patriotism of US citizens. He might be taxed with being a dreamer, he declared, but he looked forward with confidence to the time when his dreams would be embodied in actual political fact, and 'after all, circumstances will tend in that direction in which we look'.[14]

Balfour claimed that he was careful to make his words about

---

[10] Hendrick *Page* pt II p. 251.

[11] See above pp. 36–41.

[12] Dilke *Greater Britain* vol. I pp. vii–viii and 318; J.S. Mill: *Considerations on Representative Government* (London 1861); Balfour to Eleanor Balfour, June 1866, SRO GD 433/2/195; Alexis de Tocqueville *Democracy in America* (New York 1966) vol. I p. 434.

[13] *Review of Reviews* vol. 4 (Nov. 1891) p. 468; 'Mr. Balfour in Glasgow' *Times* 15 Nov. 1895 p. 6.

[14] 'Mr. Balfour on Foreign Affairs' *Times* 16 Jan. 1896 p. 10; *Review of Reviews* vol. 17 (June 1898) p. 603.

America less strong than his convictions. Anglo-Saxonism seemed to have developed more quickly in Britain than in America, at least among the wider population, so expressions suitable for British audiences might excite suspicion or ridicule on the other side of the Atlantic. Sentiment supplied an easy mark for criticism: 'But I console myself by remembering that easy criticism is usually bad criticism.'[15] He appreciated that in preaching Anglo-Saxon brotherhood he was treading on delicate ground. There were two objections to be borne in mind: the legacy of 1776, and the ethnic mix of American society.[16]

In 1898, Balfour wrote that the only perennial difficulty in the way of the Pan-Anglo-Saxon ideal was that 'from the nature of the case, American patriotism must be fed on histories of the War of Independence and their most stirring memories must be of conflicts with this country'. The fact that Americans had hitherto 'from the necessities of history' mainly fought men of their own speech and traditions did not invalidate his basic thesis. The development of a wider sense of political community took time. In the eighteenth century people had no conception of a hierarchy of patriotisms. That was why an unhappy quarrel had then proved insoluble and (with French assistance) destroyed for ever the political unity of Anglo-Saxon civilisation.[17] (Biographers who credit Balfour with definite plans for the federal re-union of Britain and the USA are in error.)[18] The tragedy was that separation had involved war – productive of triumphalism, bitterness, and enduring legends. American school-books were responsible for much ill-will. Seen in its proper perspective, however, the Declaration of Independence did not interfere with the continuity of history or the consciousness of kinship. Britain had created the thirteen colonies, and the colonists were men of English culture.[19] They had

[15] Balfour to Choate, 1 June 1905, BP 49742 ff. 122–3.
[16] Balfour *Freedom of the Seas* pp. 7–8.
[17] Balfour to Strachey, 22 July 1898, Strachey Papers S/2/4/3; 'Mr. Balfour on American Ideals and Progress' *Times* 5 July 1917 p. 8; Balfour *Opinions and Argument* p. 61; Amery *Empire in the New Era* p. ix.
[18] Young *Balfour* pp. 277–84; Judd *Balfour* pp. 315–16; Egremont *Balfour* pp. 250–1. These mistakenly ascribe to Balfour a 1909 memorandum, entitled 'The Possibility of an Anglo-Saxon Confederation', which argues that Theodore Roosevelt should campaign for the creation of a unified Anglo-American State. The memorandum was in fact sent to Balfour by Philip Kerr. See Kerr to Balfour, 3 May 1909, BP 49797 f. 1.
[19] 'Mr. Balfour on American Ideals and Progress' *Times* 5 July 1917 p. 8; Balfour to Lawrie, 14 Feb. 1921, SRO GD 433/2/25 no.78.

acted in the tradition of freedom which was their inheritance, and the English-speaking peoples had continued to develop on parallel lines. Whether friendly or quarrelsome, they could 'no more get rid of a certain fundamental similarity of outlook than children born of the same parents and brought up in the same home'.[20] Balfour evoked his conservative mentor: Edmund Burke had supported the American contention in 1776, but, if he had come back to life in 1896, he would have been pleading for an alliance to propagate Anglo-Saxon liberty and order. George Washington too would have rejoiced to see 1917.[21] At the end of the War, Balfour suggested in Cabinet that Britain adopt Thanksgiving Day. It dated from colonial times, he said: just when the harvest failed in Massachusetts, British ships had appeared laden with corn. Lord Reading replied that the Americans had evidently forgotten this, as they gave thanks each November for the fact they were no longer a British dominion. Balfour reluctantly accepted that discussion of one-hundred-and-fifty-year-old events was not now going to have much effect. In New York in 1921 he flatly said that the rebellious colonists had been right on the main issue, and Britain wrong.[22]

Before American audiences he endeavoured to address the ethnic question with equal discretion. Spiritual ties were pronounced 'more gripping than anything which could be conferred by an accident of heredity'. Admirable citizens drawn from all parts of Europe were absorbing the American spirit – a spirit rooted in British history. Only once did he come close to slipping: 'To us of Anglo-Saxon, of people of English speech.'[23] The truth was that Balfour accepted that the question of physical descent was not 'the only one which has to be taken into account', while never doubting the desirable American identity: 'These people of German or R. Catholic Irish descent have been, or are being,

---

[20] 'Balfour Sees us as Liberty's Leader' *New York Times* 6 Dec. 1921 p. 1–2; Balfour *Freedom of the Seas* pp. 8–9.

[21] 'Mr. Balfour at Bristol' *Times* 4 Feb. 1896 p. 7; 'Pilgrimage to Mt. Vernon' *New York Times* 30 Apr. 1917 p. 5.

[22] War Cabinet 506, 22 Nov. 1918, PRO CAB 23/8; Balfour to Lawrie, 14 Feb. 1921, SRO GD 433/2/25 no. 78; 'Balfour Sees us as Liberty's Leader' *New York Times* 6 Dec. 1921 p. 1–2.

[23] 'Balfour is Honored by Phil Beta Kappa' *New York Times* 18 May 1917 p. 12; 'Balfour Realizes Dream of his Life' *New York Times* 13 May 1917 p. 3; 'City's Greetings to Mr. Balfour' *New York Times* 12 May 1917 p. 2.

completely absorbed, and are subject to all the subtle influences which give to each nation its special characteristics – they are becoming as American as if their forefathers had come over in the "Mayflower".[24]

Natural alchemy was transforming diverse immigrants into 'heirs and sharers in Anglo-Saxon laws and civilisation' – but cultural assimilation could not be complete. Ancestry did have an effect, and the consequences of inter-marriage were double-edged. Thus, on the one hand, he could write that America was 'something much more than a magnified replica of Gt. Britain'. It was destined to develop on lines of its own and, like France or Germany, contribute something special to world civilisation. On the other hand, he insisted that Anglo-Saxon culture must retain a distinctive individuality through all time.[25] In other words, he was prepared to see America diverge, so long as it did not stray too far. Most Americans were of British descent (though proportionately fewer as time went on) and they were dominant in public life, but Balfour was not happy that the USA apparently liked absorbing immigrants about equal in number to the total increase by birth rate within the country. He fully supported exclusion of the 'yellow races', and he was worried about the blacks. The extraordinarily difficult problem 'of races as vigorous in constitution, as capable of increasing in number, in contact with white civilisation' was made unnecessarily embarrassing by the egalitarianism of the US Constitution.[26]

Of hyphenated Americans the most outspokenly anti-British were the Catholic Irish. Initially hopeful that exclusive Irish nationalism would dwindle, Balfour did not pay much attention to its publicised transatlantic ramifications. Warned in 1910 that the allied Irish-German vote in the USA was 'one of the greatest dangers that ever threatened the Empire', he replied that he gave it full weight – and continued to oppose Home Rule as vigorously as ever.[27] In 1916 he was 'rather painfully impressed' by reports

[24] Balfour to White, 12 Dec. 1900, BP 49742 f. 68.
[25] 2 May 1905, *PDeb* 4th Series vol. 145 col. 796; Balfour to White, 12 Dec. 1900, BP 49742 f. 68; Martin *Choate* vol. II p. 292.
[26] 'Mr. Balfour at Aberdeen' *Times* 11 Jan. 1910 p. 7; Burton 'Roosevelt' pp. 32–3; 16 Aug. 1909, *HCD* vol. 9 col. 1001.
[27] Balfour to White, 12 Dec. 1900, BP 49742 f. 68; Garvin to Sandars, 27 Jan. 1910, Garvin to Balfour, 17 Oct. 1910, Balfour to Garvin, 22 Oct. 1910, BP 49795 ff. 52, 89–90, and 101.

of the effect of the Irish rebellion on American opinion, but he was 'unwilling to believe that, if the truth about Ireland were known, there would not be a reaction in our favour'. A year later he acknowledged that American ignorance was 'invincible' on the subject. By then he himself favoured giving up southern Ireland, so it was no embarrassment to wire from Washington that the Irish Question was 'apparently the only difficulty we have to face here'. A settlement would greatly facilitate Anglo-American co-operation – and partition might do.[28] Events across the Irish Sea, not across the Atlantic, governed his retreat from the Union.[29] When he wrote that Britain had to show the world that it lived up to its own international principles, he was thinking of self-determination more for the six counties than for the twenty-six. A successful solution would indeed 'make an immense difference to American politics'[30] – but that was a bonus.

Balfour thus perceived no insuperable obstacles to the realis-ation of his vision, and Anglo-American sentiments were not too difficult to sustain, for they were widespread in Britain by the turn of the century. While Joseph Chamberlain, James Bryce, Sir Edward Grey, Arthur Lee, Admiral Fisher, Cecil Rhodes, St Loe Strachey, and W.T. Stead extolled friendship with America, no one of much importance advertised enmity. The pro-Americans heartened themselves with social bonhomie. Balfour was a sup-porter of the Anglo-American League (founded 1898), a frequent guest of the Pilgrim Society (founded 1902), and President of the British Empire section of the English-Speaking Union (founded 1918).

There were also vociferous Pan-Anglicans in the USA, where Johns Hopkins University was a centre for Anglo-Saxonist history.

---

[28] Balfour to Grey, 29 May 1916, Asquith Papers 30 f. 105; Minute by Balfour, Spring Rice to Balfour, 9 Mar. 1917, BP 49740 f. 100; Balfour to Lloyd George, 5 May 1917, Lloyd George Papers F/60/2/15.

[29] Cf. Shannon *Balfour* pp. 215–17: 'It was the American factor that finally impelled Balfour to throw his weight behind the Home Rule proposals.' This inference rests mainly on the assumption that he heeded exaggerated reports from Spring Rice in Washington in 1916. In brief: if Balfour was so sensitive to US opinion on Ireland (as Shannon claims), why did he not (i) diminish his opposition to Home Rule one jot previously, (ii) favour lenient treatment of the rebels in 1916, (iii) soften his uncompromising support for Ulster Unionism thereafter?

[30] Memo. by Balfour, 25 Nov. 1919, PRO CAB 24/93 CP 193; Balfour to Lloyd George, 10 Feb. 1920, PRO CAB 24/98 CP 681; Balfour to Alice Balfour, 9 Dec. 1921, SRO GD 433/2/75 no. 9.

Pro-British sentiment was fashionable among the educated classes of the eastern seaboard. *The New York Times* in 1917 deemed Balfour's unaffected English accent a model ambitious Americans should imitate.[31] These were the sort of Americans whom he encountered in London – Anglophiles by self-selection and self-regulation. Judging purely by his correspondence with Balfour, even Senator Henry Cabot Lodge could appear sympathetic to the cause.[32] Theodore Roosevelt (President 1901–9) was a fervent adherent, if none too consistent. Balfour was charmed when they met in 1910. John Hay (Ambassador to London 1897–8, Secretary of State 1898–1905) was another believer.[33] Cordial relations continued with Joseph Choate (Ambassador 1899–1905), who rented Balfour's London home while the owner was in Downing Street. Henry White (US Secretary in London 1883–93 and 1897–1905) was a personal friend.[34] Walter Page (Ambassador 1913–18) also inspired deep sympathy: he agreed that Anglo-Saxon sea-power was the paramount force for peace. Contacts like these encouraged Balfour in the accumulation of a record corroborative of his claim to have 'stood solid' for Anglo-American friendship.[35]

PART II: PRACTISING THE CREED

After years of quiescence, Anglo-American relations had suddenly come to prominence in 1895 in connection with a boundary dispute between Venezuela and British Guiana. The USA demanded that Britain agree to arbitration, Salisbury told Washington to mind its own business, President Cleveland said America would impose a settlement, and the result was a war scare. Balfour did

---

[31] See R. Hofstadter *Social Darwinism in Anglo-American Thought 1860–1915* (Philadelphia 1945) pp. 148–58; J. Dos Passos *The Anglo-Saxon Century and the Unification of the English-Speaking People* (New York 1903); B. Perkins *The Great Rapprochement* (New York 1968) ch. 4; 'He Talks Real English' *New York Times* 14 May 1917 p. 10.

[32] BP 49742 ff. 156–87; Cf. A.E. Campbell *Great Britain and the United States 1895–1903* (London 1960) p. 198.

[33] Burton 'Roosevelt'; Clark '*A Good Innings*' p. 109; W.R. Thayer *John Hay* (Boston 1915) vol. II pp. 163 and 221; Hay to Balfour, 22 Aug. 1898, and Balfour to Hay, 8 Aug. 1902, BP 49742 ff. 116–19.

[34] Choate to Balfour, 30 May 1905, BP 49742 ff. 120–1; Martin *Choate* vol. II p. 253; Nevins *Henry White* ch. 7; A. Strachey *St. Loe Strachey* (London 1930) p. 144.

[35] Balfour to A. Page, 29 Jan. 1926, SRO GD 433/2/16; R. Gregory *Walter Hines Page* (Lexington 1970) pp. 127–8 and 135–6; 'Balfour Realizes the Dream of his Life' *New York Times* 13 May 1917 p. 3.

not doubt who was to blame. Many Americans seemed to view war as 'an exhilarating exercise, a gentle national stimulus', while the British despatch compared 'favourably in point of *conciliatoriness* with the document to which it was a reply'.[36] Cabinet pressure, however, persuaded Salisbury to agree to conditional arbitration, and Balfour led the public reconciliation in January 1896 with an affirmation of the Monroe Doctrine and a sermon on race patriotism, which endowed Anglo-American conflict with 'something of the unnatural horror of a civil war'.[37]

American hostility had not shaken his faith. 'Gold is at the bottom of all this', he acknowledged. Bimetallism was a contentious issue in US politics, and gold monometallism was commonly denounced as a British conspiracy to hold other nations in financial servitude. His own support for a silver ratio was well known, and many Americans corresponded with him on the currency question, until Salisbury advised his First Lord of the Treasury to be more reticent. Balfour thought the importance of British cooperation was exaggerated: 'why do not the USA if they think as they do (quite rightly in my opinion) that Bimetallism is for their advantage, force Bimetallism on the world whether England likes it or not?'.[38]

Had the negotiations on Venezuela taken a different course, he once wrote, 'the history of the world would have been changed'. A new war would have revived old animosities and 'the pan-Anglo-Saxon cause would almost have had to be given up in despair'.[39]

As it was, he was elated at the turn of events just two years later. 1898 saw the heyday of the popular cult of full-blooded Anglo-Saxonism. Public opinion in Britain keenly supported the USA in the Spanish-American War, and politicians strove to match the prevailing mood. America responded with an outpouring of gratitude, and the legend was born that Britain alone had held hostile Continental Powers at bay. Balfour, who was Acting

---

[36] J.A.S. Grenville *Lord Salisbury and Foreign Policy* (London 1964) pp. 54–73; 'Mr. Balfour on Foreign Affairs' *Times* 16 Jan. 1896 p. 10; Balfour to Frewen, 3 Feb. 1896, SRO GD 433/2/13 no. 50.

[37] 'Mr. Balfour on Foreign Affairs' *Times* 16 Jan. 1896 p. 10.

[38] Balfour to Frewen, 3 Feb. 1896, SRO GD 433/2/13 no. 50; J.F. Rhodes *The McKinley and Roosevelt Administrations 1897–1909* (New York 1922) pp. 18–23; J.A. Garraty *Henry Cabot Lodge* (New York 1953) p. 140; White to Balfour, 28 Feb. and 6 May 1895, BP 49742 ff. 34–44; Salisbury to Balfour, 11 July 1896, BP 49690 f. 172.

[39] Balfour to Strachey, 22 July 1898, Strachey Papers S/2/4/3.

Foreign Secretary at both the start and finish of the War, has been praised for inaugurating the new era by reversing the Spanish sympathies of the Foreign Office in a single night.[40] On 16 April he heard that the Ambassadors of the Great Powers wanted to advise the US Government that the latest Spanish concession (an armistice in the war against Cuban rebels) removed any justification for armed intervention. He urgently ordered the Washington Embassy to refrain from giving this 'lecture on international morality': Britain must voice no judgment adverse to the United States. In so doing, he certainly prevented Ambassador Pauncefote from making a grave error, but his personal importance in regard to this incident should not be exaggerated. The German and French Foreign Ministers reacted in the same way, and Salisbury would not have done otherwise, for, whatever his private sentiments, he had no intention of offending the USA for the sake of Spain.[41]

Throughout the war, Balfour was strictly neutral in his official capacity, but privately he vowed to do all he could to bring about a firm perpetual alliance. To call for this in public (as Chamberlain did) was not very judicious, but the Americans liked it ' – they were rather coarse fibred'.[42]

Compassion for the vanquished failed to move him in August 1898. He was worried about Gibraltar. Spain, though impotent, might sometime join France in a war against Britain. The suggestion that Gibraltar be exchanged for Ceuta having fallen on deaf ears, he reacted strongly when Spain started building gun emplacements at Algeciras from which it would be possible to shell the colony. He made an offer to Madrid: if the fortifications were abandoned, Britain would guarantee the surrounding Spanish territory. If the fortifications were continued, Britain should use all its influence with America against Spain in the peace negotiations. 'A little bit of frightening' would probably be necessary too. 'I attach no value to the argument from International Law', he said:

[40] H.K. Beale *Theodore Roosevelt and the Rise of America to World Power* (Baltimore 1956) p. 94; 'Mr. Balfour in Manchester' *Times* 31 Jan. 1899 p. 10; W.S. Churchill *Great Contemporaries* p. 255; Campbell *Anglo-American Understanding* p. 36.
[41] Balfour to Chamberlain, 16 Apr. 1898, BP 49773 ff. 132–4; Perkins *The Great Rapprochement* pp. 36–41; Grenville *Lord Salisbury* pp. 199–202.
[42] R.G. Neale *Great Britain and United States Expansion 1898–1900* (Detroit 1966) p. xix; Balfour to Waldstein, 19 Apr. 1898, BP 49852 ff. 282–3; Alice Balfour's diary, 21 May 1898, SRO GD 433/2/224.

Britain should blockade Cadiz and Barcelona and raid Algeciras. He was frustrated when Salisbury insisted on less drastic methods.[43]

Annexation of the Philippines by the United States was to be welcomed. The alternative would have been German infiltration. Balfour wanted greater US involvement in Eastern Asia, as he hoped that Anglo-American guarantees might solve the Chinese problem.[44]

He found the American attitude to the Boer War in the brightest contrast to the ignorant hostility of continental opinion. (In fact American support for the British cause did not extend very far beyond the State Department.)[45]

The Isthmian Canal question was settled at this time. By the Clayton-Bulwer Treaty (1850), any canal linking the Atlantic and the Pacific was bound to be a joint Anglo-American enterprise. The USA now wanted exclusive control, and, after some vexatious negotiations, Britain conceded it in the Hay-Pauncefote Treaty (1901). Balfour was aware of the points at issue, but he was eager for agreement: 'with England at Suez and the US at Panama we should hold the world in a pretty strong grip'.[46]

'We welcome any increase of the influence of the United States of America upon the great Western Hemisphere', he declared in 1903. When the 'disreputable little republic' of Venezuela interfered with shipping, reneged on debt, and disregarded international law, Britain and Germany had mounted a blockade and seized its gunboats. Balfour was anxious to allay American jealousy – which seemed to demand all the mollification it could get. He consoled himself with the reflection that American disapproval made Germany more manageable.[47] When the US Government promoted arbitration of financial claims, he saw no reason to

---

[43] Memo. by Balfour, 19 Aug. 1898, PRO CAB 37/47 no. 63; C. Howard *Britain and the 'Casus Belli' 1822–1902* (London 1974) pp. 115–16; Neale *Great Britain and United States Expansion* pp. 72–85; Balfour to Goschen, 9 Sept. and 11 Oct. 1898, BP 49706 ff. 210–11 and 215–21.

[44] Nevins *Henry White* p. 140. See above, pp. 115–16 and 123–5.

[45] Balfour to Holls, 13 Nov. 1899, BP 49853 f. 130; J.H. Ferguson *American Diplomacy and the Boer War* (Philadelphia 1939) p. ix.

[46] Balfour to Strachey, 14 Mar. 1900, Strachey Papers S/2/4/7; Balfour to Holls, 31 Dec. 1901, BP 49854 f. 239; Beale *Roosevelt* p. 147.

[47] 'Mr. Balfour in Liverpool' *Times* 14 Feb. 1903 p. 9; Balfour to the King, 21 Oct., 15 and 18 Dec. 1902, PRO CAB 41/27 nos. 31, 38, and 39; 15 and 17 Dec. 1902, *PDeb* 4th Series vol. 116 cols. 1271–3 and 1489–90.

complain. He concluded indeed that the USA should involve itself more actively in relations between Latin America and Europe. He had no objection to the Monroe Doctrine – 'rather the reverse!' – but insofar as it sheltered 'these petty and corrupt Republics' from the consequences of their actions, it cast an obligation on the USA to 'take them in hand'.[48]

To Canada naturally attached a different degree of sensibility. The principal problem of US–Canadian relations was then delineation of the Alaskan boundary. The Klondike gold rush raised the stakes and feelings ran high. In 1903 the Americans at length agreed to arbitration by six impartial jurists of repute, three from the United States, and three from the British Empire. President Roosevelt thereupon nominated a Senator, an ex-Senator, and the Secretary for War: gentlemen (observed Balfour) 'neither judicial by position nor character, and who have one and all expressed the most pronounced opinions upon the key question'. Although the Americans had 'behaved ill', he thought it highly inexpedient for Britain to withdraw: 'all we could do was to make the best of a bad job'. The tribunal was soon deadlocked. Roosevelt arranged for him to hear from American friends that the USA was determined to prevail by whatever means necessary. In July 1903, Lodge (himself one of the arbitrators) could report that Balfour was 'thoroughly anxious to accommodate us in every possible way'.[49] Pressed again on 4 October, the Prime Minister said that he attached far more importance to the agreement of the tribunal than to any of the Cabinet questions with which he was then bothered. It would be 'little short of a disaster' if no agreement was reached. It appears that he conveyed his anxieties to his Private Secretary, who conveyed them to the British arbitrator, who acted accordingly. On 20 October the tribunal announced a 4 : 2 majority decision. The dissenting Canadian jurists led the colonial outcry.[50]

---

[48] Balfour to Lansdowne, 2 Jan. 1903, BP 49728 f. 10; 'Mr. Balfour in Liverpool' *Times* 14 Feb. 1903 p. 9; Balfour to Carnegie, 18 Dec. 1902, BP 49742 ff. 235–6; Balfour to the King, 4 May 1904, PRO CAB 41/29 no. 14.

[49] Balfour to the King, 24 Feb. 1903, PRO CAB 41/28 no. 3; Rhodes *McKinley and Roosevelt Administrations* pp. 254–9; H.C. Lodge *Selections from the Correspondence of Theodore Roosevelt and Henry Cabot Lodge 1884–1918* (New York 1925) vol. II p. 42; Garraty *Henry Cabot Lodge* p. 247.

[50] Nevins *Henry White* p. 200; Campbell *Anglo-American Understanding* pp. 334–5; Garraty *Henry Cabot Lodge* pp. 253–5.

Balfour expressed regret at the exact tenor of the ruling, but argued that the loss to Canada was 'nothing to her gain by the fact that for ever a subject of dispute has been removed between two great, two allied, two closely connected countries'. The settlement was in no way deleterious 'from a strategic point of view – the point of view in which we in this country are as immediately concerned as the great colony itself'. Nothing could absolve Britain from studying the defence of Canada whatever 'the probability, or, (as I should prefer to put it) the *im*probability of war'. There were Americans who favoured forcible annexation. He could not imagine that the majority would ever take so atrocious a view, 'but they are an excitable people'. In this 'very worst hypothesis' everything would depend on the cause of the quarrel and the state of Canadian opinion. So long as Canadians were determined to be separate, he did not think the Americans would ever risk a military operation which 'would strain even *their* power to the utmost'. Economic dependence should not be allowed to undermine that determination. For all his Pan-Anglicanism, Balfour characterised any loss of Canada to the USA as 'a great Imperial disaster'.[51]

Nevertheless the finale of the American policy of the Balfour Government was the decision to close the North Atlantic naval station and ignore the possibility of Anglo-American war in setting the strength of the Halifax and West Indies garrisons.[52] The critical questions between the USA and Britain had been settled, and resources could be better used elsewhere.

Some said Balfour's contribution to transatlantic understanding 1895–1905 was unique and inestimable. Others complained that the Conservatives would grovel to any extent to keep in with America.[53] Venezuelan arbitration, the Isthmian Canal, Alaska, military withdrawal – it was a catalogue of appeasement. These short-term losses did not trouble Balfour. He classified Anglo-American deals as investment. The USA was destined to be the

[51] 'The Guildhall Banquet' *Times* 10 Nov. 1903 p. 10; Balfour to Selborne, 1 Jan. [1905], Selborne Papers 46 ff. 5–6; CID, 29 May 1908, PRO CAB 38/14 no. 7; 6 Feb. 1911, HCD vol. 21 col. 58; 'Mr. Balfour on Unionist Policy' *Times* 9 Oct. 1911 p. 8.
[52] Perkins *The Great Rapprochement* pp. 157–8.
[53] L.M. Gelber *The Rise of Anglo-American Friendship* (London 1938) p. 19; White to Balfour, 20 Nov. 1911 and 10 Mar. 1913, BP 49742 ff. 99–104; H.C. Lodge *One Hundred Years of Peace* (New York 1913) pp. 132–5; Lodge to Trevelyan, 18 Jan. 1922, BP 49792 ff. 20–1; Burton 'Roosevelt' p. 37.

mightiest of the English-speaking communities. He ranked it in 1905 'among the greatest, if not the greatest nation in the world'. America was 'in its own despite, becoming part of the European system', for it could hardly expect to share in the cultural life of Europe without playing a part in its political life. It was almost as inconceivable that the United States should remain in isolation 'as that some vast planet suddenly introduced into the solar system should not have its perturbing influence upon other planets'.[54] When America did step out, Balfour wanted the way to be clear for it to take its proper place beside the British Empire.

In 1911, he hailed the Anglo-American arbitration treaty as a sign: 'the very fact that this seems the natural culmination of a natural progress is the greatest proof that all I have said with regard to the impossibility of dividing the destinies of the great nations is absolutely true and based upon literal fact'. The US Senate then destroyed the treaty (though motivated largely by fear of French and German insistence on equal treatment).[55]

The real test was the Great War. From the start, he emphasised the importance of bringing in the USA. The *Pax Britannica* could no longer be assured. The time for *Pax-Anglo-Americana* had come. It was a War between political philosophies – Prussian versus Anglo-Saxon – and 'I cannot doubt that in the result of that struggle America is no less concerned than the British Empire'.[56] He expected American intervention when the *Lusitania* was sunk. Discussions with the Presidential envoy, Colonel House, in 1915 and 1916, were friendly but unsatisfactory. Balfour could see no future for international peace machinery unless the USA were 'prepared actively to promote it by war or the threat of war.'[57] His hopes wore thin: 'Wilson wants votes and the country does not want war.' Jeremiads from the Washington Embassy told him that Anglo-American brotherhood was a complete delusion. Why was Britain

[54] Balfour to Hay, 8 Aug. 1902, BP 49742 f. 119; 'Mr. Balfour in Glasgow' *Times* 13 Jan. 1905 p. 8; speech of 23 June 1905 quoted in 'Mr. Balfour in America' *Times* 7 May 1917 p. 5; Balfour to Mowatt, 26 July 1900, BP 49853 f. 227.
[55] Short *Balfour* p. 295; Perkins *The Great Rapprochement* pp. 252–6.
[56] H. Asquith *Moments of Memory* (London 1938) p. 153; Digby *Plunkett* pp. 181, 189, and 192–7; Memo. by Balfour, 19 Jan. 1916, PRO CAB 37/141 no. 11; Balfour *Freedom of the Seas* pp. 3 and 7–9.
[57] Asquith *Diaries* p. 20; A.S. Link *Wilson – Confusion and Crises* (Princeton 1964) pp. 114–18; Draft Reply by Balfour, 24 May 1916, PRO CAB 37/148 no. 28.

so unpopular across the Atlantic? 'It's sad to me.'[58] His first major task as Foreign Secretary was to reply to the President's observation that the stated war aims of the belligerents were virtually the same. Spring Rice assured him that his despatch had a wonderful effect on Americans 'whom you would regard as of your make', but as for the majority: 'They live in a different world.'[59]

A month later at the Foreign Office Balfour experienced 'as dramatic a moment as I remember in all my life' when he handed the US Ambassador the text of the Zimmermann Telegram which proved that Germany would encourage Mexico and Japan to attack the USA.[60] This plus German resumption of unrestricted submarine warfare served to push America over the brink.

Though the preceding two-and-a-half years had tried his faith in Anglo-America, the Balfour Mission triumphantly affirmed it. He saw for himself 'the great resemblance between them and us even including the Irish and some of the other nationalities'. Everywhere were signs of common roots:

I feel that I am speaking to those brought up ... under one influence, in one house, under one set of educational conditions. I require no explanation of what they think, and I am required to give no explanations of what I think, because our views on great questions seem to be shared; born, as it were, of common knowledge which we know instinctively, and which we do not require explicitly to expound or to define.[61]

His tact was unfailing: if the British had been in the American position they would not have been quicker to realise the truth about the War, but now no treaty could increase Allied confidence in the United States.[62] There was in fact nothing Balfour would have prized more than a maritime alliance between America and Britain. House (whom he liked immensely) encouraged the idea, and there was a practical pretext. The Allies needed cruisers for convoy duty, but the USA was loath to divert its building programme away from capital ships. A post-war naval alliance of fixed

[58] Bertie *Diary* vol. I p. 336; Spring Rice to Balfour, Jan. 1916–Mar. 1917, BP 49740 esp. ff. 8, 25–9, 35, 44, 96, and 106; Hendrick *Page* pt II p. 251.
[59] Balfour *Essays Speculative and Political* pp. 246–55; Spring Rice to Balfour, 19 Jan. 1917, BP 49740 f. 52.
[60] Dugdale *Balfour* vol. II p. 191.
[61] Alice Balfour's diary, 17 June 1917, SRO GD 433/2/136 p. 2; 'Balfour Realizes the Dream of his Life' *New York Times* 13 May 1917 p. 3.
[62] 'America's Decision' *Times* 8 May 1918 p. 5; 'Seek No Alliance' *New York Times* 26 Apr. 1917 p. 2.

duration would protect America while its battle fleet caught up –
with Japan. There was the obstacle. Britain could not risk alienating its Far Eastern ally. Balfour realised that the new alliance
would have to be Anglo-American-Japanese and nominally anti-
German. Then France and Italy, and even Russia, might be
offended if left out. Consequently he had to suggest a multilateral
six Power treaty. Wilson refused to have anything to do with it.
'Were I in his place I should have decided as he has done', Balfour
confessed.[63] His personal relationship with the President was
always affable. Wilson's feeling for Anglo-American ties was genuine, if lukewarm, and the same could be said of Balfour's feeling
for Wilson.[64]

Balfour came back from America 'looking younger than ever,
broadened in mind and very pleased with himself'. He had
touched 'the true realities which lie at the base of our race' and
he had not found them wanting. When American troops marched
through London, he was seen waving a handkerchief with boyish
enthusiasm.[65]

He foresaw that the USA might be embarrassing in peace negotiations. He resented the way the USA continued to extend its
economic interests in South America at British expense when Britain desperately needed the income. Commercial rivalry 'however
friendly (and it is most friendly)' could be a problem. War-time
collaboration had its difficulties – but a Pan-Anglican had to
rejoice that Britain and America were closer than they had been
since the War of Independence. It raised the prospect of untold
possibilities.[66]

He assured the Imperial War Conference in 1918 that the USA
had no selfish ambitions, but was determined that freedom and
national security should come into permanent being. The devas-

---

[63] Memo. by Balfour, 22 June 1917, PRO CAB 24/17 GT 1138; Memo. by Drummond,
May 1917, BP 49687 ff. 70–4; Note by Hankey, 19 June 1917, PRO CAB 24/16 GT
1090; Ray Stannard Baker *Woodrow Wilson: Life and Letters* (London 1928–39) vol. VII
p. 162; W.B. Fowler *British–American Relations 1917–18* (Princeton 1969) p. 28.

[64] Baker *Woodrow Wilson: Life and Letters* vol. VII p. 85; Drummond to House, 9 July 1917
BP 49687 ff. 85–6; Perkins *The Great Rapprochement* pp. 78 and 291; Dugdale *Balfour* vol.
II p. 200.

[65] J.E. Wrench *Geoffrey Dawson and our Times* (London 1955) p. 151; 'Mr. Balfour on his
Mission' *Times* 29 May 1917 p. 6; 'Raymond' *Uncensored Celebrities* p. 195.

[66] Digby *Plunkett* p. 188; Balfour to Wiseman, 5 Mar. 1918, BP 49741 f. 49; 12 June 1918,
Imperial War Conference 1918 Cd 9177 pp. 19–20; 'Balfour Mission Departs' *New York
Times* 26 May 1917 p. 1.

tation of Europe made American strength and stability all the more important to international order. The world would increasingly 'turn on the Great Republic as on a pivot'.[67] He set about making a post-war settlement in which the USA would play a vital part as guarantor of the new Europe and cornerstone of the League of Nations. He even entertained hopes that America would take on especially troublesome territories: Constantinople, Armenia, and Palestine.[68]

In Paris in 1919 Balfour emphasised the immense responsibility resting on the American public 'whose services to mankind would fail of their full effect if America did not take its share in the great responsibilities of the peace'. He had anticipated that transatlantic harmony would prove more difficult to sustain immediately after the War than during it. By June 1919 he was 'of course aware of the anti-British feeling in America . . . for the Americans show no signs of concealing it'.[69] He had observed US diplomacy for over twenty years, and allowances had always to be made for a country where 'gusts of popular opinion sweep away well planned structures of policy'. The American public swayed from side to side in the most disconcerting fashion. Balfour did not encourage the suggestion that he take the Washington Embassy on retiring as Foreign Secretary. With 'its omnipresent and unscrupulous Press, its Senators who have to be separately conciliated, and its diplomatic methods, unchecked by any long international tradition', Washington was probably the most difficult theatre for diplomacy in the world.[70] 'Unfortunately', he had written in 1900, 'in their conduct of foreign affairs the American Constitution tempts, and almost obliges, the American people to be unreasonable.' It certainly seemed so in November 1919. The Treaty of Versailles was 'caught up in the wheels and cogs of party conflict'

---

[67] *Imperial War Conference 1918* Cd 9177 p. 20; Baker *Woodrow Wilson: Life and Letters* vol. VII p. 512; 'Balfour Praises our War Progress' *New York Times* 25 May 1917 p. 2; Hendrick *Page* pt II p. 251.

[68] Balfour to Lloyd George, 9 Aug. 1919, PRO CAB 24/86 GT 7949; Balfour to Gerard, 16 Feb. 1920, BP 49749 ff. 193–5; Imperial War Cabinets 43 and 47, 18 and 30 Dec. 1918, PRO CAB 23/42.

[69] 'Mr. Balfour's Appeal to America' *Times* 3 Mar. 1919 pp. 11–12; *Imperial War Conference 1918* Cd 9177 p. 20; Balfour to Mrs Murray, 6 June 1919, BP 49749 f. 96.

[70] B.J. Hendrick *The Life of Andrew Carnegie* (New York 1932) vol. II p. 181; Balfour to Grey, 29 May 1916, Asquith Papers 30 f. 105; Curzon to Balfour, 6 July 1919, BP 49734 ff. 120–3; Balfour to the King, 8 Feb. 1903, PRO CAB 41/28 no. 1.

and all common sense was 'torn to pieces in process'.[71] The USA refused to guarantee the new order. It appeared to repent of 1917 and turn its back on Europe.

Balfour felt the rebuff strongly. Anglo-American collaboration could have advanced the cause of peace to an incalculable degree. The USA would surely not abandon its high ideals, but the world would be deprived of 'that direct action which would make the assistance of the great American democracy of tenfold value could it be forthcoming'.[72]

Still he laboured on, notably helping to secure warm agreement between the British and American delegations at the Washington Conference 1921–2. Disarmament and the Far East were on the agenda, but he prayed that the Conference would 'knit the hearts of the English-speaking peoples in a closer union'. That was what the world needed.[73] He saw little point, however, in a suggestion from the Canadian statesman, Sir Robert Borden, that they should work to design a new international tribunal for the USA to join as a half-way house to League membership. Christmas with 'only lemon pop' meanwhile made him wonder if America was staying quite true to the Anglo-Saxon individualist tradition.[74]

Six months later Balfour was at the forefront of an incident which largely dissipated the goodwill won at Washington. The 'Balfour Note' of 1 August 1922 stated Government policy on war debt: Britain would ask no more from its debtors than was necessary to pay its creditors. British demands for repayment would therefore 'depend not so much on what France and the other allies owe to Great Britain as on what Great Britain has to pay to America'. Americans immediately perceived an attempt by Britain to evade its obligations and fix the whole odium of international debt-collection on the USA. A representative comment: 'Lord Balfour seems to think he can call us sheep thieves in language so eloquent that we shall not understand it.'[75]

[71] Balfour to Strachey, 14 Mar. 1900, Strachey Papers S/2/4/7; Imperial Conference, 8 July 1921, PRO CAB 32/2 p. 9.

[72] 'Case for the Coalition' *Times* 12 Dec. 1919 p. 9.

[73] 'Mr. Balfour's Return' *Times* 15 Feb. 1922 p. 12; Balfour to Trevelyan, 18 Feb. 1922, BP 49792 f. 22; 'Our Washington Advocate' *Times* 21 Feb. 1922 p. 12.

[74] Borden to Balfour and reply, 26 and 29 Nov. 1921, SRO GD 433/2/16; 'Balfour Curious as to Dry Christmas' *New York Times* 5 Dec. 1921 p. 14.

[75] Despatch by Balfour, 17 July 1922, PRO CAB 24/138 CP 4112; Middlemas and Barnes *Baldwin* pp. 133–4.

It has been suggested that the great 'Atlanticist' wrote the Note against his better judgment out of loyalty to Lloyd George. This was not the case. Balfour felt very strongly that American insistence on full repayment was not only mean but unwise. He believed (as the Note said) that to generous minds it could never be agreeable to treat war debt as an ordinary commercial dealing.[76] The world economy was hopelessly confused. Financial advisers offered nothing but platitudes. Remission of Inter-Allied debt would help restore commercial relations to normality, and by far the best plan was to write it off entirely. He had tried to sound opinion in Washington:

My impression . . . is that most far-seeing statesmen would like to liquidate international indebtedness, but that there is not the slightest chance of the public at large accepting such a policy. In this connection the ordinary American firmly holds to two dogmas – (1) America must be paid. (2) America must not be paid in goods which compete with her manufactures. How these two are to be reconciled they have not yet discovered; in fact they have not yet discovered that there is any disharmony between them.[77]

It was not right to abstain from telling the truth about the international position just because a section of American opinion – 'perhaps the largest though not the best instructed' – did not want to hear it. The deeper Europe sank into the morass the greater the need for raising the flag of unselfishness. In Cabinet there had been warnings that holding up the USA as a 'Shylock' would only make matters worse. Balfour said he was prepared to run the risk, because Britain owed it to 'the best Americans' to make a proper presentation of the facts: 'I have always held that the best opinion in America is a generous one'.[78] When it is remembered that to Balfour 'the best Americans' were almost by definition Anglophile Americans, it becomes apparent that his support for the Balfour Note was not a denial of his Anglo-American creed, so much as a consequence of it.

When the pessimists were proved right, he was privately

[76] M.G. Fry *Illusions of Security* (Toronto 1972) p. 195n; Alice Balfour's diary, 10 Mar. 1923, SRO GD 433/2/136 p. 46; Balfour to Brand, 1 Aug. 1922, SRO GD 433/2/11; 8 Mar. 1923, *HLD* vol. 53 col. 341.
[77] Balfour to Malcolm, 26 Jan. 1922, SRO GD 433/2/14 no. 5; Balfour to Severin, 5 Oct. 1925, SRO GD 433/2/22 no. 85.
[78] Balfour to Brand, 1 Aug. 1922, SRO GD 433/2/11; Cabinet 42, 25 July 1922, PRO CAB 23/30.

scathing about American behaviour and disgusted by French attempts to exploit the situation. Poincaré seemed to suggest that France should give priority to direct debt to the USA; America having fought the War purely for principles, while Britain had been defending its own interests.[79] Balfour vented his bitterness in a letter to an imaginary American correspondent. 'Is no cause unselfish for those who gain by its success?' he asked. The British people had fought promptly in 1914 for the sake of all civilisation. But, if there were a next time, perhaps they would heed the lesson now being taught them and say:

If our shores are safe, why rush too hastily to the aid of France? ... Doubtless a moment would come when we could intervene to avert a peace too perilous to ourselves. Why not wait and watch events? ... As events develop it may seem wise to fight. But if so fight as late as you can. Thus will you suffer fewer losses and receive more grateful thanks. Thus will you have more to lend, and be sooner repaid.[80]

He stood by the Note. It embodied the best policy left open to Britain by the financial views of the USA.[81]

By 1923 he accepted that no definite change in US policy towards Europe was likely in the near future. To discuss anything connecting the USA with the League was evidently pointless, but he refused to believe that Americans could really disinterest themselves from the fate of common Western civilisation. The pursuit of transatlantic sympathy must continue.[82]

On the other key issue of Anglo-American relations in the 1920s, however, he was instinctively opposed to appeasement. That issue was sea-power. Naturally he did not at all want a naval race. Apart from anything else, the material resources of the USA were such that Britain could not hope to win. Yet so long as the USA and Japan were building ships competitively, Britain could not acquiesce in a policy which might leave it in third place.[83] At

---

[79] Alice Balfour's diary, 10 Mar. 1923, SRO GD 433/2/136 p. 46; 'Inter-Allied Debts – French Reply' *Times* 2 Sept. 1922 p. 8.

[80] Draft letter to an American Correspondent by Balfour, Sept. 1922, SRO GD 433/2/11.

[81] 'Mr. Snowden on War Debts' *Times* 19 Apr. 1929 p. 17.

[82] Balfour to Lamont, 10 May 1923, SRO GD 433/2/16; 'Lord Balfour on America' *Times* 7 Nov. 1924 p. 14; 'English Speaking Patriotism' by Balfour, Apr. 1923, BP 49959 ff. 308–13.

[83] Balfour to Law, 3 Mar. 1921, Bonar Law Papers 100/3/3; Balfour to Borden, 29 Nov. 1921, SRO GD 433/2/16.

the Washington Conference, he had been happy to accept parity with the USA in capital ships. Indeed he was willing to accept parity in sea-power generally, *but* he denied that 'numerical equality of cruiser tonnage meant as between Great Britain and the USA anything that deserved to be called equality of Sea Power'. The United States stood 'solid, impregnable, self-sufficient, all its lines of communication protected, doubly protected, completely protected, from any conceivable hostile attack'. The scattered British Empire needed a much larger number of cruisers to render its lines of communication equally secure.[84] These views placed Balfour among the hard-liners on the naval question. In July 1927 it was he who drafted the Government statement which effectively dissolved the Geneva Disarmament Conference in Anglo-Saxon acrimony. 'A misfortune', he admitted, 'but one that will in due time be repaired'.[85]

Fear of direct conflict with the USA scarcely entered into this. The underlying problem was American commitment to the Freedom of the Seas, when Britain wished to retain sufficient cruisers to mount an effective blockade as a legitimate act of war. Balfour felt that the Americans had become mesmerised by a phrase. If the Freedom of the Seas were taken literally, how would they enforce the Monroe Doctrine?[86] If it merely meant that American merchants should always be free to supply any belligerent, why were they so self-righteous about it? It might be good for American trade but it was not obviously moral. The whole dispute seemed to him hypothetical and short-sighted. The USA was quite capable of defending its neutral rights in any event. Would America necessarily want strong rights for neutrals in a future war?

why are we to assume that while one branch of the English-speaking peoples is fighting for some great cause to the limits of its capacity, the other will be disputing with it over belligerent rights and neutral claims? Even if such a calamity were indeed to befall us, why assume that in

---

[84] Notes by Balfour, 19 July 1927, BP 49736 ff. 308 and 309–20; Memo. by Balfour, Cabinet 43 (Appendix), 22 July 1927, PRO CAB 23/55; Memo. by Hankey, 27 Nov. 1928, PRO CAB 24/199 CP 368 p. 8; 15 Nov. 1921, *Conference* pp. 98–100; Memo. by Salisbury, Jan. 1929, BP 49758 f. 321.

[85] Cabinets 43 and 44 (Appendices), 22 and 26 July 1927, PRO CAB 23/55; 27 July 1927, *HCD* vol. 209 cols. 1246–9; D. Carlton 'Great Britain and the Coolidge Naval Disarmament Conference of 1927' *Political Science Quarterly* vol. 83 (1968) p. 588; Balfour to Tokugawa, 8 Sept. 1927, SRO GD 433/2/22 no. 145.

[86] Balfour *Freedom of the Seas* p. 5; Memo. by Balfour, 11 Jan. 1919, BP 49750 ff. 206–7.

that event America would be the neutral and the British Empire the belligerent? I prophesy that they will throughout be on the same side; but even if this forecast is not completely fulfilled, if, for example, during the first two-thirds of the supposed world-war one of the English-speaking peoples will be making all the sacrifices, while the other is making all the money, why regard it as impossible that the first role should be played by America and the second by Britain?[87]

While this problem remained unresolved, Balfour thought Britain was right to fight shy of an all-inclusive arbitration treaty with the USA. In 1928, however, he vainly urged the Government to greet American proposals for the renunciation of war more eagerly. As a treaty the Kellogg Pact was full of holes, but it would have been wiser to accept it at once as a 'gentlemen's agreement' than to quibble. A chance to promote a little amity was allowed to slip.[88]

The following year a letter from Borden expressing concern at the poor relations between London and Washington prompted Balfour's last ever Cabinet memorandum: a draft open reply setting out the British position on arbitration and belligerent rights. The Foreign Office did not want these delicate matters aired, and he was dissuaded from sending it.[89]

It was not easy being a Pan-Anglican when the USA was determinedly isolationist. 'I don't know if the Americans are faithful to the ideal', he mused in September 1929. Anglo-American cooperation still held first place in his scale of international values: 'But it is not easy to attain, and it is not always best attained by too obviously striving for it.'[90]

CONCLUSION

Balfour was in his time the pre-eminent British representative of an enduring school of international thought. Anglo-Saxonism,

---

[87] Balfour to Borden, draft, Jan. 1929, BP 49749 ff. 276–84.
[88] Memo. by Balfour, 11 July 1928, PRO CAB 24/196 CP 223; W. Hudson and J. North (eds.) *My Dear P.M.* (Canberra 1980) p. 341; J.H. Tomes 'Austen Chamberlain and the Kellogg Pact' *Millennium* vol. 18 no. 1 (1989) pp. 17 and 23.
[89] Borden to Balfour and reply, 9 Jan. and 25 Feb. 1929, BP 49697 ff. 18–22 and 27–8; Memo. by Balfour, 4 Apr. 1929, PRO CAB 24/202 CP 89; Balfour to Chamberlain and reply, 7 and 10 May 1929, BP 49736 ff. 323–5; Balfour to Borden, 2 Jan. 1930, SRO GD 433/2/16.
[90] Dugdale *Balfour* vol. II p. 401; Balfour to Churchill, draft, 1 Jan. 1929, SRO GD 433/2/19 no. 106.

English-speaking union, and 'the special relationship' form a continuous strand. The Anglo-American creed is still heard on the lips of politicians. For intellectuals, however, it seems rather to have lost its appeal. Transatlantic harmony is dismissed by some modern studies as a simple misconception. By 1900 British and American interests had clashed in the Western hemisphere, so why ever was it assumed that they would not clash elsewhere? British leaders did not merely acquiesce in the emergence of a rival; they even encouraged the USA to extend its influence beyond the American continent. 'Myth' and 'irrational' are favoured words of the iconoclasts.[91] Balfour the irrationalist conservative would not have turned a hair.

British Pan-Anglicanism has been denounced as self-deceiving and exploitative: a desperate attempt to enlist the USA in support of flagging British Imperialism, 'a hope that world leadership could be exercised by proxy'.[92] Balfour could have countered that he had a genuine commitment to *Anglo-Saxon* world leadership. He claimed to feel loyalty to a community beyond the nation State (and his utterances did hint at an awareness that Britain might not always be the dominant partner). Britain and the USA had particular interests which might clash, but if they were sufficiently conscious of common Anglo-Saxon interests, they would probably settle their differences in a peaceful and reasonable way. An effective sense of shared loyalties could see them through all but the most severe dissensions without rupture – like a family, a party, a church, or a nation.

The significance accorded to common descent, language, and political tradition was not implausible. Biological inheritance of psychological traits is not deemed inconceivable in the case of the individual, so why categorically deny it with reference to the mass? A single language facilitates communication and may encourage common thought patterns. What other eighteenth-century nation than Britain could have served as a model for American democracy?[93]

One of the more thoughtful critiques of Anglo-Americanism distinguishes a factual liberal brand (mainly American) from

[91] R. Hyam *Britain's Imperial Century 1815–1914* (London 1976) pp. 202–4; C. Lowe and M. Dockrill *The Mirage of Power* (London 1972) vol. 1 pp. 96–9.
[92] Hyam *Britain's Imperial Century* p. 202.
[93] See H.C. Allen *The Anglo-American Relationship since 1783* (London 1959) ch. 4.

an irrational romantic brand (mainly British) and concludes:

It was one thing to argue that countries with the same political beliefs have something in common, and that they should co-operate in spreading their advantages. It was quite another to deduce some mystic sympathy from a common origin, a sympathy whose major characteristic was that it need never, and could never, be tested.[94]

Within the Balfourian view of humanity, however, such distinctions are meaningless: origin, history, culture, and belief were all inextricably interwoven. It is right that a sense of community could not be scientifically tested or proven. Who could say what part Anglo-Saxon ties (as distinct from direct national self-interest) played in US intervention in the Great War? But Balfour the metaphysician was an adept at arguing that phenomena incapable of rationalistic proof could still be true. The Anglo-American thesis is not easily demolished when it has the sort of philosophical underpinning which Balfour could provide.

Given that the abstract correctness of his principle of policy remains an open question, it is still possible to ask how accurate a perception he had of actual Anglo-American relations. It is difficult to answer with precision. So many of his statements on the subject were not objective analysis but Pan-Anglican propaganda. He was certainly alert to the increasing power and international importance of the USA. His remarkable personal and social success in Washington in 1917 and 1921 suggests a good understanding of the east-coast urban Anglo-Saxon elite and their sensitivities. About the masses (of any country) it is doubtful that he had much deep knowledge. Here is scope for misperception: Balfour would not have liked thinking about democratic influences on American foreign policy any more than he had to. Three decades of transatlantic diplomacy could not have failed to teach him something about American Anglophobia and isolationism. In 1904 he had hoped for an Anglo-American alliance before the end of the Russo-Japanese War.[95] Talk of treaty commitments was later avoided, and he was not stunned to despair by the disaster of 1919. On the other hand, he had apparently spent the previous two years happily anticipating a post-war Anglo-American world order.

In 1898, Balfour affirmed that his attitude to America rested

---

[94] Campbell *Great Britain and the United States* pp. 204–5.
[95] Balfour to Lansdowne, 11 Feb. 1904, BP 49728 ff. 172–4.

on Pan-Anglican 'opinions which I have always held, which I still hold, and which, whether their full realisation be possible in my lifetime or not, I shall certainly never abandon'.[96] So it proved. His faith did not blind him to reality, but it did imbalance his vision. Signs of Anglo-American convergence tended to be magnified: they were significant steps along the high road of history. Signs of Anglo-American divergence tended to be diminished: however formidable, they were anomalous, outmoded, or temporary. This is to put it crudely. He realised that he came across as 'a man who prophesies too earnestly what he himself hopes'.[97] The politician had always to seek the unstable equilibrium between emotionalism and cynicism.[98] This was never easily done, and, when it came to Anglo-American relations, Balfour had to contend with the greatest enthusiasm of his own political life.

[96] *The Review of Reviews* vol. 17 (June 1898) p. 603.
[97] 'Mr. Balfour in Manchester' *Times* 31 Jan. 1899 p. 19.
[98] Nicolson *Peacemaking* p. 172.

CHAPTER 8

The Balfour Declaration

A great nation without a home is not right.

Balfour 1918[1]

Balfour secured his name for posterity when, as Foreign Secretary, he signed a letter to Lord Rothschild, dated 2 November 1917:

His Majesty's Government view with favour the establishment in Palestine of a national home for the Jewish people, and will use their best endeavours to facilitate the achievement of this object, it being clearly understood that nothing shall be done which may prejudice the civil and religious rights of existing non-Jewish communities in Palestine, or the rights and political status enjoyed by Jews in any other country.[2]

This was the 'Balfour Declaration'. The assignment of the Palestine Mandate to Britain, the founding of Israel, and the continuing instability of the Middle East are all in part its legacy as shaped by subsequent strife. The Declaration provoked a sharply divided response. 'There was a great stirring of the dry bones of Israel, as if in realization of the prophetic vision of Ezekiel', wrote one Zionist. 'Lord Balfour's name has become one of the immortal realities of Palestine Restored', wrote a second. To others, the Balfour Declaration was 'a tragedy which has attracted the sorrowful attention of the whole thinking world'.[3]

Balfour opined: 'No man who is incapable of idealism is capable either of understanding the Zionist Movement or effectually contributing to its consummation.' Some may find it difficult to picture him clasping Chaim Weizmann's hand with tears in his eyes,

---

[1] Meinertzhagen *Middle East Diary* p. 9.
[2] Balfour to Rothschild, 2 Nov. 1917, British Library Add. MS 41178 f. 3.
[3] P. Goodman (ed.) *The Jewish National Home* (London 1943) p. 28; Yassky to Weizmann, 27 Mar. 1930, BP 49687 f. 27; 'Falastin' Newspaper *The Balfour Declaration* (Jaffa 1929) p. 3.

and saying, 'It is not a dream'. The Balfour Declaration has been said to carry 'a different psychological atmosphere from his other achievements',[4] but his support for Zionism was not a whim or an aberration. It was a logical corollary of his political philosophy.

The first part of this chapter examines the motives behind Balfour's support for the Balfour Declaration, looking first at his Zionism and then at the politics of the Levant. The second part considers his view of Palestine after the Declaration, the development of the Jewish National Home, and the position of the Palestinian Arabs.

PART I: MOTIVES

The Balfour Declaration was the work of the Foreign Office and the War Cabinet, and the contribution of its signatory was not especially great.[5] He is yet popularly seen as the hero or villain of the piece, and his support for the Jewish National Home after 1917 was undisguised. The first post-war Jewish settlement in Palestine was called Balfouria. Polemicists, anxious to laud or denigrate the man and his motives (as well as the deed), can find such contrasting judgments as 'Balfour was a Zionist because of his anti-Semitism', and 'Anti-semitism did not in the smallest degree enter his political philosophy.'[6]

Traditional explanations of his Zionism draw on the testimony of Blanche Dugdale (said by some to be more Zionist than the Zionists). She recorded that her uncle had a lifelong interest in the Jews and an intellectual admiration for their philosophy and culture. This seems to have grown in the telling, until Balfour is said to have made an 'extensive study of Jewish history'.[7] If he did, he was diffident about displaying his knowledge. Lady Battersea (née de Rothschild) recalled his talking at length about Jews, synagogues, and alien immigration, at a house party in 1895. Chaim Weizmann, the future leader of the English Zionist

---

[4] A.J. Balfour *Speeches on Zionism* ed. I. Cohen (London 1928) p. 28; Weizmann to Ahad Ha'am, 14 Dec. 1914, *LPCW* vol. VII no. 68; Young *Balfour* p. xvi.
[5] See L. Stein *The Balfour Declaration* (London 1961).
[6] Brendon *Eminent Edwardians* p. 121; Judd *Balfour* p. 99.
[7] Rose '*Baffy*' p. xix; Dugdale *Balfour* vol. 1 p. 433; H.M. Sachar *The History of Israel* (Oxford 1977) p. 106.

Federation, still found him to have only the most naive notion of Zionism when they met in Manchester on 9 January 1906.[8] Mrs Dugdale attributes this famous meeting to Balfour's eagerness to understand why the Zionist Organisation rejected the offer of land in East Africa. In fact, it seems to have been arranged by a leading local Conservative with an eye to the Jewish vote. Balfour found Weizmann interesting, but they did not meet again for eight years.[9]

Balfour later said that it was Weizmann in 1906 who convinced him that it was vain to seek a home for the Jewish people anywhere but in Palestine. For Jews, he argued in 1918, race, religion, and geography were uniquely inter-related. A month after the Manchester meeting, however, he had assured Israel Zangwill, who favoured the Uganda proposal, that he had not altered his view that, if the Jewish community desired such a scheme, an effort should be made to carry it out.[10] There is little evidence for the 'genuine vein of Jewish mysticism' which some claim to detect in Balfour. The reconstitution of a Jewish kingdom would be an interesting experiment, he joked, and if a King of the Jews really meant the end of the world, that would be even more interesting.[11]

Significance is often given to Scriptural knowledge acquired by young Arthur at his evangelical mother's knee. In later life, he did repeatedly acknowledge the Jewish contribution to Christian religion and culture.[12] There is no trace, however, of his citing the Old Testament in support of the Balfour Declaration. When in 1918 the anti-Zionist Beaverbrook deprecated Zionist propaganda, on the ground that the Ministry of Information had no success with religious material, Balfour was indignant: 'It is true that the Jews of Palestine were a theocracy, but surely Zionism is a purely nationalistic question, just as much as that of Poland, Esthonia or

---

[8] L. Cohen *Lady de Rothschild and her Daughters 1821–1931* (London 1935) p. 250; Chaim Weizmann *Trial and Error* (London 1949) pp. 144–5.

[9] Blanche Dugdale *The Balfour Declaration* (London 1940) p. 22; G. Alderman *The Jewish Community in British Politics* (Oxford 1983) pp. 93–6; Weizmann to Khatzman, 23 Mar. 1906, *LPCW* vol. IV no. 232.

[10] Intro. by Balfour, Nahum Sokolow *History of Zionism* (London 1919) pp. xxix–xxx; I. Friedman *The Question of Palestine 1914–1918* (London 1973) p. 6.

[11] Sachar *History of Israel* p. 106; Bertie *Diary* vol. II p. 233.

[12] Dugdale *Balfour* vol. I p. 433 and vol. II pp. 216–17; B.W. Tuchman *Bible and Sword* (London 1982) pp. 83 and 311; Stein *Balfour Declaration* p. 156; 21 June 1922, *HLD* vol. 50 col. 1018.

any other of the hundred and one nationalities who now demand our support to secure their self-determination.'[13]

It was not likely, Balfour later told his niece, that he would be less keen to satisfy Jewish nationalism than any of the others. The question remains as to why he was more keen. Proffered answers sometimes fall back on vague 'psychology': sheer intellectual curiosity, an attempt to assuage guilt, 'conscience-money paid by a wealthy man to the down-trodden'. Beaverbrook's explanation was simply to cry: 'The man was a hermaphrodite!'[14]

Balfour's attitude to Jews seems at first sight contradictory. A friend of 'Natty' Rothschild, Balfour the Semitophile maintained the innocence of Dreyfus, called on golf clubs to end their bar on Jewish membership, and deemed the Jews the most gifted people since the Greeks of the fifth century.[15] Their ranks contained 'more than their proportionate share of the world's supply of men distinguished in science and philosophy, literature and art, medicine, politics and law. (Of finance and business I need say nothing.)'[16]

Balfour the anti-Semite liked Cosima Wagner and told Weizmann that he shared many of her anti-Semitic ideas. He complained of a pompous dinner with the Sassoon family, where 'the Hebrews were in an actual majority' – 'I began to understand the point of view of those who object to alien immigration!'[17]

It was the Balfour Government which legislated to exclude 'undesirable aliens'. Balfour spoke of 'the undoubted evils which had fallen upon portions of the country from an alien immigration which was largely Jewish'. Indigent Jews from Eastern Europe were widely blamed for sustaining 'sweat-shops'. The Aliens Act 1905 was not intrinsically anti-Jewish, but he was forced into print to deny that it marked the arrival of continental anti-Semitism in England. He said he would regard such a thing as a most serious national misfortune. It was imperative to prevent anti-Semitism by all legitimate means, and, human nature being what it was,

[13] Balfour to Beaverbrook, 13 Sept. 1918, PRO FO 800/204 ff. 130–1.
[14] Stein *Balfour Declaration* pp. 159–60 and 157; Young *Balfour* pp. 388 and xvi; J.A. Kidd *The Beaverbrook Girl* (London 1987) p. 52.
[15] M. Rothschild *Dear Lord Rothschild* (London 1983) pp. 31–2 and 37–8; Vincent *Crawford Papers* p. 47; Egremont *Balfour* p. 313; Stein *Balfour Declaration* p. 157.
[16] Sokolow *Zionism* p. xxxiii. He cited Bergson, Einstein, and Freud as contemporary examples of Jewish genius (Balfour *Speeches on Zionism* p. 82).
[17] Weizmann to Ha'am, 14 Dec. 1914, *LPCW* vol. VII no. 68; S. Jackson *The Sassoons* (London 1968) p. 117.

impossible to guard against so great an evil without taking measures to prevent abuse of British hospitality.[18] Oppression of Jews
tarnished the fair fame of Christendom, he told the Commons,
and if anything could be done to diminish its effects, it would be
their duty to do it. He naturally drew attention to his Government's offer of land in Uganda as an asylum.[19] Later in the year,
he sent a message of sympathy to a protest meeting about Russian
pogroms, and instructed the St Petersburg Embassy to express
concern.[20]

Not even this philanthropic stance was unequivocal. Though the
balance of wrong-doing was on the Christian side, Jews constituted
'a formidable power whose manifestations are not by any means
always attractive'. Eastern European Jews had developed
unpleasant 'self-protecting qualities'.[21] In May 1914, Balfour
endorsed a campaign demanding civil rights for Jews in Romania,
but only after much hesitation about the inutility of empty protest
which produced international bitterness.[22] Three years later, the
Foreign Secretary refused to intercede with Russia to ameliorate
conditions in the Pale of Settlement. The fact of refusal is unre-
markable – he explained the difficulty of interfering in the domestic affairs of an ally – but he went on:

> it was also to be remembered that the persecutors had a case of their
> own. They were afraid of the Jews, who were an exceedingly clever people
> ... wherever one went in Eastern Europe, one found that, by some way
> or other, the Jew got on, and when to this was added the fact that he
> belonged to a distinct race, and that he professed a religion which to the
> people about him was an object of inherited hatred, and that, moreover,
> he was ... numbered in millions, one could perhaps understand the
> desire to keep him down ... He did not say that this justified the per-
> secution, but all these things had to be considered.[23]

---

[18] 10 July 1905, *PDeb* 4th Series vol. 149 col. 155; 'Mr. Balfour and the Aliens Bill' *Times*
11 May 1904 p. 7; 'Jewish Historical Society' *Times* 6 Feb. 1906 p. 6; Stein *Balfour Declaration* p. 165.
[19] 2 May and 10 July 1905, *PDeb* 4th Series vol. 145 col. 795 and vol. 149 cols. 154 and
178.
[20] Rothschild *Dear Lord Rothschild* pp. 32–3; 'The Outrages on Jews in Russia' *Times* 9 Jan.
1906 p. 10.
[21] Balfour to Lloyd George, 19 Feb. 1919, Lloyd George Papers F/3/4/12; Sokolow *Zionism*
p. xxxii.
[22] Open letter by Balfour, 15 May 1914, BP 49745 ff. 177–9; Balfour to Montefiore, 18
Feb. 1914, and Balfour to Rothschild, 30 Jan. 1914, BP 49745 ff. 173 and 171.
[23] Conversation between Balfour and L. Wolf, 31 Jan. 1917, PRO FO 800/210 ff. 150–2.

Pity for the victims of the pogroms was not the basis of Balfour's Zionism. His susceptibility to simple humanitarian arguments in foreign policy was slight. 'Our primary duty is to our own fellow countrymen', he had reminded Parliament during the passage of the Aliens Bill. It was the men who professed a universal cosmopolitanism who did least for their country.[24]

One of the things Balfour wanted to do for Britain was keep it 'Anglo-Saxon'. It was easy to talk of the marvellous power of assimilation, but assimilation had its limits:

If there were a substitution of Poles for Britons, for example, though the Briton of the future might have the same laws, the same institutions and constitution, and the same historical traditions learned in the elementary schools, though all these things might be in the possession of the new nationality, that new nationality would not be the same, and would not be the nationality we should desire to be our heirs through the ages yet to come.[25]

Balfour was convinced of the existence of national character – indefinable, but nonetheless real. He was also convinced that it was partly inbred. Accepting that his countrymen were an amalgam of various racial strands, he did not condemn all further immigration. Given the facility of modern transport, however, unrestricted immigration might become a great national evil, and current trends gave cause for concern.[26]

Loss of population to the colonies meant that Britain experienced net emigration. Of the incomers, the largest single group were Russian Jews. The number of Jews in Britain quintupled between 1880 and 1920 from an original 60,000. In Balfour's eyes, Jewish immigration was worrying for the reason that devout Jews married Jews. He appreciated that they were obeying what they considered binding law, but he had to regret their decision.[27] Centuries might pass without their amalgamating with the rest of the population. Serious national danger was still remote, but in the future:

a state of things could easily be imagined in which it would not be to

---

[24] 10 July 1905, *PDeb* 4th Series vol. 149 col. 178.
[25] 2 May 1905, *PDeb* 4th Series vol. 145 col. 796.
[26] 2 May 1905, *PDeb* 4th Series vol. 145 col. 797.
[27] L.P. Gartner *The Jewish Immigrant in England 1870–1914* (London 1960) pp. 274 and 280; Balfour to F. Milner, 19 July 1905, Stein *Balfour Declaration* p. 165; Cohen *Lady de Rothschild* p. 297.

the advantage of the civilisation of the country that there should be an immense body of persons who, however patriotic, able, and industrious, however much they threw themselves into the national life, still, by their own action, remained a people apart, and not merely held a religion differing from the vast majority of their fellow-countrymen, but only intermarried among themselves.[28]

Were Jews thoroughly patriotic? It was of course easier for Balfour to answer with regard to Eastern Europe. Where Jews suffered official discrimination, 'their loyalty to the state in which they dwell is (to put it mildly) feeble compared with their loyalty to their religion and their race', but it was absurd to expect outcasts to shine as patriots. The word 'race' should be noted. Assimilated Jews might argue that Judaism was a universal religion, but Balfour never doubted that the Jews were a race. 'When we talk of modern man', he once explained, ' "race" is used in a meaning which is partly psychological & historical and partly physical.' He greatly doubted that the Jewish people was ethnologically pure, but through all vicissitudes it had retained 'to the full its racial self-consciousness'. The concept of race patriotism loomed large in Balfour's thinking. Jews were as much subject to it as Anglo-Saxons. In deference to the sensibilities of assimilated Jews in war-time, he heeded advice to refrain from drawing the distinction between race patriotism and State patriotism in public, but he believed it to exist.[29] The patriotisms of a Gentile Englishman formed a congruent hierarchy – loyalty to England, to Britain, to the British Empire, to the Anglo-Saxon race, to Western civilisation, to humanity. How did Jewish race patriotism fit into this?

For Balfour loyalty was an non-rational feeling instilled by Authority.[30] In respect of some of the key forces of Authority – custom, tradition, education – the British Jew was subject to two sets of influence, one British and one Jewish. The British Jew felt a sense of community with other British Jews, but which way did he broaden his loyalties thereafter? Balfour suspected that Jews were 'torn by a double allegiance'.[31] He could not be certain that they would share to a sufficient degree the common sentiments, tastes,

[28] 10 July 1905, *PDeb* 4th Series vol. 149 col. 155.
[29] Sokolow *Zionism* pp. xxxi–ii; Balfour to Zimmern, 19 Sept. 1918, Zimmern Papers vol. 15 ff. 146–7.
[30] See above pp. 34–6.
[31] Cited in Zimmern to Balfour, 16 Sept. 1918, PRO FO 800/210 f. 163.

beliefs, and prejudices, which give rise to the loyalty on which nations are built. It was this conservative conception of political community which made Balfour a Zionist.

'Is there anyone here who feels content with the position of the Jews?' he asked the Lords in 1922. The Balfour Declaration was 'a partial solution of the great and abiding Jewish problem'. That there was a Jewish problem he had no doubt. He admitted privately to being exceedingly distressed by it. It was 'as perplexing a question as any that confronts the statesmanship of Europe'. It would remain insoluble, he told Weizmann in 1914, until either the Jews became entirely assimilated, or there was a normal Jewish community in Palestine – and he had in mind Western Jews rather than Eastern.[32] If Jewish citizenship were established in Palestine, Jews whose race patriotism exceeded their State patriotism would emigrate to their homeland. The Jews who chose to stay in their adopted country would be those for whom State patriotism was paramount. Far from undermining the position of assimilated Jews, Zionism would strengthen it, for 'any danger of a double allegiance or non-national outlook would be eliminated'. English Jews would become either Englishmen or Palestinians.[33]

Balfour thought that the vast majority of Jews throughout the world were favourable to Zionism.[34] This made it the more attractive as a scheme for ridding Gentile nations of potentially disloyal Jews, but he also had a genuine sympathy for Zionism in a positive sense. Anti-Zionist Jews he found difficult to understand, but the aspirations of Zionist Jews were immediately intelligible to him, because Zionists shared some of the basic tenets of his own social and political philosophy. Zionism and Anglo-Saxonism both rested on belief in strong consciousness of race.

Liking Jewish history 'from a Tory point of view for its length', Balfour regarded Zionists as guardians of the traditions that made unassimilated Jews a great conservative force. Their efforts to revive Hebrew culture were admirable. He approved of 'the romantic movement', which encouraged 'a deep and passionate

[32] 21 June 1922, *HLD* vol. 50 cols. 1016–17; Balfour–Brandeis meeting, 24 June 1919, *DBFP* vol. IV Appendix 2; Weizmann to Ha'am, 14 Dec. 1914, *LPCW* vol. II no. 68.
[33] War Cabinet 261 and 245, 31 and 4 Oct. 1917, PRO CAB 23/4 ff. 137 and 80; Sokolow *Zionism* p. xxxiii.
[34] War Cabinet 261, 31 Oct. 1917, PRO CAB 23/4 f. 137.

interest in the past'.[35] A community was reinforced by awareness of its common heritage, and in the natural co-operation of those who shared it lay the best hope for advance. Every nation had its national genius. When the Jews came together, the full flowering of their genius would burst forth and propagate.[36] Their national home would be a 'social commonwealth' – a community which completely harmonised with their sentiments – where they would bear corporate responsibilities and enjoy corporate opportunities of a kind which they could never possess as citizens of any non-Jewish State. In such a society, Balfour agreed, Jewish idealism would find constructive channels for expression – building a nation, rather than leading revolutionary movements.[37]

Balfour believed that Zionism would benefit the whole world by rectifying an unnatural situation:

If it succeeds, it will do a great spiritual and material work for the Jews, but not for them alone. For as I read its meaning it is, among other things, a serious endeavour to mitigate the age-long miseries created for western civilization by the presence in its midst of a Body which it too long regarded as alien and even hostile, but which it was equally unable to expel or absorb. Surely, for this if for no other reason, it should receive our support.[38]

In this examination of why Balfour supported the Balfour Declaration no mention has yet been made of political interests in the Middle East, despite their playing a major part in the decision of the British Government. This is no oversight.

'Mr. Balfour did not at first see the importance of the Zionist claim from the British point of view', reported Weizmann after an interview in March 1917. The Zionist leader had expounded the material advantages likely to accrue to Britain from the restoration of the Jewish National Home only to discover that Balfour 'strongly objected to strategic or other opportunistic considerations being brought forward as an argument for assuming the

---

[35] Frances Balfour to Betty Balfour, 8 Sept. 1895, SRO GD 433/2/314; Dugdale *Balfour* vol. II p. 216; Balfour 'Race and Nationality' p. 240.
[36] Balfour *Speeches on Zionism* p. 77; Stein *Balfour Declaration* p. 157.
[37] Sokolow *Zionism* pp. xxxi–xxxii; 21 June 1922, *HLD* vol. 50 col. 1018; Balfour–Brandeis meeting, 24 June 1919, *DBFP* vol. IV Appendix 2.
[38] Sokolow *Zionism* p. xxxiv.

responsibility for Palestine'.[39] This objection, shared by few others, was not a feint.

Balfour was not a member of the Committee on Territorial Desiderata in the Terms of Peace, and he was in the USA when the War Cabinet accepted its recommendation that Britain seek definite and exclusive control over Palestine. It was argued that Britain should use the opportunity presented by the defeat of Turkey to create a solid block of territory from the Mediterranean to the Persian Gulf, thus entrenching British dominance in the region of the Indian Ocean by completing the semi-circle of South Africa, East Africa, Egypt, India, and Australia.[40] This plan was impeded by the Sykes–Picot Agreement of 1916, which divided the post-war Middle East into British and French spheres of influence, with a small internationalised Palestine. In the light of British military efforts in the Levant, this appeared unduly generous to the French. The adoption of a Zionist policy by Britain would justify renegotiation.

Balfour was out of sympathy with the whole 'New Imperialist' scheme. He did not wish Britain to abdicate the regional supremacy it had won, but he opposed efforts to extend and formalise that supremacy. Expansion would mean antagonising France and overstretching Britain. The Sykes–Picot Agreement had been made 'for a price connected with the war' – France wanted compensation for the British Protectorate over Egypt announced in 1914 – and the price should be paid without chicanery. Balfour believed that the problem with Sykes–Picot was its failure to give anything to Italy. Otherwise it might easily have been a success. A diplomatic struggle to reduce the French share of the Levant was not worthwhile. Solid international agreement was more valuable.[41]

On first hearing Sir Mark Sykes advocate a belt of British territory across the Middle East, Balfour had been sceptical of the strategic benefits:

We have always regarded this 90 or 100 miles of desert upon her eastern

---

[39] Weizmann to Scott, 23 Mar. 1917, *LPCW* vol. VII no. 323; Stein *Balfour Declaration* p. 156.
[40] D.Z. Gillon 'The Antecedents of the Balfour Declaration' *Middle Eastern Studies* vol. 5 no. 2 (1969) pp. 133–6.
[41] Eastern Committee, 5 Dec., 11 July, 26 and 18 Dec. 1918, Milner Papers dep. 137 ff. 188, 63, 253 and 222; Memo. by Balfour, 11 Aug. 1919, *DBFP* vol. IV no. 242.

side as a stronghold of Egypt; but now you propose still further east of that to give us a bit of inhabited and cultivated country for which we should be responsible. At first sight it looks as if that would weaken and not strengthen our position in Egypt.[42]

He personally favoured a peace settlement which would give Britain no new territory north of the equator. British interests in Egypt and India would be perfectly well served by the creation of an Arab kingdom in the Hedjaz, an internationalised Jewish home in Palestine, and an 'autonomous Arab protected State' in Meso-potamia: 'They will constitute "buffer States", of all the greater value to us because they have been created not for our security but for the advantage of their inhabitants.' Indeed the protector-ate over oil-rich Mesopotamia made him uncomfortable – 'a purely imperialist war aim', he called it.[43]

Balfour's aversion to acquiring responsibilities in the Middle East only increased on his learning that administration would have to reflect the philosophy of the League Covenant. That mandates were independent nations 'in the advanced chrysalis state', with Arabs eager to set up representative government and national frontiers, seemed to Balfour utter fantasy. Neither Arabs nor Jews struck him as attractive candidates for British rule. Jews were 'not always easy to deal with'. They got dreadfully perturbed over mat-ters of small moment and were carried away by the vehemence of their passions. They would be coming from all over the world with different ideas and they were temperamentally unwilling to place full confidence in their leaders.[44]

Balfour regarded Zionism and a British Palestine as separate issues and he knew where he stood on both: 'I am an ardent Zion-ist – but . . . if only our own convenience is to be consulted I should personally like someone else to take the mandate'. At the Peace Conference, he warmly advocated that it be the United States.[45] He had wanted 'to get in the Americans' as early as January 1917, when internationalisation was still envisaged. Then he impressed on Weizmann the desirability of joint Anglo-American supervision.

[42] War Committee, 16 Dec. 1915, PRO CAB 24/1 G.46 f. 243.
[43] Memo. by Balfour, 2 May 1918, PRO CAB 24/53 GT 4774; Hankey to Balfour, 12 Aug. 1918, Cecil Papers 51071A f. 51.
[44] Memo. by Balfour, 11 Aug. 1919, *DBFP* vol. IV no. 242; Balfour to Hardinge, 29 Sept. 1920, SRO GD 433/2/5 no. 68; Balfour *Speeches on Zionism* pp. 29–30.
[45] Minute by Balfour, Curzon to Balfour, 5 Aug. 1919, *DBFP* vol. IV no. 237; Balfour to Hughes, 13 Jan. 1922, Stein *Balfour Declaration* p. 619.

It is easy to see why the idea appealed to him. The British would derive additional security without additional responsibility, if their 'natural ally' protected the Jewish National Home. When Weizmann's pro-British fervour showed itself in public, Balfour was displeased: a Zionist declaration by Britain did not imply a British protectorate.[46] In June 1919, he still talked of assigning Palestine to 'the Americans or English', but he was wasting his breath. He knew that neither Lloyd George, Curzon, the Zionists, the French, nor the Americans wanted a US mandate.[47] As for a British mandate, he was not in favour of it, but he would not oppose it.[48]

Hesitant about associating Britain too firmly with the Jewish National Home, Balfour had not so much pushed for the Balfour Declaration, as had it pushed upon him by enthusiastic New Imperialists. Leo Amery talked of 'using the Jews as we have used the Scots to carry the English ideal throughout the Middle East' and saw no point in creating 'an artificial oriental Hebrew enclave'. Balfour thoroughly disagreed (and the attribution to him of a 'dream of an alliance between the British Empire and World Jewry' is wholly erroneous).[49]

It is unlikely that Balfour's arguments for Zionism, unsupported by appeals to strategic interest, would ever have secured a British commitment to a Jewish National Home. The commitment having been made, however, his belief in the value of the work did not waver. In commending the mandate to the Lords, he begged them to send to the Jews the message that Britain desired to give them the opportunity to develop their great gifts in peace and quietness. 'Are we never to have adventures?' he asked. The House thereupon declared the mandate unacceptable. 'What does it matter if a few foolish lords passed such a motion?', said Balfour privately. 'We are partners in a great enterprise', he had told the English Zionists, 'I feel assured that we shall not fail you and that you shall not fail us.'[50]

[46] Minute by Balfour, 15 Jan. 1917, PRO FO 371/3043 f. 234; Weizmann to Scott, 23 Mar. 1917, *LPCW* vol. VII no. 323; Minute by Balfour, 20 Aug. 1917, PRO FO 371/3053 f. 370.

[47] Memo. by Balfour, 26 June 1919, *DBFP* vol. IV no. 211; Weizmann to Sacher, 20 June 1917, *LPCW* vol. VII no. 435; Sykes to Balfour, 8 Apr. 1917, PRO FO 800/210 f. 124; David Lloyd George *The Truth about the Peace Treaties* (London 1938) p. 1147.

[48] 30 July 1919, Meinertzhagen *Middle East Diary* p. 25.

[49] J. Barnes and D. Nicholson (eds.) *The Leo Amery Diaries 1896–1929* (London 1980) vol. I p. 559; C. Cross *The Fall of the British Empire 1918–1968* (London 1968) p. 279.

[50] 21 June 1922, *HLD* vol. 50 cols. 1018–19 and 1034; Weizmann *Trial and Error* p. 360; Balfour *Speeches on Zionism* pp. 30–1.

PART II: THE FUTURE OF PALESTINE

Balfour did not doubt that the creation of the Jewish National Home would have 'a reverberation throughout the coming centuries'. It was a great experiment. The World War, 'parent of infinite evils', had at least one great result.[51]

To many then and since, however, the Balfour Declaration was a disastrous document – 'a paradox, meaning nothing at all, like so many other things emanating from AJB'.[52] Did 'the establishment in Palestine of a national home for the Jewish people' signify all Palestine, or only part of it? What exactly was 'a national home'? How was a national home specifically for Jews consistent with doing nothing 'which may prejudice the civil and religious rights of existing non-Jewish communities'?

The final wording of the Declaration was an attempt to mollify both assimilationist Jews and pro-Arabs. It was therefore a 'judicious blend', which left the scope and authority of the National Home to be decided.[53] Deliberate vagueness was the policy of the Government, and Balfour adhered to it, but vagueness was not present in his own mind to anything like the same degree. He had been satisfied with the Foreign Office draft of August 1917: 'His Majesty's Government accept that Palestine should be reconstituted as the national home of the Jewish people and will use their best endeavours to secure the achievement of this object and will be ready to consider any suggestions on the subject which the Zionist Organisation may desire to lay before them.'[54] There was no ambiguous 'in Palestine' here, nor any mention of the rights of non-Jews. In these ways it reflected the attitude of Balfour more accurately than the ultimate Declaration did.

Regarding the scope of the National Home, Balfour knew what he wanted. At an interview in 1919 with Brandeis, the leading American Zionist, he entirely agreed that Palestine should be the Jewish homeland and not merely that there be a Jewish homeland in Palestine. He was rebuked by a colleague for saying as much

[51] Balfour *Speeches on Zionism* pp. 127, 121, and 22.
[52] Meinertzhagen *Middle East Diary* p. 14.
[53] Amery *My Political Life* vol. II pp. 116–17.
[54] War Cabinet, Aug. 1917, GT 1803, PRO CAB 24/24 f. 12.

on other occasions.[55] The borders of Palestine were yet to be
defined, but Balfour was not disposed to be sparing. He counselled
including land east of the River Jordan up to the Hedjaz Railway,
and northward extension sufficient to ensure control of the water
supply. Anglo-Egyptian strategic interests should not prevail. Such
protection as Suez derived from the mandate was 'merely a happy
coincidence'. The main thing was to facilitate a Zionist policy by
giving the fullest scope to economic development.[56] Preference
should be given to a Zionist public utility company to prevent con-
cessionaires (British or foreign) gaining control of land and industries. The reasoning was straightforward: 'If Zionism is to influence the Jewish problem throughout the world Palestine must be
made available for the largest number of Jewish immigrants.'
Every Jew should have the right to settle in Palestine, which Balfour saw as the future home of millions.[57]

Was the National Home to be a sovereign Jewish State? A letter
asking Balfour for a press interview on this question in 1919 was
simply endorsed, 'Not to be acknowledged.' A refusal to indulge in
prediction usually served.[58] At the Cabinet meeting which
approved the Balfour Declaration, he had said that he understood
'national home' to mean:

some form of British, American, or other protectorate, under which full
facilities would be given to the Jews to work out their own salvation and
to build up, by means of education, agriculture, and industry, a real
centre of national culture and focus of national life. It did not necessarily
involve the early establishment of an independent Jewish State, which
was a matter for gradual development in accordance with the ordinary
laws of political evolution.[59]

Balfour would never have expected abiding loyalty to the British
Empire from a real centre of Jewish national culture. Among
friends and trusted Zionists he could be frank: 'My personal hope

[55] Balfour–Brandeis meeting, 24 June 1919, *DBFP* vol. IV Appendix 2; Montagu to Balfour,
20 Feb. 1919, BP 49745 ff. 184–5.
[56] Memos. by Balfour, 11 Aug. and 26 June 1919, *DBFP* vol. IV nos. 242 and 211; 18 Apr.
1919, Bonsol *Suitors and Suppliants* p. 61; Balfour to Rothschild, 2 Jan. 1920, SRO GD
433/2/5 no. 56 (also nos. 57, 59, 66, and 68).
[57] Balfour to Curzon, 7 May 1919, *DBFP* vol. IV no. 218 n. 2; Memo. by Balfour, 11 Aug.
1919, *DBFP* vol. IV no. 242; Stephen Wise *The Challenging Years* (London 1951) p. 122;
Goodman *Jewish National Home* p. 45.
[58] Murdoch to Balfour, 23 Sept. 1919, PRO FO 800/210 f. 132; Stein *Balfour Declaration*
p. 554.
[59] War Cabinet 261, 31 Oct. 1917, PRO CAB 23/4 f. 137.

is that the Jews will make good in Palestine and eventually found a Jewish State.' Jews with strong racial idealism should develop on their own lines as a nation and govern themselves.[60] For the present, he contented himself with vague murmurings about 'a delightfully poetic idea'. A Zionist State 'may prove impossible, and in any case it is not likely to become more possible if it is prematurely discussed'.[61]

Accordingly, when Curzon warned of Arab hostility, Balfour agreed that a Jewish Government of Palestine was certainly inadmissible. A few months later, he explained that 'An increase in the numbers and economic influence of the Jews and steady colonisation must precede political favours.' The policy of the Balfour Declaration meant 'definitely building for a numerical majority in the future'.[62]

In 1917, there were in Palestine 55,000 Jews and over 650,000 Arabs. 'I was very sympathetic to Arab nationalism, too', Balfour protested later, 'though I always felt that, as far as Palestine went, Arab claims were infinitely weaker than those of the Jews.' The essential claim of the Arabs to Palestine rested on the fact that they lived there, and the post-war settlement was supposed to be based on self-determination. 'There is a technical ingenuity in that plea', Balfour conceded, but 'the deep, underlying principle of self-determination really points to a Zionist policy.' Self-determination was a commendable theory, but not one to be implemented indiscriminately.[63] He recognised that the Balfour Declaration was a flagrant contradiction of the Covenant, but in Palestine, 'We deliberately and rightly decline to accept the principle'. If the present inhabitants were consulted 'they would unquestionably give an anti-Jewish verdict'. Therefore they should not be consulted. When the USA insisted on sending a Commission to assess Palestinian wishes, Balfour thoroughly disapproved.[64]

---

[60] Meinertzhagen *Middle East Diary* pp. 9 and 104; Egremont *Balfour* p. 295.
[61] Rosita Forbes *These Men I Knew* (London 1940) p. 289; Balfour to Zimmern, 19 Sept. 1918, Zimmern Papers vol. 15 f. 147.
[62] Balfour to Curzon, 20 Jan. 1919, Lloyd George Papers F/3/4/8; Balfour to Curzon, 7 May 1919, *DBFP* vol. IV no. 218; Balfour–Brandeis meeting, 24 June 1919, *DBFP* vol. IV Appendix 2.
[63] J.L. Talmon *The Unique and the Universal* (London 1965) pp. 235 and 247; Stein *Balfour Declaration* p. 160; Balfour *Speeches on Zionism* p. 26; Meinertzhagen *Middle East Diary* p. 26.
[64] Memo. by Balfour, 11 Aug. 1919, *DBFP* vol. IV no. 242; Balfour to Lloyd George, 19 Feb. 1919, Lloyd George Papers F/3/4/12; Memo. by Balfour, 23 Mar. 1919, BP 49751 ff. 249–52.

His standard justification was that 'none but pedants or people who are prejudiced by religious or racial bigotry' could deny that the Jews were an exceptional case demanding exceptional methods. Any plebiscite on Palestine would have to consult the Jews of the world, the overwhelming majority of whom favoured Zionism under a British mandate.[65]

When Arabs complained that Britain had led them to believe that Palestine would be theirs, he reproached them for ingratitude. British skill and British blood had freed their race and established Arab kings in the Hedjaz and Mesopotamia. The claim that Britain had been unjust to the Arabs was 'almost fantastic in its extravagance'. Surely they would not grudge a 'small notch' in what was now their territory?[66]

Balfour expressed hopes for a resuscitation of Arab civilisation. 'A great, an interesting, and an attractive race' had roused itself for the first time in centuries and 'pulled off one of the most successful side shows' of the War.[67] He perceived an Arab race, Arab culture, and Arab social and religious organisation – but no Arab nation. Nationality and self-government were foreign concepts, while 'overlordship is not alien to the immemorial customs and traditions of this portion of the Eastern world'. He forgot all about Arab representation at the Paris Peace Conference and never believed in constitutional self-government for Iraq and Jordan. 'Turks and allied races naturally fall under despotic government', he said – 'however you shake them about.' Confident that even President Wilson did not seriously mean to apply self-determination to 'politically inarticulate peoples', Balfour readily disregarded the claim of the Palestinians.[68]

'I do not think Zionism will hurt the Arabs', he wrote, 'but they will never say they want it.' He did not credit them with political aspirations, but only material interests: they would welcome the Jews when they saw 'the full advantages from the influx of Jewish money'. They could also expect 'liberties which under Turkish rule

---

[65] Balfour *Speeches on Zionism* p. 26; 30 July 1919, Meinertzhagen *Middle East Diary* p. 25.
[66] 21 June 1922, *HLD* vol. 50 col. 1015; Balfour *Speeches on Zionism* p. 24.
[67] 17 Nov. 1919, *HCD* vol. 121 col. 770; Balfour *Speeches on Zionism* p. 24; Council of Ten, 17 Jan. 1919, *FRUS* PPC 1919 vol. III p. 616.
[68] Memo. by Balfour, 11 Aug. 1919, *DBFP* vol. IV no. 242; Diary, 16 Jan. 1919, Cecil Papers 51131 f. 17; Meinertzhagen *Middle East Diary* p. 104; 6 Nov. 1917, *HCD* vol. 98 col. 2041; Eastern Committee, 24 Apr. 1918, Milner Papers dep. 137 f. 13.

they never dreamed of'[69] – but that was easily said, given that Balfour doubted that Arabs ever dreamed of such things at all.

He continued to deal exclusively in bland assurance. Arabs rioted in Jerusalem in 1920. In Jaffa in 1921 they revolted. There was no need to dwell on the 'imaginary wrong' which the Jewish Home would inflict on the local population, Balfour told Parliament in 1922. Visiting Palestine in 1925, he ruled out the 'preposterous suggestion' that co-operation between Arab and Jew was impossible. The tact, patriotism, and advanced civilisation of the Jews would overcome all elements of dispute. The Balfour Declaration was a policy of peace and goodwill. 'Nothing struck me so much', he said afterwards, 'as the easy way, if they were only left to themselves, in which the Jew and the Arab get on.' In fact Balfour had encountered few Arabs during his tour – Zionist precautions and a Moslem boycott saw to that. Scores of abusive telegrams were destroyed without his knowing. Cheered by crowds of Jews wherever he went, he said it reminded him of an election tour – 'but with everybody on the same side'. Only when he passed into Syria did the atmosphere change. Six thousand Arabs stormed his hotel in Damascus, French troops opened fire, and Balfour was escorted to Beirut and a waiting ship. 'Nothing compared to what I went through in Ireland!' was his comment.[70]

It is hard to believe that Balfour's soothing utterances were rooted in conviction. Arab and Jew were not less divided than Boer and Briton had been, and, far from being optimistic about reconciliation, Balfour had favoured swamping South Africa with British immigrants. He told Jewish settlers at Benjamina that the future of Palestine depended on homogeneous co-operation of the people – and instantly corrected himself, substituting 'harmonious' for 'homogeneous'.[71] Perhaps it was a Freudian slip. Seventy thousand new settlers arrived between 1922 and 1929 bringing the Jewish proportion of the population to one fifth. An economic crisis, however, had led to net Jewish emigration in 1927.[72] In March 1928, Balfour vainly called on the Cabinet to assist the

[69] Memo. by Balfour, 11 Aug. 1919, *DBFP* vol. IV no. 242; Balfour to Curzon, 7 May 1919, *DBFP* vol. IV no. 218 n. 2; Balfour *Speeches on Zionism* p. 71.

[70] 21 June 1922, *HLD* vol. 50 col. 1015; Balfour *Speeches on Zionism* pp. 95–6, 114 and 123; Storrs *Orientations* p. 436; Weizmann *Trial and Error* pp. 396 and 400.

[71] Balfour *Speeches on Zionism* pp. 95–6.

[72] 'Palestine' *Encyclopaedia Britannica* (London 1962) vol. 17 p. 134.

Zionist Organisation in raising a loan, as he was 'not so sure' that Britain had treated the 'Cinderella' of the mandatory system very generously. For once he even invoked the defence of Suez in his cause – adding that it had certainly not influenced him in 1917. Nothing had occurred since then, he maintained, to suggest the least doubt as to the wisdom of the Balfour Declaration.[73] August 1929 saw the worst communal violence in Palestine to date. Encouraged by Mrs Dugdale, Balfour assisted Zionist efforts to restrict the scope of the subsequent Commission of Enquiry,[74] having first affirmed in an open letter to Weizmann his unshaken confidence in the policy:

of again rendering Palestine the National Home of the Jewish People. That policy is in harmony with the best opinion of Western civilization in all parts of the world. To its fulfilment is promised the support of the British Empire. That pledge has been given. Depend upon it, it is not going to be withdrawn.[75]

Within a year the British Government was starting its strife-torn retreat from Balfour's vision in an attempt to pacify the Arabs.

The story that Balfour in Palestine asked 'Who are all these people in long cloaks and white head-dresses? What are they doing in this country?' is an Arabist myth. He was not so extraordinarily ignorant as to suppose that Palestine was 'empty' after the expulsion of the Turks. It is another charge that must stand – 'He was fully aware of the Arab opposition to his policy but decided to ignore it completely.'[76] In 1906, Balfour had told Weizmann that he saw no political obstacles to Zionism, only economic ones. Later he was not sure that he did not rate the Arab question the greatest problem. He yet scorned those who turned 'a microscopic gaze to anything which happens in Palestine', but 'shut their eyes to all the world effects of this policy':[77] 'Zionism, be it right or wrong, good or bad, is rooted in age-long traditions, in present needs, in

[73] Memo. by Balfour, 5 Mar. 1928, PRO CAB 24/193 no. 71; Balfour *Speeches on Zionism* p. 128.
[74] 'The Situation in Palestine' *Times* 20 Dec. 1929 p. 15; N.A. Rose *The Gentile Zionists* (London 1973) pp. 2 and 5–6.
[75] 'Palestine – Lord Balfour's Letter' *Times* 31 Aug. 1929 p. 10.
[76] Sir George Rendel *The Sword and the Olive* (London 1957) p. 121; A.L. Tibawi *Anglo-Arab Relations and the Question of Palestine 1914–1921* (London 1977) p. 367.
[77] Weizmann to Khatzman, 9 Jan. 1906, *LPCW* vol. IV no. 195; Balfour *Speeches on Zionism* pp. 23 and 115.

future hopes, of far profounder import than the desires and prejudices of the 700,000 Arabs who now inhabit that ancient land.'[78]

CONCLUSION

'I have been a convinced Zionist', declared Balfour. So he had, and it is impossible to pass overall judgment on the individual without passing judgment on the cause. Reasoning in accordance with his fundamental political beliefs, Balfour concluded that Zionism would be good for the Jews and good for the world. Before the Great War, he had not expected to see the commencement of 'Palestinian reconstruction' in his life-time.[79] When Zionism entered the ambit of practical politics, he was certainly not going to oppose it, despite his doubts about the direct advantage of the enterprise to Britain. The righting of a wrong of nineteen centuries standing became to him an ideal.

There would be difficulties, 'but there are difficulties in whatever you do'.[80] He was not alone in 1917 in failing to foresee the persistence of Arab opposition to the Jewish National Home. In the War Cabinet, only Curzon mentioned it. Balfour persisted in the belief that Western ideas of nationalism could not take root in Arab minds. He was blinded to the severity of the problems facing Zionism by the tendency to think in racial terms which made him a Zionist in the first place.

During his last illness, he told Blanche Dugdale that perhaps nothing he had done would prove of more permanent value to the world than his support for the Jewish national cause.[81] Nearly seventy years after his death, the jury is still out.

---

[78] Memo. by Balfour, 11 Aug. 1919, *DBFP* vol. IV no. 242.
[79] Balfour *Speeches on Zionism* pp. 21–2.
[80] Egremont *Balfour* p. 295.
[81] Dugdale *The Balfour Declaration* p. 5.

CHAPTER 9

The Russian Revolution

> A clear-cut policy . . . is quite impossible, and it would be folly
> if it was tried.
>
> Balfour 1919[1]

1917 – a 'blessed date' in history.[2] The Jews had won their right
to a National Home. The USA had awakened to its global duties.
Balfour always preferred to talk of these things than of the event
for which the year is more widely remembered. As Foreign Secretary, however, he was deeply involved in formulating the British
response to the Russian Revolution.

The pursuit of his personal thought on this subject can seldom
stray far from the front-line of practical politics. Russia was in
extraordinary disarray, information was unreliable, the War over-
shadowed everything, and events were moving fast. Balfour had
his work cut out framing short-term policy which would simultaneously satisfy military requirements, fractious Allies, and discordant colleagues. He therefore tended to avoid giving a clear
lead. R.H. Ullman's standard work on Anglo-Soviet relations concludes only that Balfour's views are not easy to make out.[3] His
remarks were indeed often tentative. Only when studied together
does their consistent drift becomes apparent.

Balfour did have his own opinions on the successive phases of
the Russian question, and it is these which this chapter considers.
There are five parts, covering (i) Russia at War and the February
Revolution 1914–17; (ii) initial reaction to the Bolsheviks 1917–
18; (iii) Allied intervention in Russia during the Great War 1918;
(iv) the continuance of intervention 1919; and (v) attitudes to
Soviet Communism 1920–30.

---

[1] 17 Nov. 1919, *HCD* vol. 121 col. 767.
[2] Balfour *Speeches on Zionism* p. 127.
[3] R.H. Ullman *Anglo-Soviet Relations 1917–21* (Princeton 1961–72) vol. II pp. 296–7.

PART I: PRELUDE 1914–17

Balfour was never at ease with the Anglo-Russian Entente. When the War started, he feared the consequences of Allied victory for Indian defence, since German defeat would mean a relatively stronger Russia.[4] In public he overcompensated with extravagant rhetoric: dogged fighters, splendid organisers, the Russians would secure one great success after another. When they did not, he declared himself unable to understand why vast armies failed to accomplish more. He heard that powerful influences were at work in Russia in favour of a speedy arrangement with Germany.[5] The attitude of the Russian Foreign Office was peculiar: it appeared positively to dislike the idea of bringing Greece, Italy, and Bulgaria into the Entente. More spoils for Russia without them, he supposed.[6]

The Constantinople Agreements (1915) were intended to secure Russian loyalty. Balfour knew they had to be accepted, but he still complained. Internationalisation of the Straits would have been alright, but Russian occupation was plainly injurious to British interests, and compensation should be sought. Britain was 'fighting Russia's battles on the Gallipoli Peninsula', but rewards were uncertain. Russian sentiments were probably moved more by Constantinople than by Poland: 'If they obtained what they wanted now, they might slacken their efforts in the main theatre of war.'[7] The case did not arise.

'The nation seemed determined to fight the Germans to the end', he observed more encouragingly in 1915, 'but the people abominated the Russian Court and by no means realised what part the British had played in the war.' Rather than strive to enlighten them, however, he escaped leading the British Mission to Russia in January 1917 on the plea of ill-health.[8] By then the crisis of Tsarism was manifest. Two months later the Provisional Government was in power.

[4] Asquith *Moments of Memory* p. 153; Chirol to Hardinge, 4 Aug. 1914, L. Jaffe *The Decision to Disarm Germany* (Boston 1985) p. 46.
[5] 'Ministers on the War' *Times* 10 Nov. 1914 p. 9; War Council, 13 Jan. 1915, PRO CAB 42/1 no. 16; Balfour to Nicolson, 21 Dec. 1914, BP 49748 f. 19.
[6] Balfour to Lloyd George, 5 Mar. 1915, BP 49692 ff. 227–9; Balfour to Grey, 20 July 1915, BP 49731 ff. 47–8.
[7] War Council, 3 and 10 Mar. 1915, PRO CAB 42/2 nos. 3 and 5; Balfour to Grey, 20 July 1915, BP 49731 ff. 47–8.
[8] War Committee, 23 Dec. 1915, PRO CAB 42/6 no. 13; Hardinge *Old Diplomacy* p. 206.

Balfour afterwards insisted that if 'sanguine expectations in this country were going to make the revolution in Russia a success, it ought to have been the greatest success possible'. This was a touch disingenuous. His own speeches during 1917 brimmed with hope and enthusiasm – but it was all for America. About Russia he said nothing. It was not until March 1918 that he got around to telling Parliament what an 'optimist' he was: 'we hope from the Russian Revolution there will spring up in the future as great advantages to mankind, or to the country immediately concerned, as sprang from the French Revolution'.[9] Radical opinion was thus appeased.

This tepid response did not signify covert support for Tsarism. Balfour thought that a restored autocracy would have rendered Russia once more 'a danger to her neighbours; and to none of her neighbours so much as ourselves'. Mindful of British security in Asia, he trusted that Russia would never revert to outworn military despotism.[10]

His sympathies were with the moderate reformers, but the February Revolution appeared to fit the pattern of Russian history. Government inefficiency resulted in calamity, and disgust produced reforms. The Crimean War was followed by abolition of serfdom, the Russo-Japanese War by the Duma, and the Great War by revolution. The repeated failure of Tsardom was amazing, but the opportunity had never arisen to see whether democracy could succeed. He had previously contended that free institutions in Russia could only develop slowly on the traditional root of autocracy. Revolution was no panacea, and he was doubtful 'whether these new people will do so much better than the old'. They could surely do no worse.[11]

Increasing civil disorder and military collapse soon made even this seem debatable. Balfour did not much interest himself in schemes to coerce the Russians to keep fighting. It would not have been difficult to argue the Provisional Government into a corner, but it was wiser to act on their psychology. He stressed the political value of continuing to send guns to the Eastern Front and personally disapproved of the Allied threat to cut aid unless the Provisional Government restored order. He had no intention,

---

[9] 19 Dec. 1917, *HCD* vol. 100 col. 2011; 14 Mar. 1918, *HCD* vol. 104 col. 546.
[10] Balfour to Lloyd George, 16 July 1918, Lloyd George Papers F/3/3/18.
[11] Statement by Balfour [22 Mar. 1917], *The Lansing Papers* vol. II p. 20; 4 June 1908, *PDeb* 4th Series vol. 190 col. 249.

however, of acceding to Russian requests for a conference to define
Allied war aims and facilitate a general negotiated peace. It would
be too divisive.[12]

On 7 November, the Bolsheviks seized power in Petrograd. The
amount of attention given by Balfour to the vicissitudes of the
Provisional Government over the previous eight months had certainly not been lavish. The exploits of internationalist revolutionaries over the next eight months engaged him far more. Much as
he liked to run the Foreign Office on a loose rein, he now took
to writing the despatches to Russia himself.

PART II: FIRST REACTION 1917–18

The Bolsheviks began by calling for a democratic peace without
annexations or indemnities. They demanded a general armistice,
and threatened a separate peace if the Allies failed to co-
operate.

Balfour, at the Inter-Allied Conference in Paris, recommended
that the Russians be released from their treaty obligations. A generous gesture was more likely to incline them towards the Allies
than insistence on the letter of the law. France and Italy would
not hear of it. Balfour then telegraphed a statement expressing
broad sympathy with Bolshevik war aims, while doubting that uni-
lateral abrogation of treaties would 'commend itself to a Russian
government which can claim with justice to represent the Russian
people'. He felt that Britain could not 'swallow the Bolshevik programme whole', because it included self-determination for colonial
acquisitions, but 'the general spirit in which it desires to re-
arrange the map of Europe is in harmony with our sentiments'.
He encouraged the US President to proclaim Allied objectives of
equal high-mindedness (the result being the Fourteen Points). His
message for Lenin: 'When arms have failed, rhetoric is not likely
to succeed.'[13]

The Bolsheviks opened negotiations with Germany at Brest
Litovsk on 2 December and urged belligerent peoples to overthrow

---

[12] War Cabinets 169, 215, and 217, 26 June, 15 and 17 Aug. 1917, PRO CAB 23/3; A.
Kerensky *The Kerensky Memoirs* (London 1965) p. 389; Baker *Woodrow Wilson: Life and
Letters* vol. VII p. 149; Lowe and Dockrill *The Mirage of Power* vol. II pp. 307–8.
[13] Ullman *Anglo-Soviet Relations* vol. I pp. 23–8; Balfour to Cecil, 26 Dec. 1917, BP 49738
ff. 178–80; Baker *Woodrow Wilson: Life and Letters* vol. VII p. 453.

their Governments. This suggested to many that the Reds had to be seen as avowed enemies. Balfour dissented:

If, for the moment, the Bolshevists show particular virulence in dealing with the British Empire, it is probably because they think that the British Empire is the great obstacle to immediate peace. But they are fanatics to whom the Constitution of every State, whether monarchical or republic, is equally odious. Their appeal is to every revolutionary force, economic, social, racial, or religious, which can be used to upset the existing Political organisations of mankind. If they summon the Mahometans of India to revolt, they are still more desirous of engineering a revolution in Germany. They are dangerous dreamers ... who would genuinely like to put into practice the wild theories which have so long been germinating in the shadow of the Russian Autocracy.[14]

Even Trotsky, the dubious 'International Jew' who was First Commissar for Foreign Relations, was probably a sincere zealot rather than a traitor. Given the alternatives of working with him, defying him, or doing nothing, Balfour felt 'compelled, with whatever misgivings, to accept the first'.[15]

He maintained that the sole British interest in Russian affairs at this time was how they affected the War. The main offensive weapon left to the Allies was the blockade.[16] If Germany won control of Russian economic resources its efficacy would be fatally impaired, but Russia was not easily over-run without local compliance. The Bolsheviks would probably retain their ascendancy for a few months only, but to antagonise them needlessly would be to throw Russia into the arms of Germany. He would rather deal with them in a businesslike fashion, and 'seek to influence Russia to give to any terms of peace that might be concluded with the enemy a bias in our favour'. He declared: 'I am clearly of the opinion that it is to our advantage to avoid as long as possible an open breach with this crazy system. If this be drifting, then I am a drifter by deliberate policy.'[17]

Admittedly there were ample grounds for cutting off relations. The Bolsheviks broke treaties, repudiated debts, and openly

[14] Memo. by Balfour, 9 Dec. 1917, PRO CAB 24/35 GT 2932.
[15] War Cabinet 327, 21 Jan. 1918, PRO CAB 23/5; Balfour to Reading, 29 Apr. 1918, Milner Papers dep. 364 f. 244.
[16] David Lloyd George *War Memoirs* 2nd edn (London 1938) vol. II pp. 1555–6; Memo. by Balfour, 8 Nov. 1917, PRO FO 371/3086 f. 267.
[17] Memo. by Balfour, 9 Dec. 1917, PRO CAB 24/35 GT 2932; War Cabinet 295, 10 Dec. 1917, PRO CAB 23/4.

engaged in subversion; and they were unlikely to modify their behaviour. Transformation of international war into class war was the whole basis of their position. Their very unreasonableness was still in one respect a virtue: no other party was likely to give the Germans more trouble when it came to getting supplies out of Russia.[18]

He was therefore prepared to view them 'with a certain amount of favour'. Mainly Jews, they were without all statesmanship, but at least they showed decisiveness. Balfour felt no sympathy for the Reds. They were 'not angels of light!'. There was simply a basis for limited co-operation: 'Both the Bolsheviks and ourselves want to bring about the end of militarism in Central Europe.'[19] Accordingly:

In so far as the Bolshevists are opposing or embarrassing our enemies, their cause is our cause. In so far as they endeavour to ferment revolution in this or in any other allied country we shall thwart them to the best of our ability. In so far as they are dealing with the parts of the country where they are the *de facto* rulers, we have no desire to interfere.[20]

Balfour suffered the Bolshevik representative, Litvinov, to stay in Britain and communicated informally with the Soviet Foreign Ministry through an acknowledged intermediary.[21] Full recognition of the Bolsheviks he ruled out. Large areas currently repudiated them, so their claim to be the Government of all Russia was no better than that of various anti-Bolshevik bodies. To deal with Trotsky at all was to risk alienating counter-revolutionaries who might rule Russia tomorrow. The only way to mitigate this danger was to withhold diplomatic recognition and 'keep ostentatiously clear of internal disputes'. Balfour saw fit 'to put our *de facto* relations with all the *de facto* Governments in Russia on an equality'. His deputy, Cecil, attacked this as betrayal of anti-German Whites whom Britain should be supporting. 'To abandon friends is treachery', Balfour replied; 'To do something for your friends which they do not like is not treachery.'[22]

---

[18] War Cabinets 324, 327, and 340, 17 and 21 Jan. and 7 Feb. 1918, PRO CAB 23/5.
[19] Balfour to Wiseman, 30 Jan. 1918, PRO CAB 24/42 GT 3624 Appendix II; Imperial War Cabinet 19, 20 June 1918, PRO CAB 23/41; Jones *Whitehall Diary* p. 50; Lloyd George *War Memoirs* vol. II p. 1557.
[20] Balfour to Lockhart, 21 Feb. 1918, Milner Papers dep. 364 ff. 43–4.
[21] War Cabinets 322 and 340, 15 Jan. and 7 Feb. 1918, PRO CAB 23/5; R.H. Bruce Lockhart *Retreat from Glory* (London 1934) p. 12; Lloyd George *War Memoirs* vol. II p. 1556.
[22] War Cabinets 324 and 340, 17 Jan. and 7 Feb. 1918, PRO CAB 23/5; Ullman *Anglo-Soviet Relations* vol. I pp. 68–9; Balfour to Reading, 29 Apr. 1918, Milner Papers dep. 364 f. 244; 8 Feb. 1918, Jones *Whitehall Diary* p. 51.

Balfour wanted the Allies to avoid taking sides in Russia, but he did not accept that this meant complete non-interference. He hoped to achieve impartiality by showing willingness to work with all factions. The Bolsheviks could no more expect Britain to repudiate loyal Allies, than Britain could expect the Bolsheviks to stop promoting revolution. 'The very principles which induce us to co-operate with the Bolshevists', he wrote, 'urge us to support any forces in Russia which seem likely to offer resistance to our enemies.'[23]

PART III: INTERVENTION 1918

Balfour and Lloyd George were at one on the wisdom of tolerating the Bolsheviks, but from the French Government and the British War Office especially came insistent calls for unequivocal support for the pro-Allied counter-revolution. Balfour himself approved of retaining Allied troops to defend military stores at Archangel and Murmansk, and, in November 1917, he had advocated contact with the anti-Bolshevik General Kaledin of the Don Cossacks. The aim was to secure passage for the retreating Romanian army through south-west Russia to Mesopotamia. He deprecated premature action, however, which 'would be taken as committing us definitely to support Kaledin as against Russian Government'. In his absence, the War Cabinet decided to give Kaledin open-ended financial aid to set up a southern Russian federation. Balfour probably spoke more sincerely for himself than for his Government when he later protested that the Allies had merely grasped at 'the most shadowy chance of helping the Roumanian Army and hindering German supplies'.[24]

By January 1918 it was apparent that these anti-Bolshevik forces could offer no effective resistance to the Germans without significant Allied assistance. The inter-departmental Russia Committee recommended inviting Japan to land forces in Vladivostock, take control of the Trans-Siberian Railway, and link up with the White Russians. When the French aired similar ideas at the

---

[23] Balfour to Lockhart, Feb. 1918, Lloyd George *War Memoirs* vol. II pp. 1556–7 and Milner Papers dep. 364 f. 44.
[24] Ullman *Anglo-Soviet Relations* vol. I pp. 42–6; Balfour to Bertie, 2 Dec. 1917, Milner Papers dep. 366 f. 38 (Cf. ff. 40–1); War Cabinet 295, 10 Dec. 1918, PRO CAB 23/4; Balfour to Lockhart, 21 Feb. 1918, Milner Papers dep. 364 f. 44.

previous Inter-Allied Conference, Balfour had leant over to House and said, 'Did you ever hear of such proposals?' Now he simply referred the Committee report to the War Cabinet under a cool covering letter, pointing out that Japanese intervention would be peculiarly offensive to the Russians (on account of the Russo-Japanese War) and highly objectionable to the Americans (on account of their fear of Japanese expansionism). How could the Japanese or anybody else protect 3,000 miles of railway in a foreign and perhaps hostile country? It had to be presumed that the Bolsheviks would resist, and the Japanese would probably only occupy districts which particularly interested Japan and not extend far west.[25] The War Cabinet nevertheless thought it worth approaching Japan and the USA.

The Americans duly objected, and Balfour intimated that he agreed with them for the present. On 18 February 1918, he told the US Ambassador that the scheme had been abandoned.[26] The War Office thought otherwise.

Balfour conceded that, without intervention, organised anti-enemy influence in Russia would gradually disappear. The alternative was to trust to the inherent difficulties which a chaotic country would present to German penetration. It seemed to him 'a most serious thing to adopt any policy which might revive the moribund patriotism of Russia, and, by the very act which gives it new vigour, turn its whole strength against us'.[27] The War Cabinet, however, ordered renewed efforts to win American support for military action, and Balfour complied. Always present to his mind was the danger that the Japanese might invade Eastern Siberia of their own accord – incurring all the evils of intervention and few of the advantages.[28]

On 3 March 1918 'all previous discussion on previous lines' was rendered useless when the Bolsheviks accepted punitive German

---

[25] J. Keep (ed.) *Contemporary History in the Soviet Mirror* (London 1964) p. 293; Note by Balfour, 19 Jan. 1918, PRO CAB 24/40 GT 3421; Russia Committee, 22 Feb. 1918, PRO WO 106/1560 ff. 51–2; Balfour to Milner, 19 Jan. 1918, PRO FO 800/203 f. 294; War Cabinet 330A, 24 Jan. 1918, PRO CAB 23/13; Balfour to Rodd, 6 Feb. 1918, BP 49745 f. 6.

[26] Page to Lansing, 24 Jan. and 18 Feb. 1918, *FRUS* Russia 1918 vol. II pp. 33 and 48.

[27] Memo. by Balfour, 14 Feb. 1918, PRO CAB 24/42 GT 3624.

[28] Ullman *Anglo-Soviet Relations* vol. I pp. 88–9; Page to Lansing, 18 Feb. 1918, *FRUS* Russia 1918 vol. II p. 49; Drummond to Wiseman, 26 Mar. 1918, BP 49741 f. 68; Balfour to Lockhart, 13 Apr. 1918, Milner Papers dep. 364 f. 213.

peace terms in the Treaty of Brest Litovsk. Balfour told the Americans that he changed his mind about intervention.[29] If this was all the resistance the Reds could put up, a US–Japanese expedition to Siberia might be a risk worth taking. He began to talk about stimulating a national revival. 'Our only chance', he wrote, 'is to give the patriotic elements in the community, to whatever party they may belong, a solid Allied nucleus round which they can organise themselves'. Unabating disorder might prompt a Tsarist counter-revolution under German auspices.[30] 'The Bolsheviks have done nothing to help themselves,' he complained; 'they make it as difficult as possible for us to help them.' Still he did not give up: 'What we must if possible get them to do is to postpone the anti-bourgeois millennium until they and we have beaten the Germans.'[31] Trotsky, performing a desperate diplomatic balancing act, assured the British that he had capitulated at Brest Litovsk only to buy time.

It was intervention at Bolshevik invitation that Balfour now favoured. That way the Reds would not join hands with the enemy, and America could participate with a clear conscience. He reasoned that Bolshevik options were limited. If they accepted German domination, they could 'surely not complain of the Allies in sheer self-defence taking independent action, provided that this action does not threaten the integrity and independence of Russia'. If they fought the Germans alone, the result would be a new surrender and partition. There was a third choice: if the Bolsheviks were genuine in asserting that they wished to carry on the war, why did they not seek support from Japan?[32]

In April 1918, he thought there was a real prospect of the Bolsheviks agreeing. 'Our Russian friends' were beginning to learn that 'you cannot secure peace by fine phrases'. Trotsky was indeed discussing terms, but he kept insisting that Japan play only a

[29] Balfour to Lockhart, 21 Feb. 1918, Milner Papers dep. 364 f. 43; Seymour *Intimate Papers of Colonel House* vol. III pp. 409–10.
[30] Balfour to Reading, 15 and 29 Apr. 1918, Milner Papers dep. 364 ff. 218 and 245–6; Reading to Lansing, 25 Apr. 1918, *FRUS* Russia 1918 vol. II p. 135; Balfour to Lloyd George, 16 July 1918, Lloyd George Papers F/3/3/18; 14 Mar. 1918, *HCD* vol. 104 cols. 549–54.
[31] Balfour to Lockhart, 13 Mar. 1918, Milner Papers dep. 364 ff. 105–7; Apr. 1918, Dugdale *Balfour* vol. II p. 256.
[32] Balfour to Lockhart, 6 Mar. 1918, Milner Papers dep. 364 ff. 79–81.

subordinate role. 'No wonder there are sceptics about his sincerity', observed Balfour.[33]

In May the Germans resumed their attack. Balfour was astounded when Trotsky continued to raise objections. What 'explanation consistent with honour and patriotism' could be given of Bolshevik conduct?[34] Balfour had clearly failed to grasp the Marxist-Leninist mentality. Underlying his approach, indeed, had been the hope that the Russians, if really pressed, would hate their German invaders more than their domestic opponents. To Lenin, however, the class war was paramount – Whites, Germans, Allies; they were all so many reactionary enemies. When the German-Ukrainian offensive eased, Trotsky ceased to show any interest in Allied help. There would be no invitation from Moscow. Nor was there as yet any American approval for intervention.

The German spring offensive in the west was now thirty-seven miles from Paris. The cry arose for immediate Japanese action to re-open the Eastern Front. Balfour resisted it and warned that intervention without the USA was foredoomed to failure. The Associated Powers would be split. Japan would undertake no important expedition on its own, and American disapproval 'would be even more injurious to the moral aspect of the enterprise than it would be to the material'. It was obvious that the USA had no territorial ambitions in Russia; but Japanese motives were open to suspicion. The Russians might well treat their would-be saviours as enemies. He concluded that Allied action 'would have to be confined to what we could do at Archangel and Murmansk, and by diplomacy and promises of material and financial assistance'.[35] Exasperated interventionists thereupon tried to oust him from the Foreign Office.[36] The compromise: yet another appeal to the USA.

Events in Russia then took over. The Allied Czech Legion became embroiled with the Bolsheviks. Balfour had favoured keeping the Czechs in Russia, 'particularly as they were Slavs'. Now he joined in persuading President Wilson to send 7,000 American soldiers to Siberia to assist 7,000 Japanese in rescuing them. Then

---

[33] Balfour to Greene, 9 Apr. 1918, Milner Papers dep. 364 f. 193; 'America Day' *Times* 8 Apr. 1918 p. 3; Balfour to Lockhart, 8 Apr. 1918, Milner Papers dep. 364 ff. 185–7.

[34] Balfour to Lockhart, 4 and 6 May 1918, Milner Papers dep. 364 ff. 261 and 273.

[35] Memo. by Balfour, 29 May 1918, M. Kettle *The Road to Intervention* (London 1988) pp. 159–60; Balfour to Milner, 19 Jan. 1918, PRO FO 800/203 f. 293; War Cabinet 421, 30 May 1918, PRO CAB 23/6.

[36] Milner to Cecil and reply, 13 June 1918, Cecil Papers 51093 ff. 180–1.

it was only necessary to show that military considerations demanded more troops. By August, the Americans were in, and large-scale intervention was on.[37]

Whatever the Allies might proclaim, he appreciated that it would prove 'almost impossible to prevent intervention having some (perhaps a great) effect on Russian Parties'. When the Bolsheviks unleashed 'Red Terror' on Allied sympathisers, impartiality became a dead letter. He agreed to publicise Red outrages and hoped a non-Bolshevik military government would emerge under some outstanding Russian personality, but he was not confident. The Allies were uncoordinated and the Whites would probably soon be fighting each other.[38]

PART IV: INTERVENTION CONTINUED 1919

At the end of the Great War, the Allies were 'faced with a serious state of things in Russia'.[39] The main justification of intervention – to prevent German absorption – had no further force, but the troops were engaged. The presence of Germans, Austrians, Japanese, British, French, Czechs, and Americans compounded the ideological and nationalist conflicts of Reds, Whites, Finns, Estonians, Letts, Lithuanians, Poles, Romanians, Ukrainians, Cossacks, Georgians, Armenians, Azeris, and others.

'Russia is in a state of septic dissolution', Balfour remarked. The infection threatened to spread to Hungary, Austria, and even Germany. Militarism in its fall had shaken the whole social fabric. Inevitably each country 'according to its national characteristics' would show unmistakable signs of the ordeal. Europe faced a whirlpool of discontent; 'a wild striving for anything that is new, an unthinking desire to destroy everything that is old'. Russian society was singularly ill-equipped to withstand the storm, because it lacked the sense of national unity which prevailed in other civilised countries. Russia had been a military empire sustained by an autocracy, which had 'showed itself quite incapable of bringing

---

[37] War Cabinet 393, 17 Apr. 1918, PRO CAB 23/6; War Cabinet 409A, 11 May 1918, PRO CAB 23/14; Kettle *Road to Intervention* pp. 247, 265, and 322–3.

[38] Balfour to Lloyd George, 16 July 1918, Lloyd George Papers F/3/3/18; War Cabinets 475 and 478, 20 and 26 Sept. 1918, PRO CAB 23/7; Balfour to Eliot, 9 Sept. 1918, Milner Papers dep. 367 ff. 338–9.

[39] War Cabinet 489, 18 Oct. 1918, PRO CAB 23/8.

into existence that frame of mind which makes a great self-conscious nation independent of the particular form which its institutions may have at the moment'. Now nothing was left but an agglomeration of villages, 'lying there in Europe and in Asia', surrounded by small communities of different race, language, and religion, each of which now wanted self-determination.[40] This was the picture which Balfour had in mind when he addressed the key question: should Allied involvement continue?

Apparently ambivalent, he acquiesced in Lloyd George's plan to end hostilities but had no faith in it. The offer of negotiations at Prinkipo earnt his approval purely as a means of placating Anglo-American public opinion and putting the Bolsheviks in the wrong. He also let Churchill appeal for massive intervention, but gave him no support.[41] In the absence of a conclusive decision, Allied action against the Bolsheviks continued in a half-hearted way, dwindled, and eventually ceased – and this was essentially what Balfour favoured from the first. The position was illogical and embarrassing, but he thought a clear-cut Russian policy neither possible nor appropriate.[42]

'It seems commonly supposed', he wrote in November 1918, 'that these military expeditions are partial and imperfect efforts to carry out a campaign against Bolshevism, and to secure, by foreign intervention, the restoration of decent order and a stable Government.' That was a complete misapprehension. It was for Russians to determine their own regime: 'If Russia chose to be Bolshevik, we should not gainsay it.' Intervention was a war measure. It did not follow, however, that Britain could disinterest itself from Russian affairs. Anti-Bolshevik administrations had grown up under the shelter of Allied forces. 'We are responsible for their existence and must endeavour to support them', he maintained:

---

[40] 'National Problems' *Times* 2 Dec. 1918 p. 10; 'Case for the Coalition' *Times* 12 Dec. 1919 p. 9; 14 Mar. 1918, *HCD* vol. 104 cols. 547 and 551.

[41] C.E. Callwell *Field-Marshal Sir Henry Wilson* (London 1927) vol. II p. 167; Lloyd George *Truth about the Peace Treaties* vol. I pp. 320 and 346–7; Council of Ten, 15 Feb. 1919, *FRUS* PPC 1919 vol. IV pp. 17–18; Balfour to Churchill, 16 Feb. 1919, BP 49694 f. 158; Ullman *Anglo-Soviet Relations* vol. II pp. 127–8.

[42] Empire Delegation 8, 17 Feb. 1919, *BDFA* vol. 3 no. 50; Minute by Balfour, Curzon to Balfour, 21 Aug. 1919, and Balfour to Curzon, 27 Aug. 1919, *DBFP* vol. III nos. 399 and 405; 17 Nov. 1919, *HCD* vol. 121 col. 767.

'How far we can do this, and how such a policy will ultimately develop, we cannot yet say.'[43]

The only Bolshevik peace proposal in which Balfour showed interest was one which left all *de facto* Governments in control of the territory they currently held.[44] It seemed, however, that Bolshevism was deliberately aggressive. In his opinion, Red activities in Finland, Poland, and the Baltic States did constitute invasion rather than internal revolution. Everyone wanted 'a stable and coherent Russia in some manner comparable to the Russia that existed before the war' – but it should have new borders. National communities had 'plucked up courage to set up organisations', and it should not be assumed that they would not consolidate themselves. First axiom: 'It was one thing not to intervene in Russia; it was another to allow this tide of Bolshevism to destroy the independence and civilisation of these States.' Measures to stem the tide were also justified in self-defence. Immediate withdrawal from Russia would have entailed a serious loss of prestige. Second axiom: 'It was one thing to let the Bolsheviks 'stew in their own juice', but it was quite another to submit to being stewed in theirs'.[45]

Lithuania, Latvia, and Estonia were the objects of his especial sympathy. Distinct in race, language, and religion, and far superior to Russians in culture, they had retained their individuality despite oppression. It could not be Allied policy to deliver the Baltic provinces or Finland to their former yoke.[46] Nor should the Germans be left in control. He vainly sought Scandinavian assistance in arming and policing the new States, and called for more Allied aid.[47] A show of British naval strength in the Baltic was arranged at his instigation, and he later favoured a blockade

---

[43] Memo. by Balfour, 29 Nov. 1918, Milner Papers dep. 365 ff. 260–3; Imperial War Cabinet 45, 23 Dec. 1918, PRO CAB 23/42.

[44] I.e. The Bullitt Mission. W. and Z. Coates *Armed Intervention in Russia 1918–1922* (London 1935) p. 155; L. Fischer *The Soviets in World Affairs* (Princeton 1930) vol. I pp. 172–3.

[45] Imperial War Cabinets 45 and 41, 23 and 3 Dec. 1918, PRO CAB 23/42; Empire Delegation 1, 2, and 8, 13 and 20 Jan. and 17 Feb. 1919, *BDFA* vol. 3 nos. 43, 44, and 50; War Cabinets 511 and 489, 10 Dec. and 18 Oct. 1918, PRO CAB 23/8.

[46] Note by Balfour, 18 Oct. 1918, PRO CAB 24/70 GT 6356; War Cabinet 502, 14 Nov. 1918, PRO CAB 23/8; Imperial War Cabinet 41, 3 Dec. 1918, PRO CAB 23/42.

[47] H.R. Rudin *Armistice 1918* (Yale 1944) pp. 296, 301, and 311–12; War Cabinet 502, 14 Nov. 1918, PRO CAB 23/8; Council of Foreign Ministers, 9 May 1919, *FRUS* PPC 1919 vol. IV pp. 687–8; Memo. by Balfour, 10 June 1919, BP 49750 ff. 31–40.

of the Bolsheviks so long as they continued to fight the separatists. Containment of Bolshevism was a factor in this. It being desirable to stop the Reds driving a wedge between Finland and Poland, Balfour would have been sorry to see any peace which gave them access to the Baltic.[48] He conceded that the weakness of the new States was a problem. Russian or German suzerainty might have been the solution, had either Power been genuinely democratic. Perhaps the Baltic States would desire federal union with a reformed Russia in the future. He hoped they would federate with each other, 'and if possible join some larger Baltic aggregation including Finland and some or all of the Scandinavian Powers', but it would have to be on their own initiative.[49] Foreseeing 'a perpetual tendency on the part of renovated Russia to re-absorb these smaller communities', he wrote in May 1919: 'We shall be bound to protect them; but if the new Germany and the new Russia combine to dominate or destroy them, our task will not be an easy one.' He could only suggest making future assistance to Germany and Russia conditional on recognition of the frontiers of the new nations. In return, Russia might be offered unimpeded commercial access to the outside world, and a debt settlement apportioning the succession States a fair share of the old Empire's liabilities.[50]

In the south, Balfour supported the transfer of Bessarabia to Romania, but he dismissed the separatist Ukraine as an artifice of German Professors. Its population did not differ noticeably in race, religion, or language from that of Central Russia. Nor did the Don Cossacks.[51]

Transcaucasia was different – its peoples the victims of alien tyranny. His observations often sounded contradictory, however, for, while he *did* want Georgia, Armenia, and Azerbaijan to be independent, he did *not* want them to come under British influence. His Central Asian strategy was always to keep Russia and Britain far

---

[48] Imperial War Cabinet 37, 20 Nov. 1918, PRO CAB 23/42; Heads of Delegations, 15 and 25 July and 29 Aug. 1919, *DBFP* vol. I nos. 11, 18 (App. D), and 46; Inter-Allied Meeting, 12 Dec. 1919, *DBFP* vol. II no. 56.

[49] Note by Balfour, 18 Oct. 1918, PRO CAB 24/70 GT 6356; Imperial War Cabinet 41, 3 Dec. 1918, PRO CAB 23/42.

[50] Notes by Balfour, 9 May 1919, BP 49751 ff. 339–40.

[51] Council of Ten, 12 Jan. 1919, *FRUS* PPC 1919 vol. III p. 502; Imperial War Cabinet 41, 3 Dec. 1918, PRO CAB 23/42; Balfour to Curzon, 10 July 1919, *DBFP* vol. III no. 306.

apart. The deployment of British troops in the Caucasus therefore alarmed him, although he reluctantly conceded the need to thwart Bolshevik designs on Persia and India. He tried to foist a Transcaucasian Mandate on Italy and America. If no one else would protect the republics, it would be folly for Britain to try. Ultimately: 'If Russia is in a position to crush them, why not?'[52]

It comes as no surprise that Balfour showed less interest in anti-Bolshevik authorities in Russia proper. He did in December 1918 write a message of support for Admiral Kolchak's Government at Omsk (at the prompting of British military representatives), but he changed his mind the next day and cancelled it. By January it was plain to him that the Whites were merely leaning on foreign troops.[53] Had they been more effective, endless trouble could still have arisen from an essential inconsistency in Allied policy. Britain was backing both patriotic Great Russians and national separatists, while it was 'unfortunately true that the only Russian party which has shown itself favourable to the policy of self-determination in these non-Russian parts of Old Russia is the Bolshevist gang'.

Balfour did acknowledge some moral responsibility to the Whites, but his motives were expedient. In early 1919, he repeatedly warned that the Red Army would probably be formidable by the summer. The obvious conclusion: intervention should cease. The prudent proviso: keep quiet about it. A premature announcement of withdrawal would destroy the morale of the Whites. They would be beaten before they were attacked, 'and it might be difficult for us even to retire in dignified security'. Allied troops could hardly leave ice-bound ports until summer, and much might happen between February and June. The Soviet Government 'should at any rate be given the chance of tumbling into ruins under its own weight'. There was another good reason for maintaining small-scale intervention for a while. An all-out Bolshevik assault on Poland, Finland, and the Baltic States was what Balfour most feared. If the Reds were not to devote their whole energies

[52] Eastern Committee, 9 and 16 Dec. 1918, Milner Papers dep. 137 ff. 199–201, 208, and 210; Imperial War Cabinets 41, 42, and 45, 3, 12, and 23 Dec. 1918, PRO CAB 23/42; Ullman *Anglo-Soviet Relations* vol. II pp. 227–31; Balfour to Lloyd George, 9 Aug. 1919, PRO CAB 24/86 GT 7949.
[53] Ullman *Anglo-Soviet Relations* vol. II pp. 41–2; Balfour to Alston, 23 and 24 Dec. 1918, Milner Papers dep. 367 ff. 463–4; Council of Ten, 21 Jan. 1919, *FRUS* PPC 1919 vol. III p. 641.

to the west, it was wise to maintain pressure on them in the north, south, and east. In effect, the Whites were to be kept fighting to help secure independence for the very provinces which they wished to retain.

Outraged Whites would ultimately accuse their foreign friends of tearing Russia apart and abandoning it to Bolshevik brutality. Balfour deemed such reproach grossly unfair and sadly unavoidable. The White Russians had been extraordinarily unreasonable. Although utterly dependent on Allied help, they were quite impervious to Allied advice: 'Should we decide to leave Russia to her fate, it will not be for these gentlemen to criticise our action.'[54]

Bolshevism latterly demanded his attention in Paris primarily in its Hungarian manifestation. He supported strong steps against revolutionary Hungary, because its flouting of the armistice undermined the authority of the Peace Conference. He 'wished it to be understood that he was not animated by any consideration of Hungarian internal politics, little though he might approve of Bela Kun'.[55] For the details of Russian affairs he showed slight concern. Reassuring Curzon that an unvarying policy was inapplicable to the ever-varying phases of the Russian tragedy, he wrote in 'ever-varying phases' after crossing out 'inconsequent follies'. When Lloyd George announced the end of British intervention in November, Balfour gave him full support in Parliament. Nobody desired the continuance of Bolshevism, but who would defend the use of a single British soldier in the domestic conflicts of Russia? The Baltic and Caucasian States had been given their chance. And the rest? 'It was impossible for us to do any good in Russia', he remarked privately: 'the people were not against the Bolsheviks; indeed there was something to be said for the view that the Bolshevik government was the best Russia has ever had'.[56]

PART V: AFTERMATH 1920–30

Very little public condemnation of the Soviet regime had come from Balfour. While acknowledging that it favoured starvation,

---

[54] Memo. by Balfour, 15 Feb. 1919, BP 49751 ff. 320–1; Memo. by Balfour, 26 Feb. 1919, BP 49751 ff. 324–31; Notes by Balfour, 9 May 1919, BP 49751 ff. 335–8; Imperial War Cabinet 45, 23 Dec. 1918, PRO CAB 23/42; Empire Delegation 8, 17 Feb. 1919, *BDFA* vol. 3 no. 50.

[55] Heads of Delegations, 5, 17, 25 and 26 July 1919, *DBFP* vol. 1 nos. 3, 13,17, and 19.

[56] Balfour to Curzon, 27 Aug. 1919, BP 49734 f. 162; 17 Nov. 1919, *HCD* vol. 121 cols. 766–7; Egremont *Balfour* pp. 305–6.

murder, and wholesale execution, he restricted his objections to its external policy.[57] His comment on Churchill's anti-Red orations: 'I admire the exaggerated way you tell the truth.' Balfour was confident that he could refute Marxism-Leninism. He joked in October 1919 that he was disappointed in the Bolsheviks: 'They have gone back on all their principles.'[58] It was not until 1924 – a Labour Government, diplomatic recognition of the USSR, the Anglo-Russian Treaty, the Zinoviev letter, and a turbulent General Election – that anti-Communism entered his speeches.

Having observed over decades the rise of a 'general Socialistic feeling' in European politics, he attributed it in part to a reaction against the excesses of mid-nineteenth-century liberalism. He favoured co-operatives and profit-sharing as means of harmonising the interests of hirers and hired. 'We shall never see Socialism in a country like England', he had asserted in 1894. It was an ideology doomed to failure. History offered no example of 'a great and sudden social revolution really dealing with every relation of life coming from within a society itself'. Gradual collectivisation, however, would only demonstrate the indispensability of individual incentives. A nation reliant on trade could not risk this futile experiment.[59]

After the War, Balfour wanted Conservatives and Liberals to combine against Socialism. The Zinoviev letter confirmed that on critical occasions the Labour Party 'was really the tool of foreign criminal conspirators', and a majority Labour Government would spell ruin and even starvation.[60] Socialism meant class warfare – what good could flow from a creed based on hatred? The condition of Russia illustrated its utter failure.[61]

How was Britain to deal with the Soviets, when 'these pariahs had announced war against the civilized world, and made no secret of their intentions to set class against class and upset industry and

[57] 18 Nov. 1918, *HCD* vol. 110 col. 3175; 12 Feb. 1920, *HCD* vol. 125 col. 308.
[58] M. Gilbert *Winston S. Churchill* (London 1971–88) vol. IV p. 356; Lockhart *Retreat from Glory* pp. 12–13.
[59] 'Mr. Balfour on the Politics of the Future' *Times* 22 June 1894 p. 11; 20 Feb. 1907, *PDeb* 4th Series vol. 169 col. 871; Mackay *Balfour* p. 326; Balfour *Opinions and Argument* pp. 109–10.
[60] 'Lord Balfour's View of Coalition' *Times* 2 Nov. 1922 p. 14; 'Incompetent Folly' *Times* 17 Oct. 1924 p. 16; 'Tool of Foreign Conspirators' *Times* 28 Oct. 1924 p. 14; 'Mr. Churchill's Appeal' *Times* 26 Sept. 1924 p. 14.
[61] 'L.C.C. Election Campaign' *Times* 24 Feb. 1925 p. 14; 23 Oct. 1924, Balfour *Opinions and Argument* pp. 110–13.

the whole organism of society'?[62] Largely by ignoring them seemed to be the Balfour way.

He was content to let Lloyd George handle the Russo-Polish War. They were generally agreed on Poland.[63] Balfour did pen a celebrated despatch to Chicherin, dismissing the idea of a 'Civic Militia of Polish Workers'. It was celebrated primarily as repartee.[64]

He did not oppose Lloyd George's efforts to tame the Bolshevik Government by gradually drawing it into international society (starting with the Anglo-Soviet Trade Agreement 1921); nor did he encourage them. Why not just leave businessmen to trade as they thought fit? The seditious Soviet delegation deserved to be expelled. He suggested making the Trade Agreement conditional on some specific concession, such as an end to Russian interference in Turkey or Persia. A general undertaking to refrain from hostile action was worthless: the Bolsheviks had every motive to break their word. He attributed the Anglo-Soviet Treaty of 1924 to extremist pressure within the Labour Party. It actually envisaged a British loan to the USSR. Did the Bolsheviks think we were stupid?[65]

Balfour had in 1920 declared his hope that Britain would never formally recognise the Soviet regime. He did not change his mind, but once Labour opened diplomatic relations, he saw little point in the Conservatives breaking them off. What was to be gained by doing something sensational? Soviet Communism was a remorseless tyranny, but Britain had no right to complain of its application to the country which gave it birth. Unfortunately the essence of the Russian system was that it went beyond Russian borders. Everyone knew that the Soviets thought it their duty to destroy the British Empire. To this end they helped fund the General Strike ('an attempted revolution' which threatened to 'hand over our national heritage to be squandered amid incalculable suffering by violent and irresponsible doctrinaires'). It was a mistake to imagine that the USSR could be shepherded into the peaceable

---

[62] 'Mr. Churchill's Appeal' *Times* 26 Sept. 1924 p. 14.
[63] Cf. Anglo-French Conference, 13 Dec. 1919, *DBFP* vol. II no. 58; Conference of Ministers, 13 Oct. 1922, PRO CAB 23/31.
[64] 'Mr. Balfour's Reply to Tchitcherin' *Times* 3 Sept. 1920 p. 9.
[65] Riddell *Intimate Diary* p. 235; Conference of Ministers, 2 Sept. 1920, PRO CAB 23/22; Cabinet 62, 18 Nov. 1920, PRO CAB 23/23; 'Incompetent Folly' *Times* 17 Oct. 1924 p. 16.

circuit of the League of Nations. Soviet diplomacy was nothing but 'deliberate and authorised perfidy'. Discussion of high policy was therefore useless. The maintenance of relations merely diminished the injury which this abnormal state of affairs inflicted on individuals.[66]

He did not welcome the breach which followed the Arcos Raid in May 1927, but it did not much trouble him. The Soviets were doing 'infinite injury' to China, and the nonsense they talked about Imperialism made things harder in India, but:

I'm not much alarmed about Russia. I admit nobody knows much about it, and the most ignorant seem to be the Russians themselves. But I'm not afraid from the military point of view – they've never succeeded yet in waging a big war. I suppose you *could* draw a world picture in which they, in collaboration with the yellow races, might form some kind of economic tyranny. But that doesn't seem to be plausible.[67]

Nor could he see class war taking off. The rhetoric was not entirely empty when he proclaimed his confidence that in Britain 'with its traditions, its common sense, its love of law, its power of seeing to the essentials of a question through all the mists of argument . . . we have nothing to fear from the contrivances and intrigues of any nation under Heaven'.[68]

CONCLUSION

Perhaps the most striking thing about Balfour and the Russian Revolution is how little it seemed to worry him (aside from its effect on the War). A very different reaction might have been expected from a conservative who owned the words of Burke to be ever instructive.[69] Yet anti-Soviet hysteria passed him by. His only attack came during the 1924 Election, and that was comparatively mild.

Red Revolution made slight impact on his thought. An old man incapable of grasping the significance of the birth of a new age?

---

[66] 12 Feb. 1920, *HCD* vol. 125 col. 308; Balfour to Chamberlain, 26 Jan. 1927, BP 49736 f. 292; W. and Z. Coates *A History of Anglo-Soviet Relations* (London 1943) vol. 1 p. 284; 'Lord Balfour Defines the Issue' *British Gazette* 10 May 1926 p. 1; 17 June 1926, *HLD* vol. 64 cols. 465–74; 31 May 1927, *HLD* vol. 67 col. 688–92; Memo. by Balfour, Jan. 1927, BP 49736 f. 299.
[67] 31 May 1927, *HLD* vol. 67 col. 688–92; Sept. 1929, Dugdale *Balfour* vol. II p. 401.
[68] Dugdale *Balfour* vol. II p. 363; 17 June 1926, *HLD* vol. 64 cols. 465–74.
[69] Balfour to Strachey, 3 Mar. 1902, BP 49797 ff. 183–4.

Mrs Dugdale went so far as to concede in 1936 that her uncle showed even less understanding of the class struggle in Russia than could be expected from someone of his sheltered experience.[70]

Certainly his fixed outlook led him to view the Revolution with greater detachment than many younger and more impressionable minds. Balfour was spared any doubts about ideological Communism. It was a fallacy – a 'crazy system'. There is no sign of his ever granting it the dignity of a rival to Anglo-American 'bourgeois capitalism'. He was also spared the painful disillusionment of progressive liberals. It did not shock him to see one tyranny supplant another. The real surprise would have been the success of democracy in 1917. Russia was 'a community diverse in blood, diverse in origin, enormous in numbers, not advanced in modern civilisation, or in modern constitutional practice, suddenly brought into immediate contact and collision with the most advanced Western views'. Balfour warned in 1908 that no community could go through such trials 'without matter for infinite regret, it may be for deep condemnation'.[71] Had he later wanted a dramatic example of the catastrophic effects of introducing alien ideas into ancient societies, could he have done better than cite Marxism and Russia?

It thus becomes apparent why Balfour was a man unhaunted by the spectre of World Communism. The Socialistic trend in Western European political thought did not herald the international triumph of Bolshevism. Bolshevism was a wild and exotic off-shoot of that trend. There were still dangers. Psychological disturbances seemed universal in the post-war world. The Soviets used 'all the catchwords which unscrupulous people use to take in foolish people', and their influence on the left wing of the Labour Party was disquieting.[72] When regarded essentially as the product of a particular country and time, however, Bolshevism lost many of its terrors.

Communist historians predictably find material to support their preconceit that Balfour (and all Allied leaders) conspired from the

---

[70] Dugdale *Balfour* vol. II p. 256.
[71] 'Lord Balfour on America' *Times* 7 Nov. 1924 p. 14; 17 Nov. 1919, *HCD* vol. 121 col. 766; 4 June 1908, *PDeb* 4th Series vol. 190 col. 249.
[72] 31 May 1927, *HLD* vol. 67 cols. 691 and 688.

first to destroy Soviet power by force.[73] In truth, his initial response was not hostile, and military intervention did not commend itself to him. Under pressure from colleagues, Allies, and events, he found it necessary to reconcile himself to the policy, but keen interventionists suspected him of stalling even then. In supporting continued operations 1918–19, he aimed to contain Bolshevism within its homeland and assist small nationalities to achieve self-determination. Increased ethnic homogeneity could only help Russia to develop that sense of national unity which facilitated free co-operation and obviated the need for absolutism.

Balfour thought in terms of nations; and the Revolution was primarily Russia's affair. On the international balance-sheet, new perils of subversion and propaganda were offset by the collapse of the Russian military machine. The burden of Indian defence was not increased.[74] Never having regarded the Russians as friends, he was not too alarmed when they became loud-mouthed enemies, given that their internal turmoil made for external weakness. Balfour viewed Soviet Communism from afar – and for the time being it kept its distance.

[73] R. Page Arnot *The Impact of the Russian Revolution in Britain* (London 1967) p. 121; Keep *Contemporary History* pp. 292–3.
[74] Eastern Committee, 9 Dec. 1918, Milner Papers dep. 137 ff. 199–200.

CHAPTER 10

The Far East

> Rear-guard actions, however well fought, are apt to end in
> unconditional surrender or the unpleasant operation of dying
> in the last ditch.
>
> Balfour 1927[1]

It was in the context of Far Eastern affairs that Balfour made
his single most acclaimed appearance on the international stage.
Between November 1921 and February 1922, he led the British
Delegation to the Conference on the Limitation of Armament
held at Washington. Disarmament depended on improved
relations between the Great Powers in the Far East, where the
demise of German and Russian influence had been accompanied
by increasing tension between the remaining protagonists:
Britain, Japan, and the USA. The Conference produced three
treaties. The Five Power Treaty secured a measure of real naval
disarmament and limitation of capital ships. This was related to
the replacement of the Anglo-Japanese Alliance by the Four Power
Treaty, whereby Britain, Japan, the United States, and France
endorsed the *status quo* in the Pacific Ocean. Respect for the independence and integrity of China was confirmed in the Nine Power
Treaty.

Fear of impending war in the Pacific was thus dissipated, and
'the true Balfour, the great Balfour' stood revealed as 'the lofty
incarnation of the best of British statesmanship'. He himself
declared that the Conference was 'of absolutely unmixed benefit
to mankind' and carried no seeds of future misfortune.[2]

Balfour had been concerned with the Far East before. His first
spell as Acting Foreign Secretary coincided with the Chinese crisis

---

[1] Memo. by Balfour, 11 Jan. 1927, PRO CAB 24/184 no. 3.
[2] 'Triumph of Peace' *Times* 12 Dec. 1921 p. 10; 'Our Washington Advocate' *Times* 21 Feb.
1922 p. 12.

of 1898, and the Russo-Japanese War occurred during his premiership. In the light of his attitudes then, as well as his later involvement, this chapter explores his view of the international politics of the Far East (essentially after 1905).[3] The salient feature of the period was the expansion of Japan. His reaction to this is revealed in Part I. Part II examines his record respecting China, and Part III is concerned with his general strategy in the Pacific region.

PART I: THE RISE OF JAPAN

The outcome of the Russo-Japanese War had been very satisfactory to Balfour. Before he left office in 1905, the British Legation in Tokyo was promoted to an Embassy, and the Anglo-Japanese Alliance was strengthened. He thought 'The Yellow Peril' altogether chimerical, and willingness to contemplate 150,000 Japanese troops on the North-West Frontier (albeit in an emergency) suggests that he felt no serious apprehension about a Japanese threat to India.[4]

By the Peace Treaty of Portsmouth (New Hampshire), Port Arthur was transferred from Russia to Japan, which also gained the South Manchuria Railway and southern Sakhalin. Balfour wondered why Japan was so moderate in its demands. The Japanese then forced a protectorate on Korea. Balfour saw no objection to their annexing it (which they did in 1910).[5]

Although not obligated by the Anglo-Japanese Alliance, Japan declared war on Germany in 1914 and occupied German possessions in China and the northern Pacific. The menacing 'Twenty-One Demands' of 1915 secured the Japanese a virtual protectorate over north-eastern China. Intervention in Siberia in 1918 then allowed them to drive back Russian influence. In less than fifteen years, Russian dominance in northern China had given way to a more exclusive Japanese ascendancy.

Japan's 'profiteering' was much resented in Britain, and Balfour did not dispute the fundamental analysis: 'She is the only

---

[3] For 1898–1905 see above pp. 113–19 and 121–6.
[4] Balfour to Spring Rice, 17 Jan. 1905, BP 49729 ff. 63–4; Metternich to Bethmann Hollweg, 11 Mar. 1910, *Grosse Politik* vol. 28 no. 10375.
[5] Balfour to Lansdowne, 1 Sept. and 23 Aug. 1905, BP 49729 ff. 153–4 and 144–5; Balfour to the King, 19 July 1905, Sandars Papers c. 717 f. 88.

belligerent country among the Great Powers which, whatever happens, seems likely to come out of the war possessing both more money and more territory.'[6] He did not, however, share the widespread disgust at Japanese reluctance to assist the wider Allied war effort. While having no objection to their intervention on 'Yellow Peril' grounds (he had enquired about the possibility in 1914), he accepted that it was very unlikely that the Japanese would ever fight on the Western Front.[7] One year into the war, he publicly praised Japan, whose part had 'in its most striking aspect come to an end' with the completion of its task in the Far East. He did feel that Britain had a right to expect greater naval co-operation, but he assured Dominion statesmen that he had 'no doubt that Japan, with an eye to her own interests, is quite genuinely helping the Allies'.[8]

Where expectations are low, disappointment is avoided. Balfour never imagined that the Alliance rested on anything beyond narrow self-interest. 'Our moral obligations under the Anglo-Japanese Treaty do not exceed our legal obligations', he had said just before the Russo-Japanese War: Britain must keep its word, but further demands should be considered solely in the light of British interests.[9] He was not aggrieved when the Japanese took a similar view of their obligations to Britain during the Great War. When Japan did not volunteer naval assistance, Balfour saw no objection to bargaining for it. He urged acceptance of the agreement of February 1917, whereby Britain promised to support Japanese retention of German rights in Shantung and Pacific islands north of the equator, if Japan supported British retention of the islands south of the equator and sent a flotilla to the Mediterranean.[10]

As Foreign Secretary, he was not blind to Japanese efforts to secure dominance over Eastern Asia. He 'had nothing to say in defence' of the Sino-Japanese Treaty of 1915, when Japan had 'certainly behaved badly to China'. In 1917, he found a warning that India would probably be attacked within two years 'most

---

[6] Balfour to Milner, 19 Jan. 1918, PRO FO 800/203 f. 292.
[7] Balfour to Nicolson, 15 Oct. and 21 Dec. 1914, BP 49748 ff. 5–6 and 18–21; Balfour to Fisher, 12 Jan. 1915, BP 49712 ff. 133–4.
[8] 'Patriotism and Empire' *Times* 5 Aug. 1915 p. 8; Balfour to Milner, 19 Jan. 1918, PRO FO 800/203 f. 293; Statement by Balfour [22 Mar. 1917], *The Lansing Papers* vol. II p. 22.
[9] Memo. by Balfour, 29 Dec. 1903, PRO CAB 37/67 no. 97.
[10] Minute by Curzon, 10 Nov. 1920, *DBFP* vol. XIV no. 167n.

interesting"[11], but his statement to the Imperial War Cabinet was characteristic:

I do not think we can conceal from ourselves that there is in every quarter of the Eastern world a certain uneasiness as to whether Japan is in the future going to try and play the part in those regions which Prussia has played in Europe, – whether she is not going to aim at some kind of domination. That fear hangs over the world. I do not venture to give any opinion on that at all.[12]

Knowing that the US State Department took 'a profoundly gloomy view' of Japanese policy, he did what he could in Washington in 1917 'to combat suspicions which seemed to me, on the evidence, somewhat excessive'.[13] He may (inadvertently he maintained) have made this easier for himself. When, in 1919, President Wilson denied ever having been told about the secret treaties between the Allies, an astonished Balfour rightly insisted that he had revealed the pacts with Italy and Russia. He conceded, however, that it was just possible that he may have failed to mention the promised transfer of German rights in Shantung to Japan.[14] Allied unity demanded that he take pains to qualify American views of Japan. 'They are apparently now accepting my estimate', he observed in October 1917: 'I am now uncomfortably conscious of a certain inclination to accept theirs!'[15]

He looked askance at the idea of Japanese intervention in Russia in 1918 – mainly because he did not think it would work. Opposition to Japanese aggrandisement, as such, did not sway him. Though warned that the hegemony of Asia was at stake, he doubted that Japan could long dominate so large a country as Siberia, inhabited by 10 million of 'the best Slavs in the world'.[16] With regard to the dangers of expansionism, indeed, there was something to be said for intervention: 'the very fact that the Japanese will be forced into the open against the Germans, and their respective interests brought into open conflict, should do

[11] Balfour to Curzon, 8 May 1919, *DBFP* vol. XIV p. 565; Balfour to Curzon, 20 Sept. 1919, BP 49734 ff. 171–2; Bose to Balfour, 2 Feb. 1917, PRO FO 800/210 ff. 7–11.
[12] Statement by Balfour [22 Mar. 1917], *The Lansing Papers* vol. II p. 22.
[13] Balfour to Milner, 19 Jan. 1918, PRO FO 800/203 ff. 293–4.
[14] S. Tillman *Anglo-American Relations at the Paris Peace Conference* (Princeton 1961) pp. 9–11; Balfour to Curzon, Oct. 1919, BP 49734 ff. 188–9.
[15] Minute by Balfour, Spring Rice to Balfour, 12 Oct. 1917, BP 49740 f. 262.
[16] War Cabinet 330A, 24 Jan. 1918, PRO CAB 23/13.

much to lessen Japanese pressure in other directions'.[17] Japanese objections to the presence of token forces from other Allied Powers admittedly excited suspicions 'in the minds of the suspicious', but he had no personal complaints about Japanese diplomacy.[18]

Studied restraint was the order of the day. During the war, British policy towards Japanese expansion could only be 'one of forced acquiescence – not to obstruct, and yet not to offer any concession gratuitously'. Balfour doubted that the *status quo* in China could be defended against any sudden pressure, given 'the present condition of British political and financial helplessness'. His immediate aim was simply postponement of all important questions until after the War. Emperor Yoshihito could receive his Field Marshal's baton from the British War Mission, but Japanese statesmen were not to meet anyone with whom they might seek to negotiate.[19]

The coming of peace was not accompanied by any perceptible diminution of Balfour's politeness towards Japan. At the Paris Conference, the Japanese found him unexpectedly helpful in their efforts to keep Shantung in the face of American opposition.[20] Accepting Japan as 'the heir of Germany in China', he was anxious to honour war-time promises, although the consensus of official opinion was that Japanese retention portended the loss of most of China to British trade.[21] Once the Peace Treaty was signed, the Foreign Office judged that Britain had liquidated its obligation, and the British Delegation to the League Assembly was instructed to avoid any action which might be construed as support for Japan in respect of Shantung. Balfour proclaimed his perplexity: was he to assent to modification of the Treaty of Versailles? Was he to 'throw over' the Japanese? How was this reversal in policy to be justified? If Britain were to break its engagement, all prestige would be lost in Japan.[22]

---

[17] Balfour to Wiseman, 30 Jan. 1918, PRO CAB 24/42 GT 3624 App. II.
[18] Balfour to Milner, 19 Jan. 1918, PRO FO 800/203 ff. 292–3.
[19] Balfour to Greene, 13 Feb. 1917, PRO FO 410/66 f. 7; Balfour to Beaverbrook, 22 Apr. 1918, PRO FO 800/203 f. 324.
[20] R.H. Fifield *Woodrow Wilson and the Far East* (New York 1952) pp. 142 and 263–78; Council of Four, 28 Apr. 1919, *FRUS* PPC 1919 vol. v pp. 317–18 and 324–5.
[21] Memo. by Balfour, 2 May 1918, PRO CAB 24/53 GT 4774; W.R. Louis *British Strategy in the Far East 1919–39* (Oxford 1971) pp. 21–5.
[22] Curzon to Clive, 24 Nov. 1920, and Wilson to Curzon, 26 Nov. 1920, *DBFP* vol. XIV nos. 167 and 172.

By this time, there was in fact considerable support in Britain for the idea of throwing over Japan. With the German navy scuppered, the Anglo-Japanese Alliance no longer had an obvious military purpose, and it soured relations within the English-speaking world. Association with Japan was never popular in the Dominions, where Japanese immigrants were seen at best as cheap labour, and at worst as the advance guard of 'The Yellow Peril'. At the Imperial Conference of 1921, the Canadian Premier, Arthur Meighan, flatly demanded abandonment of a Treaty which 'makes us *particeps criminis*' in the Japanese invasion of China. When the Alliance came before the Cabinet in May 1921, Balfour had favoured its continuation. He who in 1901 had complained, 'I suppose none of us think the Japanese are more to be relied upon than European Governments', now said that he always found them true to their word.[23]

Why did Balfour tolerate Japanese expansion? Part of the answer is to be found in his attitude to the nation which bore the brunt of it – China.

PART II: CHINA

In 1919, Balfour wrote from Paris that the Chinese delegation did not deserve much sympathy. Some Foreign Office experts might hate the Japanese, but he was 'more moved by contempt for the Chinese over the way in which they left Japan to fight Germany for Shantung and then . . . tried to maintain it was theirs as the legitimate spoils of a war in which they had not lost a man or spent a shilling'.[24]

Balfour was hardly a Sinophile. He took no particular interest in Eastern culture and once chided Curzon with having become 'a mere student of effete civilisation', when the latter toured the Far East, although 'Oriental civilisations are all very well in their way and you may be quite right to study their decaying splendours.' China never fired his imagination, and during most of his life-time it required imagination to conceive of 'that ancient and

[23] I. Nish *Alliance in Decline* (London 1972) p. 335; Cabinet 43, 30 May 1921, PRO CAB 23/25; Balfour to Lansdowne, 12 Dec. 1901, BP 49727 ff. 178–9.
[24] Balfour to Curzon, 20 Sept. 1919, BP 49734 ff. 171–3; Balfour to Curzon, 8 May 1919, *DBFP* vol. VI pp. 565–6.

mysterious civilisation' playing any but a passive role in world politics.[25]

When China faced partition in 1898, he dwelt on the lack of precedent for so large an empire so little able to defend itself. How was it that a people who hated foreigners and did not fear death seemed to have no idea of real resistance to foreign attack?[26] Twenty-four years later, he could still declare:

It is impossible to apply to China the simple formulae which content us when we are dealing with Western nations. That great and ancient civilization does not easily fit into our more modern schemes of political thought, and China suffers from sources of weakness which we citizens of Western countries do not find it always easy to understand.[27]

Dealing with 'an Oriental nation of the temperament of the Chinese' tried the patience, since they were masters of obstructive tactics. He thought foreign Powers were sometimes quite justified in using force to get through to them. In 1904, he had been ready to order the Younghusband Mission to destroy the walls of Lhasa and carry off hostages if the Tibetans remained obdurate. Generally, however, the easiest sanction was occupation of some territory. He recognised that temporary occupation had a dangerous tendency to endure. Even so, he was anxious that Anglo-Japanese pledges to defend the integrity of China should not prevent other Powers taking such action to enforce treaty obligations.[28]

Although required to collaborate in the division of China into spheres of influence in 1898, Balfour never wanted formal British rule there. In the absence of compelling strategic considerations, permanent territorial occupation in the East was 'an unmixed evil' which brought responsibility for 'populations not always easy to deal with'. He reluctantly approved the lease of Wei-hai-wei in retaliation for Russian acquisition of Port Arthur, but he stressed that it was almost an island and had no population (in fact around 4,000).[29]

---

[25] Balfour to Curzon, 2 Jan. 1893, BP 49732 f. 20; 5 Aug. 1925, *HLD* vol. 62 col. 726.

[26] 5 Apr. 1898, *PDeb* 4th Series vol. 56 col. 225; Alice Balfour's Diary, 21 May 1898, SRO GD 433/2/224.

[27] 4 Feb. 1922, Conference p. 364.

[28] 9 Feb. 1927, *HLD* vol. 66 col. 63; Balfour to Spring Rice, 17 Jan. 1905, BP 49729 ff. 69–70; Balfour to the King, 15 Aug. 1904, PRO CAB 41/29 no. 32; Memo. by Balfour, P.S. 31 May 1905, PRO CAB 37/77 no. 98.

[29] 5 Apr. 1898, *PDeb* 4th Series vol. 56 cols. 226–7 and 236; Balfour to Cooper, 26 Mar. 1898, BP 49852 f. 272; Lord Charles Beresford *The Break-Up of China* (London 1899) p. 79.

The oft-repeated 'Open Door' principle was always fine by him, but, in repudiating spheres of influence, the Balfour of 1922 did not condemn the Balfour of 1898:

How did spheres of influence come into existence? Because, at a certain period of Russian and German aggression in China, other Powers, in order to prevent China from being cut up before their eyes, had to do for each other what China could not do for herself. In China's interest, as well as their own, they had to guard against their exclusion from legitimate opportunities of enterprise. This was not due so much to their own policy as to China's want of policy; not in consequence of their own strength, but of China's weakness.[30]

This is redolent of economic imperialism, but, unlike many of his contemporaries, Balfour never became excited about the Chinese market. Although not above cloaking strategic reverses in 1898 with boasts of 'a considerable harvest' of economic rights, he deemed the quarrel for concessions neither dignified nor agreeable. It was wrong to take a too purely commercial view of Chinese–British politics. The destiny of China was not going to be affected by 'the number of steel rails we export, or the number of lines which are managed by English engineers'.[31] The consequences of economic development were in any case double-edged. Balfour foresaw an era in which the ingenuity and cheapness of Oriental labour would seriously imperil Western production. China exercised his thoughts not as a marketplace but as 'the storm-centre of international politics'.[32]

In the early years of the century, he repeatedly expounded the view that the greatest dangers to European peace arose from difficulties attached to the 'existence of nations on a lower plane of civilisation and efficiency'. From Korea to Morocco, one could see a succession of States, which were 'a cause of difficulty among greater and more civilised Powers':[33]

They represent, as it were, to speak in the language of meteorology, areas of depression which inevitably produce an inrush from the outside,

[30] 8 Dec. 1921, *Conference* p. 1108.
[31] 5 Apr. and 10 Aug. 1898, *PDeb* 4th Series vol. 56 cols. 228–31 and vol. 64 col. 834; Alice Balfour's diary, 11 Aug. 1898, SRO GD 433/2/224; Memo. by Balfour, 15 Aug. 1898, PRO CAB 37/47 no. 62.
[32] Balfour to Porter, 10 Sept. 1908, BP 49860 f. 2; Memo. by Balfour, 6 Sept. 1905, PRO CAB 37/79 no. 154.
[33] 'The Guildhall Banquet' *Times* 10 Nov. 1905 p. 10; 'Mr. Balfour in Liverpool' *Times* 14 Feb. 1903 p. 9.

accompanied sometimes by dangerous tornadoes and destructive storms, and it is one of the greatest problems of modern statesmanship and modern diplomacy to see that these dangers never are allowed to culminate in internecine conflicts between civilized countries. The problem is not an easy one, for these nations cannot be left alone ... commerce makes it impossible. The desire of the trader to penetrate with his wares into these regions, the desire of the monarchs of these regions to borrow from civilized countries, and ... the augmenting competition among civilized countries for markets which are not surrounded by hostile tariffs make it a matter of international necessity that some kind of arrangement should be come to with regard to all those countries.[34]

He counselled against direct agreements. These nations merely played 'the rival civilised countries off against one another'. In principle, internationalisation of intervention was desirable, but he recognised the difficulty of creating international machinery in the case of China. He yet remained certain that it was by arrangement between the civilised countries that peace could be maintained.[35]

This stance did not change. Balfour favoured stricter regulation of foreign involvement in China, but he never had much time for the Chinese themselves. China, he argued in 1925, was not the victim of international invasions which had shattered its fabric of government. No one had attempted to impose an alien civilisation on the Chinese. They had been masters in their own house, and no substantial responsibility for their current unsatisfactory state fell upon foreign countries. China must 'pull herself together', 'put her house in order', and 'work out her own salvation'. Little was to be gained from outside advice. The behaviour of Westernised Chinese suggested a 'depressing view of the results to be expected from bringing East and West together in the hope that contact will involve comprehension!'. Chinese ills demanded Chinese remedies.[36]

Even in 1898, Balfour did not wholly rule out the possibility of Chinese self-regeneration: 'The future has many strange surprises in store for us all.' By the 1920s, he acknowledged that the tide of

---

[34] 'The Guildhall Banquet' *Times* 10 Nov. 1905 p. 10.
[35] 'The Guildhall Banquet' *Times* 10 Nov. 1905 p. 10; Balfour to Lansdowne, 2 Jan. 1903, BP 49728 f. 11; Balfour to Spring Rice, 17 Jan. 1905, BP 49729 ff. 70–1.
[36] 5 Aug. 1925, *HLD* vol. 62 cols. 727–8 and 732; Empire Delegation, 7 Dec. 1921, PRO CAB 30/1A; 27 July 1926, *HLD* vol. 65 col. 282; 4 Feb. 1922, *Conference* p. 364; Balfour to Lampson, 2 Feb. 1926, SRO GD 433/2/23 no. 156.

nationalism – 'perhaps a world movement in excess' – had reached China. Growing national self-consciousness was supplementing the age-long dislike of foreign ways, but the nationalists were making many mistakes, and the country remained in hopeless chaos.[37]

When the national aspirations of Chinese delegates at Washington seemed to verge upon pretension, Balfour was often first to correct them. It was false to suggest that China was a fully organised and stable State. It was rather in 'transition from an old to a new system, and apparently there were large tracts where, to use a homely phrase, the writ of the Government did not run'. The Chinese could not reasonably demand the right to participate in all treaties affecting their country: 'China was not in possession of material forces to enable her to carry out any policy outside her own frontier.'[38]

This hard realism had its positive side. Eager to find ways 'of compelling China to do something for herself', he suggested making tariff alteration conditional on dethronement of the Provincial Governors – only to be advised that the USA would not tolerate such interference. On his own initiative, he devised a four-Power treaty with the aim of preventing repetition of 'those acts of military or economic spoliation' which weakened China (he admitted) and caused so much international friction. This demanded continuous consultation between Britain, France, Japan, and the USA, and the internationalisation of all military intervention in Eastern Asia. It tackled covert economic penetration by proposing that financial arrangements between Chinese Governments and a signatory Power, its nationals, or agents should not be binding until communicated to the other signatory Powers. Negotiation diluted this to a mere promise to file contracts with the Conference secretariat. Much less substantial than Balfour's draft was the agreed Nine Power Treaty, which was simply another Open Door declaration.[39]

One further Balfour initiative concerning China requires special examination, as it seems at variance with his general

---

[37] 5 Apr. 1898, *PDeb* 4th Series vol. 56 cols. 237–8; 27 July 1926, *HLD* vol. 65 cols. 281–3; 5 Aug. 1925, *HLD* vol. 62 cols. 731 and 727.

[38] 2 and 8 Dec. 1921, *Conference* pp. 1052 and 1110.

[39] Empire Delegation, 7 Dec. 1921, PRO CAB 30/1A; Balfour to Lloyd George, 11 Nov. 1921, *DBFP* vol. XIV no. 415; Conference pp. 1654–5 and 1621–9.

approach. He insisted on announcing the rendition of Wei-hai-wei at the Washington Conference, despite the misgivings of the Foreign Office, the Colonial Office, the War Office, and the Admiralty. He had been directed that no concession should be made save as part of an all-round bargain with a stable Chinese Government. There was no all-round bargain and no stable Chinese Government when Balfour made his announcement. Nor was any *quid pro quo* sought from China – contrary to instructions from Curzon.[40] In truth the offer was not quite so generous as it appeared: 'certain matters of detail' would have to be settled to allow the Royal Navy continued facilities at the port (and negotiations were to last eight years), but Britain *was* pledged to surrender the lease. 'Mr. Balfour has now given up Wei-hai-wei (as he evidently always meant to do)', noted Curzon: 'I have felt all along that we have been given away.'[41]

Balfour was generally no more sympathetic to China than his colleagues, who thought it ridiculous to hand anything over as a gift when he asked for liberty to match any concession France might make.[42] He had persuaded the Empire Delegation to grant him discretion to use Wei-hai-wei as 'a political lever' in the continuing dispute over Shantung. He then said that if this were resolved, it would be folly to keep Wei-hai-wei. Seeking to justify himself to Lloyd George, he made no mention of political levers, but emphasised the risk of appearing hypocritical. If Britain had retained Wei-hai-wei after persuading Japan to give up Shantung, 'the moral position of this country would certainly have suffered in the estimation of the world'.[43]

The desire to impress American opinion was certainly a factor. He waited for the 'psychological moment' when his announcement would make the greatest impact. When the French left Washington without yielding Kwangchow-wan, they did so under a cloud. Balfour said that Wei-hai-wei was a financial drain and

[40] 1 Feb. 1922, *Conference* p. 224; Conference of Ministers, 24 Nov. 1921, PRO CAB 23/27 f. 259; Curzon to Balfour, 24 Nov., 1 Dec., and 23 Dec. 1921, *DBFP* vol. XIV nos. 446, 461, and 518.
[41] Y. Ichihashi *The Washington Conference and After* (Stanford 1928) p. 266; Minutes by Curzon, 2–3 Feb. 1922, *DBFP* vol. XIV nos. 569n, 572n, and 575n.
[42] Balfour to Curzon, 17 Nov. 1921, *DBFP* vol. XIV no. 425; Conference of Ministers, 24 Nov. 1921, PRO CAB 23/27 f. 259.
[43] Empire Delegation, 2 Dec. 1921 and 4 Jan. 1922, PRO CAB 30/1A; Balfour to Lloyd George, 4 Feb. 1922, *DBFP* vol. XIV no. 580.

dismissed it as strategically worthless, now there was no need to counter-balance Russia or Germany in northern China. In this he was at odds with the Foreign Office view 'that in easily conceivable circumstances it may possess real importance in the future'.[44] Was there no need to counter-balance Japan?

These differing evaluations of the importance of Wei-hai-wei were rooted in differing evaluations of the importance of China as a whole. The officials of the Far Eastern Department were more anxious for Britain to keep Wei-hai-wei (as they had been more anxious for Japan to leave Shantung) because they were more strongly committed to defending British interests in China. Balfour doubted that those interests had much future. He did not view the demise of European dominance in the East with relish. In 1927, he advised that Britain should threaten to blockade China rather than acquiesce in the loss of treaty rights 'at the bidding of Soviet-inspired politicians'. At the same time, he recognised that British policy was 'navigating unsound waters in the worst possible weather with no charts'. If the Kuomintang had behind it the excited passions of the Chinese people and was led with even moderate efficiency, it was 'absurd to suppose that the scattered settlements and the not less scattered policy of the Treaty Powers could offer any effective resistance'. Britain was fighting a rear-guard action in China, and 'rear-guard actions, however well fought, are apt to end in unconditional surrender or the unpleasant operation of dying in the last ditch'.[45]

Balfour had let Curzon talk him into acquiring Wei-hai-wei in 1898. He had considered retrocession immediately after the Russo-Japanese War in 1905.[46] Seventeen years later, Britain was left with a remote outpost in an unstable region where its influence had diminished. Balfour likely saw an opportunity too good to miss. At Washington, withdrawal from northern China suggested magnanimity rather than weakness.

To summarise: Balfour regarded China *per se* with a high degree of indifference. He felt little sympathy for the nationalist cause,

[44] Balfour to Curzon, 2 Feb. 1922, *DBFP* vol. XIV no. 572; Balfour to Lloyd George, 4 Feb. 1922, *DBFP* vol. XIV no. 580; 'Précis of correspondence respecting Wei-hai-wei', Empire Delegation, Jan. 1922, PRO CAB 30/2 f. 235.
[45] Memo. by Balfour, 11 Jan. 1927, PRO CAB 24/184 no. 3; Balfour to Baldwin, 10 Jan. 1927, BP 49694 f. 7.
[46] Lord Ronaldshay *The Life of Lord Curzon* (London 1927) vol. I p. 285; Balfour to Clarke, 11 Oct. 1905, BP 49702 f. 97; Lansdowne to Balfour, 20 Oct. 1905 BP 49729 f. 191.

but he was largely resigned to the loss of British influence. Consequently, his long-term objective for British policy was simply avoidance of humiliation. To him, it did not very much matter whether China became an effective empire in its own right or fell under the sway of Japan – assuming other things to be equal. But could that assumption be made when toleration of Japanese imperialism placed Britain in an invidious position in respect of the United States?

PART III: THE PROBLEM OF THE PACIFIC

In January 1921, the Anglo-Japanese Alliance Committee of the Foreign Office reported that the Far Eastern question was resolving into a duel between Japan and the USA. As keepers of the Open Door, the Americans regarded Japanese successes in China since 1905 as diplomatic defeats for themselves. They found Japanese control of Shantung a hard pill to swallow in 1919, and they disliked the mandate over Micronesia which brought Japanese power nearer to US possessions. Talk of war grew louder in Tokyo and Washington, and competitive naval building accelerated. The Committee concluded that Britain had to make a choice:

If the cardinal feature of our foreign policy in the future is to cultivate the closest relations with the United States and to secure their whole-hearted co-operation in the maintenance of peace in every part of the world, the renewal of the [Anglo-Japanese] Alliance in anything like its present shape may prove a formidable obstacle.[47]

The conditional clause encapsulates one of Balfour's unshakeable convictions. In 1898 and 1905, when Russia was feared, he had himself sought to secure American commitment to the *status quo* in China. In 1921, however, when Japan was advancing, and the Foreign Office advocated Anglo-American co-operation, he preferred to continue the Anglo-Japanese Alliance. What deflected the great Americanophile?

A clue lies in the identity of another surprising friend of the Alliance: William Morris Hughes, Prime Minister of Australia. Balfour personally detested Hughes, but their viewpoints were not

---

[47] Anglo-Japanese Alliance Committee, 21 Jan. 1921, *DBFP* vol. XIV no. 212.

dissimilar. Both desired a unified white Empire. Both would have liked an American alliance (had one been on offer). Both were mindful of Australian security.[48]

As early as September 1904, Balfour had appreciated the need for increased naval defence for Australia in the face of a Japan victorious against Russia. He hoped that growing Japanese power would strengthen Australian desire for Imperial unity.[49] An Anglo-American treaty of mutual maritime defence naturally appealed to him. It would not have been logically incompatible with British commitments to Japan. He realised, however, that in practice it would have spelt the beginning of the end of the Anglo-Japanese Alliance and produced 'a very unpleasant feeling in Tokio'.[50] He would not risk attempting so destabilising a reversal of policy until certain of success. In the meantime, he did not think the Japanese would be so foolish as to fight the USA: however great their initial victories, it could only end in the richer and bigger country building a superior fleet. Had not Grey put something in the 1911 version of the Anglo-Japanese Alliance to preclude war with America anyway?[51]

American opinion was unconvinced. The British Ambassador thought many Americans viewed the Anglo-Japanese Alliance in 1921 as British people should have viewed an American-German Alliance in 1913. Why then, it was asked, was Britain clinging to a '*mariage de convenance*' with Japan and ignoring 'our natural alliance' with the USA?[52]

Balfour would never have disputed the terminology, but he did dispute the conclusion. A paper alliance was most required precisely where there was no natural alliance. To terminate the Anglo-Japanese Alliance would be to risk turning 'a faithful friend into a very formidable enemy'.[53] It was necessary to preserve good

[48] D.H. Miller *My Diary at the Conference of Paris* (New York 1924–6) vol. 1 p. 123; W.M. Hughes *The Splendid Adventure* (London 1929) pp. 193–6, 364–71, 445 and *passim*; Nish *Alliance in Decline* p. 335.
[49] Chamberlain *Politics from Inside* p. 29; Balfour to Northcote, 22 Oct. 1904, BP 49697 f. 48.
[50] Memo. by Balfour, 22 June 1917, PRO CAB 24/17 GT 1138.
[51] Marder *Fear God* vol. II p. 350 n1; Balfour to Esher, 4 Feb. 1910, BP 49719 ff. 133–4; Balfour to Hardinge, 5 Nov. 1919, SRO GD 433/2/15 no. 32. For Grey's attempted chicane, see P. Lowe *Great Britain and Japan 1911–15* (London 1969) ch. 1.
[52] Geddes to Curzon, 24 June 1921, *DBFP* vol. XIV no. 307; Memo. by Wellesley, 1 June 1920, *DBFP* vol. XIV no. 40.
[53] Imperial Conference, 28 June 1921, PRO CAB 32/2 ff. 58–9.

relations with Japan by artificial means. Good relations with America could generally be assumed. Balfour's Pacific policy was rooted in a paradox: he could afford to be superficially pro-Japanese, because he was so fundamentally pro-American.

If the price of Japanese 'friendship' had to be paid in China, so be it. Balfour was certainly not alone in putting Australian security before Chinese interests. He was perhaps exceptional in his readiness to face the consequences. While Curzon fulminated against 'insidious and unscrupulous' Japanese imperialism[54], Balfour told the Cabinet that:

> he had talked to Lord Grey a good deal about the question, and the latter had always taken the view that His Majesty's Government must be very careful as to how far they tried to keep Japan out of China. It had to be remembered that the Japanese were not allowed to go to Australia or to New Zealand, or to California, or to the Philippines, or, in fact, to any place where there was a white population. It was, therefore, somewhat unreasonable to say she was not to expand in a country where there was a yellow race.[55]

Balfour was not in the habit of citing his predecessor as Foreign Secretary, but four years earlier he had said the same to Dominion statesmen: that Grey thought 'A nation of that sort must have a safety valve somewhere.' In giving prominence to Grey's views, Balfour was coyly presenting his own. In Paris, he had told House that with Australia and California closed to the Japanese, somewhere else would have to be found for them. Approaching the President of Brazil was House's idea – Balfour thought the fitting place was Asia. As long as the Japanese had reasonable space for emigration there, they were unlikely to risk conflict with the Anglo-Saxon Powers.[56]

Thus, when he described the Anglo-Japanese Alliance as a controlling influence over any 'imperialistic tendencies', control meant steering as well as restraint.[57] This did not imply that Britain should offer *no* resistance in China. That would have looked like abject weakness. It was not inconsistent of Balfour to promote the Open Door, but it was understandable that he did not want

---

[54] Louis *British Strategy* p. 54.
[55] Cabinet 43, 30 May 1921, PRO CAB 23/25.
[56] Statement by Balfour [22 Mar. 1917], *The Lansing Papers* vol. II p. 22; 7 Feb. 1919, Bonsal *Unfinished Business* pp. 38–9; Balfour to Esher, 4 Feb. 1910, BP 49719 ff. 133–4.
[57] Imperial Conference, 28 June 1921, PRO CAB 32/2 ff. 58–60.

to make a fuss about Shantung or to maintain a British commitment to the defence of northern China in the shape of Wei-hai-
wei. Ideally the Japanese should find absorption of China sufficiently challenging to consume all their expansionist energies. 'It
will be very interesting to see whether the Chinese will in the
long run submit to their hegemony', he had written in 1906: 'If
not, their dreams of Eastern domination must prove baseless.'[58]
British withdrawal from China and entrenchment in Australasia
was meanwhile shielded by such Anglo-Japanese amity as could
be derived from close treaty relations.

Balfour was not oblivious of the naval race, or of Canadian
pressure to improve relations with the USA. By May 1921, he
appreciated that it would probably be necessary to accede to a
conference on the Pacific and merge the Anglo-Japanese Treaty
into a more general agreement, but he hoped to retain at least
the shell of the Alliance. The Foreign Office had no such hope.
The British Delegation to Washington was provided with the draft
of a non-military agreement between Britain, Japan, and the
United States, described by its authors as necessarily 'of a somewhat anodyne nature'.[59]

During the Atlantic crossing, Balfour drafted his own tripartite
treaty, which would leave parties free to bind themselves to defend
their rights in the Far East by force. The night before the Conference opened, he gave the US Secretary of State, Charles Evans
Hughes, a frank summary of the situation with regard to the
Anglo-Japanese Alliance:

a) American sentiment
    disadvantage – *con*.
b) Japanese sense of dignity—
    Control of Japanese action—
    Sense of security of Dominions— *pro*.[60]

Balfour then presented 'the result of his personal cogitations in
the intervals of seasickness on the voyage'.[61] Respect for territorial
rights and commitment to consultation formed the first article of
the draft, which continued:

---

[58] Balfour to Ronaldshay, 3 Nov. 1906, BP 49859 f. 108.
[59] Cabinet 43, 30 May 1921, PRO CAB 23/24 f. 308; Memo. on Tripartite Agreement, 22
Oct. 1921, *DBFP* vol. XIV No.405.
[60] Memo. by Hughes, 11 Nov. 1921, *FRUS* 1922 vol. I p. 1.
[61] Memo. by Hankey, 11 Nov. 1921, *DBFP* vol. XIV no. 416.

II. If in the future the territorial rights . . . of any of the High Contracting Parties are threatened by any other Power or combination of
Powers, any two of the High Contracting Parties shall be at liberty to
protect themselves by entering into a military alliance provided (a) this
arrangement is purely defensive in character and (b) that it is communicated to the other High Contracting Party.[62]

Hughes, who wanted nothing more substantial than a joint declaration of policy, immediately objected to a treaty. Balfour simply
renamed his draft an 'arrangement' and asked if he might present
it to the Japanese. Hughes 'showed considerable disquietude', but
he need not have worried. The Japanese were not prepared to
alienate the Americans for the sake of a draft treaty which categorically ruled out any Anglo-Japanese Alliance against the only
enemy they feared.[63]

Lloyd George heard that the Balfour draft proved invaluable as
a diplomatic opening, because it convinced the Japanese of British
trust. Balfour had intended more than that:

The object of the scheme is

a) To enable the Americans to be parties to a tripartite agreement
without committing themselves to military operations.

b) To bring the Anglo-Japanese Alliance in its *original* form to an end
without hurting the feelings of our ally.

c) To leave it open to us to renew a defensive alliance with Japan if
she should again be threatened by Germany or Russia.

d) To frame a treaty which will re-assure our Australasian dominions.

e) To make it impossible for American critics to suggest that our
treaty with Japan would prevent us siding with them in the case of a
rupture or threat of rupture.[64]

It is difficult to assess how seriously Balfour rated point (c).
When it suited his purpose (in the case of Wei-hai-wei) he dismissed German and Russian threats as things of the past. He wanted
to retain as close a treaty relationship with Japan as American
and Imperial pressures would permit. His draft and its stated
objects do little to support the claim that he favoured a new secur-

---

[62] Draft by Balfour, *FRUS* 1922 vol. I p. 2.

[63] Geddes to Curzon, 24 June 1921, *DBFP* vol. XIV no. 308; Memo. by Hankey, 11 Nov.
1921, *DBFP* vol. XIV no. 416; Fry *Illusions of Security* pp. 163-7.

[64] T. Jones *Whitehall Diary* vol. I p. 182; Note by Balfour, Nov. 1921, BP 49749 ff. 221-2;
see also Balfour to Lloyd George, 11 Nov. 1921, *DBFP* vol. XIV no. 415.

ity system for the Pacific based on a constructive plan for the settlement of disputes.[65]

The accession of France turned the tripartite agreement negotiated at Washington into the Four Power Treaty, a loose arrangement of the anodyne variety. On 10 December 1921, Balfour treated the Conference to a speech which was testimony to his unimpaired powers of adaptability. First he paid tribute to the Anglo-Japanese Alliance. Two nations thus united in sacrifice and triumph could not 'take off their hats one to the other and politely part as two strangers part who travel together for a few hours on a railway train', but:

we have long come to the conclusion that the only possible way of removing those suspicions and difficulties which are some of the greatest obstacles to that condition of serene peace which is the only tolerable condition, after all, for civilized people, was that we should annul, merge, destroy, as it were, this ancient and outworn and unnecessary agreement, and replace it by something new, something effective, which should embrace all the Powers concerned in the vast area of the Pacific ... The solution is one which gives me a satisfaction which I find it difficult, which I find it impossible, adequately to express in words.[66]

When the Four Power Treaty was proclaimed, however, one observer saw only an old man accepting a bitter outcome like a gentleman: 'As the last sentence sounded and the Anglo-Japanese Alliance publicly perished, his head fell forward on his chest exactly as if the spinal chord had been severed.'[67]

The USA was now eager for naval disarmament. Japan sought to make its acceptance of the 5 : 5 : 3 overall tonnage ratio for British, American, and Japanese capital ships conditional on non-militarisation of insular possessions in the Pacific. The British responded with 'The Balfour Parallelogram' – no fortifications to be built in an area bounded by the equator and 30°N, and 110° and 180°E. Including the Philippines and Guam, and excluding Singapore, Pearl Harbour, and New Guinea, this formed the basis of Article XIX of the Five Power Treaty. With hindsight, it has been condemned for surrendering control of the north-west Pacific

[65] Balfour to Lloyd George, 4 Feb. 1922, *DBFP* vol. XIV no. 580; Dugdale *Balfour* vol. II p. 320.
[66] 10 Dec. 1921, *Conference* pp. 172–4.
[67] Putnam Weale *An Indiscreet Chronicle of the Pacific* (New York 1922) pp. 186–8.

to Japan and facilitating Japanese hegemony over Eastern Asia. Even if this occurred to Balfour, it is unlikely to have worried him much. At the close of the Conference, he said that no clause in any treaty was more happily contrived for dealing with the special difficulties of the Pacific situation than Article XIX, which ensured beyond all doubt that disarmament entailed no diminution of security on the part of any nation.[68] Was he thinking primarily of Japanese security and prohibited naval bases, or of Australian security and permitted ones?

Balfour was a staunch supporter of plans to build a major British naval base at Singapore. It was of immense importance to the Dominions, he explained in June 1921, 'as whatever fleet we might maintain, it was almost impossible to continue a situation which meant that we could not use it in those waters where it was most likely to be required'. The Japanese and US navies were now its only serious rivals. Singapore was the best location, as it 'not only covered the main entrance to the Indian Ocean from the eastward but flanked the route from Eastern Asia to Australasia'. At Washington, Balfour gained informal American approval for the base. In 1924, he warned that failure to construct it would be a disastrous mistake.[69]

It should certainly not be inferred that he left the Washington Conference a disappointed or cynical man. It had been 'a sincere attempt' to put affairs on a more friendly and stable footing.[70] He told a CID Sub-committee in 1923 that he was convinced that, as a result, peace in the Pacific Ocean was assured. Singapore had needed to be developed to fill a gap in Imperial defences, Anglo-Japanese Alliance or no. Renewal for five years would have bought time in which to construct the base, but the Washington detente served just as well and probably better. There was no question that the dropping of the Alliance involved any change of Anglo-Japanese relations: 'Japan had friendly feelings towards Britain, and those feelings were reciprocated.' Experience at Washington had shown indeed that 'the vision of a teeming population in Japan anxiously looking for an outlet oversea was fantastic'. They had

[68] 4 Feb. 1922, *Conference* pp. 366–8.
[69] J. Neidpath *The Singapore Naval Base* (Oxford 1981) pp. 42 and 71; Cabinet 50, 16 June 1921, PRO CAB 23/26 f. 49; Imperial Conference, 19 July 1921, PRO CAB 32/2 f. 424; 13 Mar. 1924, *HLD* vol. 56 cols. 759 & 765–7.
[70] Balfour to Lloyd George, 4 Feb. 1922, *DBFP* vol. XIV no. 580.

evidently found out that control of China was not feasible, and the danger from Japan to Australia 'was as nearly illusory as any danger could be'.[71] He had never expected an Oriental people to be able to combine both commercial and military qualities for long.[72] The evidence of the mid-1920s suggested that the Japanese were coming down on the side of commerce.

Further cause for rejoicing was the cordiality of transatlantic co-operation at Washington. Effusive Anglo-Americanism was suddenly back in fashion.[73] It did not last, but Balfour was confident that the Anglo-Saxon Powers would stand together if the worst happened and Japan suddenly determined to secure by force the domination of the Pacific. In 1917, he wrote: 'with or without a guarantee, popular opinion in this country would undoubtedly force us to go to the assistance of America if she were attacked by Japan'. Ten years later, he deemed the Pacific problem fundamentally absurd: if the Japanese ever attacked the British Empire, they would know that 'public opinion in America would be on the side of this country'. Every reason – material and sentimental – satisfied him that 'the Government could safely dismiss any idea of an Anglo-Japanese duel in the Far East with America holding aloof'.[74] The Pacific War of 1941–5 demonstrated that his confidence was not entirely misplaced.

CONCLUSION

According to Curzon, 'No Englishman can land at Hong Kong without feeling a thrill of pride for his nationality.'[75] Balfour never did land at Hong Kong. The nearest he went was Singapore – *en route* from Australia. Not passionately committed to the Empire in Asia, he took Britain's nineteenth-century role as 'arbiter of the East' to be a temporary engagement, and rated it correspond-

---

[71] CID Sub-committee, 16 May 1923, PRO CAB 16/46 f. 179; Cabinet 50, 16 June 1921, PRO CAB 23/26; Naval Programme Committee, 22 Nov. 1927, PRO CAB 27/355 f. 27; CID, 28 July 1922, PRO CAB 2/3.
[72] Balfour to Ronaldshay, 3 Nov. 1906, BP 49859 ff. 107–8.
[73] Balfour to Mrs Carnegie, 17 Feb. 1922, BP 49742 f. 248; 'Our Washington Advocate' *Times* 21 Feb. 1922 p. 12.
[74] CID, 28 July 1922, PRO CAB 2/3; Nish *Alliance in Decline* p. 217; Memo. by Balfour, 22 June 1917, PRO CAB 24/17 GT 1138; Naval Programme Committee, 1 Dec. 1927, PRO CAB 27/355 f. 37.
[75] Harold Nicolson *Curzon* (London 1934) p. 13.

ingly low on his list of strategic priorities.

British interests in China seemed to him relatively unimport-
ant. If he viewed Japanese expansion there with greater equanimity than Russian, there were good reasons. First, Russia had
bid for northern China at a time when the prestige of European
Powers was determined in the East. When Japan expanded, European rivalries were concentrated elsewhere, and Japan was a nom-
inal ally. Secondly, a Russo-Chinese Empire would have been a far
more formidable challenger for world supremacy than a Japanese
Empire (a specifically Eastern Asian Power, balanced between
Russia and the USA). Australia needed protection, but Japanese
sea-power could not easily become world-wide. If anyone had to
assume the mantle of Oriental dominance, better Japan than a
European Power. Thirdly, it appeared reasonable to Balfour that
Japan should expand where there were 'yellow races'. Self-
determination meant little to Asians.

To a man of these views, the Washington Conference was a
definite success. A war-scare was diffused. A ridiculous arms race
was eased. A split within the English-speaking world was healed.
Crisis averted, the progress of Far Eastern events could continue.
Maybe the Chinese would eventually 'pull themselves together',
maybe not. The Japanese might meanwhile press their influence
(commercial or military) in China, and the British would fight
their rear-guard action and build the Singapore base to defend
Australia. Faith in Anglo-America was a great comfort. So what if
the Conference failed to reduce the power of Japan or to secure
Chinese independence? Such achievements were not to be had
without tremendous efforts — efforts which the interests of the
British Empire did not warrant. Balfour felt that Anglo-Saxondom
could co-exist with Greater Japan. East was East, and West was
West.

CHAPTER 11

The League of Nations

> This suggests reflections which, if not very cheerful, are not
> wholly pessimistic.
>
> Balfour 1925[1]

'He was an enthusiast for the League of Nations and amongst the
founders . . . he will always rank high.' So ran an obituary tribute
in 1930. Later writers have endorsed it, but do the old conservative and the new internationalist sound a likely combination?[2]

Balfour did adapt surprisingly well to the post-war international
environment. His personal triumph at Washington had come
immediately after success at Geneva. A mind too long resistant
to Liberalism had apparently 'yielded at once and completely to
the social shock of war' and embraced a League of Nations, open
diplomacy, and internationalism.[3] He said he was 'confident of the
steps that are being gradually made to produce a better and
improved world – an international world'. He was 'not prepared,
seriously, to discuss with any man what the future of international
relations should be unless he is prepared to accept in some form
or another the League of Nations'. The League was 'an immense,
novel, and effective addition to the machinery of international
civilisation'.[4]

Doubts remain. Balfour always recognised that humbugging the
public was a requirement of political success.[5] In letters, he complained about having to spend a quarter of his year in a dull Swiss

---

[1] Balfour to Hankey, 23 Oct. 1925, SRO GD 433/2/17 no. 56.
[2] Earl Beauchamp, 20 Mar. 1930, *HLD* vol. 76 col. 939; F.P Walters *A History of the League
of Nations* (London 1952) vol. 1 p. 88.
[3] Kennedy *Old Diplomacy and New* p. 366; D. Wilson *Gilbert Murray* (Oxford 1987) p. 289;
'Balfour and the Americans' *New York Times* 19 Feb. 1922 III p. 25.
[4] 'Balfour Hopes Much From Conference' *New York Times* 9 Nov. 1921 p. 8; 'World Peace'
Times 12 Nov. 1919 p. 20; 24 Nov. 1925, *HLD* vol. 62 col. 841.
[5] Riddell *War Diary* p. 357.

town attending meetings 'varied only by ceremonial entertain-
ments as laborious as themselves, and perhaps not more unprofit-
able'.[6] When Lloyd George observed that Balfour was dominating
the League of Nations, Churchill replied that, if you wanted
nothing done, A.J.B. was undoubtedly the best man for the task.[7]
Lord Robert Cecil assures us in one volume of his memoirs that
Balfour was a convinced supporter of the League. In the other
volume he accuses him of a pernicious attempt to emasculate the
Covenant. *The Dictionary of National Biography* contented itself with
the observation that 'it might indeed be difficult to say' whether
Balfour's foreign policy was in the tradition of the old Europe or
of the new era of democracy.[8]

Was Balfour an idealist? Did he believe in the League of
Nations? The first part of this chapter reflects upon his mixed
credentials and his attitude to the creation of the League. The
next four parts examine his views on the major idealist objectives
with which the League was (more or less explicitly) associated:
collective security, disarmament, international law and arbitration, and open diplomacy and democratic control. From these
is distilled (in Part VI) his assessment of the functions and value
of the League.

PART I: MIXED CREDENTIALS

'Vote for A.J. Balfour and peace with all the world', declared a
1906 election leaflet. Never allowing the Liberals a monopoly on
pacific aspirations, Balfour regularly extolled peace – a jewel of
incomparable value, the basis of civilisation, the greatest of all
blessings – and deplored the disease of war.[9] He beseeched the
statesmen of Europe in 1902 to cultivate 'international tolerance,
international comprehension, and, if it may be, international
friendship and international love'. His ready way with an idealistic
phrase led him into the occasional flirtation with definite idealists,

---

[6] Balfour to Bonar Law, 2 Mar. 1923, SRO GD 433/2/19 no. 46; Balfour to Curzon, 20
Oct. 1920, BP 49734 f. 222.
[7] McEwen *Riddell Diaries* p. 353.
[8] Lord Robert Cecil *A Great Experiment* (London 1941) pp. 109 and 147, and *All the Way*
(London 1949) p. 187; *The Dictionary of National Biography 1922–1930* p. 53.
[9] 'The General Election' *Times* 3 Jan. 1906 p. 6; 'Mr. Balfour on the Situation' *Times* 7
June 1902 p. 8; 'Mr. Balfour on the Crisis' *Times* 29 Oct. 1904 p. 11; 'The Guildhall
Banquet' *Times* 10 Nov. 1905 p. 10.

but experience taught that misunderstandings were easy.[10]

In 1898, for example, he lent an ear to the International Peace Crusade. Its organiser, W.T. Stead, found him 'one of the best men in the world'. Reckoned the Minister most sympathetic to the Hague Disarmament Conference (1899), he had yet listed fundamental obstacles to success on first hearing it proposed.[11] Politely dismissive of the second Hague Conference (1907), he soon after branded the pursuit of disarmament futile.[12]

More notably, he was persuaded in 1912 to become a trustee of the Garton Foundation to promote the study of international polity and economics as indicated by the writings of the peace campaigner Norman Angell. Angell's *The Great Illusion* (1910) was a sweeping refutation of war, based on Positivist and Cobdenite ideas. Its underlying philosophy was therefore objectionable to Balfour, who especially disliked its denial of the psychological significance of the nation. With its key message, however – 'that aggressive warfare, undertaken for the purpose of making the aggressor happier, wealthier, more prosperous, is not only wrong but silly' – he was in full agreement. Under modern conditions of economic interdependence, war between Great Powers would entail material losses for all concerned, which no indemnities or annexations could compensate. Here Angell's arguments chimed perfectly with his own belief that there was no economic motive for Anglo-German conflict. Balfour hoped that the business statement contained in *The Great Illusion* would soak into the public mind and become 'part of the very tissue of ordinary political thought in all civilised countries'. Uneasy about other aspects of the book, he thought it the duty of the Foundation to see that, in furthering the cause of peace, nothing was done to weaken national sentiment or endanger national defence. Otherwise Angell's propaganda might easily do more harm than good. Dissension was inevitable. Balfour protested that Garton Foundation speakers misemployed the thesis that war was profitless to suggest that armaments were pointless. Angell ultimately broke with his

[10] 'The Guildhall Banquet' *Times* 11 Nov. 1902 p. 11; Balfour to Esher, 12 Oct. 1912, BP 49719 f. 232.
[11] Whyte *Stead* pp. 147 and 158; A. Zimmern *The League of Nations and the Rule of Law 1918–1935* (London 1936) p. 104.
[12] 14 Mar. 1907, *PDeb* 4th Series vol. 171 cols. 296–7; 16 Mar. 1909, *HCD* vol. 2 col. 947; Balfour to the Lord Mayor, 23 Apr. 1909, BP 49860 ff. 87–8.

Conservative trustees, and went on to help found the Union of Democratic Control (with which Balfour thoroughly disagreed).[13]

Balfour's involvement with the post-war League of Nations Union followed a similar course. In 1918, he agreed to be an Honorary President of the nascent 'peace group'. His niece was on the Committee, and he was on good terms with the Chairman, Gilbert Murray, who came to regard him as a pillar of the League. By 1923, however, Balfour was complaining that he never understood what role the LNU was supposed to play or how its expenditure was to be justified. He thought it should be wound up. It was not, and he resigned. He could not let his name be associated with policy statements over which he had no control.[14]

To the genesis of the League itself, his attitude had also been equivocal.

'Was it not essential that we should come to an understanding as to how international relations were to be conducted?', he asked during the War. Could we not look to an improvement which would make the gratuitous breaking of the world's peace a crime? Some coercion had to be exercised upon criminal nations if the comity of nations was to be secure.[15]

Colonel House found him interested but discouragingly argumentative when they first discussed the possibility of a 'league of democracies'. Balfour was nevertheless recommended to Wilson in 1917 as 'the most liberal member of the present British Cabinet'.[16] As Foreign Secretary, however, he simply gave his general blessing to a 'League of Peace' and handed the whole matter over to Cecil. He approved the formation of the Phillimore Committee to study schemes of international organisation, but he doubted that such speculation would be very illuminating.[17]

His speeches meanwhile responded to the spread of idealism. It was intolerable to acquiesce in the view that civilisation would

---

[13] Norman Angell *The Great Illusion* (London 1910); Balfour to Esher, 12 Oct. 1912, and Esher to Balfour, 31 Dec. 1913, BP 49719 ff. 232–4 and 258; H. Weinroth 'Norman Angell and *The Great Illusion*' *Historical Journal* vol. 17 (1974) pp. 551–74; J.D.B. Miller *Norman Angell and the Futility of War* (Basingstoke 1986) p. 45.

[14] F. West *Gilbert Murray* (London 1984) p. 187; Wilson *Murray* pp. 289–90; Balfour to Cecil, 4 June 1923, Cecil Papers 51071A ff. 87–90.

[15] 'The "Superstate"' *Times* 14 Dec. 1914 p. 12; 30 July 1917, *HCD* vol. 96 col. 1852; 'German Ambitions' *Times* 11 Jan. 1918 p. 8.

[16] Link *Wilson* pp. 114–18; Seymour *Intimate Papers of Colonel House* vol. III p. 36.

[17] Balfour to Cecil, 6 Dec. 1924, Cecil Papers 51071A f. 93; G.W. Egerton *Great Britain and the Creation of the League of Nations* (London 1979) p. 65.

go on 'oscillating between those scenes of violence and sanguinary disturbances and the intervals in which great and ambitious nations pile up their armaments for a new effort'. Mankind would slip back into bankrupt indifference unless it seized the opportunity to put international relations on a sound moral footing. At the same time, he cautioned that many countries – not necessarily or chiefly the greater nations – were still quite as disposed to quarrel as ever nations were.[18]

Balfour told the press that he regarded the League of Nations as the greatest work of the Peace Conference, but he neither helped draft the Covenant nor showed much interest in it. He did think it important that the League should be encouraged to take London as a centre of organisation.[19] This is a clue as to the way his mind was working.

PART II: COLLECTIVE SECURITY

It was in January 1916 that Balfour first circulated some 'irresponsible reflections on the part which the pacific nations might play in discouraging future wars'. One possibility was an 'Anti-War Federation'. Once the map of Europe was brought into closer harmony with the distribution of nationalities, a federation of sufficiently powerful nations might declare existing territorial arrangements inviolable. The 'Pacific Powers' could guarantee the frontiers of each other and 'everybody else's territory as well'.[20] (It was folly to imagine it possible to constitute the world with States endowed with equal powers and rights[21].) The 'League' Powers would have to bind themselves to go to war, or at least to break off all commercial and diplomatic relations with an aggressor: otherwise 'the whole arrangement, with whatever flourish of trumpets it might be introduced to an admiring world, would gradually degenerate into an ineffectual proclamation of good intentions'. Such an arrangement would be simple and definite (unlike any conditional on arbitration). If it were successful,

---

[18] 'World Peace' *Times* 12 Nov. 1919 p. 20; 'Finance & Victory' *Daily Telegraph* 1 Oct. 1918 p. 8; 1 Aug. 1918, *HCD* vol. 109 col. 713.
[19] 'League of Nations' *Daily Telegraph* 9 Dec. 1918 p. 6; Balfour to Chamberlain and Bonar Law, 13 May 1919, BP 49751 ff. 221–5.
[20] Memo. by Balfour, 19 Jan. 1916, PRO CAB 37/141 no. 11.
[21] 'League of Nations' *Daily Telegraph* 9 Dec. 1918 p. 6.

the map of the civilised world would be unchangeable and wars of conquest at an end, although stronger nations would still be free to over-run their neighbours, exact indemnities, and insist on trade concessions.

'This is a very ambitious scheme', he admitted. An Anti-War Federation might easily be vitiated by a fundamental paradox:

The members forming a 'League of Peace' must be prepared to fight for their ideals. From the very nature of the case they are nations which, however potentially powerful, detest militarism; and by every principle and instinct of their being, incline to the paths of peace. Moreover, they probably will be States enjoying free government, living in an atmosphere of domestic controversy and divided by parties. Plain treaty obligations they would, without doubt, obey. But in the most important cases of all, treaty obligations would not always be plain. The military Powers whose ambition they desire to control would not only be much better prepared for war, but would devote years of patient labour to confusing the issues; to building up technical pleas; to fostering international jealousies and embittering party strife. The very qualities which make for pacific ideals render it difficult to carry them out by the only means which are likely to be successful.[22]

Balfour's verdict on the League idea was conditional on one important respect: 'I am by no means sure that it is practicable; but I am sure that it is quite impracticable unless the USA takes a leading part.'[23] This is the key to all his pronouncements on the topic of a League of Nations between 1916 and 1919. It was immensely important that the Great War end with something being accomplished to prevent its recurrence. He believed that such hopes were realisable only if America abandoned isolation. The pacific hopes which laced his speeches were not humbug. They were the latest manifestation of his belief in Anglo-Saxon world leadership. Anglo-American unity, a League of Nations, the longed for reign of peace – such expressions were to him practically synonymous, so he mixed them into one idealistic blur.[24] It thus becomes understandable why Wilson in 1917 found him one of the least cynical politicians he had ever met.[25] Balfour would doubtless have liked a straight Anglo-American alliance best, but if the Americans

[22] Memo. by Balfour, 19 Jan. 1916, PRO CAB 37/141 no. 11.
[23] Memo. by Balfour, 19 Jan. 1916, PRO CAB 37/141 no. 11.
[24] E.g. 'America's Decision' *Times* 8 May 1918 p. 5.
[25] Frances Lloyd George *The Years that are Past* (London 1967) p. 95.

wanted to frame their international commitments in a multilateral League of Nations, he was willing to go along with them. Wilson provided the inspiration for the League, the Phillimore Committee designed its structure, and the French contributed nothing. It would work if administered by Americans and British – not otherwise.[26]

The day after the War ended, Balfour made a fervent appeal to American journalists to help build 'a temple of humanity'. Mankind saw 'spread out in bright sunshine a great fertile plain of human progress' – but it had not reached it yet. The future of the world depended on Anglo-American co-operation. They must work to foster the necessary intellectual, moral, and political development. The League of Nations, however contrived, would be insignificant in its results compared with the effect of the English-speaking press.[27]

When Wilson insisted on placing the League at the top of the Peace Conference agenda, Balfour assented, although he would have preferred just an outline statement in the Treaties, with the details of the Covenant left till later.[28] Anxious not to offend the Americans, he disliked Lloyd George's attempt to trade reservation of the Monroe Doctrine for US naval reduction. Balfour was not worried by a big American fleet; and the effective sanction of a League of Nations would be Anglo-American sea-power.[29]

The week before the US Senate rejected the Treaty of Versailles, Balfour called on all Great Powers to take an equal share of the burden of the Covenant. Reservations would threaten the whole system with ultimate dissolution, and the future would be dark indeed. Could the League exist without the USA?[30]

Exist it did, but only in 'a maimed state'. Balfour knew that collective security was sunk. To him it had really only ever meant Anglo-American security. While still declaring that Members were bound to act against an aggressor, he soon spoke of economic pressure as

[26] Betty Balfour to Alice Balfour, 28 Feb. 1919, SRO GD 433/2/277; Betty Balfour to Frances Balfour, 28 Feb. 1919, BP 49831 f. 254.
[27] 'Mr. Balfour on the New Epoch' *Daily Telegraph* 13 Nov. 1918 p. 7.
[28] Imperial War Cabinet 47, 30 Dec. 1918, PRO CAB 23/42; T.A. Bailey *Woodrow Wilson and the Lost Peace* (Chicago 1944) p. 190.
[29] P. Birdsall *Versailles Twenty Years After* (Hamden 1941) p. 142; Betty Balfour to Alice Balfour, 28 Feb. 1919, SRO GD 433/2/277; Balfour *Freedom of the Seas* pp. 10–11.
[30] 'World Peace' *Times* 12 Nov. 1919 p. 20; Memo. by Hardinge, 5 Nov. 1919, Lloyd George Papers F/12/2/3c.

the most important weapon open to the League.[31] Even this did not carry conviction. The prospects for trade sanctions were transformed by the mere existence of powerful economies outside the League. With a neutral USA, he warned, sanctions would simply change the pattern of trade; and there was no certainty that the aggressor nation would suffer most. A League blockade without American co-operation might be perilous. He therefore strongly opposed any attempt to make sanctions mandatory. To strengthen the guarantees of the League without taking stock of the degree to which it had already been weakened was extremely unwise. He thought Cecil was wasting his time with the Draft Treaty of Mutual Assistance (1923), while no one in their senses could believe that the French-inspired Geneva Protocol (1924) really gave France more security.[32]

Balfour attacked the Protocol for even suggesting that the main business of the League was to preserve peace by organising war. The reformers would only weaken the League in its task of diminishing the causes of war, without making it a satisfactory instrument for organising military operations. It was self-contradictory to say that without sanctions the League was powerless and the Covenant so much waste paper. Every sanction included in the Covenant or the Protocol depended on treaties; and if no treaties were of value, all sanctions had to be worthless: 'Do what we will, we have no choice but, in the last resort, to depend upon the plighted word.'[33] He pondered this point further:

Why did nations patiently go on making Treaties with each other all through the centuries seeing that to all appearance they broke them without the least scruple? The answer can only be that a world in which many Treaties were broken and some were kept was better than a world in which no Treaties existed at all. This suggests reflections which, if not very cheerful, are not wholly pessimistic; especially as Treaties are certainly better kept than they used to be.[34]

---

[31] 24 July 1924, *HLD* vol. 58 col. 1005; League Council, 11 and 13 Feb. 1920, *Procès-Verbal* 20/29/3 p. 7 and 20/33/2 p. 23; League Assembly, 22 Nov. 1920, *Records of the First Assembly* (Plenary) p. 188.

[32] Memo. by Balfour, 9 Feb. 1925, SRO GD 433/2/4 no. 11; CID, 4 Dec. 1924, PRO CAB 2/4; 24 July 1924, *HLD* vol. 58 col. 998; Alice Balfour's diary, 14 Mar. 1925, SRO GD 433/2/136 p. 59.

[33] CID, 19 Feb. 1925, PRO CAB 2/4; Draft statement by Balfour, [Feb. 1925], and Memo. by Balfour, 9 Feb. 1925, SRO GD 433/2/4 nos. 11 and 13.

[34] Balfour to Hankey, 23 Oct. 1925, SRO GD 433/2/17 no. 56.

If League members were true to the Covenant, there would be no need for additional collective security schemes. The Draft Treaty and the Protocol were attempts to buttress up one treaty with another. That was not, he feared, a wholly unnecessary procedure, but there had to be some reason for believing that the subsidiary treaty would be better observed than the primary one. Nations were most likely to fulfil commitments into which they had entered voluntarily on their own initiative to preserve their own interests. Freedom to combine was the best security. Perhaps arrangements like Locarno and the Little Entente would one day be superfluous: 'But meanwhile we are wise to take facts as we find them.'[35] It is doubtful that Balfour ever had any faith in collective security as an ideal system. Britain and America might have achieved something, but without the USA there was little chance of mustering preponderant power within the League. Any serious attempt to stop a war by sanctions would mark the beginning of the end: the League would fail and fall into desuetude. 'Our influence must be largely moral', he told the Assembly.[36] The League could not conceivably do any better than the five Great Powers assembled in Paris in 1919. On first attending the League Council, he immediately expressed his regret that there were only eight instead of the intended nine members. 'He hoped, however, that in spite of this drawback, the Council would ... be able to perform useful work, and make some progress to the final consummation of the aims embodied in the Covenant.'[37]

PART III: DISARMAMENT

One of those aims was disarmament. Article VIII reflected the widespread belief that (in the words of Grey) 'great armaments lead inevitably to war'.[38]

Before 1914, Balfour had frequently argued: 'great preparation for war ensures peace'. Armed forces were not the cause of war.

---

[35] 24 July 1924, *HLD* vol. 58 cols. 998–1003; 24 Nov. 1925, *HLD* vol. 62 cols. 842–3.
[36] Imperial Conference, 8 July 1921, PRO CAB 32/2 p. 11; League Assembly, 10 Sept. 1921, *Records of the Second Assembly* (Plenary) p. 188.
[37] 12 Feb. 1920, *HCD* vol. 125 col. 312; League Council, 11 Feb. 1920, *Procès-Verbal* 20/29/2/1 p. 3.
[38] Grey *Twenty-Five Years* vol. I pp. 91–2.

They were rather the only known expedient by which independence could be maintained 'in spite of the fluctuating movements of human passion'.[39] One policy alone ensured peace for Britain: 'the conviction maintained by every foreign statesman that it is dangerous to attack us'. To fail to maintain an effective deterrent was to shake the foundations of world order. Diplomacy existed on the physical force which lay behind it. Unsupported it was bound to fail at the critical moment. Countries 'that are in the nature of things defensive countries' should be as strong as possible – and Britain was one. Disarmament had to be initiated by nations which kept navies unnecessary to defend their shores.[40]

The Great War discredited such arguments in many eyes. Balfour adjusted his tone – disarmament was now 'this all-important subject' – but his opinions were quite unchanged. 'The disarmament that we all desire is one that will prevent war', he elaborated; 'the increase of armaments that we dread is the one that will increase the danger of war'. When armaments deterred aggression, they remained 'the most powerful means of securing peace, locally at all events, that human ingenuity has yet contrived'. Supposing it had been possible to restrict inventors to the development of defensive weaponry, science 'would really have given us that peace, that secure peace, for which all the world pants'.[41]

The continued existence of great armaments did not worry him. The accelerating growth of armaments did, because it denoted grave international mistrust. He blamed the post-war arms race on the Germans, whose behaviour 'had given all those who were suspicious a text on which they might preach suspicion'. The Five Power Treaty signed at Washington delighted him. Not only would naval limitation help the world out of its economic rut. It signified a turn for the better in Great Power relations and made idealism a practical proposition.[42] This way of viewing fluctuations in arms

[39] 'Mr. Balfour in Glasgow' *Times* 13 Jan. 1905 p. 8; Balfour to the Lord Mayor, 23 Apr. 1909, BP 49860 ff. 87–8; 'The Visit of the French Fleet' *Times* 14 Aug. 1905 p. 8; 2 Mar. 1908, *PDeb* 4th Series vol. 185 col. 458.

[40] 27 July 1906, *PDeb* 4th Series vol. 162 col. 113; 14 Mar. 1901, *PDeb* 4th Series vol. 90 col. 1653; 'Mr. Balfour in Glasgow' *Times* 18 Jan. 1906 p. 6; Balfour to Miss Whiting, 4 Feb. 1910, BP 49860 ff. 211–2; 9 May 1906, *PDeb* 4th Series vol. 156 cols. 1410–12.

[41] 22 Dec. 1920, *HCD* vol. 136 col. 1820; 13 Mar. 1924, *HLD* vol. 56 col. 763.

[42] 'The Washington Conference' *Times* 1 Nov. 1921 p. 12; 'Balfour Arrives' *New York Times* 11 Nov. 1921 p. 3; 15 Nov. 1921, *Conference* pp. 96–104.

levels as a barometer of international amity might explain his otherwise surprising 1919 comment that a League of Nations would be a sham if there were no disarmament.[43]

There were no short cuts: 'Disarmament is a difficult thing to carry out, except in a world where disturbances have ceased.'[44] A world disarmament conference would be hopeless, and endeavours to link disarmament with the strengthening of arbitration procedures and guarantees tried his patience. The desire to do *something* made people do very foolish things – like devise the Draft Treaty of Mutual Assistance. It was not gaps in the Covenant which haunted the imagination of those who hesitated to disarm, but concern that the Covenant would be brushed aside by force. Huge armaments were kept in being by brooding fears which had little relation to ordinary international misunderstandings. Even the most perfect method of arbitration would not touch the 'deep lying causes of hostility' which divided powerful States.[45] To demand guarantees as a condition for disarmament (as France did) was more objectionable: 'We have ourselves disarmed, or are prepared to disarm, to the lowest point of safety; and having thus reduced our own powers of defence to the utmost limits, we are being asked by Nations who have by no means imitated our example to increase our obligations to defend *them*.'[46]

Disarmament would come when the fear and jealousy which certain nations (for historic reasons) entertained against one another diminished in intensity. As the spirit of their neighbours became 'more human and more Christian', they would realise that the burden of armaments was no longer worth bearing. Balfour admitted that this was possibly overoptimistic. If nations did not moderate their passions, civilisation might tumble in the dust. That reflection itself must gradually have an effect.[47]

In the meantime, he persisted in arguing that to strengthen the naval defences of the British Empire was to safeguard peace.[48] He

---

[43] Council of Ten, 21 Jan. 1919, *FRUS* PPC 1919 vol. III p. 669.
[44] League Assembly, 10 Sept. 1921, *Records of the Second Assembly* (Plenary) p. 189.
[45] 24 July 1924, *HLD* vol. 58 cols. 997 and 1003; Memo. by Balfour, 9 Feb. 1925, SRO GD 433/2/4 no. 11; Draft Memo. by Balfour, [Jan. 1925], SRO GD 433/2/4 no. 86.
[46] Balfour to Blanche Dugdale, 10 Oct. 1927, SRO GD 433/2/227.
[47] 24 July 1924, *HLD* vol. 58 cols. 1004–5; League Assembly, 10 Sept. 1921, *Records of the Second Assembly* (Plenary) p. 189.
[48] 13 Mar. 1924, *HLD* vol. 56 col. 763.

opposed the whole principle of the Ten Year Rule as dangerous and impracticable: nobody could *ever* assert that a major war was an impossibility for the next ten years. British forces should be maintained 'in the highest pitch of perfection'.[49] Balfour was an unswerving believer in military deterrents. Disarmament? By 1927 he was frankly tired of 'this boring subject'.[50]

PART IV: INTERNATIONAL LAW AND ARBITRATION

'I am a great believer in arbitration', Balfour declared in 1918: 'Wherever I can, I encourage arbitration.' He had often said as much. Arbitration treaties offered 'a great engine for preserving the peace of the world'. They were a far more fruitful avenue than disarmament. The Permanent Court of International Justice was a 'great desideratum of the civilised community of nations'.[51]

It is therefore the more jarring to find him writing in 1925: 'The last thing I desire to do is to commit this country to a scheme of general arbitration.'[52] Many of his glowing references to arbitration had indeed been fairly transparent attempts to sugar the realist pill. He did not attach much value to the opinion of international lawyers, and his whole approach to politics was far from legalistic.[53] He deprecated, for example, any formal differentiation between the functions of the League Council and those of the Assembly, preferring to trust to tact and wise statesmanship.[54] Against this must be reckoned his eagerness to claim for the Anglo-Saxon peoples the credit for introducing legal or quasi-legal procedures to international affairs.[55]

It was in defence of British blockade policy that Balfour advanced his fundamental premise: that the obligation of international law was conditional on reciprocity. Law unsupported by

---

[49] CID, 5 July 1928, PRO CAB 2/5.
[50] Balfour to Blanche Dugdale, 26 Oct. 1927, SRO GD 433/2/227.
[51] 1 Aug. 1918, *HCD* vol. 109 cols. 712–3; 'Mr. Balfour in Glasgow' *Times* 13 Jan. 1905 p. 8; 14 Mar. 1907, *PDeb* 4th Series vol. 171 cols. 296–7; Balfour to the Lord Mayor, 23 Apr. 1909, BP 49860 ff. 87–8; 22 Dec. 1920, *HCD* vol. 136 col. 1815.
[52] Balfour to Amery, 15 July 1925, SRO GD 433/2/14 no. 32.
[53] Heads of Delegations, 29 Aug. 1919, *DBFP* vol. 1 no. 46; Balfour to Goschen, 11 Oct. 1898, BP 49706 ff. 215–6; 8 Dec. 1926, *HLD* vol. 65 col. 1335.
[54] Report by Balfour, Nov. 1920, *Records of the First Assembly* (Committees) vol. 1 p. 94.
[55] 'The Guildhall Banquet' *Times* 10 Nov. 1905 p. 10; 'The "Superstate" ' *Times* 14 Dec. 1914 p. 12; 6 Nov. 1917, *HCD* vol. 98 col. 2047; League Assembly, 13 Dec. 1920, *Records of the First Assembly* (Plenary) p. 488; Memo. by Balfour, 4 Apr. 1929, PRO CAB 24/202 CP 89.

sanctions could hardly be obeyed unless all were prepared to obey it. Otherwise it hampered everyone but the criminal. It was incumbent on international law reformers to remember that 'those countries will most readily agree to changes in the law of nations who do not mean to be bound by them'. The simple extension of international law was no certain benefit to civilisation. 'Behind law there must be power' – but the contrivance of suitable machinery would 'tax to the utmost the statesmanship of the world'. Compulsory arbitration enforced by a League of Nations would end war between civilised nations (except League war against a transgressor) – but that led straight back to the problems of collective security. Would public opinion in Member States be sufficiently united to induce them to make tremendous sacrifices for the sake of a Court verdict?[56]

Even without a formal system of enforcement, compulsory arbitration was strongly favoured by many 1920s idealists. Could a nation reasonably refuse to present its case to an international court? Balfour thought it certainly could. A court merely administered a code of laws as it found it. International law was incomplete, often disputable, and difficult to modify. An international court might find itself adjudicating on vital interests without any recognised legal principle to guide it – and without 'that larger vision which is sometimes given to statesmen'. How would a court have decided between French and German claims to Alsace-Lorraine?[57] How indeed would a court determine the appropriate level of belligerent rights at sea? He repeatedly asserted that Britain could not accept the Freedom of the Seas until the League had stopped all wars. In the meantime, continental juries always tried to limit British sea-power, and a defence based on national character was not 'very easy to handle with becoming modesty at the bar of international opinion'.[58]

Campaigners for compulsory arbitration seemed to him to be

[56] 'Mr. Balfour on Reprisals' *Times* 29 Mar. 1915 p. 10; Balfour *Freedom of the Seas* pp. 6–7 and 10; Draft Reply to Wilson, Dec. 1916, PRO CAB 37/162 no. 31; Memo. by Balfour, 19 Jan. 1916, PRO CAB 37/141 no. 11.

[57] League Assembly, 13 Dec. 1920, *Records of the First Assembly* (Plenary) p. 488; Memo. by Balfour, 4 Apr. 1929, PRO CAB 24/202 CP 89; Memo. by Balfour, 19 Jan. 1916, PRO CAB 37/141 no. 11.

[58] Conference, 13 Oct. 1918, PRO CAB 24/66 GT 5967; War Cabinet 491B, 26 Oct. 1918, PRO CAB 23/14; Imperial War Cabinet 46, 24 Dec. 1918, PRO CAB 23/41; Memo. by Balfour, 11 Jan. 1919, BP 49750 ff. 203–19.

labouring under a misconception. They noted celebrated instances of successful arbitration and concluded that a process which had proved its value should be applied universally. They failed to understand that judicial settlement had worked in those cases because the nations involved had been anxiously desirous of peace. Arbitration did not stand alone. The parties had first to agree the principles on which the tribunal was to proceed, to define the issue so as to avoid ambiguity, and to foster some confidence that the verdict would be implemented. Such arrangements had hitherto been secured by flexible diplomacy between willing governments. How could they possibly be secured between reluctant Governments by the rigid provisions of a general treaty? Would lawyers try to fix procedures for every conceivable circumstance? To construct hypothetical hard cases would be pointless and even perilous. Rigid compulsory arbitration would never be of any use.[59]

This was not to reject arbitration outright. There was a limited and imperfect form which was practical and convenient. It was not between every kind of nation that it could profitably be carried out. The prime candidates were Britain and the USA. For them Balfour favoured an arrangement 'by which every possible case of difference would be dealt with, or, at least, reported on, though only the smaller class of cases be dealt with finally'. The moral weight of arbitral judgments would be great, but there would still be room for diplomatic negotiation of major questions. A political 'safety-valve' was vital, if an international court was not to over-reach itself and lose all authority. International justice had to 'be allowed to pursue that natural development which is the secret of all permanent success in human affairs'. More and more classes of case were coming before tribunals. The wise policy was to let that process continue without impatience, while remembering that nations that did not want to keep the peace would not be bound by treaties of arbitration.[60]

---

[59] Memo. by Balfour, 4 Apr. 1929, PRO CAB 24/202 CP 89; Balfour to Borden, draft, Jan. 1929, BP 49749 f. 286; Memo. by Balfour, 11 July 1928, PRO CAB 24/196 CP 223.
[60] Balfour to Salisbury, 3 Mar. and 7 Feb. 1896, BP 49690 ff. 155 and 151–3; 16 Mar. 1911, *HCD* vol. 22 col. 2501; League Assembly, 13 Dec. 1920, *Records of the First Assembly* (Plenary) p. 488; 1 Aug. 1918, *HCD* vol. 109 cols. 712–13.

PART V: OPEN DIPLOMACY AND DEMOCRATIC CONTROL

In July 1919, the reconstituted Supreme Council of the Peace Conference discussed how they should proceed. US Secretary Lansing proposed issuing a communiqué after each meeting. Balfour dissented but offered to waive his objection 'if the communiqué was so judiciously framed as to contain no information'.[61] He had once asked President Wilson what was the function of plenary sessions open to the press. Would they not become purely a matter of form? Later he told the League that it could not possibly ask Member States to reveal the military details of alliance treaties.[62] Balfour was evidently not leading the movement to replace secret diplomacy with 'open covenants openly arrived at'. Deriding the notion 'that if only everything were said at Charing Cross with the sound of a trumpet all diplomatic difficulty would vanish', he appeared to his contemporary biographer 'a very Metternich in his enthusiasm for the sacredness of diplomatic mysteries'.[63]

Despite popular contempt, Balfour maintained, the old diplomacy carried on by confidential interviews and the exchange of notes had lost none of its value. It often had generous aims, and the world was always better for its existence. In a despatch for the League Council, however, he was willing to add that the authors of the Covenant well knew that for the solution of many international problems there was a better way; 'and they believed themselves to have found it'. The new system, which differed from the old not by substitution but by addition, 'combined frequent personal intercourse with great publicity'.[64]

He could endorse 'New Diplomacy' thus defined and cheerfully proclaim himself a great believer in conferences. Free and frank interchange of views was the best way of reaching agreement.[65] Informality and small numbers helped. This was the great advant-

[61] Heads of Delegations, 2 July 1919, *DBFP* vol. I no. 2.
[62] Council of Ten, 16 Jan. 1919, *FRUS* PPC 1919 vol. III pp. 587–8; League Assembly, 5 Oct. 1921, *Records of the Second Assembly* (Plenary) pp. 847–8.
[63] 19 Dec. 1917, *HCD* vol. 100 col. 2012; 'Raymond' *Uncensored Celebrities* p. 73 and *Balfour* pp. 196–8.
[64] 'Mr. Balfour on his Mission' *Times* 17 Feb. 1922 p. 6; A.J. Balfour: 'The League' *Headway* vol. 6 no.1 (Jan. 1924) pp. 4–5; Draft Note by Balfour, Mar. 1921, BP 49742 ff. 23–5; 'The "Old Diplomacy" and the League' *Times* 11 Oct. 1924 p. 7.
[65] 'The Washington Conference' *Times* 1 Nov. 1921 p. 12; 'The Guildhall Banquet' *Times* 10 Nov. 1903 p. 10.

age of the Council of Four in Paris. The mere presence of additional delegates would have cramped conversation. Balfour sought to foster this sort of intimacy within the League Council. By August 1921 he could report: 'The extremely friendly relations which personally exist between the members of the Council is an immense blessing' – thanks largely to his own *rapport* with the French representative, Leon Bourgeois.[66]

He even welcomed publicity 'in the true and useful form of that phrase'. The procedure of holding the first and last meetings of each session of the League Council in public was wonderfully conducive to unanimity. If no agreement was reached in private, 'the public had a right to know what arguments had been advanced by the various States, in order that it might be able to judge the merits of the question'.[67] As an example of this power of the League, Balfour cited a dispute over nationality decrees in Tunis:

Under the threat (known to all but never mentioned) that if I could not get satisfactory terms of arbitration I should have to explain the whole matter at a public seance of the Council, the Quai d'Orsay has at last given way. But as a *quid pro quo* the French Government insist that we should smooth the thing over in public as much as possible.[68]

He admitted that there was nothing radically novel about new diplomacy as he depicted it. The presence of lesser Powers and neutrals at League meetings was an innovation at which he expressed joy, professing to be deeply hurt by the suggestion that the League was an instrument of the Great Powers.[69] This would be more convincing if he had been less eager to keep the small countries well away from decision-making at the Paris Peace Conference.[70] He tended himself to address quarrelsome minor Powers as if they were naughty children.[71]

---

[66] Heads of Delegations, 1 July 1919, *DBFP* vol. I no. 1; Balfour to Alice Balfour, 31 Aug. 1921, SRO GD 433/2/76 no. 3.

[67] League Council, 11 Feb. 1920, *Procès-Verbal* 20/29/2/1 p. 3; League Council, 18 July 1922, *Official Journal* 3:8 p. 791; Egremont *Balfour* pp. 315–16.

[68] Balfour to Hankey, 29 Sept. 1922, SRO GD 433/2/2 no. 1; League Council, 2 Oct. 1922, *Official Journal* 3:11 pp. 1206–7. Other examples: Balfour to Curzon, 22 Oct. 1920, PRO CAB 24/114 CP 2009; League Council, 19 July 1922, *Official Journal* 3:8 p. 800.

[69] 'The "Old Diplomacy" and the League' *Times* 11 Oct. 1924 p. 7; League Council, 13 Feb. 1920, *Procès-Verbal* 20/31/1 p. 3; 22 Dec. 1922, *HCD* vol. 136 col. 1825; League Assembly, 10 Sept. 1921, *Records of the Second Assembly* (Plenary) p. 188.

[70] Council of Ten, 16 and 17 Jan. 1919, *FRUS* PPC 1919 vol. III pp. 587–8, 604, and 606.

[71] 'Vilna Again' *Times* 21 Sept. 1921 p. 9; League Assembly, 2 Oct. 1921, *Records of the Second Assembly* (Plenary) p. 670.

It was soon a commonplace that private tea parties were more significant than public assemblies at Geneva. Publicity was a threat – a means of embarrassing the recalcitrant, rather than a condition of normal diplomatic business. Balfour would not have had it otherwise. He thought it eminently desirable and indeed necessary that diplomatic conversations should be private and confidential. Only then could provisional arguments about delicate questions be advanced with the requisite freedom. Secret diplomacy was not a criminal operation intended to cover up dark transactions. It was merely the ordinary practice of human relations. The rules governing international life were not fundamentally different from those governing private life, and 'if everything was said everywhere and by everybody, domestic life would be impossible'.[72] Reticence was a virtue. Directly a controversy became public, fair give-and-take became extremely difficult:

How is the task of the peacemaker ... to be pursued if you are to shout your grievances from the housetop whenever they occur? The only result is that you embitter public feeling, that the differences between the two States suddenly attain a magnitude they ought never to be allowed to approach, that the newspapers of the two countries agitate themselves, that the Parliaments of the two countries have their passions set on fire, and great crises arise which may end – have ended sometimes – in great catastrophes.[73]

He might have been recalling 1899, when Joseph Chamberlain's experiment in public diplomacy ended in the Boer War. Balfour deplored 'government by rhetoric'. Not even sympathy with the cause had reconciled him to Chamberlain's platform appeals for Anglo-German-American alliance.[74] His own speeches on foreign policy were usually very discreet, any specific incident being addressed only after the event. The Washington Conference was his closest encounter with open diplomacy. On arrival, he told journalists that a conference meant an exchange of ideas and, if necessary, the modification of ideas; to express them beforehand would likely render it futile. He did consent to one big

[72] League Council, 11 Feb. 1920 and 18 July 1922, *Procès-Verbal* 20/29/2/1 p. 3 and *Official Record* 3:8 p. 791; 17 Aug. 1917, *HCD* vol. 97 cols. 1669 and 1672.
[73] 19 Mar. 1918, *HCD* vol. 104 cols. 877 and 870.
[74] Short *Balfour* p. 298; Alice Balfour's diary, 21 May 1898, SRO GD 433/2/224.

press conference – but only on condition that he not be quoted.[75]

Balfour considered details of current foreign policy to be the preserve of the few: the Prime Minister, the Foreign Secretary, and the diplomats – plus the Monarch if so inclined. (An excellent memory of foreign affairs allowed Queen Victoria to make the occasional worthwhile observation; Edward VII scarcely had the ability.)[76] The statesmen performed their duty, and the public could not know how much good they did. 'Do not suppose that we can do the work better', he said, 'by having to explain it to a lot of people who are not responsible.'[77]

Debates on foreign affairs he generally rated more prolific of evil than good. The interests of Parliamentary dialectics and those of European diplomacy scarcely ever harmonised.[78] 'Indiscreet speeches', he explained, 'the value of which we can perfectly weigh within the House, get reported and circulated abroad, or in India, or even at home in the provinces, and very often make bad blood quite unnecessarily, and raise difficulties which might easily have been avoided.' The airing of differences generated foreign misunderstanding of Britain which was a world misfortune.[79]

Parliamentary questions were also a nuisance. A ministerial answer could sew misconceptions in the minds of foreign statesmen, while it was no gain to world peace to have 670 prying eyes scrutinising the details of negotiations. Diplomats could have no confidence in a Foreign Secretary who blurted out everything. Balfour's own answers were scrupulously uninformative: 'truth is always desirable; but all truth ought not to be told at all times'. When Leader of the House, he had forbidden questions without notice on foreign affairs (except from leaders of the Opposition in exceptional circumstances) and deemed it a great reform. Beyond this, he advocated (and practised) patriotic self-restraint on the part of the Opposition, and looked to the Chamber where

---

[75] 'Balfour Hopes Much From Conference' *New York Times* 9 Nov. 1921 p. 8; 'Balfour Talks to Press' *New York Times* 17 Nov. 1921 p. 3.

[76] Notes of conversation, 30 Dec. 1899, BP 49853 ff. 18–19; Balfour to Holland Rose, 25 Jan. and 1 Feb. 1915, BP 49863 ff. 286–7 and 295.

[77] 'The Guildhall Banquet' *Times* 10 Nov. 1903 p. 10; 19 Mar. 1918, *HCD* vol. 104 col. 875.

[78] 'Mr. Balfour in Edinburgh' *Times* 23 Dec. 1898 p. 4; Balfour to Salisbury, 16 Dec. 1895, Hatfield 3M/E f. 57.

[79] *Select Committee* (1914) vol. VII para. 1707; 'Mr. Balfour in Rochdale' *Times* 18 Nov. 1896 p. 6.

interrogation was less searching. Before 1905, he repeatedly asserted that the House of Lords was the place for a modern Foreign Secretary.[80] That most laborious department was taxing even without Parliamentary aggravations. By the 1920s, he feared that modern communications might ultimately put the Foreign Office beyond the range of effective human control; the network of responsibility and calculation growing too vast for any directing mind to master it.[81] Balfour told MPs to be content with the Blue Books which gave a broad outline of what had passed in foreign policy *when it had passed*. Even then revelations were to be made with the utmost care, since Blue Books were primarily read for the purpose of putting annoying questions to the Government.[82]

Balfour clearly did not want greater democratic control of foreign policy. In the 1890s he could be candid. The phrase 'the voice of the people' was perfectly meaningless. Ordinary people were too busy with their own affairs to apprehend political complexities. They could only direct a general force. Democracy was of all forms of government the one which most required that leaders should lead – not heedless of public opinion, not subservient to it, endeavouring perhaps to mould it to the good. No people would make sacrifices for a cause in which they did not believe. The statesman needed a grasp of national psychology, but superior knowledge, experience, and (at best) wisdom were his. There was indeed nothing especially pacific about public opinion even in an age of mass armies. The British people seemed ready enough for Anglo-Russian war in 1898. Completely reversing liberal orthodoxy, Balfour then warned the Cabinet that absolute monarchs were 'just as ready to sacrifice the material interest of their country to the point of honour as Democracies'.[83]

It was rather different in America in 1917, after President Wilson had 'in a most apt and vivid phrase' proclaimed that the world must be made safe for democracy. Balfour said that the Allies had staked their last dollar on democracy as a great security

[80] 7 Feb. 1899, *PDeb* 4th Series vol. 66 cols. 114–16; *Select Committee* 1914 vol. VII para.1708; 17 Aug. 1917, *HCD* vol. 97 cols. 1669–72; 'Mr. Balfour in Edinburgh' *Times* 23 Dec. 1898 p. 4; 17 May 1904, *PDeb* 4th Series vol. 135 col. 53.
[81] J. Tilley and S. Gaselee *The Foreign Office* (London 1933) p. vii.
[82] 17 Aug. 1917, *HCD* vol. 97 col. 1672.
[83] 'Mr. Balfour on the Politics of the Future' *Times* 22 June 1894 p. 11; 'Mr. Balfour at Bristol' *Times* 4 Feb. 1896 p. 7 and 30 Nov. 1898 p. 10; Memo. by Balfour, 15 Aug. 1898, PRO CAB 37/47 no. 62.

for future peace.[84] He now genuinely rated democracy 'less monstrously bellicose than despotism', but he gave just one reason. It was only a military autocracy of the German type that could through generations pursue remorselessly the object of international domination. Democracies presumably could not achieve such fixity of purpose. Back in Europe, he added: 'Don't think that the world will be made safe for democracy merely by multiplying the number of democratic States.' Passions that arose between neighbouring democracies made them quite as prone to undertake war as if they were under other forms of government.[85] Believe that, and there is nothing to be said for democratic control as a peace policy.

The argument for open diplomacy and democracy was really the property of Radicals who believed war to be a conspiracy of the ruling classes. Balfour thought its premises false and its prescriptions worse than useless. 'It is the nations that make for war', he once said: 'It is the diplomatic representatives of the nations who have done anything that has been done in the way of preserving peace.'[86]

PART VI: RESIDUUM

All this was less than encouraging. Open diplomacy was a fallacy. Disarmament and arbitration had to wait on willingness to disarm and arbitrate. Collective security was a myth. What could the League do? Evidently far less than most people thought. Was there any point in going on?

Balfour repeatedly warned that the League would suffer more from those who sought to put too much upon it than from those who regarded it as impotent. If its supporters were overambitious, the machine would break in their hands.[87] In the Council, he strove to keep the League out of major controversies. It was not

---

[84] 'Mr. Balfour's Tribute' *New York Times* 22 Apr. 1917 p. 1; 'On the Side of Democracy' *Times* 30 May 1917 p. 6.

[85] Jones *Whitehall Diary* vol. 1 p. 69; 'Mr. Balfour Addresses Congress' *Times* 7 May 1917 p. 6; 'League of Nations' *Daily Telegraph* 9 Dec. 1918 p. 6.

[86] Imperial Conference, 8 July 1921, PRO CAB 32/2 p. 12.

[87] 'Relief for Armenia' *Times* 2 Dec. 1920 p. 13; League Council, 13 Mar. 1920, *Procès-Verbal* 20/29/6 p. 9; 'The League's Enemies' *Times* 7 Aug. 1920 p. 9; 'Mr. Balfour and the League' *Times* 22 July 1920 p. 9; League Assembly, 8 Sept. 1922, *Records of the Third Assembly* (Plenary) vol. 1 p. 70.

for the League to concern itself with revision of the Treaty of Versailles, to judge whether Germany was fulfilling its obligations, or to deal with inter-Allied debt.[88] Still less should it address the continuing conflict in the Near East. Peace settlements were not its job. The League had been constituted to preserve international health, not to deal with acute disease in the European polity.[89]

When the League was charged with large projects, such as the partition of Upper Silesia and Austrian reconstruction, Balfour yet took a leading part in their achievement and hailed victories for international organisation.[90] He also exerted himself to shepherd the Palestine mandate through the Council. The system of League mandates was not objectionable to him (save in its fantasies about early self-government). In principle, he liked the idea of placing ex-enemy colonies under international control. If the League had been 'a real thing', capable of enforcing free trade and demilitarisation, mandates could have been a breakthrough worthy of wider application. In reality, effective League supervision was full of difficulties. It was impossible to create a fiscal system whereby the League as a whole provided money for the development of mandated territories. Fixed tenure was necessary if perpetual intrigue were to be avoided. Without independent inspection, the members of the League would be helpless; with it, they would be in constant peril of coming in collision with the mandatory. The final arrangement was simply a self-imposed limitation on sovereignty, and he cannot have expected it to amount to much.[91]

He welcomed League involvement in minor disputes, such as the Åland Islands and Vilna, and in humanitarian concerns, such as typhus in Poland and the repatriation of prisoners. Even these

---

[88] League Assembly, 2 Dec. 1920, *Records of the First Assembly* (Plenary) p. 247; Balfour to Cecil, 17 July 1922, Cecil Papers 51071A ff. 71–2.
[89] League Assembly, 8 Sept. 1922, *Records of the Third Assembly* (Plenary) vol. I p. 69; League Council, 5 Aug. 1920, *Procès-Verbal* 20/29/14 p. 63; Memo. by Balfour, League Council [Aug. 1920], *Procès-Verbal* 20/29/14 Annex 95a p. 241; 'The League's Enemies' *Times* 7 Aug. 1920 p. 9.
[90] Dugdale *Balfour* vol. II pp. 309–12 and 352–5; Balfour to Cabinet, 25 Sept. 1921, PRO CAB 24/139 CP 4225; League Assembly, 28 Sept. 1921, *Records of the Second Assembly* (Plenary) p. 483; League Council, Aug.-Oct. 1922, *Official Journal* 3:11; 'The Revival of Austria' *Times* 8 Feb. 1924 p. 9.
[91] Memo. by Balfour, 2 May 1918, PRO CAB 24/53 GT 4774; Empire Delegation, 28 Jan. 1919, *BDFA* vol. 3 no.47; 'Mr. Balfour on Mandates' *Times* 6 Feb. 1919 p. 10; Council of Ten, 28 Jan. 1919, *FRUS* 1919 PPC vol. III p. 764; Memo. by Balfour, Jan. 1918, Lloyd George *Truth about the Peace Treaties* pp. 554–7.

matters could be challenging. French obstruction of the White Slavery Convention drove him to exclaim: 'What are we fit for, and what are we capable of doing?'. It was probably with a sense of relief, if not satisfaction, that he presented the report of the Council to the Second Assembly with the observation: 'It is a very dull volume'.[92]

This anti-activist line naturally met with the approval of statesmen and diplomats hostile to the League, but it would be a mistake to label Balfour their creature. When Allied Foreign Ministers (under the chairmanship of Curzon) suggested that the League take responsibility for Armenia and minorities in Turkey, Balfour led the Council in rejecting this attempt to palm off the discredit of certain failure.[93] He would have liked the League to refuse to guarantee Central European minorities as well. There were areas (like Yugoslavia) where mutual massacres seemed the only method of reaching conclusions. In such cases, the League could only reveal its impotence and make itself unpopular. He preferred that it never interfere in the domestic affairs of any State. (How, he once asked, would Britain have liked League involvement in Ireland or Egypt?)[94]

Balfour sought to restrict the functions of the League, not because he was opposed to it, but because he wanted it to work – and it could only be successful if it stayed within the limits of its severely attenuated capacities. 'What I do object to', he complained, 'is the dislike that certain Departments have to the whole idea and spirit of the League, and their obvious satisfaction in putting a spoke in its wheel.' Believing that Britain should always be represented by a Cabinet Minister versed in higher diplomacy, Balfour created for himself a role of trusted semi-autonomy which was difficult to recast in 1923. It annoyed him that the Government would not even finance a permanent British office at Geneva.

---

[92] Imperial Conference, 8 July 1921, PRO CAB 32/2 pp. 12–13; League Assembly, 29 and 10 Sept. 1921, *Records of the Second Assembly* (Plenary) pp. 517 and 190.

[93] League Council, 13 Mar. 1920, *Procès-Verbal* 20/29/6 pp. 15 and 17; Memo. by Balfour, 15 Mar. 1920, PRO CAB 24/100 CP 898; League Assembly, 22 Nov. 1922, *Records of the First Assembly* (Plenary) p. 188.

[94] League Council, 22 Oct. 1920, *Procès-Verbal* 20/29/16 p. 13; Heads of Delegations, 1 Sept. 1919, *DBFP* vol. I no. 48; 20 Apr. 1921, *HCD* vol. 140 cols. 1936–7; Imperial War Cabinet 46, 24 Dec. 1918, PRO CAB 23/41.

The French were much wiser: 'They control their League representatives but help them.'[95]

One reason why he took his League duties seriously was the faint hope that the USA might reconsider. Another factor was the need to counter the French. At first he feared that they might destroy the League. Then he feared that they might take it over.[96] There was also the fact that certain international problems *were* being settled. Balfour argued that League action could sometimes be more effective than conventional diplomacy for one simple reason: it was less bruising to national vanity. Countries found it easier to accept advice from an international organisation than from a Great Power directly. The fundamental aims of the League were consonant with British policy – both sought to prevent one nation dominating Europe – but intervention under the auspices of the League avoided some of the jealousies which independent British action would excite. In helping placate the hubris of Powers small and great, the League made a real contribution to peace. Why discard this valuable new instrument of diplomacy? Its loss would be calamitous.[97]

Beyond this, there was in Balfour a germ of genuine idealism – albeit of a modest and passive kind. To meet the popular mood it was often bloated almost out of recognition. 'The future of the world and of civilisation very largely depends upon the prestige and the growing power of the League of Nations', he proclaimed. It produced – or rather focused – 'a kind of collective sentiment which may in some respects be powerless, which may in some respects run beyond possibilities'. It had to be understood that the Covenant was merely a constitution – its success or failure depended on the political instincts of the community to which it was applied. If peace were to be preserved, it was necessary to raise the ideals and develop the common conscience of the people. International order required the citizens of each nation to

---

[95] Balfour to Hankey, 18 Jan. 1921, SRO GD 433/2/17 no. 22; Hankey to Balfour, 15 Jan. 1921, SRO GD 433/2/17 no. 23; Inter-departmental Conference, 8 Feb. 1921, PRO CAB 24/119 CP 2567.
[96] Balfour to Curzon, 22 Oct. 1920, PRO CAB 24/114 CP 2009; Inter-departmental Conference, 8 Feb. 1921, PRO CAB 24/119 CP 2567; Balfour to Hankey, 18 Jan. 1921, SRO GD 433/2/17 no. 22.
[97] Imperial Conference, 8 July 1921, PRO CAB 32/2 pp. 12–15.

consider themselves something more than citizens of that nation.[98] The idea of a developing international society was always part of his thought. He was as ready to speak of 'the Brotherhood of European nations' in 1902 as in 1919 – readier in fact, for Germany had not then shown itself to be pervaded with a philosophy absolutely inconsistent with it. He often preached the cause of 'embracing all civilized nations into one greater community of civilized thought and civilized action'.[99] He even disapproved of the Olympic Games on the ground that competition between national teams exacerbated international rivalries.[100] Europe and North America were one family of nations, and the old idea of Christendom should still be their ideal.[101] He said in 1903:

we must sometimes get depressed over the pettiness of the causes which threaten the unity of Europe; but yet let us only mark with a candid eye the progress of public opinion through these last two or three generations, and I think we shall see growing up that international spirit . . . which makes every European Power feel that it is committing a crime against civilization if it unnecessarily plunges the world into war.[102]

He once lightly prophesied that in 500 years time Europe would regard international warfare with disgust and moral disdain.[103] The Great War illustrated his contention that society could go backwards as well as forwards, but it also provided a fresh impetus to proceed. All progress was difficult to attain and not easy to maintain. General attitudes were affected by a host of factors, and the best elements in society had always to contend with all manner of misunderstanding. It was enthusiasm that moved the world, but enthusiasts could seldom be trusted to speak the truth, while their critics commonly offered nothing but the 'easy cynicism of the

---

[98] 24 Nov. 1925, *HLD* vol. 62 col. 841; 24 July 1924, *HLD* vol. 58 col. 1004; 'Mr. Balfour on National Sympathy' *Times* 6 July 1920 p. 16; 'Churches Can Hasten Peace' *New York Times* 15 Dec. 1921 p. 4; 'World Peace' *Times* 12 Nov. 1919 p. 20; 12 Feb. 1920, *HCD* vol. 125 col. 305.

[99] 'Mr. Balfour in Manchester' *Times* 11 Jan. 1902 p. 7; 'The Prime Minister at Fulham' *Times* 21 July 1902 p. 10; 'Case for the Coalition' *Times* 12 Dec. 1919 p. 9; 'The "Superstate"' *Times* 14 Dec. 1914 p. 12; 'The Declaration of London' *Times* 28 June 1911 p. 9.

[100] Balfour to Cadogan, 18 Dec. 1922, SRO GD 433/2/25 no. 64; 'Lord Balfour on Games' *Times* 5 Dec. 1924 p. 11.

[101] 'Mr. Balfour at Rochdale' *Times* 18 Nov. 1896 p. 6; 'Mr. Balfour at Bristol' *Times* 30 Nov. 1898 p. 10; 'The Guildhall Banquet' *Times* 11 Nov. 1902 p. 11 and 10 Nov. 1905 p. 10.

[102] 'The Guildhall Banquet' *Times* 10 Nov. 1903 p. 10.

[103] Short *Balfour* p. 422.

arm-chair'. Men were not mere worshippers of brute strength, and, though human nature might not change, human habits definitely did. That was the process of civilisation. Already civilised men had come some way to regarding the settlement of disputes by mutual slaughter as alien.[104] Balfour did not despair of further progress, but:

As for the League of Nations, what between the idiots who think it inherently foolish if not wicked, and the idiots who think it should be a cure for all international and many national ills, it never has behind it the sort of public opinion required to give it stability and strength. Even if it had, the difficulties in front of it would seem almost insurmountable. But we must do our best.[105]

All he asked was that people acknowledge: 'That is the path that we must pursue.'[106]

CONCLUSION

A believer in the League? An idealist? Yes, it might *indeed* be difficult to say.

To call Balfour a 'League enthusiast' is clearly misleading. It brackets him with people whose outlook on international affairs he thought deluded if not dangerous. Zealous 'peace' campaigners of the 1920s believed in collective security, disarmament, compulsory arbitration, and open diplomacy. Balfour believed in alliances, armaments, voluntary arbitration, and confidential diplomacy. While they had pinned their hopes on the League of Nations, he had pinned his on Anglo-American co-operation. His disappointment came sooner than theirs.

He believed that the League (as constituted) might be able to do a little good. It symbolised the growth of an international spirit which was definitely desirable, but it could not possibly produce enough of that spirit to generate its own motive power.[107] The League was merely a body. Humanity had to provide the soul, and

---

[104] 'World Peace' *Times* 12 Nov. 1919 p. 20; Dugdale *Balfour* vol. II p. 313; Balfour to Mary Gladstone [23 June 1883?], Mary Gladstone Papers 46238 f. 2; 'Martyrdom of Belgium' *Times* 22 July 1918 p. 4.
[105] Balfour to Fisher, 23 July 1923, Fisher Papers 65 f. 98.
[106] 'World Peace' *Times* 12 Nov. 1919 p. 20.
[107] 'World Peace' *Times* 12 Nov. 1919 p. 20.

the intellectual and moral development of civilisation was not yet sufficiently advanced.

Insofar as he believed that progress towards a more peaceful and ethical world was achievable, Balfour could still perhaps be rated an idealist – this being conditional on a weak sense of the word 'achievable'. He thought that the peoples of Western civilisation could achieve an expansion of their loyalties such that their commitment to the common interests of the international community would over-ride unenlightened national self-interest. He thought that this could gradually occur if the general evolution of human affairs went well. He did not think that politicians could achieve it now, or even do much to hasten it. When there was a will for peace, there would be a way, but no provision of ingenious ways could substitute for will.

Would-be reformers of international relations suspected Balfour of complacency. Christian Lange criticised the way he came to the League Assembly and told it that nothing could be done, while still suggesting that all was for the best in the best of possible Councils. Alfred Zimmern observed that he seemed to recommend 'a policy of Couéism – it might almost be described as the policy of the ostrich'.[108] Most idealists felt that the world simply could not wait. The Great War had in truth driven Balfour to agree, but they would probably not have liked his solution:

nothing, not the League of Nations or anything else, is going to give us peace, but the certainty of every civilised man, woman and child that everybody will be destroyed if there is war; everybody and everything. I think, perhaps, if the energies of our Research Departments in all countries are carried on with sufficient ability that that might be arrived at.[109]

The threat of community in death should surely expedite the realisation of community in life.

---

[108] League Assembly, 15 Sept. 1921, *Records of the Second Assembly* (Plenary) pp. 269–70; Zimmern *League of Nations* p. 358.
[109] CID Sub-committee, 10 May 1923, PRO CAB 16/46 p. 169

CHAPTER 12

Conclusion

When I look back, I think that my opinions have hardly ever
changed at all about anything.

Balfour 1930[1]

His thought was national, his interests were world-wide. That Britain
should be powerful and prosperous, that the Empire should gather more
closely around her, that she should be the champion of right and peace;
that her own ambitions and aspirations should fit harmoniously into the
requirements of an ever-widening and strengthening Cosmopolis, and
that he should play a worthy part in all this, was his life's aim. He was
in fact a lay-priest seeking a secular goal.[2]

Winston Churchill's panegyric is at least a valid counterpoise to
the caricature of an anaemic 'trimmer' who supposedly went
through life 'never allowing enthusiasm to colour his innate and
detached cynicism'.[3] Certainly Balfour temporised. In the organic
society of his conception, it was part of the job of politicians to
temporise. His conservatism was expedient, but it was not
unprincipled. Churchill rightly remarked on his exceptional
capacity for adjusting the ever-changing current of events to
profound and definite beliefs possessed from earlier life.
Balfour admitted to having changed appallingly little in eighty
years. Seen in a favourable light, his is a record of remarkable
intellectual integrity and even courage. He held 'to his own convictions, steering always by the same stars, diverging only so far as
was inevitable under the thrust of adverse winds'.[4] Alternatively,

---

[1] Dugdale *Balfour* vol. 1 p. 317.
[2] Churchill *Great Contemporaries* p. 238.
[3] Ryan 'Balfour' p. 421.
[4] 'Lord Balfour's Memoirs' *Times* 9 Oct. 1930 p. 15; Churchill *Great Contemporaries* p. 239.

this 'most egotistical of men' deified his own subjective universe.[5]

The fixed logic of his stance in respect of British external policy permits a measure of categorization.

Balfour was a navalist – convinced that maritime supremacy should be the strategic priority of Great Britain.

From this it follows that he was an Imperialist of a limited kind – for a global network of secure naval bases was a requirement of thalassocracy. To this he added an especial regard for white settler colonies as extensions of the Mother Country.

From this it follows that he was an isolationist in relation to Europe – for an Imperial 'Blue Water' strategy neither required nor permitted heavy intervention in most instances. This neglect of continental affairs was relative. European events had global ramifications, and Europe was the only conceivable point of departure for any direct attack on the British Isles. Still the focus of his concern was generally elsewhere. Britain was *not* the arbiter of Europe.

In subscribing to these broad strategic principles – navalism, Imperialism, isolationism – Balfour was accepting the prevailing precepts of British foreign policy in the late nineteenth century. Since the passing of Palmerston in 1865, British leaders had adopted (with varying degrees of willingness) a reserved attitude towards the continent and concentrated on Imperial interests. The threat to those interests came from Russia and France, so Britain endeavoured to keep on good terms with Germany and Austria-Hungary. In 1874, the Foreign Secretary, Lord Derby, explained that he looked to Berlin to preserve the European order and temper Russian expansionism: only if Germany provoked 'an aggressive and an unnecessary war' against France would this attitude change.[6]

Balfour firmly adhered to this way of thinking. A mind which cherished the certainties of naval mastery was easily disturbed by the putative perils of the Indian frontier, and he reasoned that there was no basis for a lasting settlement of Anglo-Russian differences in the foreseeable future. When the Franco-Russian challenge intensified, his reaction was to seek to align Britain more closely with Germany – even to the extent of joining the Triple

---

[5] [Harold Begbie] *The Mirrors of Downing Street* (London 1920) pp. 70 and 74.
[6] Kennedy *Realities behind Diplomacy* p. 80.

Alliance. This seemed to him a logical extension of the existing policy. It might mean the end of diplomatic isolation in Europe, but it was a direct response to Imperial concerns and it was not inconsistent with maritime defence. What the British had to offer was sea-power – and in this the Triplice was then much inferior to the Dual Alliance.[7]

Balfour was certainly more pro-German than was Salisbury, but he did not share the general restiveness with traditional assumptions which characterised Joseph Chamberlain and his followers. The keynote of that movement was its search for radical measures rather than its attachment to any particular alliance bloc.[8] Though the Boer War understandably sharpened his interest in defence reforms, he was not swept up in the sudden clamour for 'National Efficiency', Tariff Reform, military service, or alliance with the first Great Power which presented itself. He was even doubtful about the Anglo-Japanese Alliance initially.

During his premiership, he sought to preserve friendly relations with the Triplice, to withdraw from superfluous commitments in the Western Hemisphere, to settle outstanding colonial disputes with France when the opportunity arose, and to make good use of the Japanese. It did not prove necessary to make a commitment to Germany in order to temper Russian expansionism. The outcome of the Russo-Japanese War and the extension of the Anglo-Japanese Alliance to cover India reinforced British isolation from Europe. If there was a revolution in policy towards the continent in the first decade of the twentieth century, Balfour was not one of the revolutionaries.

By 1905, however, there were many senior figures in the Foreign Office more concerned with European equilibrium than with direct Imperial interests. They thought in terms of a continental balance of power and believed it to be seriously threatened by the growing military and industrial strength of Germany. This chimed with wider anxiety about the growth of the German fleet. From December 1905, Britain had in Grey a Foreign Secretary inclined to reassert balance of power policies by developing closer relations with the Dual Alliance.[9]

---

[7] See above, p. 117.
[8] Kennedy *Realities behind Diplomacy* p. 111.
[9] Matthews *Liberal Imperialists* pp. 203–10.

The significance for foreign policy of the change in Government was obscured by the peculiar circumstances of the year in which it occurred and by contrary tendencies in party opinion.

Balfour accepted that Britain was bound by the Entente to support French policy towards Morocco in 1905. He also held more generally that unjustifiable German aggression could warrant British intervention on the side of France – and invasion on the Moroccan pretext might well have fallen into that category. Yet the crisis was to him a temporary scare arising from implementation of the Anglo-French colonial deal. He apparently supposed that British obligations under the Entente came to an end when the Conference of Algeciras acquiesced in the increase of French influence in Morocco.[10] He did not assume that the collapse of Russia as a first-rate Power (which may have tempted the Germans to bully France) was going to be lasting – as witness his continued warnings against complacency with regard to the Indian frontier.[11] In short, when Balfour allowed British policy to take a pro-French turn in 1904–5, he never thought he was setting a course for the decade to come.

When the emergence of the Triple Entente became evident a few years later, many observers found it easier to credit Balfour and Lansdowne with its conscious initiation than to hold Campbell-Bannerman and Grey responsible. The most vociferous Germanophobes were Unionists, after all, while the most outspoken opponents of power politics and continental entanglements were Liberals. Many responsible Tories, whose strategic priorities were essentially Imperial, had reacted to German naval expansion by becoming pro-French in much the same way as Grey. Balfour did not. He argued (albeit with a touch of feigned naivety) that the maintenance of a wide margin of maritime supremacy should be for Britain a fixed principle – a matter of adding up fleet numbers without reference to foreign relations. Faced with the suggestion of an arms race, his instinct was to contest it on its own terms (and try to persuade the taxpayer that it was worth the money).

It is hard to imagine a Balfour Government cutting the naval programme as the Liberals did – but it is also hard to imagine

---

[10] See above p. 143.
[11] 15 Mar. 1906, *PDeb* 4th Series vol. 153 cols. 1459–60; 9 May 1906, *PDeb* 4th Series vol. 156 col. 1409; 12 July 1906, *PDeb* 4th Series vol. 160 col. 1162.

the Unionists winning the 1906 General Election. Historical speculation of that kind fast merges with make-believe. Suffice it to say that the diplomatic outlook of the Leader of the Opposition 1905–11 underwent no profound transformation despite his mounting concern at German sea-power. When finally told of the development of the Anglo-French Entente since he left office, he thought about Persia and Manchuria, wondered what had been gained, and denied that it was the duty of Britain to maintain the balance of power.[12] After the Agadir Crisis, he tried to adjust to the new situation by reasoning that British membership of the Triple Entente strengthened a European system of deterrence. When war broke out, he reconciled himself to its necessity by perceiving a crazy German bid for world domination.

Balfour did not in later life accept that the Great War had been inevitable: certain things had been within the power of British statesmen to attempt which might have averted it. He left them unspecified, however, and foreswore criticism. Calling Grey 'a great Foreign Secretary', he repeatedly praised his war speech of 3 August 1914 as irresistible in argument and wonderful in effect.[13]

Balfour's views on the prosecution of the conflict ran true to form. He was the leading Conservative anti-conscriptionist. He gave sympathetic consideration to proposals for military action away from the Western Front.[14] He knew the importance of defending Atlantic shipping and attached great value to the blockade as an offensive weapon. At the end of the Great War, there was a widespread feeling that the role of the Royal Navy in the conflict had been inglorious and subsidiary, but Balfour asserted: 'what history will inevitably and amply prove – the great thesis that it was the British Navy which made the victory of the British Army and the Allied Armies possible, and it was upon that unshakable foundation that the whole victory of the Allies rested.'[15]

Bonar Law had criticised him sharply in 1915 for thinking 'that this war can be carried on, as the war against Napoleon was

[12] See above p. 144.
[13] Dugdale *Balfour* vol. II pp. 80 and 119; Riddell *War Diary* pp. 31 and 357.
[14] Dugdale *Balfour* vol. II p. 130; Memo. by Balfour, 1 Feb. 1915, BP 49712 ff. 144–8; Memo. by Balfour, 27 Dec. 1915, PRO CAB 42/7 no. 5. Balfour was not a thorough-going 'Easterner' – he never imagined that campaigns outside northern Europe could be decisive – but he was very far from being a dogmatic 'Westerner'.
[15] Balfour *Opinions and Argument* p. 40.

carried on'.[16] His faith in the traditional British war strategy had indeed survived intact. The normal procedure was: (i) find allies, (ii) capture outlying territories, (iii) impose a blockade, and (iv) wait for the enemy to exhaust himself. Militarily 'forcing the decision' in 1814, 1815, and 1918 had been exceptional. 'We might have again to create a great continental army', he wrote in 1923, 'but short of that, we could play the part which we did in the Wars which ended in 1697, in 1712, in 1749, in 1760, in 1802 and 1856; but I doubt whether we could do much more.'[17]

As with military strategy, so with foreign policy. There is nothing to suggest that the War caused him to revise his basic conception of the appropriate British stance towards continental Europe. He approved the inclusion of punitive elements in the Treaty of Versailles to teach the Germans a lesson, but scorned radical schemes to destroy the economic and military strength of Germany. The French and the Germans had to learn to live with each other – and premature British guarantees would not help this process. In respect of foreign affairs, Balfour must have found the general temper of the Conservative Party more congenial in the 1920s than at any time since the 1890s. The rhetoric of Darwinian struggle had come and gone. Imperial defence and the pursuit of peace remained. It can only be guessed how he would have reacted to evidence after 1930 that (in his terms of analysis) the German Psychological Climate was going from bad to worse.

An aloof attitude to the Franco-German problem did not imply all-round complacency. One new development impressed him deeply. He was acutely aware that the effectiveness of sea-power was being eroded by the submarine and the aeroplane. Britain was suddenly 'more defenceless than it had ever been before'. Abolition of submarines was all the naval disarmament he really wanted, while the prospect of aerial invasion filled him with alarm (heightened by his distrust of the French). He strongly advocated expansion of the Royal Air Force: a One Power Standard was as necessary in the air as on the sea. But how was Britain to afford both? Viscerally averse to taking risks with defence, however remote the prospect of war – and it did seem remote to him – he

[16] D. French *British Strategy and War Aims 1914–16* (London 1986) p. 171.
[17] Balfour to Cavan, 6 July 1923, SRO GD 433/2/8 no. 22.

found the financial constraints hard to accept: 'Our position is a very unhappy one.'[18]

He did not panic. While many stalwart navalists grieved, Balfour accepted parity in capital ships with good heart. The Washington Conference was not the end of *Anglo-Saxon* naval supremacy, and he thought that *in extremis* Britain could count on the USA where it really mattered – namely, in the defence of white English-speaking communities. Thus Balfour was not merely 'the repository of the Salisbury tradition in foreign policy',[19] a dogged upholder of accepted wisdom from decades past. He also falls into the thoroughly twentieth-century category of Atlanticist. In fact, he was one of its originators: the first Prime Minister to identify friendship with the USA as Britain's most valuable international relationship (at a time when its comparative uneventfulness tended to obscure its underlying importance). He recognised the growing need of the British Empire for American tolerance and goodwill, and a personal belief in Anglo-American solidarity buttressed the whole structure of his strategic thought.

By taking a step up the hierarchy of loyalties, in anticipation of others instinctively doing the same, he shed a load of anxiety about the long-term future. In his vision of the world, Britain did not stand alone with its back to the wall. Though its rivals grew more powerful, so too did its friends, and transatlantic cooperation would become more certain and more significant as the effective community of the English-speaking peoples came to maturity. In the meantime, it was the task of British statesmen to keep control of the sea-ways and deal with international difficulties on a pragmatic basis. The USA was often no real help in this, but he found reassurance in his Anglo-American faith. It allowed him to contemplate the relative decline of British power with equanimity – and without having to revise his navalist, Imperialist, detached outlook.

If Balfour represents continuity in British foreign policy, it is not solely by virtue of his longevity and tenacity. He bridges the gap between 'splendid isolation' and 'the special relationship'. He

[18] CID, 14 and 31 Oct. 1921 and 24 May 1922, PRO CAB 2/3; CID Sub-committees, 8 May 1923, PRO CAB 16/48 p. 182 and 16 May 1923, PRO CAB 16/46 pp. 178–9; CID, 15 Oct. and 17 Nov. 1925 and 22 July 1926, PRO CAB 2/4; Naval Programme Committee, 10 Nov. 1927, PRO CAB 27/355 f. 15.
[19] Lord Beaverbrook *Politicians and the War 1914–1916* (London 1960) p. 32.

unquestionably underestimated American reluctance to assume global responsibilities in his own time, but this may be the place to cite J.M. Keynes' assessment of him as 'perfectly poised between the past and the future'[20] – which is not quite the same as being perfectly attuned to the present.

All this provides a clear pointer to where any heirs to Balfour in the realm of foreign policy are most likely to be found. At his death, he left no obvious successor. He was never a man to attract disciples, and 'Balfourism' had merely been a (frequently pejorative) term of the tariff controversy. His protégés, George Wyndham and Alfred Lyttelton, were little involved in foreign affairs and long predeceased him. As is to be expected, certain younger colleagues shared his opinions on particular issues. Baldwin and Amery famously endorsed his attitude to the Dominions, for example, but such personal comparisons cannot be pursued very far. Baldwin sounded like Balfour when talking about Imperial sentiment, national character, and parliamentary government, but he was notoriously reticent about external policy in general. Amery, with his passion for Imperial Preference, his suspicion of the USA, and his Hobbesian view of international relations, was almost the perfect Milnerite.[21] Balfour was not very supportive of France and disliked continental commitments. Was he then a proto-appeaser? The question might be asked with equal justification of practically every leading British politician of the 1920s. On the other hand, when did Neville Chamberlain ever show much interest in developing transatlantic ties?

If that be the touchstone, the man who passes the test is Winston Churchill. He had a certain *rapport* with Balfour and admired his statesmanship. It should be remembered, however, that Churchill, now widely regarded as the embodiment of Anglo-America, had not always appeared so clearly in that light and might never but for the great crisis of 1940.[22] The alliance with the USA then became a virtual necessity for Britain. It remained so in the post-war years, when Russell Kirk's cursory dismissal of Balfour as 'curiously short-sighted in his larger political prophecies and

[20] J.M. Keynes 'The Earl of Balfour' *Economic Journal* vol. 40 (June 1930) p. 336.
[21] Stanley Baldwin *This Torch of Freedom* 4th edn (London 1937) pp. 13, 21–2, 34–5, and 197; W.R. Louis *In the name of God, Go!* (New York 1992) *passim*.
[22] Gilbert *Churchill* vol. v pp. 301 and 315n.

hopes' hardly seems justified.[23] He had, after all, correctly ident-
ified the route by which Britain would ultimately escape from its
strategic dilemma. His expectations were exaggerated, it is true,
but the actual results of the transatlantic alliance should not be
undervalued. When the British Empire fell, its English-speaking
communities remained free to pursue their own way of life. It
might easily have been otherwise. Unveiling his statue in the
Palace of Westminster in 1962, Harold Macmillan praised Balfour
for laying 'the foundations of that Anglo-American understanding
which had ever since served the free world so well'.[24]

Pan-Anglicanism was but the most striking international corollary of a political philosophy firmly rooted in the Romantic conservative tradition. Loud echoes of Burke, Herder, and Coleridge
are to be heard when Balfour speaks of harmonious political communities held together by loyalty and identification.[25] Non-rational
conservatism is an abiding political theory, and Balfour's primary
arguments have not lost their coherence. Some people will find
them objectionable or absurd – as some people always did. In him,
undoubted racism (which accorded with the scientific consensus
of his day) is compounded by a vague cultural determinism. Balfour based his foreign policy on personal assumptions about indefinable national character and nebulous Psychological Climates.
What about power? What about geo-politics? What about
economics?

The concept of power is not central to a theory which views
society as the outcome of historical growth and shared traditions.
Actual nations are not the same as ideal ones, however, and Balfour never disputed that physical resources were a determinant
of national strength. He did deny that the struggle between nations
for the control of physical resources was the essence of international politics. Along with land came people, and wise statesmen
were reluctant to conquer alien populations and incur 'the evils
that follow from the agglomeration of discordant nationalities'.
He thought that the Allies were really doing Germany a favour

[23] R. Kirk *The Conservative Mind from Burke to Santayana* (Chicago 1953) p. 343.
[24] 'Balfour Statue Unveiled' *Times* 10 May 1962 p. 8.
[25] Cf. R.J. White (ed.) *The Conservative Tradition* (London 1950) pp. 114–16; D.P. Calleo *Coleridge and the Idea of the Modern State* (New Haven 1966) pp. 21, 59, 73, 76, 83, and *passim*; F.M. Barnard *Herder's Social and Political Thought* (Oxford 1965) pp. 71, 86, 117, 121, 123, 145.

when they redrew its borders in 1919 to exclude non-Germans.[26]

This emphasis on human loyalties set Balfour apart from balance of power theorists. It helps explain why he was not one of the Edwardian advocates of a Triple Entente to rectify the equilibrium of Europe. He seldom mentioned the continental balance of power except to dismiss it as an anachronism in an age of developed nationalism. He seemed to assume that military expansion in total disregard of nationality was virtually a thing of the past in Western Europe. He certainly found it extremely hard to credit that German leaders were out 'to restore the Germanic Empire of Charlemagne'.[27] If he thought it unlikely that Germany would ever seek to annex or permanently subjugate France, he was not compelled to draw a very close connection between Franco-German antagonism and the defence of British naval supremacy.

British Imperialism demanded that he grant considerations of nationality far less weight outside Europe. 'Politically inarticulate peoples' far away might be conquered for reasons of power. Commitment to Anglo-Saxon global ascendancy placed Balfour in an ambiguous (if not hypocritical) position: Anglo-Saxons had sometimes to descend to power politics in order to protect the world from Powers who knew no better.

It was always the remote control of naval supremacy which commended itself to him, however, so confident was he that maritime power satisfied the main strategic needs of the British Empire. From the 'Blue Water' studies of Admiral Mahan, an Englishman could learn 'more of the external history of his country than he could collect from all the tomes referring to the same subject by which they have been preceded'. This did not stop him accusing Mahan of pushing his conclusions about the influence of sea-power on history 'a little too far'.[28] Geo-political thinking, even in its most congenial form, was too mechanistic for him.

In any case, geo-politics proper pointed in the same direction at global level as Pan-Anglicanism. After 1919, Halford Mackinder himself was prescribing an Anglo-American alliance as the best hope for prolonging the ascendancy of the maritime powers.[29] The

---

[26] Memo. by Balfour, 19 Jan. 1916, PRO CAB 37/141 no. 11.
[27] Balfour to Churchill, 22 Mar. 1912, BP 49694 ff. 75–6.
[28] Balfour to Mahan, 20 Dec. 1899, BP 49742 ff. 253–4.
[29] G. Parker *Western Geopolitical Thought in the Twentieth Century* (London 1985) p. 27.

English-speaking world as a whole had resources to rival those of any challenger.

This underlying assurance may partly account for Balfour's lack of interest in schemes to develop the economic strength of the British Empire. The close connection between industrial wealth and military-political power did not escape him. He simply doubted that governments could significantly affect the course of technological and social change which ultimately determined the relative wealth of nations. His own efforts were directed towards education and science. The Education Act (1902) was 'intimately bound up with our greatness as a nation and our Imperial position in the world'. The Department of Scientific and Industrial Research and the Committee of Civil Research were pet projects of his Lord Presidency. He repeatedly emphasised the need for the application of science to industry. Britain did not compare altogether favourably with Germany and America in this regard. Scientific knowledge would mould the future, and 'if we lack either the imagination or the knowledge we cannot help being at a disadvantage with those who are possessed of both'.[30] For the fundamentals of national prosperity he thus showed clear concern. Of the value of active economic policy, as such, he remained unconvinced.

His foreign policy analyses rarely included economic factors of any sort. Certainly not for him the motto: 'Trade follows the Flag'. Balfour rather feared the tendency of the *flag* to follow *trade*. He would have been happier if Western commerce had remained on the fringes of foreign communities and never interfered with their politics. Diplomats had enough to do without chasing contracts. Balfour took no interest in the commercial side of the Foreign Office.[31] He once confessed: 'I am unfortunately not a man who has had any opportunity of actually dealing with manufactures or commerce or trade or industry in the direct practical manner which a man has to do who earns his livelihood.'[32]

In 1929, a suggestion that the centre of human interest was gradually shifting from politics to economics struck him as profound, but he had never given much credence to economic theories

---

[30] 'Mr. Balfour in Manchester' *Times* 15 Oct. 1902 p. 5; Young *Balfour* pp. 446–8.
[31] Steel-Maitland to Lloyd George, 17 Jan. 1919, Lloyd George Papers F/36/3/3.
[32] 'London School of Economics' *Times* 26 Feb. 1906 p. 14.

of international relations. In his experience, it was simply not the case that all wars were economic wars. Ambition, religion, and territorial and racial feeling all caused conflict.[33]

He had read Marx by 1885 and admitted its intellectual force, but the theoretical distinction between capital and labour was wholly untenable in reality – so argued his unpublished critique of the principles of economics: 'Making and Marketing'. Balfour thought that failure to apprehend the proper relation of economic science to politics was one of the great problems of the age. Economics said a little about one part of human behaviour with exceptional clearness. Its rare objectivity tempted some to exaggerate its claims, but economics could not broaden its province without including great fragments of psychology, sociology, history, and geography, and foregoing its exactitude. Its very barrenness for the student of social character was a condition of its value – yet it was on social character that economic theory itself rested. There was no such thing as a universal economic law, independent of custom, taste, character, knowledge, and belief. The narrow science of economics could never therefore secure primacy over the all-encompassing art of politics. Economic determinism ignored the infinite variety of human impulse and conduct.[34]

Pseudo-scientific approaches to politics seemed to Balfour descriptively inadequate and prescriptively pernicious. A strong nation did not seek domination over weaker nations whenever it could – but when it *would*. It would, moreover, when it thought it should. Ruthless *Realpolitik* was practised by countries which *believed* in ruthless *Realpolitik*. That was the tragedy of Imperial Germany. Nations acted in accordance with their beliefs.

Whose beliefs? Those of the nation as a whole. The opinions of individuals were not logically quantifiable or commensurable, but it was the non-rational influence of man on the beliefs of his fellow men which made social life possible.[35] The herd instinct, personal example, personal ascendancy, corporate authority, custom, tradition, fashion, heredity, and even telepathy served to create a

---

[33] Balfour to Butler, 27 Dec. 1929, BP 49742 f. 226; 8 Aug. 1918, *HCD* vol. 109 cols. 1625–6.

[34] A.J. Balfour 'Land, Land Reformers, and the Nation' *The Report of the Industrial Remuneration Conference* (London 1885) p. 34; 'Making and Marketing' *c.* 1906–8 BP 49954 ff. 5–6, 17–19, 30–4 and 56–9; Balfour 'Politics and Political Economy'.

[35] A.J. Balfour *Familiar Beliefs and Transcendent Reason* (London 1925) p. 12.

climate of opinion which (though subtle and elusive) was not an empty abstraction, but a meaningful expression of shared beliefs. It was this national attitude which the successful statesman (consciously or unconsciously) interpreted. Thus Balfour's conception of foreign policy, though certainly not democratic, was essentially popular. 'Wax and parchment, treaties, protocols, and exchanges of notes', he said, 'all these have a meaning, a purpose, and a result only if there be behind them these sentiments of the great populations concerned, which alone can make them effective.'[36] Political progress was fundamentally governed not by politicians but by the moral and intellectual condition of the people. This model of politics demanded a strong sense of social responsibility and international morality on the part of the individual – especially the influential individual. 'So far as I can observe the forces that make for peace or war in this our great Western civilization', declared Balfour in 1905, 'you will find them on the platform, you will find them in the Press, you will find them, perhaps, even in the professorial chair.'[37] Those who said that world politics was an amoral struggle for wealth and power risked making it so.

Why are human relations at international level so readily subjected to reductionism? Balfour could not accept that the prime motive of man was greed or the lust for power. Unlike Milner, he did not pretend to have discovered the 'law of Life and Progress'. For him, the object of politics was simply the preservation of social life as an end in itself. He did not think in institutional or legal terms. The 'State' he mentioned hardly at all; the 'Nation' not very often. 'Community' was the word – and he applied it to all self-conscious human groups from the family to civilisation. Social life was a network of loyalties which placed a man within a hierarchy of communities of various scope, formality, and cohesiveness. The laws of life in common were similar at every level. The first fact of international relations was plain enough: 'Like members of the same family, we have got to live together.' Family life could be the greatest of blessings or the most serious of curses: 'The principles underlying international action do not differ fundamentally from those underlying family behaviour.'[38]

[36] 'The Prime Minister at Fulham' *Times* 21 July 1902 p. 10.
[37] 'The Visit of the French Fleet' *Times* 14 Aug. 1905 p. 8.
[38] Balfour *Opinions and Argument* pp. 84–5; 'Mr. Balfour at Bristol' *Times* 30 Nov. 1898 p. 10; Balfour to Camp, 1 Dec. 1927, SRO GD 433/2/22 no. 189A.

People – individuals and nationalities – were differentiated by distinctive Psychological Climates born of heredity and environment. They thought in different ways. Some understood each other, liked each other, and came to care about each other. The extension of social sympathy allowed them to tolerate their peculiarities, resolve their differences, and co-operate. Others would never understand each other and had best keep well apart. Balfour thought that the peoples of Europe and North America did form a viable community and should work at strengthening it. The statesman had to 'look beneath the surface of what are called facts and figures to those truths which are more fundamental even than ordinary facts and figures, the fundamental facts of human nature, of the feelings of nation to nation, of communities to communities'.[39] Some national feelings were far from rational. Germany had suffered a fit of insane egotism. France was chronically suspicious and vain. Every nation had its own developing character, its own ideas and idiosyncrasies. No nation saw itself as others saw it. That was the irreducible problem of international relations.

Artificial 'internationalism' was no answer. You did not widen effective social loyalties by weakening them. You could not create an international community by destroying national communities. Patriotism was noble, while what passed under the name of enlightened cosmopolitanism was often in practice indistinguishable from selfish indifference. It was natural and right that people should look at their own nation with different eyes from which they looked at other nations. Increased objectivity was never a guarantee of better relations in any case. Feeling was the key. How could a man follow the political and national struggles of his fellow men in other countries with profound sympathy and deep comprehension unless he shared their passions as well as studied them?[40] At the inaugural meeting of the British (later Royal) Institute for International Affairs, Balfour warned against expecting too much from political science:

There were people so cool and indifferent in their intellectual outlook that they were quite ready to study ... foreign politics, or any politics – without a trace of passion or a trace of sympathy for the actors. They

---

[39] 'Mr. Balfour on his Mission' *Times* 17 Feb. 1922 p. 6.
[40] Balfour *Nationality and Home Rule* pp. 10–11; 'Mr. Balfour on National Sympathy' *Times* 6 July 1920 p. 16.

treated politicians as though they were beetles and great communities as though they were hives of bees. That was quite sound scientifically, but unfortunately the temper of mind which made that scientific attitude so easy was one which destroyed the sympathy without which no knowledge could be acquired of any community.[41]

Balfour proclaimed mutual understanding the essential basis of all good human relationship and the surest safeguard of peace. But he had to admit: 'Verily it is even more difficult for nations than for individuals to acquire the gift of reciprocal comprehension.'[42]

[41] 'Mr. Balfour on National Sympathy' *Times* 6 July 1920 p. 16.
[42] Balfour *Opinions and Argument* pp. 84–5; 'Mr. Balfour in Manchester' *Times* 31 Jan. 1899 p. 10; Balfour to Hügel, 3 Jan. 1916, BP 49864 f. 241.

Bibliography

PRIVATE PAPERS

H.O. Arnold-Forster Papers, British Library.
H.H. Asquith Papers, Bodleian Library.
A.J. Balfour Papers, British Library.
Balfour of Whittingehame Muniments, Scottish Record Office.
Viscount Bertie of Thame Papers, British Library.
Viscount Cecil of Chelwood Papers, British Library.
H.A.L. Fisher Papers, Bodleian Library.
Mary Gladstone Papers, British Library.
Andrew Bonar Law Papers, House of Lords Record Office.
David Lloyd George Papers, House of Lords Record Office.
1st Earl of Midleton Papers, British Library.
Alfred Milner Papers, Bodleian Library.
Gilbert Murray Papers, Bodleian Library.
3rd Marquess of Salisbury Papers, Hatfield House.
J.S. Sandars Papers, Bodleian Library.
2nd Earl of Selborne Papers, Bodleian Library.
St Loe Strachey Papers, House of Lords Record Office.
Alfred Zimmern Papers, Bodleian Library.

STATE PAPERS

Public Record Office: Papers of the Cabinet Office, the Foreign Office, and the War Office.

British Documents on the Origins of the War 1898–1914 (London: Her Majesty's Stationery Office 1926–38).
Documents on British Foreign Policy 1919–1939 1st Series (London: Her Majesty's Stationery Office 1947–85).
British Documents on Foreign Affairs: Reports and Papers from the Foreign Office Confidential Print 1st Series Part II (University Publications of America 1989).
Documents Diplomatiques Français 1871–1914 1st and 2nd Series (Paris: Ministère des Affaires Etrangères 1929–59).
Die Grosse Politik der Europäischen Kabinette 1871–1914 (Berlin: Deutsche Verlagsgesellschaft für Politik und Geschichte 1922–7).
Papers relating to the Foreign Relations of the United States (Washington: Department of State).
Conference on the Limitation of Armament, Washington, 12 Nov. 1921 – 6 Feb. 1922 (Washington: Government Printing Office 1922).

Procès-Verbal of the Council of the League of Nations.
Records of the Assembly of the League of Nations.
League of Nations – Official Journal.

PARLIAMENTARY PAPERS

Parliamentary Debates 3rd and 4th Series.
House of Commons Debates 5th Series.
House of Lords Debates 5th Series.

Report from the Select Committee on the House of Commons (Procedure) (1914)
Report 378 vol. vii pp. 593–909.
Imperial War Conference 1917: Extracts from Minutes of Proceedings (1917) Cd
8566 vol. xxiii pp. 319–481.
Imperial War Conference 1918: Extracts from Minutes of Proceedings (1918) Cd
9177 vol. xvi pp. 691–942.
*Conference of Prime Ministers and Representatives of the United Kingdom, the
Dominions, and India 1921: Summary of Proceedings* (1921) Cmd 1474
vol. xiv pp. 1–69.
Papers Respecting Negotiations for an Anglo-French Pact (1924) Cmd 2169 vol.
xxvi pp. 187–367.
Imperial Conference 1926: Summary of Proceedings (1926) Cmd 2768 vol. xi
pp. 545–605.

NEWSPAPERS AND MAGAZINES

British Gazette.
Daily Mail.
Daily Telegraph
Fortnightly Review.
National Review.
New York Times.
Quarterly Review.
Review of Reviews.
Times.

BOOKS AND ARTICLES

Albrecht-Carrie, R. *Italy at the Paris Peace Conference* (Hamden: Archon
1966).
Alderman, G. *The Jewish Community in British Politics* (Oxford: Clarendon
1983).
Alderson, B. *Arthur James Balfour: The Man and his Work* (London: Grant
Richards 1903).
Allen, H.C. *The Anglo-American Relationship since 1783* (London: Adam and
Charles Black 1959).
Amery, J. *The Life of Joseph Chamberlain* vol. IV (London: Macmillan 1951).

Amery, L.S. *The Empire in the New Era* with a Foreword by Lord Balfour (London: Edward Arnold 1928).
My Political Life (London: Hutchinson 1953).
Andrew, C. *Theophile Delcassé and the Making of the Entente Cordiale* (London: Macmillan 1968).
Angell, Norman *The Great Illusion* (London: Heinemann 1910).
Anonymous *Home Rule ?'s Answered* (London: Liberal Publication Department 1913).
Arnold-Forster, M. *The Rt. Hon. Hugh Oakeley Arnold-Forster: A Memoir* (London: Edward Arnold 1910).
Page Arnot, R. *The Impact of the Russian Revolution in Britain* (London: Lawrence and Wishart 1967).
Asquith, Lady Cynthia *Diaries 1914–1918* (London: Hutchinson 1968).
Asquith, H. *Moments of Memory* (London: Hutchinson 1938).
Bagehot, Walter *The English Constitution* with an Intro. by Lord Balfour (Oxford: Oxford University Press 1928).
Bailey, T.A. *Woodrow Wilson and the Lost Peace* (Chicago: Quadrangle 1944).
Baker, Ray Stannard *Woodrow Wilson and World Settlement* (London: Heinemann 1923).
Woodrow Wilson: Life and Letters (London: Heinemann 1928–39).
Baldwin, Stanley *This Torch of Freedom* 4th edn (London: Hodder and Stoughton 1937).
Balfour, Alice *Twelve Hundred Miles in a Waggon* (London: Edward Arnold 1895).
Balfour, A.J. 'The Indian Civil Service: A Reply' *Fortnightly Review* vol. 28 no. 128 (Aug. 1877) pp. 244–58.
'A Speculation on Evolution' *Fortnightly Review* vol. 28 no. 131 (Nov 1877) pp. 698–704.
'The Philosophy of Ethics' *Mind* vol. 3 (1878) pp. 67–86.
A Defence of Philosophic Doubt (London: Macmillan 1879).
Mr. Gladstone's Scotch Speeches (Edinburgh: Blackwood 1880).
'Morley's *Life of Cobden*' *Nineteenth Century* vol. 11 no. 59 (Jan. 1882) pp. 40–55.
'Berkeley's Life and Letters' *The National Review* vol. 1 (1883) pp. 85–100 and 299–313.
'Green's Metaphysics of Knowledge' *Mind* vol. 9 (1884) pp. 73–92.
'Land, Land Reformers, and the Nation' *The Report of the Industrial Remuneration Conference* (London: Cassell 1885) pp. 336–68.
'Politics and Political Economy' *National Review* vol. 5 (1885) pp. 361–7.
The Religion of Humanity (Edinburgh: David Douglas 1888).
British Industries and International Bimetallism (London: Effingham Wilson 1892).
A Fragment on Progress (Edinburgh: David Douglas 1892).
The Currency Question (London: Effingham Wilson 1893).

The Nineteenth Century (Cambridge: Cambridge University Press 1900).

Economic Notes on Insular Free Trade (London: Longman and Green 1903).

Negotiation and Imperial Trade (London: Conservative Central Office 1904).

Reflections suggested by the New Theory of Matter (London: Longman and Green 1904).

Essays and Addresses 3rd edn (Edinburgh: David Douglas 1905).

Fiscal Reform (London: Longman and Green 1906).

The Foundations of Belief 9th impression (London: Longman and Green 1906).

Decadence (Cambridge: Cambridge University Press 1908).

'Race and Nationality' *Transactions of the Honourable Society of Cymmrodorian* (1908–9) pp. 237–42.

'Creative Evolution and Philosophic Doubt' *Hibbert Journal* vol. 9 (1911) pp. 1–23.

Aspects of Home Rule ed. L. Magnus (London: Routledge 1912).

Nationality and Home Rule (London: Longman and Green 1913).

The British Blockade (London: Darling 1915).

The Navy and the War (London: Darling 1915).

Theism and Humanism (London: Hodder and Stoughton 1915).

The Freedom of the Seas (London: Fisher Unwin 1916).

Essays Speculative and Political (London: Hodder and Stoughton 1920).

Theism and Thought (London: Hodder and Stoughton 1923).

'The League' *Headway* vol. 6 no. 1 (Jan. 1924) pp. 4–5.

Familiar Beliefs and Transcendent Reason (London: Oxford University Press 1925).

Opinions and Argument (London: Hodder and Stoughton 1927).

Speeches on Zionism ed. I. Cohen (London: Arrowsmith 1928).

Chapters of Autobiography (London: Cassell 1930).

Balfour, Lady Frances *Ne Obliviscaris; Dinna Forget* (London: Hodder and Stoughton 1930).

Bannister, R. *Social Darwinism: Science and Myth in Anglo-American Social Thought* (Philadelphia: Temple University Press 1979).

Barnard, F.M. *Herder's Social and Political Thought* (Oxford: Clarendon 1965).

Barnes, George *From Workshop to War Cabinet* (London: Jenkins 1924).

Barnes, J., and Nicholson, J. (eds.) *The Leo Amery Diaries 1896–1929* (London: Hutchinson 1980).

Bärtschi, H.E. *Die Entwicklung vom Imperialistischen Reichsgedanken zur modernen Idee des Commonwealths im Lebenswerk Lord Balfours* (Aarau: Verlag H.R. Sauerländer 1957).

Bates, J.V. *Sir Edward Carson* with an Intro. by A.J. Balfour (London: John Murray 1921).

Beale, H.K. *Theodore Roosevelt and the Rise of America to World Power* (Baltimore: Johns Hopkins Press 1956).

Beaverbrook, Lord *Men and Power 1916–1917* (London: Hutchinson 1956).

Politicians and the War 1914–1916 (London: Oldbourne 1960).

[Begbie, Harold] *The Mirrors of Downing Street: Some Political Reflections by a Gentleman with a Duster* 12th edn (London: Mills and Boon 1920).

Benson, A.C. *Land of Hope and Glory* (London: Boosey and Hawkes 1902).

Beresford, Lord Charles *The Break-Up of China* (London: Hooper 1899).

Bernhardi, Friedrich von *Germany and the Next War* transl. by A.H. Powles (London: Edward Arnold 1912).

Bertie, Lord *The Diary of Lord Bertie of Thame 1914–1918* (London: Hodder and Stoughton 1924).

Birdsall, P. *Versailles Twenty Years After* (Hamden: Archon 1941).

Birkenhead, Lord *Contemporary Personalities* (London: Cassell 1924).

Birrell, Augustine *Things Past Redress* (London: Faber 1937).

Blake, R., and Cecil, H.P. (eds.) *Salisbury: The Man and his Policies* (Basingstoke: Macmillan 1987).

Blunt, W.S. *My Diaries* (London: Secker 1919–20).

Bolt, C. *Victorian Attitudes to Race* (London: Routledge and Kegan Paul 1971).

Bonsal, S. *Unfinished Business* (London: Michael Joseph 1944).

Suitors and Suppliants: The Little Nations at Versailles (New York: Prentice-Hall 1946).

Borden, H. (ed.) *Robert Laird Borden: His Memoirs* (London: Macmillan 1938).

Bourne, K. *The Foreign Policy of Victorian England 1830–1902* (Oxford: Clarendon 1970).

Brendon, P. *Eminent Edwardians* (London: Secker and Warburg 1979).

Brett, M.V. and O. (eds.) *Journals and Letters of Reginald, Viscount Esher* (London: Nicholson and Watson 1934–8).

Bridge, F.R. *Great Britain and Austria-Hungary 1906–1914: A Diplomatic History* (London: Weidenfeld and Nicolson 1972).

Bridges, Sir Tom *Alarms and Excursions: Reminiscences of a Soldier* (London: Longman and Green 1938).

Bruce, Stanley M. 'The British Commonwealth of Nations' *International Conciliation* no. 228 (Worcester, Mass.: Carnegie Endowment for International Peace 1927).

Bryce, James *Impressions of South Africa* 3rd edn (London: Macmillan 1899).

Buckle, G.E. (ed.) *The Letters of Queen Victoria* 3rd Series vol. III (London: John Murray 1932).

Buell, R.L. *The Washington Conference* (New York: Appleton 1922).

Bülow, Bernhard von *Memoirs* (London: Putnam 1932).

Burk, Kathleen *Britain, America and the Sinews of War 1914–1918* (Boston: Allen and Unwin 1985).

Burton, D.H. 'Theodore Roosevelt and his English Correspondents: A Special Relationship of Friends' *Transactions of the American Philosophical Society* New Series vol. 63 pt 2 (Philadelphia 1973).

Caine, Hall (ed.) *King Albert's Book* (London: Daily Telegraph 1914).

Calleo, D.P. *Coleridge and the Idea of the Modern State* (New Haven: Yale University Press 1966).

Callwell, C.E. *Field-Marshal Sir Henry Wilson: His Life and Diaries* (London: Cassell 1927).

Cambon, Paul *Correspondance 1870–1924* (Paris: Editions Bernard Grasset 1940).

Campbell, A.E. *Great Britain and the United States 1895–1903* (London: Longman and Green 1960).

Campbell, C.S. *Anglo-American Understanding 1898–1903* (Baltimore: Johns Hopkins Press 1957).

Campbell, J. *F.E. Smith, First Earl of Birkenhead* (London: Jonathan Cape 1983).

Carlton, D. 'Great Britain and the Coolidge Naval Disarmament Conference of 1927' *Political Science Quarterly* vol. 83 (1968) pp. 573–98.

Carr, E.H. *The Twenty Years' Crisis 1919–1939* (London: Macmillan 1942).

Carr, Wildon H. *Henri Bergson: The Philosophy of Change* (London: Jack 1912).

Cecil, Lady Gwendolen *Life of Robert, Marquis of Salisbury* (London: Hodder and Stoughton 1922–32).

'Cecil, Hugh' [Ernest Newman] *Pseudo-Philosophy at the End of the Nineteenth Century: An Irrationalist Trio: Kidd – Drummond – Balfour* (London: London University Press 1897).

Cecil, H.P. 'The Development of Lord Robert Cecil's Views on the Securing of a Lasting Peace 1915–19' (Oxford: DPhil thesis 1971).

Cecil, Lord Robert *A Great Experiment* (London: Jonathan Cape 1941). *All the Way* (London: Hodder and Stoughton 1949).

Chamberlain, Sir Austen *Down the Years* (London: Cassell 1935). *Politics from Inside* (London: Cassell 1936).

Chamberlain, Austen, and Balfour, A.J. *The Unionist Party and Future Policy* (London: Harrison 1922).

Chilston, Viscount 'Balfour: The Philosopher at the Helm' *Parliamentary Affairs* vol. 13 (1959–60) pp. 442–57.

Chirol, Valentine *The Far Eastern Question* (London: Macmillan 1896).

Christie, C.H.P. *Mr. Balfour and Conceivable Cures for Imagined Ills* (London: Effingham Wilson 1903).

Churchill, Randolph S. *Winston S. Churchill* vols. I and II (London: Heinemann 1966–7).

Churchill, W.S. *Great Contemporaries* (London: Thornton Butterworth 1937).

Clark, A. (ed.) *'A Good Innings': The Private Papers of Viscount Lee of Fareham* (London: John Murray 1974).

Coates, W. & Z. *Armed Intervention in Russia 1918–1922* (London: Gollancz 1935).

A *History of Anglo-Soviet Relations* (London: Lawrence and Wishart 1943).

Cohen, L. *Lady de Rothschild and her Daughters 1821–1931* (London: John Murray 1935).

Coogan, J.W. *The End of Neutrality: The United States, Britain, and Maritime Rights 1899–1915* (Ithaca, N.Y.: Cornell University Press 1981).

Cox, Harold *Mr. Balfour's Pamphlet: A Reply* (London: Fisher Unwin 1903).

Crook, D.P. *Benjamin Kidd: Portrait of a Social Darwinist* (Cambridge: Cambridge University Press 1984).

Cross, C. *The Fall of the British Empire 1918–1968* (London: Hodder and Stoughton 1968).

D'Abernon, Viscount *Portraits and Appreciations* (London: Hodder and Stoughton 1931).

Darwin, F. (ed.) *The Life and Letters of Charles Darwin* (London: John Murray 1887).

Darwin, J. 'Imperialism in Decline? Tendencies in British Imperial Policy between the Wars' *Historical Journal* vol. 23 no. 3 (1980) pp. 657–79.

David, E. (ed.) *Inside Asquith's Cabinet: From the Diaries of Charles Hobhouse* (London: John Murray 1977).

Dawson, W.H. *Germany under the Treaty* (London: Allen and Unwin 1933).

Deakin, Alfred *The Federal Story* (Melbourne: Robertson and Mullins 1944).

Dickinson, G. Lowes *The International Anarchy 1904–14* 2nd edn (London: Allen and Unwin 1937).

Dictionary of National Biography 1922–30 (London: Oxford University Press 1937).

Digby, M. *Horace Plunkett: An Anglo-American Irishman* (Oxford: Blackwell 1949).

Dilke, Sir Charles *Greater Britain* (London: Macmillan 1868).

Dilks, D. *Curzon in India* (London: Hart Davis 1969–70).

Dos Passos, J.R. *The Anglo-Saxon Century and the Unification of the English-Speaking People* (New York: Putnam 1903).

Dugdale, Blanche *Arthur James Balfour* (London: Hutchinson 1936).

The Balfour Declaration: Origins and Background (London: Jewish Agency for Palestine 1940).

Dugdale, E.T.S. *Maurice de Bunsen: Diplomat and Friend* (London: John Murray 1934).

Eckardstein, Hermann von *Ten Years at the Court of St. James 1895–1905*, transl. by G. Young (London: Thornton Butterworth 1921).

Egerton, G.W. *Great Britain and the Creation of the League of Nations* (London: Scolar 1979).

Egremont, M. *Balfour* (London: Collins 1980).

d'Egville, Howard *Imperial Defence and Closer Union* (London: King 1913).

Elcock, H. *Portrait of a Decision: The Council of Four and the Treaty of Versailles* (London: Eyre Methuen 1972).

Elers, G. *The Memoirs of George Elers, Captain in the 12th Regiment of Foot (1777–1842)* (London: Heinemann 1903).

Encyclopaedia Britannica (London: Encyclopaedia Britannica 1962).

Engelenburg, F.V. *General Louis Botha* (London: Harrap 1929).

'Falastin' Newspaper *The Balfour Declaration: An Analysis* (Jaffa: Falastin 1929).

Ferguson, J.H. *American Diplomacy and the Boer War* (Philadelphia: University of Pennsylvania Press 1939).

Fest, W. *Peace or Partition: The Habsburg Monarchy and British Policy 1914–1918* (London: George Prior 1978).

Fifield, R.H. *Woodrow Wilson and the Far East* (New York: Crowell 1952).

Fischer, L. *The Soviets in World Affairs* (Princeton: Princeton University Press 1930).

Fisher, L. *An Unfinished Autobiography* (London: Oxford University Press 1940).

Fitzhardinge, L.F. *The Little Digger 1914–52: William Morris Hughes* (Sydney: Angus and Robertson 1979).

Fitzroy, Sir Almeric *Memoirs* (London: Hutchinson 1925).

Foot, M.R.D. *British Foreign Policy since 1898* (London: Hutchinson 1956).

Forbes, Rosita *These Men I Knew* (London: The Right Book Club 1940).

Fowler, W.B. *British–American Relations 1917–18: The Role of Sir William Wiseman* (Princeton: Princeton University Press 1969).

Fraser, P. *Lord Esher: A Political Biography* (London: Hart-Davis MacGibbon 1973).

French, D. *British Strategy and War Aims 1914–16* (London: Allen and Unwin 1986).

Friedman, I. *The Question of Palestine 1914–1918* (London: Routledge and Kegan Paul 1973).

Fry, M.G. *Illusions of Security: North Atlantic Security 1918–22* (Toronto: University of Toronto Press 1972).

Garraty, J.A. *Henry Cabot Lodge* (New York: Alfred Knopf 1953).

Gartner, L.P. *The Jewish Immigrant in England 1870–1914* (London: Allen and Unwin 1960).

Garvin, J.L. *The Life of Joseph Chamberlain* vols. I–III (London: Macmillan 1932–4).

Gelber, L.M. *The Rise of Anglo-American Friendship: A Study in World Politics 1898–1906* (London: Oxford University Press 1938).

Gibbs, N.H. *The Origins of Imperial Defence* (Oxford: Clarendon 1955).

Giddings, Franklin *Democracy and Empire* (New York: Macmillan 1900).

Gifford, P. and Louis, W.R. *Britain and Germany in Africa* (New Haven: Yale University Press 1967).

Gilbert, M. *Winston S. Churchill* vols. III–VIII (London: Heinemann 1971–88).
   Exile and Return: The Emergence of Jewish Statehood (London: Weidenfeld
   and Nicolson 1978).
Gillon, D.Z. 'The Antecedents of the Balfour Declaration' *Middle Eastern
   Studies* vol. 5 no. 2 (1969) pp. 131–50.
Gilmour, D. *Curzon* (London: John Murray 1994).
Goldstein, E. *Winning the Peace: British Diplomatic Strategy, Peace Planning,
   and the Paris Peace Conference* (Oxford: Clarendon 1991).
Gollin, A.M. '*The Observer*' *and J.L. Garvin 1908–14* (London: Oxford Uni-
   versity Press 1960).
   Proconsul in Politics (London: Blond 1964).
   Balfour's Burden: Arthur Balfour and Imperial Preference (London: Blond
   1965).
Goodman, Paul (ed.) *The Jewish National Home* (London: Dent 1943).
Goodman, Paul, and Lewis, A. (eds.) *Zionism: Problems and Views* (London:
   Fisher Unwin 1916).
Gordon, D.C. *The Dominion Partnership in Imperial Defence 1870–1914*
   (Baltimore: Johns Hopkins Press 1965).
Goudswaard, J.M. *Some Aspects of the End of Britain's 'Splendid Isolation'
   1898–1904* (Rotterdam: Brusse 1952).
Gregory, R. *Walter Hines Page: Ambassador to the Court of St. James*
   (Lexingon: University Press of Kentucky 1970).
Grenville, J.A.S. *Lord Salisbury and Foreign Policy* (London: Athlone 1964).
Grey, Sir Edward *Twenty-Five Years 1892–1916* (London: Hodder and
   Stoughton 1925).
Gwynne, S. (ed.) *The Letters and Friendships of Sir Cecil Spring Rice* (London:
   Constable 1929).
Gwynne, S., and Tuckwell, G. *The Life of the Rt. Hon. Sir Charles W. Dilke*
   (London: John Murray 1918).
Hall, H. Duncan 'The Genesis of the Balfour Declaration of 1926' *Journal
   of Commonwealth Political Studies* (1962).
Halperin, V. *Lord Milner and the Empire* (London: Odhams 1952).
Hamilton, Lord George *Parliamentary Reminiscences and Reflections 1886–
   1906* (London: John Murray 1922).
Hammond, W.J. *Thoughts on Mr. Chamberlain's Proposed Fiscal Policy*
   (London: Effingham Wilson 1903).
Hancock, W.K. and Poel, J. van der (eds.) *Selections from the Smuts Papers*
   (Cambridge: Cambridge University Press 1966).
Hankey, Lord *Diplomacy by Conference* (London: Ernest Benn 1946).
   The Supreme Command 1914–1918 (London: Allen and Unwin 1961).
   The Supreme Control at the Paris Peace Conference 1919 (London: Allen and
   Unwin 1963).
Hardinge, Lord *Old Diplomacy* (London: John Murray 1947).
Harris, P. *Life in a Scottish Country House: The Story of A.J. Balfour and
   Whittingehame House* (Whittingehame: Whittingehame House Pub-
   lishing 1989).

Harrison, Frederic *The Philosophy of Common Sense* (London: Macmillan 1907).

Hartley, S. *The Irish Question as a Problem in British Foreign Policy 1914–18* (Basingstoke: Macmillan 1987).

Hayashi, Tadasu *The Secret Memoirs of Count Tadasu Hayashi* ed. A.M. Pooley (London: Eveleigh Nash 1915).

Headlam, C. (ed.) *The Milner Papers: South Africa 1899–1905* (London: Cassell 1933).

Headlam-Morley, Sir J. *A Memoir of the Paris Peace Conference 1919* (London: Methuen 1972).

Hearder, H., and Loyn, H. (eds.) *British Government and Administration: Studies Presented to S.B. Chrimes* (Cardiff: University of Wales Press 1974).

Heever, C.M. van den *General J.B.M. Hertzog* (Johannesburg: A.P.B. 1946).

Heindel, R.H. *The American Impact on Great Britain 1898–1914* (Philadelphia: University of Pennsylvania Press 1940).

Hendrick, B.J. *The Life and Letters of Walter H. Page* (London: Heinemann 1924).

The Life of Andrew Carnegie (Garden City, N.Y.: Doubleday and Doran 1932).

Hewins, W.A.S. *The Apologia of an Imperialist* (London: Constable 1929).

Hofstadter, R. *Social Darwinism in Anglo-American Thought 1860–1915* (Philadelphia: University of Pennsylvania Press 1945).

Holland, B. *The Life of Spencer Compton, Eighth Duke of Devonshire 1833–1908* (London: Longman and Green 1911).

Holland, R.F. *Britain and the Commonwealth Alliance 1918–1939* (London: Macmillan 1981).

House, E.M. and Seymour, C. *What Really Happened at Paris* (London: Hodder & Stoughton 1921).

Howard, C. *Britain and the 'Casus Belli' 1822–1902* (London: Athlone 1974).

Hudson, W. and North, J. (eds.) *My Dear P.M.: R.G. Casey's Letters to S.M. Bruce 1924–29* (Canberra: Australian Government Publishing 1980).

Hughes, W.M. *The Splendid Adventure: Empire Relations within and without the Commonwealth of Britannic Nations* (London: Ernest Benn 1929).

Hurst, M. (ed.) *Key Treaties for the Great Powers 1814–1914* (Newton Abbot: David and Charles 1972).

Hyam, R. *Britain's Imperial Century 1815–1914: A Study of Empire and Expansion* (London: Batsford 1976).

Ichihashi, Y. *The Washington Conference and After* (Stanford: Stanford University Press 1928).

Jackson, S. *The Sassoons* (London: Heinemann 1968).

Jaffe, L.S. *The Decision to Disarm Germany: British Policy towards Postwar German Disarmament 1914–1919* (Boston: Allen and Unwin 1985).

Jebb, R. *The Imperial Conference* (London: Longman and Green 1911).

Jenkins, R. *Asquith* (London: Collins 1964).

Joll, J. *1914: The Unspoken Assumptions* (London: Weidenfeld and Nicolson 1968).

Jones, Thomas *Whitehall Diary 1916–1925* ed. K. Middlemas (London: Oxford University Press 1969).

Jordan, W.M. *Great Britain, France and the German Problem 1918–39* (London: Oxford University Press 1943).

Judd, D. *Balfour and the British Empire: A Study in Imperial Evolution 1874–1932* (London: Macmillan 1968).

Keep, J. (ed.) *Contemporary History in the Soviet Mirror* (London: Allen and Unwin 1964).

Kendle, J.E. *The Colonial and Imperial Conferences 1887–1911* (London: Longmans 1967).

Kennan, G.F. *American Diplomacy 1900–1950* (Chicago, 1951).

Kennedy, A.L. *Old Diplomacy and New 1876–1922: From Salisbury to Lloyd George* (London: John Murray 1922).

Salisbury 1830–1903 (London: John Murray 1952).

Kennedy, P.M. *The Rise and Fall of British Naval Mastery* (London: Allen Lane 1976).

The Rise of Anglo-German Antagonism 1860–1914 (London: Allen & Unwin 1980).

The Realities behind Diplomacy (London: Fontana 1981).

Kerensky, Alexander *The Kerensky Memoirs* (London: Cassell 1965).

Kettle, M. *The Allies and the Russian Collapse* (London: Andre Deutsch 1981).

The Road to Intervention (London: Routledge 1988).

Keynes, J.M. 'The Earl of Balfour' *Economic Journal* vol. 40 (1930) pp. 336–8.

Kidd, Benjamin *Social Evolution* new edn (London: Macmillan 1895).

The Control of the Tropics (New York: Macmillan 1898).

Individualism and After (Oxford: Clarendon 1908).

Kidd, J.A. *The Beaverbrook Girl* (London: Collins 1987).

Kimche, J. *The Unromantics: The Great Powers and the Balfour Declaration* (London: Weidenfeld and Nicolson 1968).

Kirk, R. *The Conservative Mind from Burke to Santayana* (Chicago: Henry Regnery 1953).

Lansing, R. *The War Memoirs of Robert Lansing* (London: Rich and Cowan 1935).

The Lansing Papers 1914–1920 (Washington: Department of State 1939–40).

Lentin, A. *Guilt at Versailles: Lloyd George and the Pre-History of Appeasement* (London: Methuen 1985).

Lewis, R. *Enoch Powell: Principle in Politics* (London: Cassell 1979).

Link, A.S. *Wilson: Confusion and Crises 1915–16* (Princeton: Princeton University Press 1964).

Lloyd George, David *War Memoirs* 2nd edn (London: Oldhams 1938).
The Truth about the Peace Treaties (London: Gollancz 1938).
Lloyd George, Frances *The Years that are Past* (London: Hutchinson 1967).
Lockhart, R.H. Bruce *Memoirs of a British Agent* (London: Putnam 1932).
Retreat from Glory (London: Putnam 1934).
Lodge, H.C. *One Hundred Years of Peace* (New York: Macmillan 1913).
Selections from the Correspondence of Theodore Roosevelt and Henry Cabot Lodge 1884–1918 (New York: Scribner 1925).
Louis, W.R. *British Strategy in the Far East 1919–39* (Oxford: Clarendon 1971).
In the Name of God, Go!: Leo Amery and the British Empire in the Age of Churchill (New York: Norton 1992).
Lowe, C., and Dockrill, M. *The Mirage of Power* (London: Routledge and Kegan Paul 1972).
Lowe, P. *Great Britain and Japan 1911–15* (London: Macmillan 1969).
Lyons, F.S.L. *John Dillon* (London: Routledge and Kegan Paul 1968).
Macartney, A., and Cremona, P. *Italy's Foreign and Colonial Policy* (London: Oxford University Press 1938).
McEwen, J.M. (ed.) *The Riddell Diaries 1908–1923* (London: Athlone 1986).
Mackay, R. *Balfour: Intellectual Statesman* (Oxford: Oxford University Press 1985).
Malcolm, Ian *Lord Balfour: A Memory* (London: Macmillan 1930).
Vacant Thrones (London: Macmillan 1931).
Marais, J.S. *The Fall of Kruger's Republic* (Oxford: Clarendon 1961).
Marder, A.J. *From the Dreadnought to Scapa Flow* vol. 1 (London: Oxford University Press 1961).
Marder, A.J. (ed.) *Fear God and Dread Nought: The Correspondence of Admiral of the Fleet Lord Fisher of Kilverstone* (London: Jonathan Cape 1952).
Marlowe, J. *Milner: Apostle of Empire* (London: Hamish Hamilton 1976).
Martin, E.S. *The Life of Joseph Hodges Choate* (London: Constable 1920).
Matthews, H.C.G. *The Liberal Imperialists* (Oxford: Oxford University Press 1973).
Maxse, L.J. *Politicians on the War-Path* (London: The National Review 1920).
Mee, C.L. *The End of Order: Versailles 1919* (London: Secker and Warburg 1981).
Meinertzhagen, R. *Middle East Diary 1917–1956* (London: Cresset Press 1959).
Middlemas, K., and Barnes, J. *Baldwin* (London: Weidenfeld and Nicolson 1969).
Midleton, Lord *Records and Reactions 1856–1939* (London: John Murray 1939).
Mill, J.S. *Considerations on Representative Government* (London: Parker and Bourn 1861).

Miller, D.H. *My Diary at the Conference of Paris* (New York: privately printed 1924–6).
Drafting the Covenant (New York: Putnam 1928).
Miller, J.D.B. *Norman Angell and the Futility of War* (Basingstoke: Macmillan 1986).
Milner, Viscountess *My Picture Gallery* (London: John Murray 1951).
Monger, G. *The End of Isolation* (London: Nelson 1963).
Morgan, K.O. *Consensus and Disunity: The Lloyd George Coalition Government 1918–1922* (Oxford: Clarendon 1979).
Morgan-Brown, H. *Balfourism: A Study in Contemporary Politics* (London: Fisher Unwin 1907).
Morison, E.E. *The Letters of Theodore Roosevelt* vol. VII (Cambridge, Mass.: Harvard University Press 1954).
Morley, John *Recollections* (London: Macmillan 1917).
Morris, A.J.A. *The Scaremongers: The Advocacy of War and Rearmament 1896–1914* (London: Routledge and Kegan Paul 1984).
Mosley, L. *Curzon: The End of an Epoch* (London: Longman and Green 1961).
Naamani, I.T. 'The Theism of Lord Balfour' *History Today* vol. 17 no. 10 (1967) pp. 660–6.
Neale, R.G. *Great Britain and United States Expansion 1898–1900* (Detroit: Michigan State University Press 1966).
Neame, L.E. *General Hertzog* (London: Hurst and Blackett 1930).
Neatby, H.B. *William Lyon Mackenzie King* (Toronto: University of Toronto Press 1963).
Needham, J. *Science Religion and Reality* with an Intro. by Lord Balfour (London: Sheldon 1926).
Neidpath, J. *The Singapore Naval Base* (Oxford: Clarendon 1981).
Nelson, H. *Land and Power: British and Allied Policy on Germany's Frontiers 1916–1919* (London: Routledge and Kegan Paul 1963).
Nevins, A. *Henry White: Thirty Years of American Diplomacy* (New York: Harper 1930).
Newsome, D. (ed.) *Edwardian Excursions: From the Diaries of A.C. Benson 1898–1904* (London: John Murray 1981).
Newton, Lord *Lord Lansdowne* (London: Macmillan 1929).
Retrospection (London: John Murray 1941).
Nicolson, Harold *People and Things* (London: Constable 1931).
Curzon: The Last Phase (London: Constable 1934).
Peacemaking 1919 new edn (London: Constable 1945).
King George the Fifth (London: Constable 1952).
Nish, I. *The Anglo-Japanese Alliance* (London: Athlone 1966).
Alliance in Decline (London: Athlone 1972).
O'Brien, P. 'The Costs and Benefits of British Imperialism 1864–1914' *Past and Present* no. 120 (1988) pp. 163–200.
Oldroyd, D.R. *Darwinian Impacts* (Milton Keynes: Open University Press 1980).

Parker, G. *Western Geopolitical Thought in the Twentieth Century* (London: Croom Helm 1985).

Pearson, Karl *Reaction! A Criticism of Mr. Balfour's Attack on Rationalism* (London: William Reeves 1895).

Percy, Lord Eustace *Some Memories* (London: Eyre and Spottiswoode 1958).

Perkins, B. *The Great Rapprochement: England and the United States 1895–1914* (New York: Atheneum 1968).

Pigou, A.C. *The Great Inquest* (London: 'The Pilot' 1903).

Pinto-Duschinsky, M. *The Political Thought of Lord Salisbury 1854–68* (London: Constable 1967).

Pollock, Sir Frederick 'A.J. Balfour, the Foundations of Belief' *Mind* New Series vol. 4 (1895) pp. 376–84.

Ponsonby, Arthur *Democracy and Diplomacy* (London: Methuen 1915).

Pribram, A.F. *England and the International Policy of the European Great Powers 1871–1914* (Oxford: Clarendon 1931).

Pusey, M.J. *Charles Evans Hughes* 3rd edn (New York: Columbia University Press 1963).

Pyrah, G.B. *Imperial Policy and South Africa* (Oxford: Clarendon 1955).

Rayleigh, Lord *Lord Balfour in his Relation to Science* (Cambridge: Cambridge University Press 1930).

'Raymond, E.T.' [E.R. Thompson] *Uncensored Celebrities* (London: Fisher Unwin 1919).

Mr. Balfour (London: Collins 1920).

Portraits of the New Century (London: Ernest Benn 1928).

Rendel, Sir George *The Sword and the Olive* (London: John Murray 1957).

Repington, C.C. *The First World War* (London: Constable 1920).

Rhodes, J.F. *The McKinley and Roosevelt Administrations 1897–1909* (New York: Macmillan 1922).

Rich, N., and Fisher, M. (eds.) *The Holstein Papers* (Cambridge: Cambridge University Press 1955–63).

Riddell, Lord *Lord Riddell's War Diary* (London: Nicholson and Watson 1933).

Lord Riddell's Intimate Diary of the Peace Conference and After (London: Gollancz 1933).

More Pages from My Diary (London: Country Life 1934).

Ridley, J., and Percy, C. (eds.) *The Letters of Arthur Balfour and Lady Elcho 1885–1917* (London: Hamish Hamilton 1992).

Robbins, K. *Sir Edward Grey* (London: Cassell 1971).

Robson, W.S. et al. *The Premier's Fiscal Doctrines* (London: Black 1905).

Rohl, J. *1914: Delusion or Design* (London: Elek 1973).

Rolo, P.V.J. *Entente Cordiale* (London: Macmillan 1969).

Ronaldshay, Lord *The Life of Lord Curzon* (London: Ernest Benn 1927).

Root, J.D. 'The Philosophical and Religious Thought of Arthur James Balfour' *Journal of British Studies* vol. 19 no. 2 (1980) pp. 120–41.

Rose, K. *The Later Cecils* (New York: Harper and Row 1975).

Rose, N.A. *The Gentile Zionists: A Study in Anglo-Zionist Diplomacy 1929–39* (London: Frank Cass 1973).

Rose, N.A. (ed.) *'Baffy': The Diaries of Blanche Dugdale 1936–47* (London: Vallentine Mitchell 1973).

Roskill, S. *Hankey: Man of Secrets* (London: Collins 1970–2).

Rothschild, M. *Dear Lord Rothschild* (London: Hutchinson 1983).

Rudin, H.R. *Armistice 1918* (Yale University Press 1944).

Ryan, A.P. 'Arthur Balfour' *History Today* vol. 2 (1952) pp. 421–7.

Sachar, H.M. *The History of Israel* (Oxford: Blackwell 1977).

Said, E.W. *Orientalism* (London: Routledge and Kegan Paul 1978).

Salter, Sir Arthur *Personality in Politics* (London: The Right Book Club 1948).

Seymour, Charles *Letters from the Paris Peace Conference* (New Haven: Yale University Press 1965).

Seymour, Charles (ed.) *The Intimate Papers of Colonel House* (London: Ernest Benn 1928).

Sforza, Count Carlo *Europe and the Europeans* (London: Harrap 1936).

Shannon, C.B. *Arthur J. Balfour and Ireland 1874–1922* (Washington: Catholic University of America Press 1988).

Shastri, Vamadeo 'Brahmanism and the Foundations of Belief' *Fortnightly Review* vol. 64 no. 347 (Nov. 1895) pp. 682–98.

Shaw, Lord *Letters to Isabel* (London: Cassell 1921).

Short, W.M. (ed.) *Arthur James Balfour as Philosopher and Thinker* (London: Longman and Green 1912).

Shotwell, J.T. *At the Paris Peace Conference* (New York: Macmillan 1937).

Sidgwick, A. and E. *Henry Sidgwick: A Memoir* (London: Macmillan 1906).

Smith, P. (ed.) *Lord Salisbury on Politics* (London: Cambridge University Press 1972).

Sokolow, Nahum *History of Zionism* with an Intro. by A.J. Balfour (London: Longman and Green 1919).

Spender, J.A. *The Foundations of British Policy* (London: Westminster Gazette 1912).

The Statesman's Year-Book 1903 (London: Macmillan 1903).

Steed, H. Wickham *Through Thirty Years 1892–1922* (London: Heinemann 1924).

Stein, L. *The Balfour Declaration* (London: Vallentine Mitchell 1961).

Steiner, Z.S. *The Foreign Office and Foreign Policy 1898–1914* (Cambridge: Cambridge University Press 1969).

Stevenson, D. *The First World War and International Politics* (Oxford: Oxford University Press 1988).

Storrs, Ronald *Orientations* (London: Nicholson and Watson 1945).

Strachey, A. *St. Loe Strachey: His Life and his Paper* (London: Gollancz 1930).

Sullivan, M. *The Great Adventure at Washington* (London: Heineman 1922).

Swinton, Lord *Sixty Years of Power* (London: Hutchinson 1966).

Sydenham, Lord *My Working Life* (London: John Murray 1927).

Sykes, A, *Tariff Reform in British Politics 1903–1913* (Oxford: Clarendon 1979).

Talmon, J.L. *The Unique and the Universal* (London: Secker and Warburg 1965).

Taylor, A.J.P. *From the Boer War to the Cold War: Essays on Twentieth Century Europe* (London: Hamish Hamilton 1995).

Taylor, R. *Lord Salisbury* (London: Allen Lane 1975).

Thayer, W.R. *John Hay* (Boston: Houghton Mifflin 1915).

Tibawi, A.L. *Anglo-Arab Relations and the Question of Palestine 1914–1921* (London: Luzac 1977).

Tilley, J., and Gaselee, S. *The Foreign Office* (London: Putnam 1933).

Tillman, S. *Anglo-American Relations at the Paris Peace Conference* (Princeton: Princeton University Press 1961).

Tocqueville, Alexis de *Democracy in America* transl. H. Reeve and F. Bowen (New York: Alfred Knopf 1966).

Tomes, J.H. 'Austen Chamberlain and the Kellogg Pact' *Millenium Journal of International Studies* vol. 18 no. 1 (1989) pp. 1–27.

Treitschke, G.H. von *Politics* transl. Blanche Dugdale and T. de Bille, with an Intro. by A.J. Balfour (New York: Macmillan 1916).

Tuchman, B.W. *Bible and Sword: How the British came to Palestine* (London: Macmillan 1982).

Turner, J. *Lloyd George's Secretariat* (Cambridge: Cambridge University Press 1980).

Ullman, R.H. *Anglo-Soviet Relations 1917–21* (Princeton: Princeton University Press 1961–72).

Vansittart, R. *The Mist Procession* (London: Hutchinson 1958).

Vereté, M. 'The Balfour Declaration and its Makers' *Middle Eastern Studies* vol. 6 no. 1 (1970) pp. 48–76.

Vincent, J. (ed.) *The Crawford Papers: The Journals of David Lindsay, 27th Earl of Crawford and 10th Earl of Balcarres 1871–1940* (Manchester: Manchester University Press 1984).

Waley, S.D. *Edwin Montagu* (London: Asia Publishing House 1964).

Wallas, Graham *Human Nature in Politics* 3rd edn (London: Constable 1914).

Wallis, J.P.R. *Fitz: The Story of Sir Percy FitzPatrick* (London: Macmillan 1955).

Walters, F.P. *A History of the League of Nations* (London: Oxford University Press 1952).

Warman, R.M. 'The Erosion of Foreign Office Influence in the Making of Foreign Policy, 1916–1918' *Historical Journal* vol. 15 no. 1 (1972) pp. 133–59.

Weale, Putnam *An Indiscreet Chronicle of the Pacific* (New York: Dodd and Mead 1922).

Weinroth, H. 'Norman Angell and *The Great Illusion*: An Episode in Pre-1914 Pacifism' *Historical Journal* vol. 17 (1974) pp. 551–74.

Weisgal, M.W. (ed.) *The Letters and Papers of Chaim Weizmann* Series A (London: Oxford University Press 1968–).

Weizmann, Chaim *Trial and Error* (London: Hamilton 1949).

Wemyss, Lady Wester *The Life and Letters of Lord Wester Wemyss* (London: Eyre and Spottiswoode 1935).

West, F. *Gilbert Murray: A Life* (London: Croom Helm 1984).

White, R.J. (ed.) *The Conservative Tradition* (London: Nicholas Kaye 1950).

White, T. de V. *Kevin O'Higgins* (London: Methuen 1948).

Whyte, F. *The Life of W.T. Stead* (London: Jonathan Cape 1925).

Wilkinson, H. Spenser *Thirty-Five Years 1874–1909* (London: Constable 1933).

Williams, R. Harcourt (ed.) *Salisbury–Balfour Correspondence 1869–1892* (Hertford: Hertfordshire Record Society 1988).

Williams, R.H. 'The Politics of National Defence: Arthur James Balfour and the Navy 1904–1911' (Oxford University DPhil thesis 1986).

   Defending the Empire: The Conservative Party & British Defence Policy 1899–1915 (New Haven: Yale University Press 1991).

Williamson, S.R. *The Politics of Grand Strategy: Britain and France Prepare for War 1904–1914* 2nd edn (London: Ashfield 1990).

Wilson, A. *The Strange Ride of Rudyard Kipling* (London: Secker and Warburg 1977).

Wilson, D. *Gilbert Murray* (Oxford: Clarendon 1987).

Wilson, J. *C.B.: A Life of Sir Henry Campbell-Bannerman* (London: Constable 1973).

Wilson, K. *Empire and Continent: Studies in British Foreign Policy from the 1880s to the First World War* (London: Mansell 1987).

Wilson, K. (ed.) *British Foreign Secretaries and Foreign Policy: From Crimean War to First World War* (London: Croom Helm 1987).

Wise, Stephen *The Challenging Years* (London: East and West Library 1951).

Woodward, D.R. 'The British Government and Japanese Intervention in Russia during World War I' *Journal of Modern History* vol. 46 (1974) pp. 663–85.

Wrench, J.E. *Geoffrey Dawson and our Times* (London: Hutchinson 1955).

Young, K. *Arthur James Balfour: The Happy Life of the Politician, Prime Minister, Statesman, and Philosopher 1848–1930* (London: Bell 1963).

Zebel, S.H. *Balfour* (Cambridge: Cambridge University Press 1973).

Zeman, Z.A.B. *A Diplomatic History of the First World War* (London: Weidenfeld and Nicolson 1971).

Zimmern, Alfred *The League of Nations and the Rule of Law 1918–1935* (London: Macmillan 1936).

Index

317